MUSLIM COOKING WITH MUHAMMAD
MUSLIM COOKBOOK, NUTRITION & HEALTH GUIDE
VERSION ONE of FIVE
©BY RAWIYAH SPHERE OF WRITERS™

Aubrey M. Muhammad, Editor
Cover illustration by Pierre Tra Bi
Graphic Illustrations by Aubrey M. Muhammad

Printed by
Sterling Pierce Co., Inc.
East Rockaway, New York

Published by Rawiyah Sphere Of Writers™
ISBN Number: 1-4276-0085-6

Printed in the United States of America

MUSLIM COOKING WITH MUHAMMAD
MUSLIM COOKBOOK, NUTRITION & HEALTH GUIDE
VERSION ONE of FIVE
NUTRITION & HEALTH
Complement To HOW TO EAT TO LIVE
by The Honorable Elijah Muhammad

TABLE OF CONTENTS

GREETINGS

In the name of Allah who came in the person of Master Fard Muhammad, HIS exalted Christ the Honorable Elijah Muhammad, and THEIR divine reminder in our midst today the Honorable Minister Louis Farrakhan Muhammad.

As Salaam Alaikum.

PURPOSE

Muslim Cooking With Muhammad© has been compiled by the Rawiyah Sphere of Writers™ to assist us who desire to eat to live with the right foods and to properly prepare them. There are a few aberrations of the teachings like a handful of fried foods and Potatoes (pg. 74) should be eaten only in frigid zones above the Ohio Valley. The books "How To Eat, One and Two" should be diligently referred to. This initial version is aimed at our constituency of door to door friends outside of the Mosque, whom have some of the least nutritional eating habits, like fast food and is intended to introduce us to adjusting our ways of cooking to maximize the benefit of healing and nutritional foods.

In the introduction we will answer "Why is it necessary to eat to live?", "What foods to eat and avoid," and "How to eat to live a healthier, happier and longer life."

INTRODUCTION

Master Fard Muhammad diagnosed us in 1930 as being in a miserable state and condition, weighing other than ourselves, high blood pressure, rheumatism (Rheumatoid arthritis), headaches, pain in all joints, chills, grippe (pronounce 'grip') (flu), fever, foot ailments, toothaches and cannot walk up to the store and get pills from the doctor.

We had a diet of soul food which we were forced to eat during slavery. Our slavemasters would feed us just enough to keep us going and to keep us alive to maximize our prime productivity years. They determined it would be more productive, for them, to work us as hard as he possibly could day and night for 5 to 6 years and burn us out until death or injury over took us, than to let us live out our full lives they already limited. They fed us through what is called a Pork Barrel. They would chop up a sick or rotten pig (to save money) and dump it in a pork barrel. This is where we concocted pig guts (chitterlings or chitlins), pig feet, knuckled, tail, ears, neck, and think of any other part possibly to eat. We would sometimes kill a prime cattle and act like it died from natural causes so we could have a better grade meat. The pork barrel is a modern term used in politics for a government project or appropriation that yields jobs or other benefits to a specific locale and patronage opportunities to its political representative who has been compromised. The pork was just enough to survive to keep us like the walking dead. Ten ounces of swine, sounds 1/60th of an ounce of our 7 1/2 ounces of original brains or spiritual atoms and takes away 3% of our beauty appearance. We can be robbed successfully with 1/3rd (or 2 1/2 ounces) of unsound brain. At this rate we can be robbed of unsound-meaning not mentally healthy-brain with 93.75 pounds of poison animal and our beauty appearance destroyed with 20 pounds of poison animal.

Keep in mind that the Capitalist World's Medical Profession, scientists and other wise Muslim Sons (Caucasian Shriners and Masons) have taken a Hippocratic Oath that binds them to ethical professional behavior as new physicians. It should be called the Hypocritical Oath because they do not inform us of the truth that will perfect us. If they revealed the truth, they would have to become Muslims in order to service us. Which in turn would require them to give more of themselves instead of this world's ethos of the common people serving and looking up to professionals. They support bankers, food processors and drug producers who keep us in bad health so the Medical Profession entrepreneurs can profit off our ignorance and the scientists don't want to lose their jobs due to funding being cut off. They are analogous to men who are stamped engineers, yet relate to you with the knowledge of electronic technicians. The same tricknology is used by the F.D.A. in the food pyramid where they prescribe three to five—sometimes eight! meals a day to keep you sick because you never fully digest what you have ate. Often when I'm discussing the program of "How to eat to live" people say "I already eat one meal a day." Then their protruding bellies jiggle to testify against them. I clarify the concept we're presenting by saying "Any amount of food consumed at any time is what we are considering a meal." One molecule of sugar is enough to begin the digestive process. For good health, during a twenty four hour period a consecutive two hours should be dedicated to eating one meal. Preferably between the hours of 4 p.m. and 6 p.m.. The less we eat and the longer the period between the meal the better it is for us.

WHY WE EAT TO LIVE

Eat a single meal. Nursing mothers and children under 16 eat two a day. Or, if we're sick, eat when required. But basically everyone should eat a single meal a day or every two days, no matter what anyone says. The more idle our stomachs are the longer they will last. The more we tax our stomachs, the sooner they will wear out. We can drink water, preferably mineral water, Coffee (pg.299) or Tea (pg.301) between our one meal. Years ago we were taught to fast a minimum two to three days the end of each month or as much as we could, the longer the fast the better for us. In modern times not only is there poisons and pesticides in the foods, but the food itself is being grafted, cloned and Allah knows what else. We should fast a minimum five days the end of each month or three days the end of each two weeks or two days each weekend. Pick your favorite time, because there is death closing in all around us. Fasting cleans the poisons and toxins out of us.

Food processors take the naturalness out of food so they can obtain the red meat taste they acquired in the caves and hillsides of Europe. They bleach the flour, rice and sugar. This depletes the food of its nutrients. They then take the extracted nutrients and put it in vitamin pill and cream cosmetic form, which we now need because we're undernourished. The processed foods have been robbed of nutrients which will make us tired, due to undernutrition. We eat the same amount of food but we don't get the usual and expected nutrients which have been processed out. They also inject hormones and steroids in animals to speed growth, and increase production of eggs, milk and meat. This swells us up. Nothing in nature is fat. It is lean and averaged. You never see a fat lion or even an elephant. If its bigger its proportional to mass. Food producers have taken advantage of our excessive & compulsive lives. We eat to please our eyes, smell and palette instead of our delicate digestive tract.

Although eating to live cleans us out, the spiritual thinking is what gives us the youthful spirit, look and increases our awareness. It regenerates our body cells to youth and life. We inhale a finer quality mist of air. The living proof is the body regeneration, illumination of the mind and transmutation of the emotions to righteousness of the followers of the Honorable Minister Louis Farrakhan. Fasting purifies the blood which functions our brain with glucose and oxygen. The proper food helps. When we give our digestive system a break, it gives us a break. Purified blood, a low metabolism, slow breathing, an empty digestive tract and clear more aware mind with lighter and sharper movements are the results of fasting. But many of us only see the self-denial aspects of proper lifestyles. Like "Oh no I can't be like you Mooslems. You can't do this and you can't do that!" Its not what we can't do, its the benefits of being ourselves which gives us secure, richer, younger, cleaner, longer and happier lives than what Satan's world has to offer, death, alcohol accompanied partying and comedy at the expense of someone else's confident self-image being destroyed.

This rebellious world has increased the type of products that are grafted or genetically engineered. They would like to graft everything possible to control it. The food manufactures don't want to appropriately label altered foods. The grafted man can't graft himself back into his original form so he has decided to graft us along with him.

Fasting is the best way to reduce stress. The foods in the provided list (pg.13) are the best tonic to help. Proper food provides the nutrients that strengthen glands, organs, and the nervous system to meet daily challenges with stamina. We reduce our effectiveness to convey high energy through our bodies when we consume food products robbed of nutritional value because of mineral-poor soils, over processing, grafting and transportation.

B-vitamins are very effective for handling stress because they work together to promote optimal functioning of the nervous system. These nutrients also help mood swings, anxiety and depression. It has been shown in animal studies that B-complex vitamins have antiaggressive and muscle-relaxing effects. Navy beans and brown rice are examples of food containing all the B-complex vitamins.

Stress causes the blood sugar to rise and fall repeatedly. During a down cycle, the adrenal glands sense the lack of blood sugar and secrete a hormone that breaks down protein mass in the body to make more sugar for energy. However, additional protein is needed to compensate for this protein breakdown. Blood sugar fluctuations also cause mood-swings and mental confusion. All minerals are essential for a healthy adrenal system. They support the adrenal glands, which help handle stress by applying a steady stream of fuel to the body. The adrenal glands also secrete adrenaline which stimulates quick action in "flight or fight" situations. Consume the stress-reducing minerals found in such foods as whole grains (pg.188) and wheat germ. Vitamin C also reduces stress, oranges are full of vitamin C. See different sources of vitamin C (pg.13).

We must take our time and prepare our own food and don't rush our meals. Rushing the consumption of food can block the secretion of hydrochloric acid needed to digest food and can lead to ulcers and other stomach malfunctions. Do not eat on the run. Eat in pleasant surroundings and chew your food well to break down food. Digestion is helped when we avoid drinking liquids with meals since it dilutes the digestive juices and washes down the enzymes. Then the food deteriorates while awaiting a new production of digestive juices.

We must change our perceptions to a good one. Stop eating all day. Take a day off from work and sit down at a table and eat a tremendous amount of food, sweets and drinks until we can't take another bite. We will see how ridiculous it is to eat too much food. If we smoke, chain smoke about three cigarettes and ask ourselves "How do we feel? Why are we doing what we are doing?" Its silly isn't it? Yes it is. We know its silly. But you may say "Well Brother Muhammad, these vices make me feel good!" That may be your perception. But we may ask you "Why do you feel bad in the first place?" You can't answer us because the answer is inside you. You are just like Dorothy in the Wizard of Oz™. She travelled all over the strange land seeking the way back to Kansas until finally she was told that all she had to do was tap her slippers together three times and she would be home. All we have to do is accept our own and be ourselves. Peace and happiness is an internal meeting with the Creator which is manifested without, in other people. See "Elaborations on the Proper Way of Handling People by the Honorable Elijah Muhammad; See yourself in other people. (pg.3)

Prayer, exercising (See Muhammad's Work In™ by Rawiyah Sphere of Writers©), meditation, or simple deep-breathing exercises can relieve stress. Don't do extravagant heavy-weight "work outs" all day to excrescent our muscles trying to look like an image of a doctored (altered through a computer graphics program Photo Shop™ to look enhanced) photo of a weight lifter in popular magazines. Those superfluous muscles require blood flow which it draws away from our brains and digestive system. Don't emotionally overextend ourselves by worrying about work place competition while at home then worrying about domestic strife while at the work place and then trying to regain a normal reaction to challenges by popping pills. There are 3 billion prescriptions a year in the United States of America.

We must change our perceptions about Working In™ (working out). We must see it as a process of internally conditioning ourselves. The energy from our center degree or stage flows best through a purified vessel. Water cleans out the digestive system and hydrates us. Stagnant water is poison. Dust gathers when something is not being kept up. By not Working In™ (working out) we are stagnant in our physical development and by not eating properly, we are poisoning our systems. By not studying we are limiting our thinking. Think about that. Nature purifies the Earth, by the will of Allah. We abuse it by our will to disobey. We associate food with moods and eat to satisfy our palate and not our delicate digestive system. Its easier to teach a filthy lowdown dance than a healthy improving exercise. Some people memorize senseless, idle and negative songs easier than positive principles.

Stress can lead to irritability, anxiety, depression, headaches, stomach disorders, premature aging and hair loss. It might also lead to more serious problems such as colitis and cancer.
Worrying about our hair becoming grey is what causes it to grey prematurely. The Honorable Elijah Muhammad says the food we eat keeps us here or takes us away. Just as we need good food we need the right knowledge. Allah knows us and revealed what is best for us. The key is to ease the system by extracting the most nutrients from the easiest foods to break down. Disease is not necessarily a virus that enters your body and effects you. It should be more thought of as a discomfort to our health do to negative thoughts or dis-ease a lack of ease; trouble.

The priority of nutrients required by our bodies is as follows: First **glucose** a monosaccharide sugar occurring widely in most plant, especially fructose rich fruit and vegetables and animal tissue. It is the principal circulating sugar in the blood and the major energy source of the body. Second is **starch** a naturally abundant nutrient carbohydrate found chiefly in the seeds, fruits, tubers, roots, and stem pith of plants, notably in corn, potatoes, wheat, squash, bread, beans and rice, and varying widely in appearance according to source but commonly prepared as a white, amorphous, tasteless powder. And third and lastly is **proteins** which are fundamental components of all living cells and include many substances, such as enzymes, hormones, and antibodies, that are necessary for the proper functioning of an organism. They are essential in the diet of animals for the growth and repair of tissue and can be obtained from foods such as meat, fish, eggs, milk, and legumes. The navy bean has 12 of our body's 18 nutritional requirements. Amino acids help us because there is not one body process in which they do not have influence. There are more than 32 amino acids that have been reported. However, there are only eight which are called essential. They are: leucine, isoleucine, lysine, methionine, phenylalanine, tryptophan, threonine and valine. If we get these eight in our food, our bodies can manufacture all the rest. The other amino acids play as an important part in the health of our bodies as the eight we must get in our foods. Navy beans (pg.82) and whole wheat bread have all the 20 essential amino acids we need to survive. Amino acid is an organic compound containing both an amino group and a carboxylic acid group especially any of the 20 compounds that link together by peptide bonds to form proteins.

NAVY BEAN (1 1/2 cup-cooked beans)

Calories	259	
Protein	17	grams
Fat (TTAL Lipids)	1	gram
Fatty Acids	.5	gram
Cholesterol	0	gram
Carbohydrate	49	grams
Total Dietary Fiber	83	grams
Sodium	4	grams
Potassium	876	grams
Thiamin	.45	grams (milli)
Riboflavin	.11	grams (milli)
Niacin	3.3	grams (milli)
Pantothenic Acid	.47	grams (milli)
Vitamin B-6	.24	grams (milli)
Foliate	259	grams (milli)
Iron	5.4	grams (milli)
Calcium	138	grams (milli)
Phosphorous	320	grams (milli)
Magnesium	124	grams (milli)
Zinc	2.1	grams (milli)
Copper	.28	grams (milli)

SAMPLE OF PROPERTIES IN FOODS

Many vegetables are good to eat. Steam them a few minutes so they remain crisp. We need the enzymes contained in them, and boiling vegetables in long stews strips them of their chlorophyll, which is to plants what melanin is to people. Fiber found in whole wheat bread, garlic and apples flush the body system of its own excretions of tissue cells or cell change.

Eat foods that contain phytochemical-built in plant-based antioxidant that get rid of free radicals, the negative by-products in our bodies that destroy cells and cause cancer, heart disease and early aging. The prefix phyto means plant.

• Olive oil - Olive oil can lower the level of undesirable LDL cholesterol while maintaining (or slightly raising) the level of beneficial HDL. And recently Spanish researchers found that the antioxidents in olive oil might ward off colon cancer.

• Tomatoes - The consumption of tomatoey foods has been linked to a decrease incidence of cancers. This is due to lycopene, an antioxidant found in tomatoes, including Tomato Soup (pg.87) and tomato juice.

• Apples - Researchers in London found that men who ate five or more apples a week had stronger lungs than those who didn't. Scientists theorize that the phytochemical quercetin guards lungs from cellular damage. And soluble fiber and pectin in apples help lower LDL levels.

• Chilies - Capsaicin, the hot stuff in peppers, is a phytochemical believed to inhibit carcinogenic molecules from attaching to DNA. Capsaicin also clears sinuses, speed up metabolism and releases a short-lived endorphin kick.

• Garlic - Garlic contains allicen, a chemical that shows some antibiotic properties. It also has anticoagulant properties and can act as an antioxidant and an anti-inflammatory.

• Broccoli - Broccoli is low in calories, high in fiber and rich in potassium, iron, calcium, vitamins C and A, and phytochemical that may protect against cancer and heart disease.

ADDITIONAL FOOD WITH POSITIVE PROPERTIES

•Ginger - Ginger fights nausea. It also may help control stomach ulcers, protect against symptoms of colds and flu, and reduce allergy symptoms.

• Bay - To ward off migraines, put a few bay leaves into your soup. Bay leaves contain compounds called parthenolides, which inhibit migraines. A bay leaf can also help the body use insulin more efficiently.

• Peppermint - Rub a few crushed leaves on our bodies to relieve back pain, headache and hives-a skin condition characterized by intensely itching welts and caused by an allergic reaction to internal or external agents, an infection, or a nervous condition. To fight indigestion, toss the crushed leaves into our tea or coffee.

• Basil - Crush a few basil leaves into a hot drink, or sprinkle some on our food. Basil acts as a natural expectorant to relieve coughs and chest congestion. It also helps lower blood pressure.

• Dill - To ease stomach gas, add 2 teaspoons of mashed dill to a cup of tea; plus the chlorophyll helps kill bad breath.

FOOD PERCEIVED AS BAD, YET UNDER THE PROGRAM OF "HOW TO EAT TO LIVE" AND UTILIZED IN MODERATION, HAVE GOOD PROPERTIES

• Coffee - Experts now generally agree that there is no consistent scientific evidence to prove coffee is detrimental to our health. From a health standpoint, coffee is a harmless substance. Coffee (pg. 300) may even be good for us. Freshly brewed coffee contains antioxidant compounds that may carry as much power as vitamins C and E. In part, the seductive smell of brewed coffee is caused by these compounds.

• Eggs - Although, egg yolks are one of the most concentrated sources of cholesterol in the diet (about 213 milligrams each), research strongly suggests that, for most folks, dietary cholesterol is not the primary enemy in the battle against high blood cholesterol. Instead, saturated fat—most concentrated in fatty cuts of meat and full-fat dairy products—is the main dietary suspect in the artery-clogging process. Limit saturated fat in our diet and it will help towards lowering our blood cholesterol.

• Fat - Fat can be healthy if we eat the right kind in moderation. The recommendation to keep fat in our diet to no more than 30 percent of daily total calories still stands. But that leaves plenty of room for "good" fats, such as omega-3 fatty acids, which have potential disease-preventing properties. Researchers have discovered that omega-3, found mainly in fish, may relieve the inflammation of arthritis and reduce the risk of heart disease and stroke. Japanese researchers found that people who do not eat fish daily have 3 to 5 times the risk of certain cancers.

Recently researchers have been focusing on the role that DHA (docosahexaenoic acid), one kind of omega-3 fatty acid, plays in everything from ensuring proper infant brain development to possibly preventing a decline in brain function due to aging. Though DHA is not currently found in infant formulas, many nutritionist are pushing for it to be a standard ingredient. To make processed formulas resemble mother's milk manufactures include DHA. The best milk for infants is breast milk which naturally contains DHA. Salmon and trout are among the richest sources of omega-3.

Monounsaturated fat is found in olive oil. Studies show that diets rich in "monos," like the Mediterranean diet, can lower the risk of heart disease and help control blood-sugar levels in noninsulin-dependent diabetics. Some experts even say it's okay if fat in the daily diet goes as high a 40 percent, if most of it comes from healthy monos.

Antioxidant components are found in olive oil. These include polyphenols, beta-carotene and alpha-tocopherol, which may play a role in reducing the risk of certain cancers. And as Minister Ava Muhammad stated at the Harlem Office State Building on 125th Street, Harlem, NY 1-9-2001 (paraphrased) "Cancer is when the cells of our bodies no longer nourishes by their normal means, but begin to feed off the other cells in our systems." A sort of cannibalism.

A substance called resveratrol which is produced by grapes (pg. 295) to fight fungi, is a natural pesticide that has been found in Japanese animal studies to reduce fat and cholesterol levels in the blood. Additional sources of resveratrol are red or purple grape juice and raisins that are artificially dried. Because sunlight can destroy this chemical, even though sun-dried grapes are good for us. Grapes also contain quercetin, which has displayed cancer-fighting properties in laboratory animals. High levels of this chemical are found in red grapes, red and yellow onions, broccoli and yellow squash. It appears that quercetin is inert until acted on by bacteria in the digestive system or by yeast in a wine fermenting vat. (This example is given only to better understand the process. As we know it is forbidden for Muslims to consume any form of toxins including alcohol wines.) It then turns into what may be one of nature's more potent anti-carcinogens. Carcinogen is a cancer-causing substance or agent.

Garlic and onions (pg.73) have medicinal powers in these related bulbs, which contain many organic sulfur compounds. In laboratory test tubes these sulfur compounds kill bacteria, fungi and viruses. Inside the body, aged garlic extract appears to slow blood coagulation time, which could reduce the risk of clots and heart disease. We eat the whole garlic to obtain the best properties in garlic. Garlic's blood-thinning properties reduce the mortality and incidence of nonfatal reinfarctions of heart attacks.

Several epidemiological studies in China have pointed to reduced stomach-cancer risk in those eating diets rich in vegetables of the onion family. These include chives, shallots and leeks.

When researchers at Rutgers University in New Jersey fed green tea from Japan to mice, skin cancers in the rodents (caused by ultraviolet light) were reduced by about 50 percent. Fung-Lung Chung, associate chief of the Division of Chemical Carcinogenesis at the American Health Foundation in Valhalla, N.Y., has been studying a chemical in green tea called epigallocatechin gallate (EGCG). Chung's group has found that this powerful antioxidant protected mice against lung cancer.

Inuits (Eskimos) in Greenland consume vast quantities of fat yet have remarkably low death rates from heart disease. One reason is that the Inuit diet includes abundant fish—salmon (pg.280), herring and others—rich in unusual oils that scientists label omega-3 fatty acids. If consumed for a long period, these fish oils appear to thin the blood, lower cholesterol, reduce inflammatory reactions, lessen the risk of atherosclerosis and, according to recent animal research, may protect against colon cancer.

Eat cruciferous foods like broccoli (pg.71) and related vegetables—cabbage (pg.72), Brussels sprouts (pg.72), watercress, and other—so named because of the cross-shaped arrangement of their flower petals. in March 1992 a team of scientists at John Hopkins University in Baltimore announced that a sulphur-rich chemical in broccoli called sulforphane may be a significant part of the anti-carcinogenic action of broccoli. Cruciferous vegetables have chemicals called indoles that can block certain cancer-causing agents. Indole speeds up the breakdown of the hormone estrogen, which is a risk factor for breast cancer. In mice the cruciferous indole substantially reduces the incidence, size and multiplicity of spontaneous mammary tumors.

Eat citrus fruits (pg.178), long loved as an excellent source of vitamin C has other health-enhancing chemicals. Pectin found in citrus fruits lowers blood cholesterol levels. A 1% drop in cholesterol causes about a 2% drop in the risk of heart disease. It lowers the plaque levels in arteries. Pectin is a soluble fiber found only in the citrus fruit itself, not in the juice.

Any one of the following 5 foods contain the same amount of vitamin C as an orange (pg.178):

1.   1 cup strawberries (pg.178)
2.   1 half papaya (pg.170 & 178)
3.   1 red bell pepper (pg.187)
4.   1 kiwi fruit (pg.178)
5.   1 cup broccoli (pg.71)

When preparing foods use vegetable oil, corn oil, pure butter (pg.44), olive oil (pg.46) or whatever good vegetable oil we choose. Do not eat fried nor food that is baked all day long or hard baked, if you can avoid them. Fried foods are hard on our digestive system and will cut our life short. Simply bake our food till its done.

SUMMARY OF FOODS TO EAT

small navy bean	red potatoes (frigid-zones residents)
small pink, red or brown beans	peppers (all)
string or green beans	onions
june peas	olives
white cabbage	radishes
red cabbage	brown rice (cooked well)
broccoli	whole wheat bread
garlic	rye bread (after hard labor)
cauliflower	lake trout
parsley	red salmon
corn (on cob, not hominy)	smelt
celery	sardines (Portuguese)
asparagus	red snappers
cucumbers	porgies
egg plant	perch
okra	herring
spinach (a little bit)	pickerel
carrots	bass
squash	white bass
tomatoes	whiting fish
lettuce	pike
turnip root	smoked fish
rutabaga (a little bit)	lamb
most any raw fruit	tuberculosis free beef

13

FOODS WE DO NOT EAT

It is not best to eat foods which require alkaline and acid digestive medium together. Acid and alkaline don't mix. Starchy foods: corn, potatoes, wheat bread, and rice require alkaline. Protein foods: meat, fish, eggs, milk, and beans (nut seeds) require acid and pepsin.

Sweet potatoes are full of gas, don't eat them. White potatoes are food for people who live in frigid zones but are too starchy for you and me. They laden us with too much starch and fat which are friends to diabetes. A white potato will raise our blood sugar higher than pure sugar will. Allah forbids us to eat peas. No blackeye peas either. Do not eat leafy greens (tough). No beans except the small navy bean do we eat. This small little brown or white navy bean is valued to be very high in protein, fats and starches. And it is safe food for prolonged life. The lima bean, says the Honorable Elijah Muhammad, "will burst the lining of the stomach and intestines of a Texas bull." Do not eat them either small or large ones.

Cook our whole wheat bread (pg.188) thoroughly done two or three times or at least toast it. It should be ground very fine. Rye bread is okay for the hard working man, even then it should twice. Eat whole wheat and not bleached white flour which has been robbed of all its natural vitamins and proteins.

We are flatly forbidden to eat corn bread. It is only digestible by animals. Never eat fresh hot corn muffins or hot cakes and syrup. When we eat half-cooked bread, it shortens our life. As all bread will rise again in our stomachs and intestinal walls.

Do not eat the highly rich soy bean flour. These beans are for cattle, not human beings. The oil from soy beans is not good for our stomachs. Soy protein—via soybeans, tofu, tempeh or soy milk is loaded with unneeded protein. In the case of soy milk it is lower in protein, calcium, riboflavin and vitamin A than cow's milk. (See Final Call Newspaper™ Vol.22, #19, Feb.11, 2003: pg. 29 "Is Soy Milk Okay?" Get Fit To Live with Audrey Muhammad)

Olestra is a grafted oil. It may cause abdominal cramping and loose stools. Olestra inhibits the absorption of some vitamins and other nutrients. To make up for this, water soluble vitamins A,D,E and K have been added to olestra chips. Also this is because olestra isn't broken down or digested by the body. It just zips on through. Although Olean could replace fat in ice cream, tables spreads, salad dressings and cheeses, uses beyond snack chips and crackers will require separate FDA review and approval. FDA approval for chips and crackers was granted after 150 studies, some short, some long, with more than 8,000 adults and children. Some tasters complained of a lingering aftertaste. Perhaps, though, a statement in the Procter & Gamble® press kit says it best: "Still, Olean is a replacement for fat, not for common sense." With regular fat the body's digestive enzymes break off the spokes of fatty acid from their core, and the body absorbs them. With Olean, so many fatty acid spokes are crowded around the core that the digestive enzymes can't find a breaking point. So Olean doesn't release any fat or calories. Its like putting plastic in our digestive systems. (See Newsday™, Wednesday, Jan. 31, 1996 for a reproduction graphic comparison between Olean and regular fat).

Here's how it works:

Regular Fat
The Body's digestive enzymes break off the spokes of fatty acid from their core, and the body absorbs them.

CORE

FAT & CALORIES

DIGESTIVE ENZYME

DIGESTIVE ENZYME.

Olean
With Olean, so many fatty acid spokes are crowded around the core that the digestive enzymes can't find a breaking point.

CORE

DIGESTIVE ENZYME

So Olean doesn't release any fat or calories

Reproduced from **Newsday** Wednesday, January 31, 1996

Old bread is better for the stomach than fresh cooked bread or fresh cooked cakes.

Brown the rice thoroughly in or on top of the stove with a little butter of oil to keep it from sticking. Keep stirring it.

Pastries and cakes are not good for our stomachs—not the kind made with crusts of white flour and sweetened with white sugar. Use brown sugar (Raw™) and whole wheat flour for our pie, crumb and cobbler crusts (pg.231).

Virtually all fruits are good. Except processed fruits and fruit in the can laden with heavy syrup. Sundried are okay. The fruit is better raw than cooked. Positively do not eat nuts.

SUMMARY OF FOODS TO AVOID

pork   pastries

sweet potatoes (gaseous)	cooked fruit
white potatoes (except frigid zone)	candy
black eyed peas	highly rich soybean flour
speckled peas	fish that weigh over 50 pounds
field peas	shrimp
red or brown peas	oysters
split peas	clams
hominy grits	lobsters
pop corn	squid
hot dogs	raw fish
peanut butter	octopus
kale	squirrel
collard greens	opossum or possum
mustard	rabbit
turnip salad	deer (venison)
lima beans	fried or hard cooked foods
white (bleached) flour	half-done bread
white sugar	hot cakes (pancakes)
corn bread	fast foods

HERBIVORES LIVE LONGER THAN CARNIVORES

Vegetables and grains that are low in fat tend to be high in nutritional value. Fish has more fat than vegetables but also tends to be a good source of protein. Some fish is also very low fat as well. Meat in its various forms usually has the most fat and protein.

In a study done in Britain the relative weight was examined of "meat eaters" vs. "fish eaters" vs. "vegetarians or vegans" (who eat no animal products at all). The data for the study was compiled from 3,947 men and 17,158 women who were solicited from vegetarian and health food stores and publications. The heaviest were the "meat eaters". The "fish eaters" averaged seven pounds lighter than the "meat eaters". The lightest were the "vegetarians" who were 10 to 13 pounds lighter than the "meat eaters".

The conclusion is that if we are striving to manage our weight then we should increase our consumption of vegetables and fish and decrease our consumption of meat.

High protein requirement is a myth to make money on meat and health care to treat its consumption. When we are born, moma's milk has 2.38% protein, after 6 months it reduces to 1.3%. Also the by-product of meat protein metabolism is ammonia. Meat contains uric acid which the kidneys extract as urine. If you must eat meat—which after reading this section you should understand that contemporary meat isn't even food, but is filler—eat the cleanest, such as healthy and tuberculosis free beef, raised by personal farmers on hands-on, interactive organic farms. The lamb is best. Most beef is too coarse for your stomachs. The lamb is a much finer-grain meat. Eat small young pigeons which have never flown from their nest. Do not eat any bird that has been free to fly around and look for its own food. Chickens are not fit to eat. You have to nurse them so carefully to keep them away from filth, the kosher Empire™ chickens are best, you are permitted to eat them. The Rabbis watch, feed, inspect and sacrifice them peacefully with the utmost care and diligence. Don't eat ground meat unless you see it ground. Do not buy the Christian's ready-prepared ground meats or any ready ground meat. Buy the quality meats you like, and have them ground by the Orthodox kosher butchers through their meat grinders. If you want to find good food, such as lamb, beef or even chicken, buy it from the strictly orthodox Jew. Be certain it is a Kosher market because some Jews eat the pig. It is best to exclude meat from our diet.

THE REAL MAD ANIMAL DISEASE (PORK)

I know a pork sounded mind relative, who has consumed pork for probably 55 years. Please do not eat pork. We lose our senses. Imagine the actions of someone trying to justify the lost of their senses. Just as it is difficult for a physically disabled (blind, crippled, etc.) person to perform fully in life, it is ten times worse for a spiritually disabled (sounded mind) person. Please stop eating pork and its by-products. Its like a young person who drinks alcohol. After a while they become tolerant to the alcohol so they have to consume more to achieve a buzz or state of drunkenness. Or a punch drunk boxer returning to the ring. It is a tragedy.

Pigs contain many toxins, worms and latent diseases and they are prone to illnesses than other animals. They will eat anything. Influenza (flu) is one of the illnesses which pigs have in common with humans. Sausage, a hodge podge of pig parts, contains parts of pig lungs, so those who eat pork sausage tend to be effected more during epidemics of influenza. Pig meat also contains excessive amounts of imidazole compounds, that are an inhibitor of histamine-a compound released from cells of the immune system in human beings as part of an allergic reaction, which can lead to itching and inflammation; growth hormone, which promotes inflammation and growth; sulphur containing mesenehymal mucus, which leads to swelling and deposits of mucus in tendons and cartilage, resulting in arthritis, rheumatism and further degeneration of cartilage. Pork consumption can also cause gallstones and obesity, probably due to its high cholesterol and saturated fat content. The pig is the primary carrier of the taenia sodium worm, which is found in its flesh. This type of tapeworm can pass through the intestines and affect many other organs including our brains, and is incurable once it reaches beyond a certain stage. One in six people in the U.S. and Canada has trichinosis from eating trichina worms which are found in pork, many people have no symptoms to warn them of this, and when they do, they resemble symptoms of many other illnesses. The rat, an animal along with the cat and dog, which the pig is grafted from, also harbors this disease. There are many other worms, germs diseases and bacteris which are commonly present in pigs.

Pigs are biologically similar to humans, and their meat is said to taste similar to human flesh. Imhotep grafted the pig and Musa prescribed it for the caveman to utilize as medicine and to heal sores due to their blood diseases and injuries from in-fighting in the caves. Pigs have been used for dissection in biology labs due to the similarity between their organs and human organs. People with insulin-dependent diabetes usually inject themselves with pig insulin.

MODERN MEAT
Meat in America
Beef is an 80 billion dollar industry. It is bad enough that cows are scavengers, but are also mechanically mass produced on traumatic farm prisons. They live and sleep in their own manure with 100,00 other cows. They are prematurely grown to full size in 4 years. They only graze 6 months after birth on a prison farm. Were in the wild or olden times with concerned farmers they use to graze all their lives and mature in a full 12 years.

On mass production prison farms they are fed corn, which is hard for them to digest, so it has to be consumed with baking soda to make it digestible, which accounts for half the country's sale of baking soda. The corn feed is laced with antibiotics to fight the bacteria that is in the manure they sleep in. The cows are injected or fed hormones and steroids to speed the growth process and increase their size. They are mentally and spiritually in hell.

Meat manufacture lobbyists like the National Meat Association™ and the National Meat Institute™ fight the U.S.D.A. so they don't have to spend money on safety, testing and hygiene, which increases profits for them and presents this useless eating material passed off as meat to an unaware public. Meat is grey and tasteless, especially when koshered. They inject red dye for the color and the uric acid, which becomes urine, gives meat its taste. Refer to the movie The Matrix® were the character Cipher is negotiating how he will benefit betraying his comrades released from the enslaving Matrix, with the computer generated agent Williams over a steak and red wine dinner. He describes the steak as an illusion that appears real and attractive to his brain but he knows its a computer image impressed in his mind by the Matrix. As he sticks the nonreal steak in his mouth he tastefully says "ignorance is bliss."

WHAT AMERICANS EAT

Americans are shopping more consciously and eating lighter. Among the key findings from Parade's® sixth survey of the nation's eating and food-buying habits:
• 91% of the respondents say they've changed their food-buying habits in the last two years, primarily by comparing prices more and reading labels.
• 90% of the respondents are concerned about saturated fat in their diets, and most (85% of women, 77% of men) are doing something to cut down: 67% are opting for low-fat versions of the foods they

usually eat, while 41% are using non-fat alternatives.

• 88% are concerned about cholesterol, 82% about salt.

• Chips are everyone's favorite snack—chosen by 40% of men, 39% of women and 37% if children. (for women and children, fruit is No.2; for men, cookies).

• In the 12 months prior to the survey, twice as many women as men (38% vs. 19%) went on at least one diet. Overall, 550 of the 2215 respondents lost weight—an average of 17.6 pounds. Meanwhile, 602 gained weight—an average of 13.6 pounds.

• 53% of Americans are more likely to purchase a brand-name product; 28% say they'll pay more for it. And 69% buy convenience foods, though they cost more.

• 82% of the men shop for food, and 39% say they're the principal food shoppers in their household.

• 68% of the respondents (73% of those earning more than $40,000) shop at warehouse/club food stores.

[Parade's® survey of 2215 men and women was conducted in March 1997 by the independent firm of Mark Clements Research, Inc. The overall sample was selected to conform to the latest available U.S. Census data for men and women aged 18 to 65.]

Questions? If we had purchased the rights, for millions of dollars, to promote, consult and manage Steve Mcnair, Tiger Woods, high scoring Hockey star Markus Naslund of the Vancouver Canucks, WBA heavyweight champ Roy Jones Jr., Venus & Serena Williams, Derek Jeter, Olympic figure skating champion Sarah Hughes and Allen Iverson what would we suggest they eat? How do we maintain our cars, stereos and appliances? Accordingly how we desire, which would have detrimental effects or by the instruction manual which insures the best performance by the maker and servicer? Look at what and how trainers feed pedigree dogs, horses, and other sport and service animals. Now contrast that with we feed pet animals, some of which are lucky to even get fed.

TURNING ON OURSELVES

Eat from our proper Tropic level in the food chain.

There Are Three Tropic Levels:
* One - Grass, weeds and plants.
* Two - Herbivores: Humans, cows, insects and snails.
  Decomposers: Moss and mushrooms.
* Three - Carnivores: Lions, birds (predator) and snakes.

In The Sea Its:
* Predator sharks, whales, etc.
* Red snapper, whiting, etc.

* Scavengers: Crabs, lobsters, clams, catfish, etc.

* Water carries minerals we ALL require between it's loosely knit molecules.
* A pig will eat anything.

When we turn on our own tropic level we contribute towards:

Entropy - The gradual disordering of energy that threatens Earth. The energy needed to
combat it is sunlight, given to us by photosynthesis.

Photosynthesis - The process in green plant and certain other organisms by which
carbohydrates are synthesized from carbon dioxide and water using light as an
energy source. Most forms of photosynthesis release oxygen as a byproduct.
The green coloring matter in the leaves of plants called chlorophyll is essential in
this process. It is analogous to the melanin in our skin and sap is analogous to
blood in our circulatory system.

When the Sun is not present the sap sinks down into the tree roots. When the Sun rises the sap flows up
to the leaves and photosynthesis continues. The Sun & moon draws the water from the ground, drag-
ging minerals with it, through the roots, then through tree and the nutrients form fruits. When we are
asleep the blood sinks down into our bodies (root) when we are awake the blood flows up into our
brains (leaves) to function in the thinking process. When we have good thought (proper cultivation) we
produce fruits that sustain life.

Entropy also is a measure of the loss of information in a transmitted message.

By eating the fruits and vegetables we obtain fixed nitrates the plants have secured from the soil. We
secure 10% of what we eat and excrete the other 90% as waste matter eliminated from the bowels. A
cow does this also with the grass. When we turn on the cow we now have to go through 99% of it's
meat to secure **ONLY 1%** of the nutrients it ate. Remember, it only obtained 10% of the nutrients from
the grass. Now we have to digest more material while getting less. Processed foods have lost the most
nutritional value. Which is why we must choose natural foods that have the most nutritional value,
while being the easiest to digest (extract nutrients). The Honorable Elijah Muhammad said we must
preserve our digestive system. Which develops a new layer of mucous every 2 weeks. If it doesn't the
stomach acids would dissolve our digestive system. This is one of the reasons its hard to lose fat which
insulates our systems from the excess levels of acid we've accumulated from years of unbalanced eating. We must turn our system alkaline with fruits and vegetables to more efficiently lose fat. Ease the
system by reducing the time it works. Let it simply digest one full meal at a time. Give it a 24 hour
break and only fill up again when our entire system has completely digesting what we ate. We die when
our digestive system can no longer process food, and brain no longer function effectively; eat to live.

We are what we eat. We actually take on the characteristics of what we eat. A cow is easily lead in the wrong direction. A chicken is frightened easily, a pig just doesn't care! At least Snappers (pg.258 & 274) have courage and aren't that damaging to our digestive system. Fruits and vegetables that have been grafted aren't the best to eat, seedless grapes and oranges are sterile and can't reproduce themselves. We have seeds in us. The woman an egg and the male has sperm. The grapefruit was grafted from an orange and lemon for people who couldn't tolerate the lemon's acidity to obtain it's digestive system and blood cleaning properties.

Do we have Original thinking (truth) or grafted thinking (lies-which are manipulations of the truth)?

Accept our own and be ourselves. If we trip being ourselves, we will really stumble all over the place trying to be somebody else.

ENERGY

The energy in food comes from fixed nitrogen N2, occurring in various minerals and in all proteins, which is replenished in the soil by naturally allowing the fields to rest and grow.

* Since 1900 50% of the fixed nitrogen has been depleted from the soil. This was purposely done to sell nitrogen N2 used in a wide variety of important manufactures, including ammonia, nitric acid, TNT, and especially as petroleum based fertilizers back to the farmers of the mineral depleted soils.

Per the 12 units of energy the Sun gives the Earth, the cow naturally retains .5 units of the energy. By applying artificial fertilizers, etc. this number is increased. This brings to mind the controversy Oprah Winfrey was involved in when she mentioned she would no longer eat beef, due to the mad cow disease present in them, and a drop in beef sales occurred. Beef manufactures sued her in Texas, but loss due to the great amount of money Oprah has at her disposal to present the harmless image she portrays in the public which generated sympathy for her in the eyes of the jury. The point being made is that the Ten Percenters undermine the natural economy so they can control us through their artificial one. Another example is the case of Dr. Kervorkian, dubbed "Dr. Death" because of his practice of applying painless methods to end the life of suffering elders or others who were slowly dying in pain due to being hooked up to life maintaining machines. He sincerely sought to aid the consenting families of these patients. But the problem was the life-maintaining machine manufactures and hospitals who provide the high cost equipment were losing these vegetable state or totally dependent patients, whom they advised the grieving families there was a "possibility" their loved ones could recover, but truly were cash cows to health care providers and Dr. Kervorkian was cutting them off from the exploitive relationship the health care system strives to increase. Another example of the exploitive relationship is to think of how many poor people we know who can't have our loved ones in these nearly vegetable states, to remain on these high cost machines with the hope they will recover and the health care provider advise us to remove them from the machines because the chance of recovery is "highly not probable", because they want the machines reserved for the wealthy, abandoned and insured ones. We must provide family structure and nutrition for our people from babies to elders.

The process of energy trapped by plants fuels us. The process of photosynthesis stores energy in sugars and starches, energies we need to survive.

PHOTOSYNTHESIS

only 1% of the Sun's energy is photosynthesised

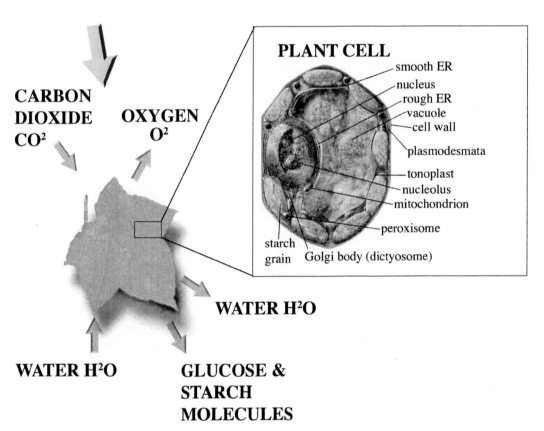

SUN

ENERGY RAYS

CARBON DIOXIDE CO²

OXYGEN O²

PLANT CELL

- smooth ER
- nucleus
- rough ER
- vacuole
- cell wall
- plasmodesmata
- tonoplast
- nucleolus
- mitochondrion
- peroxisome

starch grain   Golgi body (dictyosome)

WATER H²O

WATER H²O

GLUCOSE & STARCH MOLECULES

Of the total plant energy 5% of it that concerns us is in agricultural and only 1% of this is passed up the entropic levels to feed us.

TROPIC LEVELS
(For people who eat livestock)

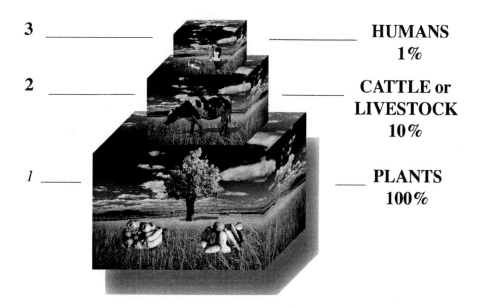

3 _____   _____ **HUMANS**
                                                     1%

2 _____   _____ **CATTLE or**
                                                     LIVESTOCK
                                                     10%

1 _____   ____ **PLANTS**
                                            100%

•*Units Joules per degree 1 is entropy, which never decreases, flows and increases total energy.*

When humans skip meat (cows, etc.) we get 10% of energy per unit. Therefore eat directly from our lower tropic level. We must let the soil from which we extract from rest a cycle or season. We must rotate the crop types. George Washington Carver developed this technique to perfection at Tuskegee with Booker Tee Washington whom sent us back to the plantations to redeem our people and teach practical, frugal and efficient methods of agriculture to better us. Allah gave them the answer.

* The word doctor literally means teacher.

Eating to Live purifies the blood, easing our system. Our heart is a pump, pumping 1,400 gallons of blood a day received from the veins into the arteries, thereby maintaining the flow of blood through the entire circulatory system.. The kidneys are a pair of organs, functioning to maintain proper water and electrolyte balance, regulate acid-base concentration, and filter the blood of metabolic wastes, which are then excreted as urine. The liver detoxifies the blood. It is an organ that secretes bile and is active in the formation of certain blood proteins and in the metabolism of carbohydrates, fats, and proteins. The Most Honorable Elijah Muhammad says the blood is the fluid of life.

STOP EATING ALL DAY

Eating all day takes our life fluid away from functioning efficiently. Deepak Chopra in the Seven Spiritual Laws of Success explains the process by which a molecule of sugar is ingested. Imagine the process involved with foods which conflict with our systems.

> To metabolize one molecule of sugar, by itself, requires infinite organizing power. A cell has to immediately send orders to the pancreas to start secreting insulin, send orders also to the pancreas to start secreting growth hormone, a whole symphony has to be orchestrated. The cell is a conscious entity.

Our thinking is balanced when we find the common thread in life. The answer is the God Allah in people. Our basic problems stem from our perception of God as only a spirit. He couldn't be present in people, especially me! We think. This thought justifies our rebelliousness to each other and neglect of our body or vessels. We really can't stand to see God through each other when its our faults he manifest through one to the other. So how collectively important is the flesh? we figure. In a selfish individualistic way we may improve it, but collectively we must cherish it for the allotted time we are assigned to it. The Creator knows what's best for us and has given us the keys to unlock the answers.

Eat the best foods. We are the best in creation. Food is an investment. What value do we give ourselves? Do we see ourselves as just some person or a Divine manifestation of All mighty God Allah. Relax, we can never under eat, if we balance the meal. We have a spiritual value and when we pollute our bodies and mind we rob our people of a better us. We have been taken off course and need guidance back to a righteous body and mind. Eating to Live reduces our sickness to only once a year. It reduces stress and helps us to think better, thereby increasing our value and time we can contribute to the Mission.

CONCLUSION

Master Fard Muhammad and the Most Honorable Elijah Muhammad gave us simple instructions to prolong life. Allah reveals the message of grace, blessings and chastisement to whom He pleases. It is up to us to act upon it and be grateful. Holy Quran, Sura 5-The Food, verses 111-115: (111)"And when I revealed to the disciples, saying, Believe in Me and My messenger, they said: We believe and bear witness that we submit." (112)"When the disciples said: O Jesus son of Mary, is thy Lord able to send down food(knowledge) to us from heaven(state of submission to Allah)? He said: Keep your duty to Allah if you are believers." (113)"They said: We desire to eat of it, and that our hearts should be at rest, and that we may know that thou hast indeed spoken truth to us, and that we may be witnesses thereof." (114)"Jesus, son of Mary, said: O Allah, our Lord, send down to us food from heaven which should be to us an ever-recurring happiness to the first of us and the last of us, and a sign from Thee, and give us sustenance and thou art the Best of the sustainers." (115)"Allah said: Surely I will send it down to you, but whoever disbelieves afterwards from among you, I will chastise him with a chastisement with which I will not chastise any one among the nations."

The elaborations and recent studies presented in this nutrition section is to put pressure on our minds, in regards to recommitting ourselves to eating to live. Although this is an extensive cookbook and nutrition guide, look forward to our expanded versions.

Version II will contain more recipes and nutritional information; Version III will include the Cooking & Baking School. This is Version One in a series of Five.

TABLE SETTING

Just as good food sets the tone for the evening, so does a table.

All these rules assume that we have a collection of silver. If we don't, we need not worry, and certainly don't hesitate to serve more than just one course because of lack of tableware. In between courses you can wash up whatever is needed or simply ask guests to keep a knife or a fork. The French use special knife-and-fork rests for just this purpose. Fine Nigerian Table mats are used in the examples below.

TWO STYLES OF TABLE SETTINGS

1. The first thing to do is to see that the cloth is clean and straight. If place mats are utilized, put one for each setting, placing each setting opposite one another.

2. Fold napkins and place on mat at the right. If there are guest place second large napkin at the right of the first napkin to be utilized on the lap.

3. Or we can do something fancy like making the napkin into a fan shape and putting it in the middle of each place setting or stuffing it into a large goblet. Glasses for drinks and water are always to the right of the setting. Butter plates, when utilized, are to the left.

4. Next is the silverware. Place soup spoon on the first napkin. Dinner fork to the left of soup spoon, place knife on the mat at our left.

5. Put salt and pepper on table. If we're going to serve at once, we may complete our table setting with a plate of toast, cheese, chutnies and relishes. But if we aren't ready to serve, then leave it off until we are ready. If there are more than four guests, use two plates of toast.

6. Most important, whether for guests or when we're just family, remember always to have our plates, serving bowls and platters warm whenever we are serving hot food. It is so unpleasant to have nice hot food congealing on a cold plate after it is served. Warm everything in a low heated oven or on the back of the stove, if we have room; if not, a radiator, a hot plate, and even the drying cycle of a dishwasher make excellent plate warmers.

SERVING

1. Have the family or guest to come into the dining room. Have each to stand at our place with the chair in back of us until the prayer has been said, then we may be seated.

2. The soup is served with the dinner plate under the soup bowl. Place it in the center of the mat in front of the person from the right.

3. After the soup is finished, remove the plate, bowl and spoon. If we have a plate salad we may serve it after we remove the soup plate.

4. Bring the food in on each plate. Milk, for those who desire it, is always served with the dinner. Place glass near the upper right hand corner of the place mat.

5. After we have finished, remove both dinner and salad plates, and serve the dessert. If the dessert is cake or plate pie, serve it on a dessert plate with the fork to the right of it; with the handle and small end of the dessert facing us. Place it in the center of the mat and more of a dessert drink may be served if desired.

6. When dessert is finished, remove everything from the table; also remove crumbs, with a flat blade-type utensil. Lightly scrape them into a napkin held-with our hand, under the edge of a table.

7. Bring in the cream and sugar for coffee. If we have an electric coffee maker or better a thermal carafé, we may serve the coffee at the table. If not, bring coffee in cup on a serving tray with spoon on each saucer.

8. After coffee is finished, remove cups, cream and sugar, and serve water.

9. Bring in a pitcher of water and glasses. Pour each a glass. Refill the pitcher and put it on the table.

TABLE ETIQUETTE

Master Fard Muhammad and the Most Honorable Elijah Muhammad instructs us in the 24 Principles of Islam: #2 "A Muslim is polite and courteous"; #10 "A Muslim is clean in mind, body and action"; and #15 "A Muslim knows what to say, how to say it, when to say it, where to say it, and whom to say it to." We must be right and exact with our manners at the table. A cultured person can detect whether we've been taught to eat properly. For example: To eat without making much sound of the lips, to grasp the fork and knife properly, to drink quietly, to utilize the napkin properly, to make no noise with any of the implements of the table, and to eat slowly and chew the food thoroughly. Teach these principles to our children, and then they will feel at their ease at the most exquisite tables in the land. Sitting at a dining table quickly reveals the level of refinement of us, and those of us who have not been educated in table etiquette can feel "out of place." It can be embarrassing to some of us, if we feel others registering our deficiency at this setting. God forbid someone is "soaking in" our lack of training of the essentials table etiquette. We should never accept more food than we plan to eat. The only foodstuff remaining on the table after our courses should be the garnishes. It is a sin to waste food. The knife should never be UTILIZED to carry food to the mouth, but only to cut it up into small mouthfuls; then place it upon the plate at one side, and take the fork in the right hand, and eat all the food with it. When both have been utilized finally, they should be laid diagonally across the plate, with both handles towards the right hand; this is understood by well-trained and alert waiters to be the signal for removing them, together with the plate.

It is wise instruction to keep the mouth shut closely while chewing the food. It is the opening of the lips which causes the "smacking" which seems very disgusting. Chew our food well, but do it silently, and be careful to take small mouthfuls. The knife can be utilized to cut the meat finely, as large pieces of meat are not healthful, and appear very indelicate. Have a knife and a fork for each course, so that there need be no replacing of them after the breakfast and dinner is served. Be cautious not to clatter our knives and forks upon our plates, and utilize them with out noise. When passing the plate for a second helping, lay them together at one side of the table, with handles to the right. When we are helped to anything, do not wait until the rest of the company are provided, as it is not considered good manners. Soup is always served for the first course, and it should be eaten with dessert spoons, and taken from the sides, not the tips, of them, without any sound of the lips, and not sucked into the mouth audibly from the from end of the spoon. Never ask to be helped to a soup a second time. The host or hostess may ask us to take a second plate, but we should politely decline. Fish Chowder (pg.89), which is served in soup plates, is an exception to this rule, and is considered proper to take a second plateful if we desire.

Another generally neglected obligation is that of spreading butter on our bread as it lies on our plate, or slightly lifted at one end of the plate. It is better to cut it, a bit at a time, after buttering it, and put piece by piece in our mouth with our finger and thumb. Never help ourselves to butter or any other food with our own knife or fork. It is not considered good taste to mix food on the same plate. Salt must be left on the side of the plate and never on the tablecloth.

We can be flexible with these rules, they aren't etched in stone. A Cream type cake (pg.209) and anything of similar nature should be eaten with fork and knife, never bitten. Asparagus (pg.72 & 140), if it is fit to be set before us, the whole of it may be eaten. Pastry (pg.232) should be broken and eaten with a fork, never cut with a knife. Fish (pg.267) should be eaten with a fork. Peas (pg.155) and beans require the fork only; however food that cannot be held with a fork should be eaten with a spoon. Potatoes (pg.74 & 157), if mashed, should be mashed with a fork. Green corn (pg.73 & 151) should be eaten from the cob; but it must be held with a single hand.

Olives (pg.171), Celery (pg.73 & 150), Radishes (pg.166), and relishes of that kind are to be eaten with the fingers. Fish is to be eaten with the fork, without the assistance of the knife; a bit of bread in the left hand sometimes helps one to master a refractory morsel. Fresh fruit (pg.166) should be eaten with a silver-bladed knife, especially pears, apples, etc. Berries are to be eaten with a spoon. It is not proper to drink with a spoon in the cup; nor should one ever drain a cup or glass. Bring the glass perpendicularly to the lips, and then lift it to a slight angle. Do this easily. It is far better for the digestion not to drink liquids until the meal is finished. Drink gently, and do not pour it down our throat like water turned out of a pitcher nor guzzle.

RECEPTION

The guest should be received with a warm reception. Have a (host)brother or (hosts)brothers wait for them at the street entrance to show them where to park or valet park for them. The host should open the doors for all (female guest)sisters, carry any heavy bags and escort the guests to the host house or premise. Brothers(host) and sisters(host) can take coats and packages to a storage area, preferably out of site, then treat guest to any planned activities for the day.

The brothers(men) should seat the sisters(women) first at the table then be seated ourselves. Unfold our napkin and lay it across our lap in such a manner that it will not slide off upon the floor; a brother should place it across our right knee. When soup is eaten, wipe the mouth carefully with the napkin, and use it to wipe the hands after meals—if, in the Asiatic tradition, steamed rags aren't furnished at this time. Steamed rags should be steamed until slightly damp in the top compartment of a chinese bamboo steamer and handed out on saucers at the table; handle rags with prongs.

Spoons are sometimes utilized with firm puddings, but forks are the better style. A spoon should never be turned over in the mouth. The knife should be held freely by the handle only, the forefinger being the only one to touch the blade, and that only along the back of the blade at the root, and no further down.

At the conclusion of a course, where they have been utilized, knife and fork should be laid side by side across the middle of the plate.

The host or hostess should offer everything at the left of the guest, that the guest may be at liberty to use the right hand.

Our teeth are not to be picked at the table; but if it is impossible to hinder it, it should be behind the napkin. We may pick a bone at the table, but, as with corn, only one hand is allowed to touch it; yet we can easily get enough from it with knife and fork, which is certainly the more elegant way of doing it; we are, however, on no account to suck or slurp our finger after it.

If we are in doubt as to the best way to do a thing, let our conscious (wife or husband) be our guide and follow what is most rational; Allah will always give a hint, and that will be the proper etiquette. Be comfortable and at ease towards enjoying the dinner, and making ourselves agreeable to the company or guest, whom are the most important people in the premise at the moment and all attention, courtesy and protocol should be focused on them. There is reason for everything in polite usage; thus the reason why we don't blow a thing to cool it, is not only that it is an inelegant and vulgar action intrinsically, but because it may be offensive to others, and it, moreover reveals, haste, which, whether from greedi-ness or a desire to eat and run, is equally objectionable. The best training is to watch experienced host, speak to waiters, and get books from the library and internet on etiquette.

In conclusion, if we seat ourselves properly at the table and take reason into account, we will do well. We must not pull our chair too closely to the table, for the natural result is the inability to utilize a knife and fork without inconveniencing our neighbor at the table; the elbows are to be held well in and close to our side, which cannot be done if the chair is too near the table. We should not lie or lean along the table, nor rest our arm upon it. Nor are we to touch any of the dishes. We must not tap our fingers on the table or play with utensils or any object, unless it is a business meeting where a prototype or sample of a business product in a napkin is passed around to anyone desiring to inspect it. Always sneeze or cough into a napkin away from the table. If we cross-talk with someone at the opposite side of a big table, make sure we don't interfere with the neighbor's, flanking us, conversation; if a member of the family, we can perform all duties of hospitality through helpers, and wherever there are helpers or aiders, neither family nor guests are to pass or help from any dish. Lastly, when rising from our chair leave it where it stands, only moving it to allow someone to pass. When leaving the residence the brothers escort the sisters out and carry the heavy packages to vehicles, load it and hold the doors open until the sisters are seated, then wait for an affirmation they are prepared to have to the door closed; the impediment to safely closing the door usually is a belt from an overcoat or the bottom material of a dress draped over the bottom opening of the vehicle where the bottom of the door closes shut. Clear any traffic obstacles from the perimeter of the premises. And send off the guests with a blessed farewell.

KITCHEN HEALTH SUGGESTIONS

SANITATION ADVICE

The Honorable Elijah Muhàmmad teaches us in the 12th Principle of Islam that "A Muslim keeps his person clean, as well as his living quarters." Our kitchens must be immaculately clean.

Once we have gotten into the routine of food preparation and cooking recipes, we usually take safety for granted; think over this, we are handling food, the phone rings, we answer the phone, converse, hang up, then go back to handling food. I witnessed this in a restaurant, which has since closed. This information deals with proper food handling and keeping. Use fresh, high quality ingredients and now we will explain how to keep them safe to consume. Share this information with family and friends.

Firstly, we must be conscious of undetectable dangers. Food poisoning is very common and it should be the responsibility of everyone who prepares food to do all we can to prevent poisoning ourselves, families and friends.

FOODBORNE ILLNESSES

Most of foodborne illnesses are caused by bacteria. Although, viruses, protozoa and trichinae are other microorganisms that may contribute to illnesses.

ABOUT BACTERIA

Bacterium are unicellular organisms that take in nutrients, produce waste, have the power to move spontaneously, may be free-living, and multiply quickly. Of the many types here are a few that negatively affect us: Pathogenic bacteria is a group name for the bacteria that are capable of causing disease (see pg.34). This group of bacteria may cause illness from living and multiplying in food or they may utilize food (without flourishing in it) as the means in which they are transferred to us.

Many bacteria produce toxins in foods as they multiply. This toxin is very powerful and will cause illness and even death. Botulism toxin is the worst and most deadly characterized by nausea, vomiting, disturbed vision, muscular weakness, and fatigue. Other toxins will cause various degrees of illness which are almost always thought to be something other than food poisoning.

Bacteria thrives on food, moisture and warmth to multiply. Many bacteria must also have air, but others do better without air. All the bacteria that cause foodborne illness prefer foods of a proteinaceous nature such as milk, meat, poultry, eggs and seafood. Bacteria must have moisture to flourish. Dry foods such as sugar, flour, cookies and dry baked goods inhibit bacterial growth and are not good environment for bacteria to flourish. All bacteria grow best at a warm temperature from 60°F to 120°F. Pathogens, the foodborne illness causing bacteria, grow best at about 98.6°F body temperature.

All food prepared within the temperature range of 45°F to 145°F is a potential source of bacterial infection. If the food remains within this temperature range for 2 to 4 hours it may be contaminated and could possibly cause illness.

Heat can kill bacteria. However, clostridium botulism bacteria will survive unless processing methods are adhered to. This bacteria grows best without air in a sealed can or jar. Baking or cooking does not mean that food is free from infection. Freezing will not kill bacteria. Bacteria will not flourish when frozen, but will continue to grow when the food is thawed.

STAPH (pronounced STAF) FOOD POISONING

The toxin produced by the bacterium staphylococcus aureus (staph) is the most common cause of food poisoning. Staph bacteria grows well in high salt concentrates and in high sugar concentrations. It will also survive freezing. Since it is the toxin that is poison and not the bacteria itself—food poisoning may occur even after the bacteria has been killed by heat.

Symptoms in people who have Staph poisoning will appear on an average of 2 to 3 hours and include salivation, nausea, vomiting, abdominal cramps, diarrhea, headaches, muscular cramps, sweating, chills and prostration. These symptoms may last for 1 to 2 days.

The most common source of Staph bacteria is the human body. Even healthy people carry the bacteria in our mouths, throats, noses, pimples and infected wounds. When an infected person does not utilize proper food handling techniques they may transmit the Staph bacteria to food.

Staph is transmitted by:
1. The infected person passing the Staph bacteria to the food.
2. The Staph bacteria grows and produces the toxin.
3. The toxin causes food poisoning in everyone who eats it.

Protein based foods are the most likely to be infected with the Staph bacterium. Foods that are ground or chopped such as ground meat are contaminated from the food handler, tables, equipment. Eggs utilized in a recipe could be contaminated if they were held in a bowl which had been utilized to hold contaminated ground meat, etc.

Foods contaminated with Staph bacteria usually look, smell and taste normal.

Staph bacteria can be killed by heating to 165°F, but the toxin it has produced will still cause food poisoning.

Seven ways to prevent Staph bacteria poisoning:

1. Keep food clean and free of the bacteria in the first place.
2. Keep food hot at least 140°F or cold at least 45°F.
3. Cool cooked or baked food rapidly to a safe temperature.
4. Do not cough or sneeze on food.
5. Do not touch our mouth or nose while preparing food.
6. Keep all cuts, sores and infections treated and covered while preparing food.
7. Sanitize the tools and the work table utilized.

SALMONELLA FOOD POISONING

Salmonellosis is the infection caused by the salmonella bacteria. This bacterium does not develop a toxin and must be ingested in order to cause food poisoning.

Although symptoms in people who have salmonellosis are much like Staph poisoning, salmonellosis symptoms take an average of 12 to 24 hours to appear.

Salmonella bacteria come from:

1. The intestine tract of humans.
2. Human feces and sewage.
3. The intestine tract of animals.
4. Animal feces and sewage.

Salmonella bacteria can be killed by heating food to 165°F. However, foods may be contaminated after cooking and therefore the following precautions are a must.

1. We should wash and dry our hands before handling food.
2. We should wash and dry our hands after visiting the toilet.
3. We should wash and dry our hands after handling raw meat.
4. We should wash and dry our hands after touching any object that is suspect of being dirty.
5. Work area surfaces should be scrubbed and sanitized before and after utilizing for the preparation of foods.
6. Insects and rodents must be kept under control.
7. Pets must be limited to a tank or cage in a controlled area.
8. Keep foods hot at 140°F and cold at 45°F.
9. Plumbing should be kept in good working order to prevent contamination from sewage.
10. Dirty or cracked eggs should never be utilized.
11. Poultry should be rinsed well and cooked at a high temperature.
12. All meat (especially ground and rolled) and fish should be cooked thoroughly.

PERFRINGEN FOOD POISONING

Perfringens are found everywhere. They are in the intestine tract of humans and animals, feces, sewage, manure, soil and dust.

Clostridium perfringens causes gastrointestinal illness. In perfringens poisoning toxin and large numbers of the bacterial cells must be ingested.

Symptoms occur within 8 to 22 hours and are much the same as those of Staph except usually no vomiting.

Perfringens may be controlled by:
1. Do not handle cooked meat after handling raw meat.
2. Utilize separate work surfaces for raw meats and other menu items.
3. Washing our hands after visiting the toilet.
4. Keep our kitchen dust free.
5. Keep food hot at 140°F and cold at 45°F.
6. Cool foods that are hot as rapidly as possible and do not let set at room temperature.

PREVENT FOOD POISONING

1. Wash our hands up to wrist.
2. Do not reuse containers or utilize containers for something other than which they are intended. (Do not utilize a salt shaker to hold anything other than salt.)
3. Never store caustic materials in the kitchen.
4. Keep flies and other insects out of the kitchen.
5. Get rid of rusted cans, swollen cans and dented cans. Do not feed their contents to pets.
6. Get rid of home canned products that are not fresh. (The canning recipe should tell us the maximum time to keep an item, mark the containers with dates.)
7. Follow home canning methods to the letter.
8. Do not keep anything that is molded.
9. Sanitize our work area and inside our refrigerator regularly.
10. Keep our glasses, plates, utensils clean and dust free. (Wash and rinse in very hot water.)
11. Do not store pesticides near foods.
12. Keep the floors, walls and ceiling of our kitchens clean and dust free.
13. Store dry foods in a clean, insect free place. Do not store near water pipes or under sewer pipes.
14. All opened packages should be stored in closed and labeled containers.

15. Always utilize the oldest packages first. Put fresh boxes and cans to the back of the storage shelf.
16. Check and make sure that our refrigerator is at 40°F or below. Make sure our freezer is at 0°F.
17. Allow for good air circulation around items in the refrigerator.
18. Divide large portions of food into small sizes for faster cooling.
19. Date everything in the freezer and utilize the oldest first.
20. Keep garbage areas out of the kitchen.
21. Keep screens on doors and windows in good condition. Seal cracks and holes in walls. Utilize pest controls regularly and safely.
22. Keep our dishwasher clean and in good running order.
23. Insist that everyone maintains good personal hygiene.

WAYS TO AVOID LETHAL BACTERIA

Here is how pregnant women can reduce your chances of listeria (rod-shaped, gram-positive bacterium) infection:
1. Avoid soft cheeses such as feta, mozzarella, goat, brie, Camembert, blue-veined and Mexican.
2. If you must utilize soft cheeses, cook them to boiling.
3. Hard cheeses as well as processed, cream and cottage cheese and yogurt are fine if kept properly refrigerated.
4. Utilize only pasteurized dairy products. Hard cheese made from unpasteurized milk should be aged at least 60 days.
5. Eat only thoroughly cooked meats, poultry and seafood.
6. Thoroughly reheat meats from deli counters, including hot dogs, salami and cold cuts.
7. Avoid or cook to steaming ready-to-eat foods from stores and delis.
8. Wash raw vegetables before eating.
9. Keep uncooked meats separated from all other foods.
10. Wash hands, knives and cutting boards after handling uncooked foods.
11. Keep counter tops, utensils and the inside of your refrigerator clean.

BUYING AND STORING PRODUCE

Tomatoes: The redder, the better. For eating raw, splurge on a greenhouse variety. For cooking, the best value is an ordinary plum tomato. Keep any tomato out on the counter until its fully ripe.
Grape: Store grapes in pierced plastic bags in the refrigerator. Don't wash them first, since the dusty residue provides a protective layer.
Peaches, nectarines & plums: The flesh should give a bit near the stem when pressed. If the fruit is hard, put it in a loosely closed paper bag at room temperature for several days; the fruit emits ethylene gas, which speeds ripening.

Eggplant: To make sure an eggplant isn't dry inside, tap on it with your knuckles. If it sounds hollow, don't buy it.

Pears: Unlike summer pears, which turn yellow or crimson as they mature, most varieties we will find in winter remain brown or green. To tell if a pear is ready to eat, see if it gives slightly near the stem when pressed. If the fruit's base is soft, the pear is probably overripe.

WHAT CHEFS BUY

Sometimes chefs rely on out-of -season produce. Without peppers, Eggplant and parsley we would have to completely pare down our cooking styles.

In the winter utilize cold-storage produce. Zucchini, acorn and butternut squash, turnips and rutabagas have thick skins and even after two months in storage, they are still fresh and moist. But, we can also utilize Mexican watermelons and Peruvian asparagus as minor ingredients.

Most chefs have a philosophical objection to out-of-season produce, which grafting or genetic altering may never overcome. It goes out of the cycle of nature to serve summer fruits in January.

BAKING SUBSTITUTION

Apples, Tart
Granny Smith or Gravenstein
Apples, Sweet & Tart
McIntosh or Jonathan
Apple Pie Spice, 1 teaspoon
1/2 teaspoon ground cinnamon plus 1/4 teaspoon ground nutmeg,
1/8 teaspoon ground allspice, and dash ground cloves or ginger.
Almonds, roasted
Sesame seeds, roasted

Baking Powder
1/2 teaspoon cream of tartar & 1/4 teaspoon baking soda
Butter
Apple Sauce (pg.250) or prune purée
Buttermilk, 1 cup
1 cup milk & 1 3/4 tablespoons cream of tartar or sour cream or low-fat yogurt
Butternut Squash
acorn squash
Light Cream, 1 cup

7/8 cup milk & 3 tablespoons butter

Heavy Cream, 1 cup

3/4 cup milk & 1/3 cup butter

Chocolate, unsweetened, 1 ounce

3 tablespoons cocoa & 1 tablespoon butter(cold)

Chocolate, unsweetened pre-melted, 1 ounce

3 tablespoons cocoa & 1 tablespoon corn oil

Chocolate, Semisweet, 1 ounce

1 ounce unsweetened chocolate & 1 tablespoon Raw™ sugar or 3 tablespoons

cocoa & 1 tablespoon Raw™ sugar & 1 tablespoon butter(cold)

Condensed Milk, Sweetened

1 cup powdered milk, 1/3 cup hot water, 1/2 cup Raw™ sugar & 1 tablespoon butter

(Blend ingredients until smooth; refrigerate)

Cornstarch

Unbleached flour, up to a few tablespoons, for thickening

Corn Syrup, 1 cup

1 cup Raw™ sugar & 1/4 cup boiling water. (dissolve)

Cream Cheese

Cottage Cheese blended with cream

Currants

Gooseberries or raisins

Dates

Raisins

Egg, 1 whole

2 egg whites; 2 egg yolks & 1 tablespoon water;

or 1/4 cup frozen egg product, thawed.

Evaporated Milk

Light cream or half-and-half

Flour, for thickening, up to a few tablespoons only

Tapioca or cornstarch, or 1 whole egg or 2 yolks or

2 whites (for cooked sauces)—whisk vigorously

Flour, Whole Wheat, 1 cup

2 tablespoons wheat germ & enough white flour to make 1 cup

Fruit Liqueur, 1 tablespoon

1 tablespoon fruit juice.

Ginger, powdered

Mace & lemon peel, finely grated

Gingerroot, grated, 1 teaspoon

1/4 teaspoon ground ginger & Pinch white pepper dash lemon juice

Half-and-Half

3 tablespoons melted butter & enough milk to make 1 cup.

Honey, 1 cup

1 1/4 cups Raw™ sugar & 1/4 cup more liquid

Kiwi Fruit

Strawberries & a splash of lime juice

Lemon

Lime (the juice from a fruit = 1 tablespoon grated rind (zest)

Lemon Juice

Vinegar or lime juice

Lemon Peel, finely grated

Lime or orange peel

Mace

Allspice or cloves or nutmeg (all 4 are interchangeable)

Mango

Peach with a little lime and allspice

Mascarpone Cheese, 8 ounces

8 ounces regular cream cheese, whipped with a little butter

Mayonnaise

Sour cream or yogurt & a splash of lemon juice

Milk

Fruit juice plus 1/2 teaspoon baking powder added to flour

Molasses, 1 cup

1 cup honey or 3/4 cup Raw™ sugar & 1/4 cup liquid, and increase spices.

Nuts

Bran

Oil, 1 tablespoon

1 1/4 tablespoon butter

Peanut Butter

Tahini

Pears

Apples

Prunes

Dates or raisins or dried apricots (all 4 are interchangeable)

Pumpkin

Acorn squash or butternut squash or turban squash

Raspberries

Blackberries

Shortening

Butter
Sour Cream, 1 cup
1 cup yogurt or 1 tablespoon lime juice & enough evaporated milk to make 1 cup

or 6 ounces cream cheese plus 3 tablespoons milk
Sugar, Granulated White, 1 cup
1 cup superfine sugar or 1 cup packed brown sugar or

1 cup Raw™ sugar or 2 cups powdered sugar, sifted
Sugar, Brown, 1/2 cup
1/2 cup white sugar plus 2 tablespoons molasses
Yeast, Dry, 1 envelope
1/2 cake compressed yeast, crumbled

PERCEPTIONS

Many people perceive exercising to lose weight is better than diet. Yet, we are composed of what we eat. Proper dieting cleanses the body.

Running World©, January 1997

On a light jog we take an average 1,700 steps per mile. (Some of us average 575 paces jogging and 510 paces trotting per mile.)

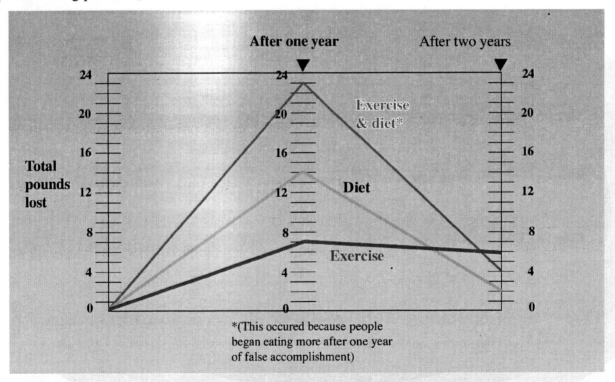

This is a long-range program we must see ourselves ten years from now being happier because of what we have decided to do today. After one year people perceive that they have arrived by meeting a one year goal. Don't confuse activity with accomplishment.

ONE YEAR PLAN TO ADJUST NUTRITION PROGRAM TO ONE MEAL A DAY

Firstly, we must SEE ourselves eating one meal a day and reaping the benefits of Eating To Live.

Let positive supportive friends know our "give up" (bad habits) goal. It will put pressure (good) on us. Be mindful that all goals and transitions are to be phased in so as to not shock our systems. Adjust our nutritional program to one meal a day over a period of time. It took years to gain the weight by small "extras" to satisfy hunger associated with emotional circumstances which turned into random eating and allowing "convenient" snacks and foods to become our program or habit. It will take months to years to refine our actions and to discipline our stomachs. People with a lot of fat can die from the toxins which have accumulated in our bodies over the years. Because when we abruptly fast, from this condition, our bodies digest all the food in our digestive systems, then our bodies feed off the only thing left, the fats and toxins which have deposited over the years by eating the wrong foods. The layer of fat has developed to prevent high acid levels, caused by eating the wrong foods, from corroding our systems. This is why it seems we can hardly lose weight. We must transform our system to alkaline base before fat will dissolve. Detoxification is phased in. [Refer to Audio tape Science of "Fat Reduction" Muslim Cookbook Version II™]

ONE YEAR GOAL OF ONE MEAL A DAY

Firstly, get a blank journal to document our progress. Write in it that we will be successful in accomplishing this goal in one year because we deserve the best conditioning the Creator has to offer. HE only helps those who strive. "And whoever strives hard, strives for himself. Surely Allah is Self-sufficient, above (need of) (His) creatures." The Holy Qurán, Sura 29; vs 6.

Break our goals down into 30 day intervals. Taking things in steps gives a sense of accomplishment when we complete a part. We must be serious about being refined, because if we don't see an immediate change we may be discouraged. Putting the process into intervals gives us a chance to see a small change. Some people confuse activity with accomplishment. We are doing something but aren't getting anything completed. We must stick to our plan. Remember a stick is utilized to guide a young sapling (baby tree) straight as it grows so it will have a symmetrical appearance at its maturely. A pine tree is an example of a tree that when straightened has a better appearance then when grown crooked. The stick represents discipline. It is when we reap the harvest of a finely cultivated cherry tree that we have an appreciation for the early discipline in cultivating that cherry tree. Take our time and be patient. It took us years to get into bad shape and it will take us months to years to get into the best condition. Yet, we will see constant improvement when we are consistent.

ONE YEAR GOAL OF ONE MEAL A DAY

* During the first **30** days we want to cut out all snacks. A snack is any food eaten between a meal. "Any amount of food consumed at any time is what we are considering a meal." One molecule of sugar is enough to begin the digestive process. The substitute for snacks is water, coffee or tea.

* During the next 30 days—which is up to day **60**—we want to limit ourselves to just three meals a day.

* During the next 30 days—which is up to day **90**—we want to enjoy ourselves to eating only home cooked food (if practical). Take food to work.

* During the next 30 days—which is up to day **120**—we want to cut back on meat and increase our fish consumption.

* During the next 60 days—which is up to day **180**—we want to limit ourselves to simply two meals a day. Either cut out dinner or lunch. We want to decrease processed food (food in the can, or any ready made food). And we want to increase our vegetable consumption.

* During the next 30 days—which is up to day **210**—we want simply two meals a day of whole wheat bread, navy bean soup, the right vegetables, the right fish, fruit and the right desserts.

* During the next 50 days—which is up to day **260**—we want to do a one day watermelon or juice fast.

* During the next 30 days—which is up to day **290**—we want to limit ourselves to one meal a day for three days.

* During the next 30 days—which is up to day **320**—we want to do a one day fast without food, then the next day a watermelon or juice fast.

* During the next 40 days—which is up to day **360**—we want to limit ourselves to simply one meal a day as a basic eating habit. We want to perform a two day fast at the end of each month.

TWO YEAR PLAN

* During the next year we want to plan our one meal a day with a three day fast at the end of each month.

THREE YEAR PLAN

* During the next year up to year three we want to have achieved our one meal a day with a two day fast at the end of each week as a standard practice. We should fast 5 days the end of each month, or 3 days the end of each two weeks or two days the end of each week.

After this time we may begin fasting for longer days. We would suggest a seven day fast once in a while. Do as many as we can.

Muslims have been following the program of "How To Eat To Live" since Master Fard Muhammad introduced it to us in the 1930s. It has helped produce the most healthiest and beautiful people on the planet.

KEEP PLANNING

LIFE'S GOAL= To fill empty jar with rocks

Family & Work=

Health=

Errands & Play=

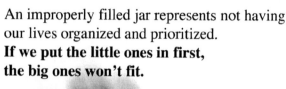

MOTTO= Big rocks first, then the little rocks will fit.

An improperly filled jar represents not having our lives organized and prioritized.
If we put the little ones in first, the big ones won't fit.

A properly filled jar represents having our lives organized and prioritized.
When we put the big ones in first, the little ones will fill in the spaces.

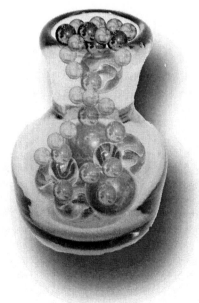

Adapted from "7 Habits of Highly Effective People"

INGREDIENTS: HOW TO UTILIZE THEM

SHORTENINGS, FATS AND OILS (AVOIDING PORK)

Taking short cuts. With the introduction of the process of hydrogenation in 1910 manufacturers of the all-hydrogenated oils (cottonseed oils) began to realize the advantage of grafting and developing new products rather than finding substitutes for lard.

In regards to swine, be on the look-out for pork fat, we have to look for lard, shortening, animal fat and the like. As for shortening, we have to look-out for the word vegetable shortening, pure vegetable shortening, butter and the like. As for animal meat, be on guard for pork, ham, bacon and the like. As for gelatin, we have to discern whether it source is from animal or plant. If the source of gelatin is animal, then we have to be concerned whether the animal was the pig or not. The least expensive animal to raise is the pig and therefore the Ten Percenters and lower members of their exploitive economic and social food chain (Food Chain=Exploit peoples ignorance with products which maintain an unaware state) utilize it and it's by-products in every field of industry.

Types of shortenings:

There are multiple types of shortening, depending on the context to the utilization of the word, as well as the contents of ingredients.
1. All butter shortening: Some breads are found with the label as "all butter shortening". This means that the source of shortening is butter. It is understood that butter is prepared from milk fat, particularly cows.
2. Animal shortening: The source of the fat is an animal one, however, the fat can be of one animal or a combination of several, depending on the economics and the quality. As long as lard is the least expensive of all animal fats, it is used.
3. Butter crust or top shortening: There are a few types of breads on the market that contain on their labels a quotation like "butter crust" or "buttertop". Such type of bread may contain any other shortening mixed with the dough. However, butter has been added to the surface or crust so as to give it a better color, appearance and taste. [Bake our own Bread (pg.188)].
4. Lard shortening: There are some types of breads that contain lard as their main shortening or as one of the other shortenings. Lard is the white solid or semisolid rendered fat of a hog.—lard transitive verb. larded, larding, lards. 1. To cover or coat with lard or a similar fat. 2. To insert strips of fat or bacon in (meat) before cooking. 3.a. To enrich or lace heavily with extra material; embellish. b. To fill throughout; inject. —lardy adjective.
5. Pure vegetables shortening: The source of this type of shortening is plants. However, we should be mindful that the source is mainly coconut oil which has a high degree of saturation.

6. Shortening: If the term shortening is used as such, it means that the fat is a mixture of animal and vegetable sources. The animal sources could be one or a combination of beef, mutton (The flesh of fully grown sheep) and pork fat (lard). If lard is the least expensive of the fats listed it will be utilized.

7. Vegetable shortening: The source of this type of shortening is plants, particularly coconut oil, If the word "pure" is not utilized with "vegetable shortening" there is no assurance that animal fats have not been added, even at the rate of 5% to 10%.

TERMS TO KNOW CONCERNING SHORTENING

1. Emulsion—A suspension of small globules of one liquid in a second liquid with which the first will not mix; example: an emulsion of oil and vinegar.

2. Emulsification—A process of lowering the surface tension or the physical breaking up of the large particles of an immiscible liquid into smaller ones that remain suspended in another liquid. An agent which has this ability is called an emulsifier. Examples of this would be bile salts, lecithin and diglycerides. The process of emulsification of fat by the action of these agents facilitates its digestion. For this reason the food industry adds emulsifiers to certain foods, that if they are that hard on the digestive system we shouldn't put them in us in the first place.

3. Diglyceride (DG)—It is a glyceride which contains two molecules of fatty acids. This type of fat is utilized in the food industry to increase the degree of emulsification before it is hydrolyzed.

4. Hydrogenate—To combine with or subject to the action of hydrogen, especially to combine (an unsaturated oil) with hydrogen to produce a solid fat.

5. Lard—It is purified internal fat from the abdomen of the pig. It is a soft white unctuous mass; slight characteristic odor, bland taste.

6. Lard oil—It is the oil derived from lard at a low temperature. It contains olein and stearin and it is colorless or pale yellow. It is utilized as a lubricant, in the manufacturing of soap, oiling wool and illuminant.

7. Lecithin-lecithol—A mixture of the diglycerides of stearic, palmitic and oleic acids linked to the choline ester of phosphoric acid. Its scientific name is phosphatidylcholine (PC). The commercial grades contain 2.2% by weight. It is found in all living organisms (plant and animals), the plasma membrane of plant and animal cells. It is a significant constituent of nervous tissue and brain substance. It is isolated from egg yolks and obtained from soybeans as a bi-product in the manufacture of soybean oil. It is UTILIZED in chocolate, margarine and in the food industry in general. It is also utilized in pharmaceuticals and in cosmetics. In medical us it is utilized as a lipotropic agent. It emulsifies fat before it is digested.

8. Fatty acids—Any of a large group of monobasic acids, especially those found in animal and vegetable fats and oils. Characteristically made up of saturated or unsaturated aliphatic

compounds with an even number of carbon atoms, this group of acids includes palmitic, stearic and oleic acids.

9. Phospholipid (PL)—The other name for it is phosphatide. It is substituted fat containing a phosphoric residue, nitrogenous compounds and other constituents in addition to fatty acids and glycerol. Examples of phospholipids would be lecithins, sphingomyelins, cephalins and plasmalogens.

10. Polyunsaturated fats (PUFA)—Are those compounds that have two or more unsaturated linkages or double bonds. Interesting are linoleic acid (two double bonds), linolenic acid (three double bonds) and arachidonic acid (four double bonds). The PUFA are essential for growth, reproduction, health of the skin and proper use of fats. They are essential because the body cannot synthesize them and hence has to have them daily from the diet. PUFA are better for health than the saturated fatty acids, i.e., liquid oils are better for health than solid fats. Examples of unsaturated acids:
    A. Arachidonic Acid
    B. Linoleic Acid
    C. Linolenic Acid
    D. Oleic Acid

11. Saturated fat—The carbon's of the fatty acids in fats are having single bonds. Saturation of fatty acids in fats amounts to the firmness and solidification of fats at room temperature. The most common in animal fats are palmitic and stearic acids.

12. Shortening—Shortening is a general term referred to the solid fats and liquid oils.

THE SUPREME OIL

Olive oil is cholesterol-free and helps to lower the body's overall cholesterol level without the loss of beneficial fats. It also enables the digestive system to function more efficiently and promotes bone growth.

Utilize the purest oils like condiments, as a top note to a dish. There's nothing like the lush bouquet of a fine oil, so we cook most foods with olive oil.

Select a good oil:
* Here's a test for "true virginity." Insert a drop of oil in a glass bowl and refrigerate for a few days. if it crystallizes, its probably an authentic extra virgin oil. If it forms a block, it's likely to be chemically refined oil with some first-pressed oil added. A buttery consistency indicates refined oil extracted from the pulp of pressings.
* Seek a knowledgeable merchant. Many gourmet grocers will not sell an oil unless they have personally sampled it. Question the grocer about an oil's qualities; he or she should also know the year it was harvested.

* Learn the language of oil. Familiarize ourselves with the main regions of oil-producing countries; in Italy, for example, the two prime places are Liguria and Tuscany.

* Care for the oil. Light, heat and air can turn it rancid. Store it in a cool, dark place, tightly sealed. When we buy oil in the can, transfer it upon opening to a glass or glazed terracotta jar. Do not refrigerate. Do not close airtight, let the bottle breathe a little by plugging it with a paper towel or cloth.

* Olive oil does not improve with age and is best utilized when newly pressed. Observe the harvest date on the label.

COMPARING THE OLIVE OILS

Olive oil is available in a wide variety of flavors, colors and aromas, depending on the soil type, climate and time of harvest. Its greatest significant variable is the acidity level. Extra virgin, the most highly regarded oil, has the lowest acidity level, which accounts for its superior flavor. Virgin oil has a slightly higher level, as well as some small imperfections in aroma and flavor. Olive oil, sometimes referred to as "pure olive oil," has the highest level and must be refined and blended with virgin oil before it can be consumed.

When choosing oils we must develop our own taste and rely on the requirements of the dish we're preparing:

Virgin olive oil is obtained from the mechanical pressings of the olives, using no chemical solvents, at room temperature conditions, which preserve the natural flavor and color of the fruit. It is utilized to add flavor to refined olive oil and is rarely sold alone in the United States.

COLOR: Yellowish green to deep green.

TASTE: A good flavor, with some slight imperfections (e.g., may have an acid or bitter aftertaste). Golden oils tend to have a more delicate, nutty flavor, while greener oils are more pungent and "leafy"; however, this varies depending on soil, type, climate and harvesting time of the olives.

ACIDITY: More than 1 gram and less than 3.3 gram oleic-free fatty acid per 100 gram oil.

PRICE: $4.00 to $25.00 for a pint bottle. (moderate priced.)

Extra virgin olive oil is produced the same way as virgin oil, extra virgin has an exceptionally pure, full flavor. Its low acid level contributes contributes to the smoothness of the taste. Since it offers the most diverse range of aromas and flavors and is made in little quantities, this olive oil is a greater expense than the others. It loses some of it's robust flavor when heated, so utilize it at room temperature (e.g., on salads or tossed with pasta).

COLOR: Ranges from golden to yellowish green or deep green.

TASTE: Has an all-around, perfect taste, which, like virgin oil, can be delicate, ripe and/or nutty (mostly in the case of golden oils) or pungent, leafy and/or peppery (greener oils).

ACIDITY: Extra virgin has the lowest acidity level of any olive oil—a maximum of 1 gram of olei-free fatty acid per 100 gram oil.

PRICE: $4.90 to $40.00 for a pint bottle. (most expensive).

Olive oil was previously known as "pure olive oil," this is a blend of virgin olive oil and oil that has been refined on account of imperfect flavor or high acidity. The proportion of virgin olive oil to refined oil relies on the flavor desired by the maker. Due to it's mild taste and relatively low cost, this oil is mainly suitable for heavy-duty high-temperature cooking.

COLOR: Pale yellow to golden.

TASTE: Light with some olive undertones and blander than virgin or extra virgin varieties.

ACIDITY: Less than 1.5 gram oleic acid per 100 gram oil.

PRICE: $3.00 to $12.00 for a pint bottle. (least expensive).

HOW TO TASTE OILS

First pour a little oil into a clear wine-type glass and examine it's aroma and color. Take a little amount in the mouth, keep it there and breathe in slightly (through the mouth) to experience the full flavor of the oil. Check its texture and how it eases down the throat, as well as any aftertaste it has. Prepare the palate for the next type of oil tasting by drinking a sip of sparkling water and a piece of Bread (pg.188) or a Cracker (pg.204).

A FEW OLIVES UTILIZED FOR EXTRA VIRGIN OILS

Black Greek (Greece)

Kalamata (Greece)

Bella di Cerignola (Italy)

Picholine (France)

Arbequina (Spain)

OTHER OLIVES

Alphonso   Gaeta   Mission   Moroccan   Raw Green   Sicilian

A RANGE OF FLAVOR

It is not always the color that is indicative of the quality of an oil. Extra virgin can come in a green or yellow hue yet have distinct and unique flavors. Find a favorite by tasting.

FATS

Fats are solid at room temperature and are made from vegetable or animal products or a combination of both. Some solid fats are hydrogenated vegetable fats, lard, butter and margarine. Hydrogenated fats are the most common shortening utilized in baking goods. Margarine or butter is utilized for flavor and to modify textures and consistency. Their creaming qualities are not as good as hydrogenated fats.

Drippings are fats usually obtained by cooking fat meats.

OILS

Oils are fats that are liquid at room temperature and are usually vegetable origin. Salad oil has been processed to stay clear when refrigerated; cooking oils become cloudy. The frequently utilized oils are corn, cottonseed, olive, peanut, walnut, soybean and safflower. Vegetable oils are utilized for salad dressings, cooking fat and in some baked products.

FLOURS

Whole wheat flours: Previously whole wheat flours needed to be blended with white flours in order to bake with them. But now with the advent of a newer process of milling which produces a flour which can be utilized alone with great success in bread and even cakes. In many speciality and health food stores we can obtain whole wheat pastry flour, an extra fine grind of the entire wheat flour which is essential in making fine cakes and pastries. When doing all our baking, sift the whole wheat flour many times, up to five to make it light enough for baking.

Through the imposition, of this culture, of white-flavorless-flour, on us. We first taste whole wheat flour and perceive it as strange. When in fact the robust and distinct flavor is fine. If we are not use to the flavor, add extra sweetness to make it more agreeable. Particularly if we are utilizing whole wheat flour in a recipe that calls for white flour. In this situation we substitute whole wheat flour for white, almost a cup of whole wheat for a cup of white, we need a little less whole wheat than white because whole wheat absorbs more moisture than white.

All-purpose flour: This is the most common flour utilized. Its usually a blend of hard and soft wheats to have the best appearance in baking. The terms white, wheat or plain flours are synonymous.

Gluten: Yeast breads rely upon wheat flour, rich in protein called "gluten," which makes dough strong and elastic. It is capable of expanding much, forming a network of hundreds of tiny pockets to hold the yeast-producing gases which would otherwise escape from the dough.

LEAVENINGS

Leavenings are substance that form bubbles of gas (carbon dioxide) or physical leavenings like steam and air. The gas, air or steam expands when a batter or dough is heated, making baked products light and affecting grain and texture.

Leavening agents include yeast, baking powder, soda (plus a food acid) and eggs.

Yeast is a little plant that produces carbon dioxide from sugar when temperature and moisture are favorable for its growth. Yeast is available in two forms—active dry and compressed. Before active dry yeast is utilized, soften it in hot-warm water (110°F) for 5 to 10 minutes. Soften compressed yeast in lukewarm water of other liquid (85°F) for the same time. It is best to allow yeast to rise dough for long hours. Today we have fine bread-machine yeast which can be added dry to the flour and give the bread a good texture.

Baking powder can be SAS-phosphate (double acting), phosphate or tartrate type. The double-acting type releases a tiny amount of gas when mixed with liquid, the major part when heated. Phosphate type gives off some gas when combined with liquid and the remaining when heated. Tartrate type reacts almost entirely when mixed with the liquid. The gas formed expands when the batter is heated.

Baking soda gives off gas when combined with a food acid such as buttermilk, sour milk, molasses, lemon juice or vinegar. 1/4 teaspoon of baking soda plus 1/2 cup sour milk is equivalent to 1 teaspoon baking powder (double-acting).

Beaten eggs or egg whites: Are often utilized to leaven; they enclose air which is forced to expand in a hot oven.

EGGS

Slightly beaten eggs are whole eggs beaten with whisk only long enough to break up the yolks and allow streaks of yellow and white. Utilized to thicken custards and to coat foods with (yellow) egg crumbs.
Beaten eggs are whipped till whites and yolks are mixed. Utilized to give light texture to batters and doughs and as a binder in salad dressings and baked products.
Well-beaten egg yolks are beaten until thick, fine and literally yellow-lemon colored foam is developed. Utilized in sponge cakes. Stiffly beaten egg whites are beaten till peaks stand up straight, but are still glossy and moist. Egg whites are to be beaten to soft peaks, until the peaks droop over slightly. Sugar is gradually added while beating to stiff peaks. This increases the air-holding (fluff) property of the egg whites. So-called Angel cake is leavened by expansion of air trapped in egg whites and by steam during baking. Souffles, Macaroons, Mouses and chiffon pies all depend on stiffly beaten egg whites for light-

ness. [See Meringue-Pie Topping (pg.236)].

THICKENING AGENTS

Cornstarch: may be blended with sugar or cold liquid before adding to hot mixture. Cook and stir constantly till thick and bubbly. But remember cornstarch will lock our digestive systems up. Flour may be thoroughly mixed with fat before liquid is combined. Or it can be blended with cold liquid or sugar before mixing with hot mixture. Cook and constantly stir till thickened and bubbly.

Tapioca: Quick-cooking tapioca is utilized in recipes presented herein. Its added to the liquid mixture. No soaking is required. Heat right to boiling; please don't over cook. Let cool without stirring. When utilizing pearl tapioca, use double the amount and soak several hours. Cook till substance is clear.

Eggs: are slightly beaten when utilized for thickening. Then add to a hot mixture, stir small amount of hot mixture into eggs; now stir egg mixture into remaining hot mixture. Cook and stir constantly over low heat.

Arrowroot: is very expensive and is not always available. It must be dissolved in water first and is utilized similar to cornstarch. It is clear and almost tasteless and gives a nice gleam to food.

Beurre manié: is French for "handled butter." To thicken a sauce or soup that is already cooked, make a beurre manié by blending equal amounts of flour and softened butter, blending them together fast with your fingers. Add the mixture, a little at a time, to a hot sauce, stirring after each addition, until it is absorbed and you have the desired thickness.

MILK

The pasteurized milk we get today spoils before it turns sour. To "sour" pasteurized milk, when needed, add 1 tablespoon white vinegar or lemon juice to 1 cup of milk and let stand at room temperature 10 to 15 minutes.

Skim milk: has most of the fat (cream) removed.

Low-fat or Non-fat milk: contains not more than 0.1% milk fat. It is skim milk which still retains a little of the cream. It taste more like whole milk and looks less anemic than skim milk, although it's not rich.

To 'Scald' milk: Heat it slowly in a small pan or pot until little bubbles appear around the edges, but before the milk begins to boil-up.

Homogenized milk: is pasteurized milk that has been mechanically treated so the globules of cream will not separate from the rest of the milk and rise to the top.

Buttermilk: is the part that remains after sweet or sour milk has been churned and the fat removed. Cultured buttermilk is the soured product after pasteurized skimmed milk is treated with a suitable lactic acid bacteria culture.

Evaporated milk: is the whole cow's milk from which 60% of the water has been extracted. It is homogenized and placed in cans. Sweetened condensed milk is made by evaporating half the water

51

from whole milk and adding enough corn or cane sugar to preserve it. It is then heated, cooled and canned.

Dry whole milk solids: are what is left after all the water has been removed from whole milk. They can be reconstituted with water or another liquid.

Yogurt: is fermented milk, served on its own, plain or combined with fresh fruit. It can be utilized in salad dressings (pg.186) and is a perfect lower-calorie substitute for sour cream.

BOUQUET GARNI

Bouquet Garni: means a bouquet for garnish—parsley, thyme and bay leaf being traditional ingredients; also mint leaves or Chervil, dill, citrus rind and zest can be placed strategically on or near the dish to highlight or complement the setting.

RETURN TO THE LAND OF CHEESE

In every part of the Western world cheese is made. Cheese can be allocated into two main classes— Ripened cheese in which the curd is made through the action of rennet and Natural cheese in which it is formed by means of lactic acid. When rennet comes in contact with milk, the milk casein coagulates, drawing together in a semi-solid mass. This is called curd the part of milk that coagulates when the milk sours or is treated with enzymes and is used to make cheese. The watery substance remaining is the whey. The dissimilarity among the diversity of cheeses are due to source of milk, whether from the cow, sheep or goat, the temperature and conditions of ripening, harmless organisms such as bacteria and mold added to help development of flavor and texture. Cheese furnishes Vitamins B2 and calcium. Its not difficult to digest, but rest in the stomach until its proteins are digested to a liquid.

Most varieties of cheese are made by the rennet method except cream cheese, which is usually made by the lactic acid method or technique. This means that pure cultures of lactic acid are added to milk to begin the transition of lactose (milk sugar) to lactic acid.

Cheese can also be allocated into soft and hard types. The distinction between them is the amount of moisture or whey left with the curd. Its not only the degree of whey in the cheese that determines the differences in type, however, but rather untangibly such collective factors as the quality of the milk, the length of the aging process, the humidity and temperature of the place where the cheese is ripened and the difference in molds from one cave or cellar to another. Soft types are Brie, cream and Camembert. Hard types are Romano, Swiss and Parmesan. Between these two groups are varieties which may be described as semi-soft, such as Muenster, Brick and Bleu cheese. And finally, semi-firm like Cheddar, Gruy'ere and the blue cheeses Stilton, Roquefort and Danish blue.

American Cheddar: or just plain cracker-barrel cheese is one of the best we can purchase. We can get wedges varying in color from pale yellow to deep orange and in flavor from mild to very sharp. It is an all-purpose, full-flavored, natural, good-keeping cheese.

Bleu Cheese: is a strong, salty-flavored, soft cheese with mold veins running through it. It is the American version of Roquefort. Serve it as a spread, sprinkle over green salad, add to French dressing or serve with fruit.

Brie: A subtle, well-ripened is the comfortable American cheese we utilize for toasted cheese sandwiches.

Camembert: is a foil-wrapped single-portion triangular shaped cheese, just soft enough to spread and tart enough to have character.

Gouda Cheese: is a flatted sphere-shaped cheese, with bright red coat that peels off when cut. It is creamy yellow with a salty nut-like flavor made from whole or partially skimmed milk. Good for sandwiches or for dessert with fruit or crackers.

Limburger: A soft white cheese with a very strong odor and flavor. It is eaten as a sandwich snack with fruit.

Provolone: is a smoky pungent Italian cheese, pear-shaped, yellow-tan in color and with rope marks. BEFORE PURCHASING WE MUST DISCERN WHETHER IT IS MADE FROM THE PIG OR WATER BUFFALO.

Parmesan and Romano: are hard Italian-style cheeses, good for grating. Grate only as needed, to obtain the best flavor.

Swiss Cheese: is the supreme cheese. It is pale yellow, has a mild nut-like flavor and big, even, round holes.

Processed cheese is natural cheese that has been ground up, pasteurized, remixed and packaged. Cheese food is a mix of various ground cheeses with whey solids, whey albumin, seasonings, water and color. Cheese spreads are made by adding gums, liquid and fat to processed cheese. Although low in calories it has less nutrient value than natural cheese and lacks its texture and fine flavor. We therefore avoid processed cheeses.

GLOSSARY OF TERMS

Absorb: To take in by chemical or molecular action.
Adding: To increase the amounts of ingredients.
Albumen: The white of an egg.

Bain Marie: A double boiler utilized for melting and cooking puddings.
Bag out: To press dough, batter or frosting from a conical shaped cloth, parchment sheet or paper bag.
Bake: To cook covered or uncovered in an oven or oven-type appliance. For meats cooked uncovered, it is called roasting.
Baking Powder: A mixture of baking soda, starch and at least one slightly acidic compound such as

cream of tartar that works as a leavening agent in baking by releasing carbon dioxide when mixed with a liquid, such as milk or water.

Baking Soda: Is pure bicarbonate of soda. It has a slight alkaline taste and products leavened only with baking soda must be processed and baked quickly in order to manifest the desired strength of the baking soda.

Baste: To moisten foods during cooking with pan drippings or a specific sauce to increase flavor and prevent dehydration.

Beat: To make mixture smooth by adding air with a brisk whipping or stirring motion, utilizing spoon or electric mixer.

Batch: The whole contents of a recipe.

Blanch: To precook in boiling water or steam to prepare foods for canning or freezing or to loosen skin.

Blend: To thoroughly mix two or more ingredients until smooth and uniform with a spoon, fork, whisk or electric mixer.

Braise: To cook slowly with a small amount of liquid in tightly covered pan on top range or in oven.

Bread: To cover, coat or roll with crumbs. Usually the food is first dipped in milk or whipped egg before cooking.

Broil: To cook by direct heat, usually in broiler or over coals.

Boil: To cook in liquid at boiling temperature where bubbles rise to the surface and break. For a full rolling boil, bubbles form rapidly throughout the blend.

Boiling point: Water boils at 212°F.

Candied: To cook in syrup or sugar when applied to ginger and carrots. For fruit or fruit peel, to cook in thick syrup till clear and well coated.

Caramel: Sugar heated above its melting point so that it takes on an amber color.

Caramelize: To melt sugar slowly over low heat until it becomes brown in color. Describes the color change in heated sugar.

Chill: To place in refrigerator to reduce temperature.

Chocolate: A product of the roasted, fermented, shelled and ground Cacao bean-seeds, often combined with a sweetener or flavoring agent. Cacao trees grow only 20° north and south of the equator and mainly in West Africa and Latin America. A beverage made by mixing water or milk with chocolate. A small, chocolate-covered candy with a hard or soft center.

Chop: To cut in small pieces about the size of peas with knife, chopper or blender.

Cinnamon: Is ground from the inner-bark of a type of laurel tree. Cinnamon varies in strength and loses its flavor with age.

Clarify: The removal of extraneous material from a liquid.

Clove: A clove is the dried bud of a species of myrtle grown in Zanzibar and the East Indies.

Cool: To remove from heat and let stand at room temperature until it is no longer warm to the touch.

Cream: 1. The yellowish fatty component of unhomogenized milk that tends to accumulate at the surface. 2. To beat with a spoon or electric mixer till mixture is soft and smooth. When applied to blending shortening and sugar, mixture is beaten till light and fluffy.

Crystallization: The forming of sugar into crystals.

Cut in: To mix shortening with dry ingredients utilizing pastry blender or knives.

Develop: To mix a bread type dough to increase its elasticity by the development of the flour's gluten.

Dice: To cut food in small cubes of uniform size and shape.

Dissolve: To disperse a dry substance to form a solution. Or the act of liquefying a solid.

Docking: To punch holes in a yeast dough in order to insure an inside texture without large holes.

Dredge: To sprinkle or coat with flour or other fine substance.

Dust: To sprinkle flour on a working surface to keep dough from sticking. Bread flour is best.

Egg: A fresh egg is made up of three parts: the shell is 12%, the white is 59%, the yolk is 30%. An egg white has .2% fat content. An egg yolk has 31% to 32% fat content. An egg white has 12% protein. And egg yolk has 17% protein.

Egg wash: To brush on a mixture of fresh egg and water to make breads and rolls have a shine to their crusts.

Emulsified Shortening: Shortening to which an emulsifier has been added. This shortening will hold moisture in baked goods.

Enrobe: To coat with icing, chocolate. Cakes, cookies and pastries are enrobed with a coating.

Flake: To break lightly into small pieces.

Flour: The wheat grain has three main parts. The bran coating is about 13%. The embryo or germ is about 13%. The embryo or germ is about 2%. The endosperm is about 85%. The endosperm consists of protein, starch, fat, water, sugar and mineral matter. White flour is milled from the endosperm. The bran consist of fiber. The germ is vitamin-rich.

Fold: To add ingredients gently to a mixture. Utilizing a spatula, cut down through mixture; go across bottom of bowl and up and over, close to the surface. Turn bowl frequently for even distribution.

Fermentation: The forming of carbon-dioxide gas in dough which causes the dough to rise.

Fry: To cook in hot shortening. Pan frying is to cook in a small amount of shortening. Deep-fat frying is to cook immersed in a large amount of shortening.

Full-sheet pan: A term to describe a flat baking pan that is usually 16-inches by 18 1/2-inches.

Ginger: Ginger is made from the root of a herb grown in China, India, Australia and South Africa.

Glaze: A mixture applied to food which hardens or becomes firm and/ or adds flavor and to give a glossy surface to baked items by brushing on a liquid.

Glucose: A very thick corn syrup. In most instances a light corn syrup can be substituted in the recipe.

Gluten: The insoluble wheat protein left after hydration. Gluten is the elastic substance that assists in trapping CO2 gas in bread dough. The strength of the flour's gluten determines the toughness of the dough or batter. Bread dough requires a high gluten strength while cake batter requires low gluten strength.

Grate: To rub on a grater that separates the food into very fine fragments.

Greasing: The process of applying a thin coating of shortening inside a bread, cake or pie pan to prevent sticking.

Honey: Honey is produced by bees from the nectar of flowers. The flavor of honey depends on the kind of flowers the bees find. Clover is what most people consider the best.

Hygroscopic: The power or potential to attract moisture.

Hydrogenate: To combine with or subject to the action of hydrogen, especially to combine (an unsaturated oil) with hydrogen to produce a solid fat.

Incorporating: The act of mixing ingredients together in a recipe.

Icing: A term used to describe the sweet coating on a product. A term used instead of saying "frosting".

Jell: To become firm or gelatinous; congeal.

Jerk: 1. To cut (meat) into long strips and dry in the sun or cure by exposing to smoke. 2. Being related to a method of barbecuing meat that has been seasoned and wrapped in leaves of the allspice tree.

Knead: To work the dough with the heel of the hand with a firm pressing, folding motion.

Leavening: A substance which, when exposed to liquid or heat, produces a gas causing aeration before or during baking.

Lecithin: A gum by-product of soybeans. Phospholipids are the active portion of the lecithin molecule. Lecithin is utilized in small amounts to cause better mixing, a release agent, a dispersing agent, a fat emulsifier and increases water solubility of all ingredients.

Maltodextrins: A starch that is utilized as a fat replacement. Controls sweetness, helps moisture control, alters mouth feel (provides body) and weakens the gluten in flour making the product soft longer.

Marinate: To allow a food to saturate in a liquid to tenderize and/or to add flavor.

Melba Sauce: A sauce made from raspberries.

Mince: To cut or finely chop food into very small fragments.

Milk: Milk is variable in composition. An average composition is: Fat 3.75%, milk protein 3.46%, mineral matter .75%, lactose 4.70% and water 87.34%. Milk has a fairly high sugar content which aids browning in baked items. The milk fat with the sugar enriches and tenderizes baked goods.

Mix: To combine ingredients, usually by stirring, till evenly distributed.

Mixing: The blending of ingredients into a mass.

Mixing times: Mixing times have a direct effect on leavening of the product. Yeast, baking powder and baking soda cannot do their functions if the mixing times are not correct.

Cakes and Cookies—The proper result of baking powder and baking soda is determined by acid and heat. If the batter or dough is allowed to over mix and get too hot the carbon dioxide gas will be released and will escape before the product is baked.

Under mixing may cause uneven disbursement of the powder and dense grain, holes, tunnels and lack of volume may result.

Nutmeg: Nutmeg is ground from the nut of the Nutmeg tree. Nutmeg comes from the East and West Indies. Mace comes from the same fruit's outer hull.

Oil: Pure vegetable oil, olive oil and palm oil are utilized in baking. Vegetable oil is utilized in sponge type cakes and to make solid shortening and margarine. Olive oil is utilized in bread making. Palm oil is utilized to make solid vegetable shortening and margarine.

Over mix: To mix longer than the recipe can tolerate.

Over proof: To let doughs rest too long after moulding into loaves and rolls.

Panbroil: To cook uncovered on hot surface, removing fat as it begins to accumulate.

Panfry: To cook in small amount of hot shortening.

Pit: To remove pits from fruits.

Poach: To cook in hot liquid, being mindful that the food keeps its shape while cooking.

Press: A cookie press is utilized to flatten cookie dough and sometimes leave an imprint.

Precook: To cook food partially or completely before final cooking or reheating.

Proof: To let yeast type doughs rise before baking.

Quiche: A rich unsweetened custard baked in a pastry shell often with other ingredients such as vegetables or seafood.

Retard: To slow down the rising process of a yeast raised product.

Retarder: A cool place to slow down the rising process of a yeast raised product.

Retarding: To keep a dough cool so that the yeast or leavening agents will not work.

Roast: To cook uncovered without water added, usually in an oven.

Rounding: To shape bread dough into a tight ball. Rounding puts bread dough in a proofing stage, before the final shape is made.

Salt: Salt is sodium chloride. It adds a flavor of its own to baked items and also slightly enhances the flavors of the other ingredients. Salt has a retarding effect on yeast and a toughening effect on gluten.

Sauté: To brown or cook in a small amount of hot shortening.

Scald: To bring to a temperature just below the boiling point where small bubbles form at the edge of the pan.

Scaling: Weighing the ingredients on a scale.

Scallop: To bake food, usually in a casserole, with sauce or other liquid. Crumbs are often sprinkled on top.

Scrape the bowl: The act of cleaning partially mixed ingredients from the sides of the mixing bowl.

Score: To cut narrow grooves or slits part way through the outer surface of food.

Sear: To brown the surface of meat very quickly by intense heat.

Set or Set-up: Terms used to describe something that changes consistency usually upon cooling, such as gelatin. These terms can also mean to get something ready.

Shelf life: A term utilized to describe the freshness life of a product.

Shortening: Shortening is the fat utilized in baking. Butter, vegetable shortening, margarine and lard are shortenings.

Shred: To rub on a shredder to form small, narrow pieces.

Sift: To shake one or more dry ingredients through a fine mesh called a sieve or sifter.

Sifting: To shake dry ingredients through a sieve to allow the finest particles to remain.

Simmer: To cook in liquid over low heat at a temperature of 185°F to 210°F where bubbles form at a slow rate and burst before reaching the surface.

Soft peaks: To beat egg whites or whipping cream till peaks are formed as the beaters are raised, but tips curl over.

Steam: To cook in steam with or without pressure. A small amount of boiling water is utilized, more water being added during steaming process if necessary.

Steep: To extract color, flavor or other qualities from a substance by leaving it in liquid just under the boiling point.

Stew: To simmer slowly in a small amount of liquid.

Stiff peaks: To beat egg whites till peaks stand up straight when the beaters are raised, but are still moist and glossy.

Stir: To mix ingredients with a circular motion until well blended, of uniform consistency or dissolved.

Sugar: Granulated sugar, powdered sugar and brown sugar are the most common sugars utilized in baking. Refined sugar comes from sugar cane or sugar beets. Cane and beet sugar is called sucrose and are equally sweet. Sugar in the raw is best.

Syrup: Light and dark corn syrup, glucose, molasses and honey are the most common syrups utilized in baking. Flavored simple syrup is a common sauce. Pure maple syrup is best.

Temperature: The degree of cold or heat.

Tempering: To regulate a liquid temperature to a desired level.

Tender: A term to describe the texture of a baked item.

Texture: The inside size of grain or smoothness of a baked item.

Toss: To mix ingredients lightly.

Truss: To secure fowl or other meat with skewers to hold its shape during cooking.

Under mix: To mix a recipe too little.

Under bake: To bake a product too little.

Vanilla: Any various tropical American vines of the genus Vanilla in the orchid family, especially V. planifolia, cultivated for its long narrow seedpods from which a flavoring agent is obtained.

Venison: The flesh of a deer used as food.

Vinegar: An impure dilute solution of acetic acid obtained by fermentation beyond the alcohol stage and used as a condiment and preservative.

Wash: To brush a liquid over the top of any baked item, before, during or after baking. This causes a crust effect. Water, egg, oil and milk are common washes.

Wet peak: A stage where the meringue peak folds over.

Whip: A whisk utilized to beat egg whites, sauces and heavy creams. Also means to beat ingredients together rapidly to incorporate air and produce expansion, as in heavy cream or egg whites.

Whipping: Using a hand whisk or mixer attachment to beat ingredients.

Xanthan gum: A natural gum of high molecular weight produced by culture fermentation of glucose and utilized as a stabilizer in commercial food preparation.

Yeast: Yeast is a living micro-organism of the fungi family of plants. Yeast is the primary rising ingredient in bread. Yeast should be stored at 40°F or below and has a thermal death point of 120°F. Yeast can be purchased as fresh compressed, dried or instant dried.

Zest: The outer rind of oranges, lemons and limes. The zest contains the oil of the fruit.

MEASURES, WEIGHTS AND CONVERSIONS

TABLE

mg = milligram

g = grams (dry measure)

kg = kilograms

dl = deciliter

L = liters

tbsp. = tablespoon

tsp = teaspoon

c = cup

oz = ounce

lb = pound

pt = pint

qt = quart

LIQUID & DRY MEASURE EQUIVALENTS

a pinch = slightly less than 1/4 teaspoon

dash = a few drops less than 1/8 teaspoon

60 drops = 1 teaspoon

3 teaspoons = 1 tablespoon

16 tablespoons = 1 cup

2 tablespoons = 1 liquid ounce = 1/4 deciliter

1/3 cup = 5 tablespoons & 1 teaspoon

7/8 cup = 3/4 cup & 2 tablespoons

1/2 cup = 8 tablespoons = 4 ounces = 1 deciliter

1/4 cup = 4 tablespoons

1 cup = 1/2 pint

2 cups = 1 pint = 1/2 liter = 16 ounces

4 cups = 1 quart ≈ 1 liter

1 gram = 1000 milligram

28 grams = 1 ounce

454 grams = 1 pound

4 quarts = 1 gallon = 3 3/4 liters

8 quarts (dry) = 1 peck = 7 1/4 kilogram

4 pecks (dry) = 1 bushel

OTHER EQUIVALENTS

2 cups butter = 1 pound

2 cups water = 1 pound

4 cups flour = 1 pound

2 cups granulated sugar = 1 pound

2 2/3 cup powdered sugar = 1 pound

4 cups confectioners' sugar = 1 pound

1 cup honey = 3/4 pound

1 cup molasses = 13 ounces

3 cups apples (raw), sliced = 1 pound

1 2/3 cups apples (cooked), chopped = 1 pound

2 1/2 cup raisins = 1 pound

4 tablespoon dry yeast = 1 ounce

2 cups dates = 1 pound

3 cups onions (medium), chopped = 1 pound

4 cups grated cheese = 1 pound

1 cup shortening = 1/2 pound

1 cup uncooked rice = 2 cups cooked rice

8 to 10 large egg whites = 1 cup

16 large egg yolks = 1 cup

2 large eggs = 1/2 cup

3 medium eggs = 1/2 cup

5 large eggs = 1 cup

fresh bread crumbs (pg.188), 4 sandwich slices = 2 cups loosely packed

dry bread crumbs, 4 sandwich slices = 3/4 cups

1 cup white flour = 1 cup fine whole wheat flour

1 cup white flour = 1 cup pastry whole wheat flour

1 cup white flour = 7/8 cup stone ground whole wheat flour

1 cup sugar = 1 cup honey with 1/4 cup less liquid

1 cup sugar = 1 1/3 cup maple syrup or sugar

1 cup sugar = 1 cup Raw™ sugar = 1 cup brown sugar

1 pound figs or dates = 2 3/4 cup = 2 2/3 cup (cut up)

1 pint heavy cream = 4 cups whipped cream

1 egg is equal in leavening effect to 1/2 teaspoon baking powder

1 cup shortening or butter = 2/3 cup vegetable oil

BUTTER, SHORTENING, CHEESE AND OTHER SOLID FATS

1 tablespoon = 1/8 stick = 1/2 ounce

2 tablespoons = 1/4 stick = 1 ounce

4 tablespoons = 1/2 stick = 2 ounces = 1/4 cup

8 tablespoons = 1 stick = 4 ounces = 1/2 cup = 1/4 pound

16 tablespoons = 2 sticks = 8 ounces = 1 cup = 1/2 pound

32 tablespoons = 4 sticks = 16 ounces = 2 cups = 1 pound

GRANULATED SUGAR

1 teaspoon = 1/6 ounce

1 tablespoon = 1/2 ounce

4 tablespoons = 1 3/4 ounces = 1/4 cup

5 tablespoons = 2 1/4 ounces = 1/3 cup

1/2 cup = 3 1/2 ounces

Abroach: Opened or positioned so that a liquid, such as juice, can be let out.

Abstemious: Eating and drinking in moderation.

Acidulate: To make or become slightly acid by adding, vinegar, lemon, etc.

Air-dry: To dry by exposure to the air.

A la carte: A term utilized on menus to indicate that a meal is ordered dish by dish, each of which has a separate price. (French)

Antipasto: An appetizer usually consisting of ingredients, such as smoked meats, cheese, fish and vegetables. (Italian)

Au gratin: Covered with bread crumbs and sometimes butter and grated cheese and then browned in an oven. (French)

Au Jus: A French expression meaning "with the juice" (pronounced "oh zhu"), it is a term applied to meat, usually roast beef, which is served in its own juices.

Baba: A leavened rum cake, usually made with raisins, fruit or fruit juices. (French, Polish or Russian)

Barbecue: As commonly utilized, to cook on a grill over intense heat, usually a live fire made with charcoal or wood, sometimes called "charcoal broiling." True barbecuing requires basting with a sauce as the meat or items cooks.

Bechamel Sauce: A white sauce of butter, flour and milk or cream. (French)

Bisque: A rich, creamy soup made from meat, fish or shellfish. Also a thick cream soup made of pureéd vegetables. And ice cream mixed with crushed macaroons or nuts. (Perhaps French)

Blancmange: A flavored and sweetened milk pudding thickened with cornstarch, flour or gelatin and usually shaped in a mold. (French)

Bombe: A dessert consisting of two or more layers of variously flavored ice cream frozen in a round or melon-shaped mold. (French)

Borscht: A beet soup served hot or cold, usually with sour cream. (Russian)

Bouillabaisse: A highly seasoned fish stew made of several kinds of fish and shellfish. (French)

Café au laite: Coffee served with hot milk. (French)

Caffé Americano: The European approach to American-style coffee: A shot of espresso combined with steaming hot water.

Caffé Latte: Steamed milk laced with rich, full-bodied shot of espresso and topped with a delicate crown of foamed milk. (Italy)

Caffé Mocha: Intensely flavored mocha syrup and espresso are mixed with steamed milk and finished with a cloud of whipped cream.

Café noir: Coffee served without cream or milk. (French)

Canape: A cracker or a small, thin piece of bread or toast spread with cheese, meat or relish and served as an appetizer. (French)

Cannoli: Pastry shells filled with sweetened ricotta cheese or pudding mixture. (Italian)

Caper: The bud of the caper bush pickled and utilized as a pungent condiment in sauces, relishes and various other dishes.

Caramel: 1. A smooth, chewy candy made with sugar, butter, cream or milk and flavoring. 2. Burnt sugar, utilizing for coloring and sweetening foods.

Caviar: The roe of a large fish, especially sturgeon, that is salted, seasoned and eaten as a delicacy or relish.

Charlotte: A dessert of fruit filling, whipped cream, custard, gelatin or other filling usually in a ladyfinger, bread, cake "crust". Popular form is Charlotte Russe. (French)

Chateaubriand: A double-thick, tender center cut of beef tenderloin, sometimes stuffed with seasonings before grilling. (French)

Chutney: A pungent relish made of fruits, spices and herbs.(Hindi)

Cider vinegar: Vinegar made from fermented cider.

Coq au vin: A dish of chicken cooked in red wine. (French)

Coquille: A scallop-shaped dish or a scalloped shell in which various seafood dishes are browned and served. (French)

Court bouillon: A poaching liquid for fish whose ingredients usually include water, vinegar or wine, diced vegetables and seasonings. (French)

Crepe suzette: A thin dessert pancake usually rolled with hot orange or tangerine sauce and often served with a flaming brandy or curacao sauce. (French)

Croissant: A rich, crescent-shaped roll of leavened dough or puff pastry. (French)

Croquette: A small cake of minced food, such as poultry, vegetables or fish, that is usually coated with bread crumbs and fried in deep fat. (French)

Crouton: A small crisp cubed-piece of toasted or fried bread. (French)

Dahl: A thick creamy East Indian stew made with lentils, onions and various spices. (Hindi)

Daikon: A white radish of Japan, having a long root that is eaten raw, pickled or cooked. (Japanese)

Demitasse: A small cup of strong black coffee or espresso. Also the small cup utilized to serve this drink. (French, Arabic tast)

Dolma: A cabbage or grape leaf stuffed and cooked with ingredients such as ground beef, minced lamb, herbs or rice. (Turkish)

Du jour: Utilized on menus to indicate feature "of the day". As, soupe du jour (soup), carte du jour (meal). (French)

Dulcet: Sweet to the taste. (Latin)

Empanada: A Spanish or Latin-American turnover with a flaky crust and a spicy or sweet filling.

En brochette: On a skewer kabob-style. (French)

Encrust: To cover with or as if with a crust. (French)

Enchilada: A tortilla topped or rolled with highly seasoned filling. Served with chili-seasoned tomato sauce. (Mexican)

Endive: An Indian plant cultivated for its crown of crisp, succulent leaves utilized in salads. Also called frisee. And a variety of the common chicory cultivated to produce a narrow, pointed cluster of whitish leaves utilized in salads. Also called witloof. (French)

Espresso: A strong coffee brewed by forcing steam under pressure through darkly roasted, powdered coffee beans. (Italian)

Filet Mignon: A small, round very choice cut of beef from the loin. (French)

Fillet: Strip of lean meat or fish without bone.

Flambe: To drench with a liquor, such as brandy and ignite or served flaming in ignited liquor. (French) (Forbidden by Muslims)

Fondue: A hot dish made of melted cheese and wine and eaten with bread. Also a similar dish, especially one consisting of a melted sauce in which pieces of food, such as bread, meat, or fruit, are dipped or cooked: chocolate fondue. And finally, a souffle usually made with cheese and bread crumbs. (Swiss national dish) (French)

Fondant: A sweet, creamy sugar paste utilized in candies and icing's. Also a candy containing this paste. (French)

Foo yong: An omelet with shrimp, crab, lobster, chicken or vegetable such as bean sprouts, green pepper and onion. (Chinese)

Frappe: A frozen, fruit-flavored mixture that is similar to sherbet and served as a dessert or appetizer. Also a beverage, usually a liqueur, poured over shaved ice. (French)

Fricassee: A stew of meat or poultry in gravy. (French & Latin)

Frijoles: Beans. (Mexican)

Garbanzos: Chick peas. (Spanish)

Garnish: To decorate (prepared food or drink) with small colorful or savory items, such as parsley, cilantro, mint or citrus fruit slices especially lemons. (Egyptian)

Gherkin: A West Indian vine having prickly, mature fruits that are sold as curiosities. The immature fruits are widely utilized for pickling. The small cucumber. (Dutch)

Ginger beer: A nonalcoholic drink similar to ginger ale but is stronger and flavored with fermented sugar.

Glaze: To glaze or coat with a thin sugar syrup. (French)

Hors d'oeuvre: An appetizer served before a meal. (French)

Ice: A dessert consisting of sweetened and flavored crushed ice.

Julienne: Consommé or both garnished with long, thin strips of vegetables. [adjective] Cut into long, thin strips. (French)

Kebab: Shish kebab.

Kolacky: A square, sweet bun with a fruit or poppy seed filing. (Czechoslovakian)

Kosher also Kasher

1. Judaism. a. Conforming to dietary laws; ritually pure. b. Selling or serving food prepared in accordance with dietary laws.

Kuchen: A coffeecake raised with yeast, often containing fruits and nuts. (German)

Kugelhof: Raisin-studded sweet bread baked in a special mold. (German)

Kumquat: A fruit, having an acid pulp and a thin, edible rind. It is the smallest of the citrus fruits. (Chinese)

Linder torte: A spicy rich chocolate-nut pastry filled with jam or preserves with a lattice top. (German)

Lox: Smoked salmon: (German)

Lyonnaise: A dish, usually potatoes, cooked with onions. (French)

Macaroon: A chewy cookie made with sugar, egg whites and almond paste or coconut. (French)

Macerate: To toss fruits in sugar and lemon, wine or a liqueur and let them stand to absorb the flavors.

Maitre d'hotel butter: A sauce of butter, lemon juice, chopped parsley, seasonings. (French)

Maize: A light yellow to moderate orange yellow. (Spanish, Cariban)

Maraschino Cherries: Cherries bleached and cooked in syrup with bright color and maraschino flavor added. (Italian)

Marzipan or marchpane: A confection made of ground almonds or almond paste, egg whites and sugar, often molded into decorative shapes. (German)

Minestrone: A thick soup of Italian origin containing assorted vegetables, beans, pasta such as vermicelli or macaroni and herbs in a meat or vegetable broth. (History) The thick vegetable soup known as minestrone did not come by its name because of its ingredients or their shape but rather because of service, something highly valued by many restaurant patrons. (Italian)

Mocha: 1. A rich, pungent Arabian coffee. 2. Coffee of high quality. 3. A flavoring made of coffee often mixed with chocolate. (Arabic)

Monosodium glutamate: A powder with little or no flavor of its own utilized to enhance other food flavors. Accent™ is an example. (Not recommended)

Mornay: Being or served with a white sauce flavored with grated cheese and seasonings: eggs mornay. (French-perhaps after Philippe de Mornay)

Mostaccioli: Short, tubular pasta with slanted ends. (Italian)

Moussaka: A Greek dish consisting of layers of ground lamb or beef and sliced eggplant topped with a cheese sauce and baked. (from Arabic)

Mousse: Any of various chilled desserts made with flavored whipped cream, gelatin and eggs. Also a molded dish containing meat, fish or shellfish combined with whipped cream and gelatin. (French)

Mousseline: A hollandaise sauce to which whipped cream has been added. Also an aspic containing whipped cream. (French)

Mutton: Meat from a sheep more than one year old.

Natural food: Food that does not contain any additives, such as preservatives or artificial coloring.

Oaten: Of, made of or containing oats, oatmeal or oat straw.

Olio: A heavily spiced stew of meat, vegetables and chick peas.

Paella: Classic saffron rice dish made with chicken, seafood and vegetables. (Spanish)

Pareve: Prepared without meat, milk or their derivatives and therefore permissible to be eaten with both meat and dairy dishes according to dietary laws.

Parfait: A flavored custard made with whipped cream and syrup frozen without stirring. Also, ice cream layered with syrup, whipped cream, fruit, etc., in a parfait glass (a tall narrow glass with a short stem.) (French)

Parmigiana: Made or covered with parmesan cheese. (Italian)

Pasta: 1. Paste or dough made of wheat flour, eggs and water, often formed into shapes and dried and used in a variety of recipes after being boiled. 2. Prepared dish containing pasta as its main ingredient. (Italian)

Pasteurize: To preserve food by heating sufficiently to destroy undesirable microorganisms but not enough to greatly change chemical composition. Mainly applied to milk and fruit juices.

Pâté: 1. A meat paste, such as pâté de foie gras. 2. A small pastry filled with meat or fish. (French)

Penuche: A fudge like confection of brown sugar, cream or milk and chopped nuts. [variant of panocha] (Mexican)

Persimmon: An orange-red fruit that is edible only when completely ripe. (Algonquian)

Petit Four: A small, square-cut, frosted and decorated piece of pound cake or sponge cake. (French)

Pilaf also pilaff, pilau, pilaw or pilav: A rice dish with meat or poultry and vegetables or raisins and spices. Fried in oil then steamed and seasoned. (Oriental and Turkish-Persian)

Poisson: Fish. (French)

Polenta: A thick mush made of cornmeal boiled in water or stock. (Italian)

Pot-au-feu: A dish of boiled meats and vegetables. (French)

Pot de creme: Delicate chilled dessert pudding, often chocolate, served in little cups. (French)

Poult or poulet: A young fowl, especially a turkey, chicken or pheasant. (French)

Praline: A confection made of nut kernels, especially almonds or pecans, stirred in boiling sugar syrup until crisp and brown. (French)

Prosciutto: An aged, dry-cured, spiced Italian ham that is usually sliced thin and is served without cooking. (Italian)

Pureé: To mash to a smooth blend. The result-the mashed substance-is also referred to as a pureé. (French)

Quahog or quahaug: An edible clam of the Atlantic coast or North America, having a hard, rounded shell. (Narragansett)

Queen olive: A large, edible variety of olive not utilized as a source of oil.

Quiche Lorraine: Savory hot custard tart containing bacon, onions and cheese. (French)

Quinine water: A carbonated beverage flavored with quinine.

Ragout: A well-seasoned meat or fish stew, usually with vegetables. (French)

Ratafia: 1. A sweet cordial flavored with fruit kernels or almonds. A biscuit flavored with ratafia. (French perhaps of West Indian origin)

Ratatouille: A vegetable stew, usually made with eggplant, tomatoes, zucchini, peppers and onions, seasoned with herbs and garlic and served hot or cold. (French)

Ravioli: Miniature pillows of noodle dough, stuffed with mixtures of chopped meat, cheese or other foods (often spinach), then boiled. Served with seasoned sauce. (Italian)

Roulade: A thin slice of meat rolled up with or without a stuffing, then cooked. (French)

Roux: A mixture of flour and fat that is cooked, sometimes till the flour browns and is utilized to thicken soups and sauces. (French)

Sacher torte: Spiced chocolate cake layered with apricot jam and frosted with chocolate. (German)

Sake: A Japanese wine made from fermented rice. (Japanese)

Samp: Cornmeal mush. (New England)

Sand pear or Asian pear, Chinese pear: A chinese tree of the rose family, having edible, globose, firm, juicy fruit.

Sashimi: Thin slices of raw fish served with soy sauce and grated wasabi, a kind of horse-radish. (Japanese)

Sauerbraten: A pot roast of beef marinated in vinegar, water, wine and spices before being cooked. (German)

Scaloppine also scaloppini: Small, thinly sliced pieces of meat, especially veal, dredged in flour, sautéed and served in a sauce. (Italian)

Scampi: Large shrimp broiled or sautéed and served in a garlic and butter sauce. (Italian)

Smorgasbord: A buffet meal featuring a varied number of dishes. (Swedish)

Sorrel: A plant having acid-flavored leaves sometimes used as salad greens or cooked and resulting drained-liquid a soft drink. (Jamaican)

Souffle': A light, fluffy baked dish made with egg yolks and beaten egg whites combined with various other ingredients and served as a main dish or sweetened as a dessert. (French)

Soupcon: A very small amount; a trace. (French)

Soup du jour: A soup featured by a restaurant on a given day. (French)

Spatzle or spaetzel: A type of noodle made from batter pressed through a colander and cooked in boiling water. (German)

Sterilize: To destroy microorganisms by boiling, dry heat or steam.

Stroganoff: Usually beef sliced thin and cooked with sauce of broth, sour cream and seasonings.

(Russian)

Strudel: Very thin, flaky pastry spread with filing, usually fruit, rolled and baked. (German)

Subgum: A dish made with mixed vegetables. (Chinese)

Succotash: A stew consisting of kernels of corn, lima beans and tomatoes. (Narragansett)

Succulent: Full of juice or sap; juicy.

Sukiyaki: A Japanese dish of sliced meat, bean curd and vegetables seasoned and fried together. (Japanese)

Tabasco pepper: A very pungent pepper grown principally in the Gulf Coast states for use in hot sauces.

Table d'hote: 1. A communal table for all the guests at a hotel or restaurant. 2. A full-course meal offering a limited number of choices and served at a fixed price in a restaurant or hotel. In this sense, also called prix fixe. (French)

Tempura: A dish of vegetables and shrimp or other seafood dipped in batter and fried in deep fat. (Japanese)

Teriyaki: A dish consisting of grilled or broiled slices of marinated meat or shellfish. (Japanese)

Thyme: A pungent, aromatic herb utilized in seasonings.

Torte: A rich cake made with many eggs and little flour and usually containing nuts. It can be layered with filling and frosting. May indicate many layers. (German, Italian)

Tortellini: Small ring-shaped pasta stuffed usually with meat or cheese and served in soup or with a sauce. (Italian)

Tortilla: A thin unleavened cake, prepared from coarse cornmeal and baked on a hot sheet of iron or slab of stone. Usually eaten hot topped or filled with ground meat, cheese and various sauces. (Mexican)

Truffle: A European fungus that grows underground. Utilized as a seasoning or garnish. Also a rich chocolate candy, especially one made of a mixture including chopped nuts, rolled into balls and covered with cocoa powder. (French)

Truss: To bind wings and legs of poultry to body. Or to lace body cavities of poultry to hold in stuffing.

Unleavened: Made without yeast or any other leavening agent.

Vegetable wax: A waxy substance of plant origin, as that obtained from certain palm trees.

Welsh rabbit or Welsh rarebit: Melted cheese, usually mixed with milk, ale or beer, an served over toast or crackers.

Wiener Schnitzel: A thin breaded veal cutlet. (German)

Wild Rice: Wild rice, also known as Indian rice or water oats, is not a rice at all, but the seed from a grass that grows wild along the edges of lakes in Minnesota, Wisconsin and Southern Canada.

Worcestershire: A piquant sauce of soy, vinegar and spices.

Wrasse: Any numerous chiefly tropical, often brightly colored marine fishes of the family Labridae, having spiny fins, thick lips and powerful jaws and often valued for food. (Cornish and Welsh)

Wurst: Sausage. (German)

Yakitori: A dish of marinated chicken pieces, grilled on skewers. (Japanese)

Zabaglione: Foamy egg dessert, wine flavored served hot or cold. (Italian)

STEAMING VEGETABLES AND COOKING BEANS

Some of us were brought up on overcooked, soggy and worst, from the can, vegetables and have never acquired the taste of a good vegetable. But, we will soon discover the same vegetables, properly cooked to keep flavor, color, shape and texture are not only good for us but very tasty.

To Steam Vegetables: Steam vegetables brief enough that they become tender and only slightly lose their shape and color and have a crispness or crunchiness to them. A double section steamer has two parts; a top part which is a covered basket that holds the vegetables to be steamed and a bottom section which holds water that is boiled to create steam that cooks the vegetables as it rises up through the top section. Add a bit of olive oil and salt to the water in the bottom section utilized to create steam, it will give the vegetables a slight gleam. Also add a sprig of parsley to the water to give the vegetables back some of the color they lose through the steaming procedure.

BASIC METHODS FOR COOKING VEGETABLES

ARTICHOKES, FRENCH or GLOBE:

Step1: Wash; peel the coarse fibers from the stem; remove the tough bottom leaves, then slice off about an inch from the leaves top; with scissors, snip off the prickly tops of the remaining side leaves.

Step 2:To Cook: Plunge the artichokes into a very large pot filled with boiling water and boil them gently until done. Allow 20 to 30 minutes; they are done when an outer leaf pulls off easily and the bottom is tender when pierced with a fork.

Alternative Step 2:To Steam:Steam them 25 to 35 minutes.

Step 3: Drain them upside down.

Step 4: Serve them hot or warm, with melted butter or Hollandaise on the side, or cold with French Dressing or Mayonnaise seasoned with lemon juice and a bit of prepared mustard.

The Art Of Eating An Artichoke: Begin by using our fingers to eat a whole cooked artichoke by removing one leaf at a time and pulling it between our teeth to remove the soft, tender flesh at the base.

Throw away what's left. When all the fleshy leaves have been removed, utilizing a small knife to scrape away and discard the hairy "choke" that covers the base. The final part is the best; the heart, which is the tenderest, sweetest part of an artichoke.

JERUSALEM ARTICHOKE:
Step 1: Wash; Peel with a peeler; leave whole or slice.
Step 2:To Cook: Cook covered in small amount of boiling water. Cook 15 to 35 minutes.
Alternative Step 2:To Steam: Steam 12 to 30 minutes; test often by piercing them with the point of a knife; they should be a bit resistant in the center, but not so hard.

ASPARAGUS:
Step 1: Wash the asparagus and break stalks-they will break where tender part starts; pare bottom half.
Step 2: Plunge the spears into a large pot of boiling water and boil gently until the bottoms are just tender when pierced with a knife. Begin testing after 4 to 8 minutes, depending on the thickness of the stalks.
Alternative Step 2: Steam whole spears 4 to 8 minutes.
Step 3: Drain and serve with melted butter, Hollandaise Sauce or Cheese Sauce.

STRING or GREEN BEANS:
Step 1: Wash; remove ends, (Strings have been bred out of most varieties-which use to have to pulled out). Leave them whole or cut them in diagonal strips.
Step 2:To Cook: Cook covered in a small amount of boiling water 5 to 10 minutes.
Alternative Step 2:To Steam: Steam 7 to 12 minutes. The beans should be bright-light green and crunchy.

NAVY BEAN:
Step 1: Rinse and sort beans. Cover beans with water and let soak overnight or boil 2 minutes, cover and let set 1 hour before going to next step. Then drain beans and rinse thoroughly, until water runs clear.
Step 2: Place in a large pot with water. Bring to a boil over high heat, immediately turn down heat. Simmer 1 hour or until tender. Drain the water and replace with boiling fresh water a few times during cooking. The beans should be a pale-beige or light-almond color when finished cooking.
Step 3: Add salt and oil to taste in the last 15 minutes of cooking. (Salt added at the beginning of simmer will dry beans out)

BEETS:
Step 1: Wash thoroughly. Always cook beets whole, and leave a bit of the stem on-to prevent the root from bleeding. Do not pare.
Step 2:To Cook: Drop the beets into enough boiling water to cover them, and cook them, uncovered,

until they are tender and remain bright red, allowing 30 to 60 minutes, depending on the age and size of the beets.

Alternative Step 2:To Steam: Steam 35 to 60 minutes.

Peel and slice only after cooking. After cooking, run under cold water and the skins will peel off easy. They can be served with butter or a little lemon juice.

Beets, Pared:

Step 1: Wash thoroughly Pare and slice or cube. Or pare and shred.

Step 2: To Cook Pared:Cook covered in small amount of boiling water. Cook 12 to 20 minutes.

Alternative Step 2:To Steam Pared: Steam 15 to 20 minutes.

BROCCOLI:

Step 1: Wash; cut off and discard the tough end of stems and coarse outer leaves; split rest of stalk almost to flowerets.

Secure stalks in bundle, utilizing a folded strip of foil. Stand up in one inch of boiling water.

Step 2:To Cook: Cover and cook 10 to 15 minutes.

Broccoli, Cut:

Step 1: Cut stalk in one inch pieces.

Alternative Step 2:To Cook: Cook stalks in a large pot of boiling water for 3 to 4 minutes; add flowerets. Cook 8 to 12 minutes total.

Alternative Step 2:To Steam: Steam stalks 2 to 3 minutes; add flowerets. Steam 10 to 13 minutes total.

BROCCOLI RABE:

Step 1: Wash; cut off the bottoms of the stalks.

Step 2: Steam for 6 to 8 minutes.

Step 3: Drain and serve with garlic sauteéd in extra virgin olive oil.

BRUSSELS SPROUTS:

*Step 1:*Wash; remove any wilted or yellow leaves. Score the stem ends so the cuts form an (X). Halve large sprouts.

Step 2:To Cook: Cook covered in a small amount of boiling water 7 to 10 minutes.

Alternative Step 2:To Steam: Steam 10 to 13 minutes.

Step 3: Drain.

CABBAGE:

Step 1: Wash; cut the cabbage in half; cut away and discard the hard, whitish core.

Step 2:To Cook: Cook covered in a small amount of boiling water 8 to 15 minutes.

Alternate Step 2:To Steam: Steam 6 to 13 minutes.

Step 3: Drain.

Cabbage, chopped or sliced:
Step 1: Wash; roughly chop or slice thin.
Step 2:To Sauté: Heat some olive oil in a skillet over a medium-high flame; sauté 10 to 12 minutes or until tender-crisp.

CARROT:
Carrots have a lot of natural sugar contained in them, so the less we do to them, the more they will do for us.
Step 1: The carrot can be pared, scrubbed good without paring, sliced diagonally, cubed or leave them whole, if they are small.
Step 2:To Cook: Cook covered in small amount of boiling water. Whole carrots 15 to 20 minutes; sliced carrots 10 to 12 minutes.
Alternate Step 2:To Steam: Steam whole carrots 17 to 22 minutes; sliced carrots 10 to 15 minutes.

CAULIFLOWER:
Step 1: Remove the leaves and some of the woody stem; wash; leave it whole or separate into flowerets.
Step 2:To Cook: Cook covered in small amount of boiling water; whole for 15 to 22 minutes; flowerets for 8 to 15 minutes.
Alternative Step 2:To Steam: Steam whole for 20 to 25 minutes; flowerets for 10 to 15 minutes.

CELERY:
Step 1: Cut off leaves; trim roots; scrub thoroughly, slice outer branches; cut hearts lengthwise.
Step 2:To Cook: Cook covered in small amount of boiling water 10 to 15 minutes.
Alternative Step 2:To Steam: Steam 10 to 15 minutes.

CORN:
Step 1: Husk the corn; pull off the silky threads; rinse; leave whole or if too long for the pot break them in two with our hands.
Step 2:To Cook: Drop them into a large pot of boiling, unsalted water; cover the pot and let the water return to a boil again, then turn off the heat and keep pot covered. After 6 to 8 minutes, remove enough ears for a first serving. The remaining corn can be kept warm in the water for another 10 minutes without it becoming tough.

Corn On The Cob:
Step 1: Husk the corn; pull off the silky threads; rinse; cut the corn from the cob with a sharp knife.
Step 2: In a skillet, heat the kernels in butter and seasonings, or milk for 4 to 7 minutes.

EGGPLANT:

Step 1: Wash, pare—if skin is tough; cut into 1/2 inch slices.

Step 2: Dip in beaten egg, then in fine whole wheat bread crumbs.

Step 3: In a skillet over a medium flame, brown slowly on both sides in hot oil or butter for 4 to 5 minutes total.

GARLIC:

Step 1: Break a few cloves off of a bulb of garlic; smash the cloves, the skins will peel away easy; cut off the tough stem end; slice, chop or mince garlic.

Step 2:To Sauté: Sauté in a little olive oil till golden brown.

Step 3: Sprinkle sauteed garlic over most vegetables.

OKRA:

If we don't prefer the slippery texture of cooked okra, sauté or stew it. (Stew it in dishes that include tomatoes.)

Step 1: Wash; snap or cut off stems.

Step 2:To Cook: Cook covered for 10 minutes.

Alternative Step 2:To Steam: Steam for 10 minutes.

Alternative Step 2:To Sauté: Cut large pods in 1/2 inch slices and prepare as for eggplant sautéed.

ONIONS:

Rinse onions in water to take away bite when serving raw.

Step 1: Quarter or leave small onions whole.

Step 2:To Cook: Cook in small amount of water 20 to 30 minutes.

Alternative Step 2:To Steam: Steam 20 to 30 minutes.

Alternative Step 2:To Sauté: Sauté in a skillet with a little extra virgin olive oil till golden brown; about 10 minutes.

PEPPERS (Sweet Red & Green peppers):

Step 1: Wash; slice into 1/4 inch slices or strips.

Step 2: Sauté in a little extra virgin olive oil 5 to 7 minutes.

RED POTATOES:

(for small-medium potatoes)

Step 1: Scrub thoroughly; leave skins on. Or wash and pare lightly. Cook whole, quarter or cube.

Step 2:To Cook: Cook covered in boiling water; whole for 25 to 35 minutes; quartered for 20 to 25 minutes; cubed for 10 to 15 minutes.

Alternate Step 2:To Steam: Steam; whole for 25 to 35 minutes; quartered for 20 to 25 minutes; cubed for 10 to 15 minutes.

RUTABAGAS (Yellow Turnip):
Cook like Red Potatoes. See above.

SPINACH:
Step 1: Wash extra carefully due to the dirt and tiny rocks caught in the leaves; cut purple stem ends.
Step 2: Steam 3 to 5 minutes.

SUMMER SQUASH (Soft):
Step 1: Wash; pare lightly or leave skins on; cut in 1/2 inch slices or cube.
Step 2: Cook covered in small amount of boiling water 10 to 20 minutes.

ZUCCHINI (Summer-Soft):
Step 1: Wash; don't pare; cut in 1/2 inch slices.
Step 2: Sauté in a little oil, covered for 5 minutes; then uncover and cook, turning slices until tender; cook about 10 minutes total.

BUTTERNUT OR ACORN SQUASH (Winter-Hard):
Step 1: Wash; cut in half; remove seeds.
Step 2:To Bake: In a buttered dish, bake cut side down in a 350°F oven for 35 to 40 minutes; turn cut side up; bake till done; 50 to 60 minutes total.
Alternative Step 2:To Cook: Pare or cube; cook covered in a small amount of boiling water for 15 minutes.

HUBBARD SQUASH (Winter-Hard):
Step 1: Wash; cut into serving sections; don't pare; arrange on baking sheet; season and dot with butter; cover with foil.
Step 2:To Bake: Bake in a 350°F oven for 1 hour and 15 minutes; testing with a knife for tenderness.
Alternative Step 2:To Cook: Wash; cut into serving sections; don't pare; cook covered in small amount of boiling water for 15 to 20 minutes.
Alternative Step 2:To Steam: Wash; cut into serving sections; don't pare; steam for 15 to 20 minutes.

TOMATOES:
Step 1: Wash ripe tomatoes.
Step 2:To Peel: Submerge in boiling water for about a minute, then cool under cool water; peel with sharp knife; cut out stems, chop or leave tomato whole.
Step 3: Cook slowly, without adding water, covered; add seasoning and sauté onions, peppers and garlic; cook a total 8 to 12 minutes.

TURNIP (Roots):

Cook like red potatoes. See Red Potatoes.

DISCLAIMER

You should consult a physician in all matters relating to health before making any significant lifestyle or dietary changes. The information contained in or made available through this series of five cookbooks is intended to help you make informed decisions about your health.

The nutrition information provided for each recipe is determined by an analysis utilizing Muhammad's Program of "How To Eat To Live". Please purchase copies of the Honorable Elijah Muhammad's Books One and Two titled 'How To Eat To Live'.

LIST OF SOURCES & ACKNOWLEDGEMENTS

NUTRITION

- Master Fard Muhammad
- The Most Honorable Elijah Muhammad
- The Honorable Minister Louis Farrakhan
- Mother Tynetta Muhammad
- Dr. Alim Muhammad
- Minister Ava Muhammad
- Minister Nelson Muhammad
- Takayuki Shibamoto - Professor in department of Environmental Toxicology at University of California at Davis.
- Wanda Howell of University of Arizona.
- Stanley Segall - Professor of Nutrition & Food at Drexel University.
- Sara Lippmann
- Shirley Mandel
- Norman Salem Jr. - Researcher with National Institute of Health.
- Terrance Leighton - Biochemist at University of California at Berkeley.
- The Standard Deviants, Video Course Review "The Nutty, Nougat Filled World Of Human Nutrition" Cerebellum Corporation.
- Peak Energy, The High-Oxygen Program For More Energy Now!, by Daniel Hamner, M.D. and Barbara Burr.
- The Supreme Wisdom-The Problem Book:Section 6:9.

KITCHEN HEALTH SUGGESTIONS

- Susan Edelman
- Centers for Disease Control and Prevention, www.cdc.gov

RECIPES (adaptations)

- Many are adaptations from classical and traditional sources.
- M.G.T. of The Muhammad Mosque and The Lost Found Members Of The Nation Of Islam In The West.
- The Final Call Newspaper™, Deloris Ali Muhammad - National Cooking Instructress of the Nation of Islam.
- The Fannie Farmer Cookbook™, 12th edition, Alfred A. Knopf, New York 1980
- Food Day™ Newsday™ contributing authors Marge Perry & Bev Bennett.
- The Great Chili Book, by Mark Miller

- Fruit, a Connoisseur's Guide and Cookbook, by Alan Davidson.
- Best Recipes Of The Great Food Companies, Compiled by Judith Anderson.
- Skinny Spices, by Erica Levy Klein.
- Spices and Herbs Around The World, Elizabeth S. Hayes
- The Spices Of Life, by Troth Wells
- Condiments, by Jay Solomon.
- Cooking Under Wraps, by Nicole Routhier.
- Flatbreads and Flavors, by Jeffrey Alford.
- The Forgotten Art of Making Old-Fashioned Pickles, Relishes, chutnies, Sauces & Catsups, Mincemeats, Beverages & Syrups; published Dublin, N.H.; Yankee 1978.
- The Complete Book of Sauces, by Salley Williams.

RECIPES (adaptations) VERSION II
- Red Hot Peppers, by Jean Andrews
- Meatless Mexican Home Cooking, Nancy Zaslavsky
- Essential Flavors, by Leslie Brenner
- 100 Simple Sauces, by Carl Jerome

INGREDIENTS: HOW TO UTILIZE
Ahmed H. Sakr
Gutrie, H.A. - Introductory Nutrition

THE SUPREME OIL
Pamela Street - Self Magazine
Bruce Cohn - Owner of Sonomas BR. Cohn Winery
Michele Anna Jordan - The Good Cook's Book Of Oil & Vinegar

GLOSSARY OF TERMS (and Basic Definitions)
The American Heritage Dictionary Of English Language, 3rd Edition

STEAMING VEGETABLES & COOKING BEANS
Pete Napolitano - Produce Pete's "Farmacopeia"

MUSLIM COOKING WITH MUHAMMAD
MUSLIM COOKBOOK, NUTRITION & HEALTH GUIDE
VERSION ONE of FIVE
RECIPES

MUSLIM COOKING WITH MUHAMMAD
MUSLIM COOKBOOK, NUTRITION & HEALTH GUIDE
VERSION ONE of FIVE
RECIPES

TABLE OF CONTENTS

NOTES ON RECIPES

1. Wash all vegetables, fruits and beans before utilizing.
2. All salt utilized for these recipes are vegetable salt or coarse kosher salt.
3. Black and other peppercorns are roasted-if desired and mostly freshly ground in a peppermill.
4. Most spice seeds are usually roasted, cooled and ground
5. All citrus juices like lemon and lime should be freshly squeezed.
6. Tomatoes strained means the chopped tomatoes are processed through a Foley Mill™ where the skin and seeds are strained out and a pureé results.
7. Remember to prevent food from sticking to a pan always heat pan first then add cold oil. Remember the saying "Hot pan, cold oil, food won't stick."
8. For calorie watchers substitute yogurt for the sour cream.
9. Bake casseroles in a shallow-pan, not a deep-pan, to ensure even baking.
10. Utilize Muhammad's Farms™ products and Muhammad's™ products.

1. SOUPS

FISH BROTHS

Fish stock should be saved for fish soups & chowders or for sauces to be utilized with seafood. When prepared, it should always be set aside an hour or two, then utilized to poach the fish; or as a substitute of water in making fish sauces.

FISH STOCK PLAIN

2 pounds fish trimmings (bones, tails)	1 bay leaf
2 quarts water	1 teaspoon salt

Step 1: Wash trimmings thoroughly in salted water.

Step 2: Pour water into deep saucepan; add fish, salt and bay leaf; cover; simmer 30 minutes.

Step 3: Strain and set aside for utilization in preparing fish recipes.

VEGETABLE STOCK

Vegetable stock is the substance in which vegetables have been cooked. It contains many nutritional vitamins and minerals. Utilize stocks from highly flavored vegetables like celery, cabbage, turnips, and carrots sparingly and with discretion, and please do not cook vegetable stocks for more than 30 minutes or they may become bitter. Utilize instead of water or meat stock in many soups.

COURT BOUILLON

2 quarts water	1 large onion, chopped
2 teaspoons butter or olive oil	2 sprigs parsley
6 crushed peppercorns	1 large carrot, chopped
2 whole cloves	3 stalks celery, chopped
1 bay leaf	2 teaspoons vinegar

Step 1: Peel and chop vegetables.

Step 2: Melt butter in deep saucepan over medium flame; add chopped vegetables; sauté 5 minutes or until golden brown; add water, crushed peppercorns, cloves, bay leaf, parsley and vinegar; cover and simmer 30 minutes.

Step 3: Strain and set aside for utilization in boiling fish.

THE INCREDIBLE NAVY BEAN

Some tips on bean cuisine are these:

• After soaking, rinse beans thoroughly, in several changes of water. This helps prevent gassiness from beans. Then after they boil for a few minutes, drain again and replace with fresh boiling water.

• Never salt beans until they are almost done, or else they will stay hard longer or may never soften.

• Cook beans until they make a creamy gravy of their own; chewy, undercooked dried beans can cause colic in you.

• A roasted chili pepper will give a pot of beans a spark.

←——————————————————————→

PLAIN BEANS™

1 pound dried navy beans	4 quarts water
1/2 teaspoon salt	

1 small dried ancho chili pepper, toasted, seeded & stemmed and crumbled

Step 1: Rinse and sort beans. Cover beans with water and let soak overnight or boil 2 minutes, cover and let set 1 hour before going to next step. Then drain beans and rinse thoroughly, until water runs clear.

Step 2: Place in a large pot with water. Bring to a boil over high heat, immediately turn down heat. Simmer 1 hour or until tender. Drain the water and replace with boiling fresh water a few times during cooking.

Step 3: Add salt to taste and chili pepper in the last 15 minutes of cooking.

←——————————————————————→

TRADITIONAL BEAN SOUP™

(This is a standard procedure for making flavored and multi ingredient bean soup. follow this procedure for the following recipes.)

2 cups navy beans	1 large onion, chopped
1 tablespoon sugar	1 green bell pepper, chopped
3 stalks celery, chopped	1 garlic clove, minced
1/4 cup corn oil	1 teaspoon Hungarian paprika
2 cups strained tomato purée	1 teaspoon sage
1/4 teaspoons black pepper	1/2 teaspoon salt

Step 1: Rinse and sort beans. Cover beans with water and let soak overnight or boil 2 minutes, cover and let set 1 hour before going to next step. Then drain beans and rinse thoroughly, until water runs

clear.

Step 2: Place in a large pot with water. Bring to a boil over high heat, immediately turn down heat. Then after they boil for a few minutes, drain again and replace with fresh boiling water. Add seasonings and oil. Simmer 1 hour or until tender.

Step 3: Add in the last 15 minutes of cooking, tomatoes, chopped vegetables and salt. It is ready when beans are easily mashed. Add more boiling water if needed.

Step 4: If you like, strain through a Foley™ food strainer, or eat them whole in a chunky or rustic style. Serve with toast and cheese (pg.132). Soup will naturally thicken immediately after its done, just add boiling water.

MILD BEAN SOUP™

2 cups navy beans

2 tablespoons clarified butter

1 stalk celery, chopped

2 carrots, chopped

1 cup strained tomato purée

1/2 teaspoon rosemary

1/2 teaspoon salt

1/8 teaspoon Muhammad's Red Hot Sauce™ (pg.307)

1 tablespoon Muhammad's Seasoning™ (pg.307)

1 large onion, chopped

1 cup green bell pepper, chopped

1 cup red bell pepper, chopped

5 bay leaves

1/2 teaspoon thyme

1/2 teaspoon sage

Step 1: Rinse and sort beans. Cover beans with water and let soak overnight or boil 2 minutes, cover and let set 1 hour before going to next step. Then drain beans and rinse thoroughly, until water runs clear.

Step 2: Place in a large pot with water. Bring to a boil over high heat, immediately turn down heat.Then after they boil for a few minutes, drain again and replace with fresh boiling water.

Step 3: Add seasonings and butter. Simmer 1 hour or until tender.

Step 4: Add in the last 15 minutes of cooking, tomato purée, chopped vegetables and salt. It is ready when beans are easily mashed. Add more boiling water if needed.

Step 5: If you like, strain through a Foley™ food strainer, or eat them whole in a chunky or rustic style. Serve with toast and cheese. Soup will naturally thicken immediately after its done, just add boiling water.

THAI SOUP™

2 cups navy beans

2 carrots, chopped

1 cup strained tomato purée

1 teaspoon thyme, finely chopped

1/4 teaspoon black pepper

5 bay leaves

83

Salt to taste
1/4 cup Muhammad's™ Thai Sweet & Sour Sauce (pg.307)

SAUTEÉD VEGETABLES

2 tablespoons clarified butter	1/2 cup green bell pepper, chopped
1 medium onion, chopped	1 stalk celery, chopped
1/2 cup red bell pepper, chopped	
1 serano chili pepper, roasted, skin & seeds discarded, and finely chopped	

Step 1: Rinse and sort beans. Cover beans with water and let soak overnight or boil 2 minutes, cover and let set 1 hour before going to next step.

Step 2: Then drain beans and rinse thoroughly, until water runs clear. Place in a large pot with water. Bring to a boil over high heat.

Step 3: Drain water from beans again and replace with fresh boiling water; bring to boil over high again, immediately turn down heat.

Step 4: Add thyme, thai sauce, black pepper and bay leaves; simmer 1 hour or until tender.

Step 5:For The Sauteéd Vegetables: Meanwhile heat butter until it sizzles in a heavy skillet over medium flame; sauté onions, celery, serano chili, green and red bell peppers.

Step 6: During the last 15 minutes of cooking the beans, add carrots, tomato purée, sauteéd vegetables and salt. It is ready when beans are easily mashed. Add more boiling water if needed. If you like, strain through a Foley™ food strainer, or eat them whole in a chunky or rustic style. Step 7:Serve with toast and cheese. Soup will naturally thicken immediately after its done, just add boiling water.

◄─────────────────────────────────►

SWEET BEAN SOUP™

2 cups navy beans	1 large onion, chopped
2 to 4 tablespoons brown sugar	2 cloves garlic, minced
2 stalks celery, chopped	2 cups green bell pepper, chopped
3 carrots, chopped	2 to 4 tablespoons maple syrup
Salt to taste	
1/3 cup olive oil	
1/4 teaspoon Muhammad's Red Hot Sauce™ (pg.307)	
2 tablespoons Muhammad's Seasoning™ (pg.307)	

Step 1: Rinse and sort beans. Cover beans with water and let soak overnight or boil 2 minutes, cover and let set 1 hour before going to next step. Then drain beans and rinse thoroughly, until water runs clear.

Step 2: Place in a large pot with water. Bring to a boil over high heat, immediately turn down heat. Then after they boil for a few minutes, drain again and replace with fresh boiling water.

Add seasonings. Simmer 1 hour or until tender.

Step 3:For The Sauteéd Vegetables: In a skillet over a high flame, sauté onions, garlic, green & hot pepper, and celery in olive oil.

Step 4: Add in the last 15 minutes of cooking, sautéed & chopped vegetables and salt. It is ready when beans are easily mashed. Add more boiling water if needed.

Step 5: If you like, strain through a Foley™ food strainer, or eat them whole in a chunky or rustic style. Serve with toast and cheese. Soup will naturally thicken immediately after its done, just add boiling water.

DELICIOUS BEAN SOUP™

2 cups navy beans

1/3 cup corn oil

3 stalks celery, chopped

3 carrots, chopped

1 teaspoon turmeric

2 teaspoon paprika

1/4 teaspoon fresh black pepper

1/4 teaspoon Muhammad's Red Hot Sauce™ (pg.307)

2 onion, chopped

2 cups strained tomato purée

1 green bell pepper, chopped

2 garlic cloves, minced

Salt to taste

Step 1: Rinse and sort beans. Cover beans with water and let soak overnight or boil 2 minutes, cover and let set 1 hour before going to next step. Then drain beans and rinse thoroughly, until water runs clear. Place in a large pot with water. Bring to a boil over high heat, immediately turn down heat.

Step 2: Add seasonings. Simmer 1 hour or until tender.

Step 3:For The Sauteéd Vegetables: In a skillet over a high flame, sauté onions, garlic, green & hot pepper sauce, and celery in oil.

Step 4: Add in the last 15 minutes of cooking, tomato purée, sautéed & chopped vegetables and salt. It is ready when beans are easily mashed. Add more boiling water if needed. If you like, strain through a Foley™ food strainer, or eat them whole in a chunky or rustic style. Serve with toast and cheese. Soup will naturally thicken immediately after its done, just add boiling water.

BEAN & ONION SOUP™

2 cups navy beans

1/4 cup olive oil

1 teaspoon parsley, chopped

1/4 stick butter

1/2 teaspoon salt

1/2 teaspoon Muhammad's Red Hot Sauce™ (pg.307)

2 onion, chopped

2 red onions, chopped

4 garlic cloves, minced

1/2 fresh ground black pepper

Step 1: Rinse and sort beans. Cover beans with water and let soak overnight or boil 2 minutes, cover and let set 1 hour before going to next step. Then drain beans and rinse thoroughly, until water runs clear. Place in a large pot with water. Bring to a boil over high heat, immediately turn down heat.

Step 2: Add seasonings. Simmer 1 hour or until tender.

Step 3:For The Sauteéd Vegetables: In a skillet over a high flame, sauté onions, garlic, and hot pepper in oil & butter.

Step 4: Add in the last 15 minutes of cooking, sautéed & chopped vegetables and salt. It is ready when beans are easily mashed. Add more boiling water if needed. If you like, strain through a Foley™ food strainer, or eat them whole in a chunky or rustic style. Serve with toast and cheese. Soup will naturally thicken immediately after its done, just add boiling water.

√ Bean & Onion Soup With Cheese

Delete *butter.* Place soup in individual serving baking bowls and top with grated *Parmesan cheese.* Place in a 400°F oven until cheese is golden brown.

———————————————————————————————————→

RED BEANS™

1 pound dried red beans	4 quarts water
1 teaspoon fresh thyme, minced	Salt to taste
3 tablespoon butter	
1/4 teaspoon black pepper	
1 teaspoon Muhammad's Seasoning™ (pg.307)	

Step 1: Rinse and sort beans. Cover beans with water and let soak overnight or boil 2 minutes, cover and let set 1 hour before going to next step. Then drain beans and rinse thoroughly, until water runs clear.

Step 2: Place in a large pot with water. Bring to a boil over high heat, immediately turn down heat. Simmer 1 hour or until tender. Drain the water and replace with boiling fresh water a few times during cooking.

Step 3: Add salt to taste, seasoning, pepper and fresh thyme in the last 15 minutes of cooking. Serve hot with butter.

←———————————————————————————————————

VEGETABLE SOUPS

CREAM OF ARTICHOKE SOUP

4 large Jerusalem artichokes

2 tablespoons butter

2 tablespoons unbleached flour

Salt to taste

Dash of Muhammad's Red Hot Sauce™ (pg.307)

Dash of mace

1 cup cream

1/2 cup milk

Step 1: Peel the artichokes with a potato peeler and drop them into cold water acidulated with a tablespoon of lemon juice. Reserve 1/3 of an artichoke to dice fine just before serving and utilize as a garnish.

Step 2: Bring 5 cups water to boil and add the remaining artichokes, cut in half. Boil them briskly, for about 30 minutes or until they are just soft.

Step 3: Put the artichokes and cooking liquid in a Foley™ mill or food processor and purée.

Step 4: Melt the butter in a large pot, stir in the flour, hot sauce, and mace, and cook, stirring until smooth and thick. Just before serving, add cream, milk, and salt and reheat. Put a little of the saved diced artichoke in each bowl of soup.

⟵——————————————————⟶

TOMATO SOUP

2 stalks celery, chopped

1 green bell pepper, chopped

3 whole cloves

Fresh ground black pepper

Dash of baking soda

2-3 pounds tomatoes, chopped or strained & puréed

1 carrot, sliced

1 onion chopped

2 tablespoons lemon juice

Salt to taste

Step 1: Place tomatoes and 1 cup of water in a soup pot. Add the vegetables, cloves and baking soda. Bring to the boiling point, reduce heat, and simmer for 15 minutes.

Step 2: Strain and season with lemon juice and salt and pepper to taste.

⟵——————————————————⟶

CABBAGE SOUP

1/2 head cabbage, roughly sliced

4 garlic cloves, chopped

2 carrots, sliced

2 celery stalks, sliced

1/4 teaspoon ground black pepper

1 teaspoon thyme

7 parsley sprigs (tied with 1 bay leaf)

2 onions, chopped

2 turnips (or red potatoes), sliced

1 teaspoon marjoram

1 tablespoon butter

1/4 cup olive oil

2 quarts water

2 cups cooked navy beans, puréed (pg.71)

2 tablespoons Muhammad's Seasoning™ (pg.307)

Pinch Muhammad's Chili Pepper™ (pg.307)

Step 1: Place the water in a kettle and bring it to the boil.

Step 2: For The Sauteéd Vegetables: In a skillet over a high flame, sauté the garlic, onions, and celery in olive oil.

Step 3: Add all the ingredients into kettle. Simmer partially covered for 20 minutes.

Step 4: Discard parsley bundle. Serve with French bread slices toasted.

CREAM OF TOMATO SOUP

4 cups milk or light cream	2 cups strained tomatoes
1/2 cup French Bread crumbs (pg.195)	1/4 teaspoon baking soda
1 onion stuck with 5 cloves	4 tablespoons unsalted butter
4 parsley sprigs (tied with 1 bay leaf)	Salt to taste
2 teaspoons Raw™ sugar	Freshly ground pepper

Step 1: Put the light cream or milk in a pot and add the French bread crumbs, onion with cloves, parsley bundle, and sugar. Simmer gently over medium heat for about 5 minutes.

Step 2: Remove from heat and discard the onion with cloves and parsley bundle and bay leaf, leave one parsley sprig in soup. Add the tomatoes and baking soda and simmer gently for 15 minutes.

Step 3: Put through a Foley™ mill or purée with hand mixer.

Step 4: Return to pot, add the butter and salt and pepper to taste, and reheat, stirring until the butter melts and the soup is hot.

SQUASH SOUP

1 cup mashed cooked winter squash	2 tablespoons butter
1 quart milk	1/2 teaspoon ginger
2 tablespoon grated onion	3 tablespoons unbleached flour
Salt to taste	(opt.) 1/8 tsp. white pepper

Step 1: Mix the squash, milk, onion, and ginger in a pot and cook over moderate heat about ten minutes.

Step 2: Melt the butter in a small pan, stir in the flour, and cook several minutes until smooth and thick. Pour a little of the soup into the butter-flour mixture, stirring until blended, then slowly pour into the soup. Add salt and pepper. Continue cooking, stirring frequently, until very hot.

FISH SOUPS

CLASSIC FISH CHOWDER™

2 pounds whiting or red snapper	2 onions, thinly sliced
3 medium potatoes, peeled & fine diced	2 cups cream or milk
2 tablespoons olive oil	2 tablespoons butter
4 cups Fish Stock (pg.80)	Salt to taste
Freshly ground white pepper	

Step 1: Heat the oil, add onions, and cook over low heat until golden. Stir in the potatoes and toss till well coated. Add the fish stock.

Step 2: Wipe fillets with a clean damp clothe; cut the fish in chunks or strips; remove dark meat; add it to the pot, and simmer, partially covered, for 15 minutes, or until the fish is cooked through and the potatoes are tender. Stir in the cream or milk and heat slowly, without boiling. Just before serving, stir in the butter, add salt and pepper to taste, and heat until butter melts. Serve with Plain Cheese Thins (pg.137).

√ Savory Fish Chowder

Omit the *cream* and substitute 4 cups *strained tomatoes*. Add 1/2 teaspoon *marjoram* or *thyme* along with the tomatoes. Serve with Plain Cheese Thins (pg.137).

WHITING CHOWDER™

One and a half pounds whiting fillets	2 red potatoes, finely diced
1 onion, chopped	4 tablespoons flour
3 stalks celery, chopped	1 teaspoon Worcestershire sauce
4 tablespoons butter	1/4 teaspoons white pepper
3 cups water	Salt to taste
1 quart of milk	

Step 1: Wipe fillets with a clean damp clothe; place fish in deep kettle; cover with one and a half cups cold water; simmer over medium flame 10 minutes. Place fish in bowl and remove skin & dark meat; flake; reserve fish stock for use later.

Step 2: Place butter in deep kettle over medium flame; add onions; sauté 5 minutes or until golden brown; add potatoes, celery and one and a half cups water; cover, cook 15 minutes or until potatoes and celery are tender.

Step 3: Blend flour in small mixing bowl with half of the quart of milk; when smooth, add the other half of the quart; then add to cooked potatoes and celery; add fish and fish stock; heat to boiling point but do not boil. Season with salt and pepper.

Step 4: Serve hot in preheated bowls. Garnish each serving with thyme sprigs or parsley.

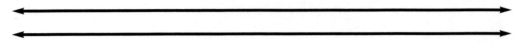

2. SEASONINGS, HERBES, SAUCES, RELISHES & STUFFINGS

SEASONINGS

All spices and seasonings should be stored in an airtight container in a cool dry place for up to 3 months; the pungent aroma begins to diminish after 3 weeks.

PARTY MIX SEASONING™

1 part dry mustard

1 part Parmesan or Romano cheese (optional)

4 parts Muhammad's Garam Masala™ (pg.307)

Step 1: Blend all ingredients together and sprinkle on a party mix of pretzels, crackers and chips; Bake in a preheated 350°F oven for 10 minutes.

←——————————————————————————→

FIVE-SPICE SEASONING™

(For Asian cooking)

2 teaspoons star anise, ground

2 teaspoons Szechwan pepper, ground

1 teaspoon cinnamon, ground

2 teaspoons fennel seed, ground

1 teaspoons cloves, ground

Step 1: Blend all ingredients together and utilize with Asian dishes.

←——————————————————————————→

GALANGAL (LAOS) POWDER™

(For Asian cooking)

1 part ginger, finely grated

1 part cardamom, roasted & ground

Step 1: Blend all ingredients together.

←——————————————————————————→

FRUIT SPICES™

apples with cinnamon or nutmeg

peaches with ginger

pears with cloves

oranges with cinnamon or cloves

sliced grapes with allspice or nutmeg

←——————————————————————————→

INDIAN DESSERT BLEND™

For East Indian Desserts

2 tablespoons cardamom   2 tablespoons allspice

2 tablespoons cinnamon   1 tablespoon powered sugar

Step 1: Blend all ingredients in a mortar.

Step 2: Use with desserts, Shortbread Pie Crust (pg.236) or Cookie Seasoning (pg.226).

←——————————————————————————→

GINGER COOKIE SPICE™

4 tablespoons ginger   2 tablespoons nutmeg

1 tablespoons cloves, ground

Step 1: Blend all ingredients in a mortar.

Step 2: Use with desserts, Ginger Snaps (pg.227) or Pie Crust (pg.231) .

←——————————————————————————→

ZAATAR™

(For Middle Eastern cooking)

1 part savory   1 part sumac

1 part sesame seed, roasted & mashed

Step 1: Blend all ingredients together in a mortar.

←——————————————————————————→

HUNAN SEASONING™

Chinese

1 tablespoon garlic, finely minced   1 tablespoon cilantro, finely chopped

1 tablespoon ginger, finely minced

1 to 2 tablespoons Mustard (pg.108)

1/2 tablespoon Muhammad's Red Hot Sauce™ (pg.307)

1 tablespoon Szechuan peppercorns, roasted & ground

2 tablespoons Tahini (pg.94)

Step 1: Blend all ingredients together in a mortar.

√ Chinese Vegetable Seasoning

Use 1 teaspoon Hunan Seasoning™ *(pg.92)* with *1 tablespoon non-alcohol dry sherry* as a flavoring ingredient in sauteéd vegetables or in stir fries.

EASTERN SPICE MIX™
Khmeli Suneli
(For Eastern Georgian cooking)

12 parts coriander seed, roasted & ground	1 part fenugreek seed, roasted & ground
6 parts dried parsley	2 parts dried mint
2 parts fennel seed	
2 parts dried oregano or thyme	
4 parts dried calendula (pot marigold) petals, or 2 to 3 saffron threads, ground	

Step 1: Blend all ingredients together in a mortar or spice grinder.

Step 2: Mix ingredients together in a bowl and utilize with Eastern Georgian dishes.

®BARBECUE SPICE & BASTING SAUCE™ BLENDS

√ Barbecue Marinade I

Blend in Barbecue Spice & Basting Sauce™ (pg. 307) with non-alcohol white wine & onions.

√ Barbecue Marinade II

Blend in Barbecue Spice & Basting Sauce™ (pg.307) with vinegar & soy sauce.

√ Barbecue Marinade III

Blend in Barbecue Spice & Basting Sauce™ (pg.307) with a Citrus Sauce.

√ Barbecue Basting Sauce

Blend in Barbecue Spice & Basting Sauce™ (pg.307) with 1 1/4 cup Ketchup (pg.109), 1/4 cup olive oil, & 1 tablespoon minced garlic. Baste with the sauce during the last 10 minutes of cooking.

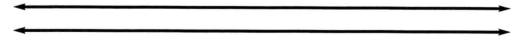

FINE HERBES

FINES HERBES™

1 to 2 parts parsley	1 part tarragon

| 1 part chervil | 1 part chives |

Step 1: Mince herbes together and mix.

HERBES DE PROVENCE™

| 4 parts fresh thyme leaves | 4 parts fresh summer savory |
| 2 parts fresh lavender 1 part fresh rosemary leaves | |

Step 1: Mince herbes together and mix. Once prepared, mix may be used fresh or dried in salad dressings, vegetables, soups, fish & breads.

HERBES DE PROVENCE II™

4 parts fresh thyme leaves	4 parts fresh summer savory
2 parts fresh lavender	1 part fresh rosemary leaves
1 part fresh fennel	1 part fresh basil
2 parts fresh oregano	1 part fresh sage

Step 1: Mince herbes together and mix. Once prepared, mix may be used fresh or dried in salad dressings, vegetables, soups, fish & breads.

MEDITEREANNAN SPICE BLEND™

1 part Mexican oregano	1 part thyme
1 part sage	1 part parsley
1 part black pepper	2 bay leaves, powdered

Step 1: Mince herbes together and mix.

TAHINI™

1/4 cup sesame, seeds, roasted & mashed
1 to 2 tablespoons corn oil

Step 1: Blend oil and mashed seeds together and mix.

√Tahini Substitute™
Substitute sesame seeds with *unsalted sunflower seeds.*

®MUHAMMAD'S SALAD TOPPING MIX™ BLENDS

√ ®Muhammad's Vegetable Seasoning™

Use *1 teaspoon ®Muhammad's Salad Topping Mix™ (pg.307)* with *1 tablespoon non-alcohol dry white wine* as a flavoring ingredient in sauteéd vegetables and fish.

√ ®Muhammad's Fish & Vegetable Marinade™

Use *1 tablespoon ®Muhammad's Salad Topping Mix™ (pg.307)* with *1/2 cup non-alcohol dry white wine* as a marinade for fish and vegetables.

MOROCCAN MINT MIX™
Middle Eastern

2 tablespoons dried mint leaves, crumbled

2 tablespoons sesame seeds, toasted

1/2 tablespoon onion flakes

2 tablespoons garlic

1/2 tablespoon lemon peel, finely grated

Step 1: Blend all ingredients together in a mortar.

√ Vegetable Seasoning™

Use *1 teaspoon Moroccan Mint Mix™* with *1 tablespoon non-alcohol dry red wine* as a flavoring ingredient in sauteéd *string beans.*

√ Moroccan Scrambled Eggs™

Use *1/2 teaspoon Moroccan Mint Mix™* with *4 scrambled eggs* on *4 slices Whole Wheat Herb Bread, toasted (pg.192)*

SAUCES

THE GREAT CHILE SAUCE

• The smaller the chilies the hotter.

• Anchos provide fruity flavors of wild cherries and dried plums.

• Mulatos have tones of liquorice and tobacco.

• Smoke chilies and tomatoes to add smoke flavor.

• Roast to give a robust flavor. Use a butane torch, grill or broiler; quickly burn skin black-without burning flesh; sweat in a paper bag; peel and discard skin.

SUBSTITUTES

CHILE or CHILI PEPPERS, HOT
-habanero, Jamaican, Scottish

-Fresno

-jalapeño

-serrano, medium or small

CHILI or CHILI PEPPERS, MILDER
-green, red, yellow

-Anaheim or chili verde

-banana peppers or Hungarian wax peppers

-poblano (called ancho when dried)

←——————————————————————————→

•Dried chilies are more intense in flavor.

To Make a Powder out of Dried chilies:

Step 1: Place a few dried ancho and New Mexican chilies on a baking sheet and toast them in a 350˚F preheated oven for 6 minutes.

Step 2: Stem and seed them; break into pieces.

Step 3: Grind in a spice grinder or mortar.

(Note:Add powder to water, oil, or juice before adding to other ingredients over heat so as to not burn the powder.)

To Make a Sauce out of Dried chilies:

Step 1: Stem and seed them.

Step 2: Roast them in a skillet for 3 minutes making sure not to scorch or over-roast or they will be bitter.

Step 3: Then place in hot water, that has been brought to the just before boiling point, and soak for 20 minutes. If after 20 minutes the water is bitter, discard it, but use the chilies.

Step 4: Pureé and add a little soaking water or fresh water or tomato juice.

•Bass, baritone or low tone sauces are:roasted & smoked processed; they are earthy, woodsy or smoky tones.

•Tenor or the middle tones are mainly fruity like dried cherries or plums from chilies like ancho and casabel.

•The high notes or soprano are derived from the hot and citrus ones like Jamaican or habanero.

•The Vocabulary of flavors are:

Berry, dried cherry & plum, chocolate, citrus, coffee, fruit, liquorice, prune, raisin,

96

spice, tannin, tea and tobacco.

Themes are:

Earthiness, smokiness, stemminess and woodiness.

•Use chilies first for flavors, then for heat. The heat blocks flavors.

ASIAN GINGER SAUCE™

1/4 cup light soy sauce

3 tablespoons ginger, grated

1 tablespoon sesame oil

2 tablespoons peanut oil

Dash of Muhammad's Red Hot Sauce™ (pg.307)

1/4 cup white wine vinegar

2 cloves garlic, minced

Step 1: Blend ingredients together. Let stand for a few hours.

Step 2: Serve with steamed broccoli, asparagus or broiled fish.

CHEESE SAUCE™

4 tablespoons butter or olive oil

4 tablespoons unbleached flour

1/4 teaspoon ground black pepper

Salt to taste

1/4 teaspoon mace

1 tablespoons grated onion

2 cups milk

1 cup grated Cheddar cheese

Step 1: Melt butter in medium sauce pan. Blend in flour, onion, salt pepper and mace. Slowly stir in milk. Cook over low heat, stirring frequently until sauce thickens and boils, about one minute. Add grated cheese. Continue to cook over low heat, stirring frequently until cheese melts.

Step 2: Serve over puréed navy bean (pg.71), Baked Potato (pg.157) , Macaroni, broccoli or Salmon Patties (pg.281) and croquettes.

WHITE SAUCE OR BECHAMEL SAUCE™

(White sauce may be used to prepare creamed fish and as a
basis for preparing a variety of seasoned sauces.)

2 tablespoons butter

1 cup rich milk heated

Salt to taste

2 tablespoons unbleached flour

1/8 teaspoon ground white pepper

Pinch Mace

Step 1: Melt the butter in a heavy-bottomed saucepan. Stir in the flour and cook, stirring constantly, until the paste cooks and bubbles a bit, but please don't let it brown—about 2 minutes.

Step 2: To attain a smooth sauce, in a extra pot, have the milk hot when we add it to the butter and flour, continuing to stir as the sauce thickens. Bring to a boil. Add salt and pepper to taste, lower the heat, and cook, stirring frequently for 2-3 minutes more. Remove from the heat. Serve hot.

Step 3: We can cool this sauce for later utilization; in that case, cover it with wax paper or pour a film of milk over it to prevent a skin from forming.

√ **Celery White Sauce™**

Add *1/2 cup minced celery.*

√ **Cheese White Sauce™**

Stir in *1/2 cup grated Cheddar cheese* during the last 2 minutes of cooking.

√ **Curry White Sauce™**

Add *1 teaspoon Muhammad's Curry Seasoning™ (pg.307).*

√ **Egg White Sauce™**

Add *2 hard-boiled eggs, chopped fine. (pg.125)*

√ **Golden White Sauce™**

Remove sauce from heat just before serving; fold in *1 well-beaten egg* ; stir briskly until the hot sauce incorporates and cooks the egg.

√ Garnish with sprigs of fennel, dill, mint or cilantro.

◄───────────────────────►

TOMATO SAUCE™

5 tablespoons olive oil	6 tomatoes, strained
1/2 onion, minced	1 carrot, chopped
1 1/2 teaspoon thyme	1/2 cup parsley, chopped
Ground black pepper	Salt to taste
Pinch baking soda	

Step 1: Heat oil in sauté pan, add onions. Cook, stirring, for 1 minute. Add thyme, tomatoes, baking soda, carrot and pepper. Simmer for 15 minutes. Add parsley and salt.

Step 2: Cook 15 to 30 more minutes until thick. Serve hot over steamed fish, pasta or rice or in pizza..

◄───────────────────────►

TOMATO SAUCE FOR PASTA™

2 tablespoons olive oil	6 tomatoes, strained
1 tablespoon basil, chopped fine	1 carrot, minced or 1 tsp. Raw™ sugar
5 tablespoons butter	Ground black pepper
Salt to taste	Pinch baking soda

Step 1: Heat oil in a heavy-bottomed saucepan. Stir in tomatoes, baking soda, carrot or sugar, pepper and basil. Simmer for 15 minutes; cook 15 to 30 more minutes until thick, then stir in butter and salt.
Step 2: Serve with whole wheat pasta.

√ **Marinara Sauce™**

Cook *1 onion, chopped, 2 cloves garlic, chopped,* and *1/4 teaspoon Muhammad's Red Hot Sauce™ (pg.307)* in the heated oil for 3 minutes before adding the remaining ingredients.

← — — — — — — — — →

HOLLANDAISE SAUCE™

3 egg yolks	1 stick unsalted butter, room temp.
1 tablespoon lemon juice	1/8 teaspoon white pepper
Salt to taste	

Dash of Muhammad's Red Hot Sauce™ (pg.307)

Step 1: Utilize a double boiler or a metal bowl placed over very hot, but not simmering, water.
Step 2: Place the egg yolks in the boiler top, and beat with hand mixer until smooth. Add the lemon juice and gradually add in the soft butter. Slowly stir in 2 tablespoons hot water, hot sauce & white pepper and salt. Mix for 1 minute. The sauce will thicken.
Step 3: If it curdles, whisk in a teaspoon or two of boiling water, a drop at a time. If its still curdled put an egg yolk in a warm bowl and add curdled sauce very slowly, whisking till smooth. Serve immediately, or refrigerate.

√ **Hollandaise Sauce Mousse line™**

Fold in 1/4 cup of *heavy cream*, whipped, and sprinkle a dash of *mace* on top, just before serving.

← — — — — — — — — →

CLASSIC AIOLI™
(PRONOUNCED "I-oh-lee" a mayonnaise type sauce.
Used here as an accompaniment to vegetables)

3 egg yolks	5 garlic cloves, minced
1 1/2 cups extra virgin olive oil	1 tablespoon lemon juice
Salt to taste	1/2 teaspoon white pepper

Step 1: Place the yolks in a tall glass.
Step 2: Place some salt on minced garlic and mash with the side of a knife until they are incorporated into a paste. Add this to the yolks. pour the oil on top of this. With a hand blender place the blending blade through oil down to the yolks and blend till creamed. Then move up glass till oil begins to incor-

porated into a smooth sauce.

Step 3: Add lemon juice, blend well, and correct seasoning with pepper. Serve on baked red potatoes, fish, hard-cooked eggs, green beans or broccoli.

⟵————————————————————————————————⟶

SEAFOOD AIOLI™

(PRONOUNCED "I-oh-lee" a mayonnaise type sauce.

Used here as an accompaniment to steamed fish)

2 egg yolks   1/2 tablespoon garlic, chopped

2 cups extra virgin olive oil   3/4 tablespoon lime juice

1/2 tablespoon ginger, finely grated   1/2 teaspoon white pepper

1/2 teaspoon salt

1/2 teaspoon yellow chili pepper, roasted , skin & seeds discarded, and finely chopped

Step 1: Place the yolks in a tall glass.

Step 2: Place some salt on minced garlic and mash with the side of a knife until they are incorporated into a paste; add this to the yolks; then add ginger and chili; pour the oil on top of this. With a hand blender place the blending blade through oil down to the yolks and blend till creamed. Then move up glass till oil begins to incorporated into a smooth sauce.

Step 3: Add lime juice, blend well, and correct seasoning with pepper. Serve on baked red snapper, fish cakes, hard-cooked eggs, or steamed salmon.

⟵————————————————————————————————⟶

ANCHOVY SAUCE™

3 tablespoons non-alcohol white wine   1 bunch parsley, coarsely chopped

1 clove garlic   3 anchovy fillets

1/3 cups extra virgin olive oil   1/2 teaspoon salt

1/4 teaspoon black pepper

1/2 cup Basic Wheat Bread, crumbs (pg.188)

Step 1: Soak the bread crumbs in white wine for 10 minutes, then squeeze out the excess moisture with hands.

Step 2: Pureé the crumbs, parsley, garlic and anchovies in a food processor. With machine running, add the oil a little at a time, and process until thick and smooth. Season with salt and pepper.

Step 3: Utilize with baked and grilled fish.

⟵————————————————————————————————⟶

HORSERADISH HERB SAUCE™

1/2 cup sour cream   1/3 cup horseradish, grated

1/3 cup white wine vinegar

1/3 cup Mayonnaise (pg.183)

1/2 teaspoon salt

1/4 dill pickle, minced

1 tablespoon dill, chopped

1/4 teaspoon white pepper

Step 1: Mix all ingredients together in a bowl.

Step 2: Chill in refrigerator for several hours. Return to room temperature before serving.

Step 3: Utilize with baked and grilled fish, vegetables or as a salad dressing.

INDONESIAN SOY SAUCE™

1/2 cup soy sauce

3 tablespoons dark corn syrup

1/4 cup dark brown sugar

1 tablespoon molasses

Step1: Blend ingredients together.

SAUCE FOR FISH™

1 stick butter

1/4 cup non-alcohol white wine

1/4 cup parsley

1/2 teaspoon salt

1/4 cup white raisins

1/4 cup sunflower seeds

1 tablespoon fresh thyme, chopped

1/4 teaspoon black pepper

Step 1: Melt butter in a skillet over medium flame and sauté sunflower seeds a minute; add raisins and remaining ingredients; reduce flame and cook until it reduces to a thick sauce, stirring often. Serve hot over cooked fish .

HARISSA SAUCE™
(Tunisian Chili Sauce)
(For Tunisian cooking)

1 whole head (bulb) garlic, peeled

1 tablespoon olive oil

1 tablespoon cumin seeds, roasted & ground

1 tablespoon coriander seeds, roasted & ground

1 tablespoon caraway seeds, roasted & ground

3 small red chilies, roasted , skin & seeds discarded

3 small red chilies, seeded (if dried, soak first)

3 tablespoons fresh coriander (cilantro)

1 teaspoon dried mint

Step 1: Blend all ingredients together in a mortar or food processor and utilize with Tunisian fish or rice dishes.

√**Harissa II**™

Omit dry mint; omit 1/2 tablespoon cumin seed; add *1/2 teaspoon salt* and use an additional *1/2 tablespoon caraway seed.*

√**Tunisian Harissa Spread**™

Blend with*1/2 cup sour cream* and use as a Fish Sandwich spread (pg.284)

MUSLIM CHILI SAMBAL™
Indonesian

7 cloves garlic, minced

2 teaspoons Raw™ sugar

2 teaspoons salt

1/2 tablespoon water (Optional)

2 red chili peppers, roasted, skin & seeds discarded, and finely chopped

6 scallions, minced

1 tablespoon tamarind pureé

Step 1: Combine together in a bowl; Add water, if needed; mix well until sugar dissolves. Let sit for an hour.

Step 2: Utilize with Indonesian vegetable & fish dishes.

MUSLIM FENUGREEK PASTE™
Libya

3 cloves garlic, minced

1/2 teaspoon salt

2 tablespoon lime juice

2 yellow chili peppers, roasted, skin & seeds discarded, and finely chopped

1 teaspoon fenugreek seeds, soaked in water a 24 hours, then dried some

2 tablespoons cilantro, chopped

1/4 teaspoon black pepper

Step 1: Combine ingredients together in a bowl; mix well.

Step 2: Pureé in a blender. Let sit for an hour.

Step 3: Utilize with Libyan vegetable dishes and as a filler accompaniment with vegetables in pitas and bread wraps.

TAHINI SAUCE™
(Middle Eastern Sauce)
(For Middle Eastern cooking)

2 cloves garlic, minced

1/3 cup Tahini (pg.94)

3 tablespoons lime juice

1 tablespoon light soy sauce

Step 1: Blend all ingredients together in a mortar or food processor and utilize with Middle Eastern dishes. Serve on Fish or as a Meatless sandwich spread or vegetables dip or salad dressing.

$$\longleftrightarrow$$

TAHINI SAUCE II™
(Middle Eastern Sauce)
(For Middle Eastern cooking)

1/2 cup sesame seeds, toasted & mashed

1 tablespoon light soy sauce

(1/2 to 1) cup water

1/4 cup green onions, sliced

1 teaspoon ginger, minced

1 tablespoon corn oil

1/2 yellow chili pepper, roasted , skin & seeds discarded, and minced

Step 1: Heat corn oil in a small heavy-bottom saucepan over a medium flame; add green onions & ginger; cook 1 minute; then add chili pepper, mashed sesame seeds, water (start with 1/2 cup) and soy sauce; stir constantly and cook until thick. Serve hot.

Step 2: Utilize with Middle Eastern dishes. Serve on Fish or as a Meatless sandwich spread or vegetables dip or salad dressing.

$$\longleftrightarrow$$

RAITA™
Eastern Indian

1/2 cup sour cream

1/2 teaspoon honey

1/2 teaspoon coriander, roasted & ground

1/3 teaspoon salt

1 teaspoon cumin seeds, roasted & ground

1 teaspoon salt, for coating cucumber

1 tablespoon cilantro leaves, finely chopped

1/2 large tomato, seeded and finely diced

1 small cucumber, peeled, seeded, cut in 1/4-inch dices

1/2 green chili pepper, roasted , skin & seeds discarded, and minced

Step 1: Place cucumber in a strainer, sprinkle salt over to coat, toss well, and let stand for 15 minutes. Then rinse off salt, and pat dry with paper towels.

Step 2: In a bowl, combine the cucumber with all the remaining raita ingredients. Stir to mix well, and refrigerate. It will keep for 5 days. Serve with Samosas, steamed vegetables & rice.

√ **Heavenly Raita™**

Omit coriander, tomato and cilantro. Add *1/4 cup fresh mint leaves.*

ACHAR SAUCE™
Eastern Indian

2 pounds tomatoes, finely chopped

1 tablespoon cilantro, chopped

1 teaspoon cumin seeds

1/2 teaspoon salt

1 teaspoon fenugreek seeds, soaked in water a 24 hours, then dried some

2 yellow chili peppers, roasted, skin & seeds discarded, and finely chopped

1 teaspoon turmeric

2 teaspoons mustard oil or olive oil

Step 1: Heat a heavy-bottom saucepan over a low flame; add cumin seeds and fenugreek seeds; roast a few minutes; remove from heat to cool; grind in grinder or mortar.

Step 2: Heat mustard or olive oil in saucepan, over medium flame; add tomatoes, turmeric, ground fenugreek and cumin, yellow chilies and salt reduce flame and simmer until it has reduced by one-third or until thick, stirring frequently.

Step 3: Remove from heat, stir in cilantro.

Step 4: Utilize with East African vegetable and soup dishes.

CREOLE SAUCE™
Complex

1 tomato, diced

1 tablespoon olive oil

1 tablespoon butter

1/4 cup celery, minced

1 cup tomatoes, crushed

1/4 cup + 2 tablespoons water

1 tablespoon dried parsley leaves

1/4 teaspoon salt

1/8 teaspoon black pepper

1/4 teaspoon cayenne pepper (Thai)

2 garlic cloves, minced

1/2 green bell pepper, seeded & diced

2 tablespoons non-alcohol dry red wine

1 onion, diced

1/4 cup okra, chopped

1 tablespoon Worcestershire Sauce

1/2 tablespoon dried Mexican oregano

1/4 teaspoon onion powder

1/8 teaspoon white pepper

1/4 teaspoon dried ancho chili pepper, toasted, seeded & stemmed and crumbled

2 teaspoons Muhammad's Red Hot Sauce™ (pg.307)

Step 1: Heat butter and oil in a heavy-bottom saucepan over a high flame. Add onion, garlic, green bell pepper, diced tomato, celery and okra; sauté about 10 to 12 minutes; reducing flame to medium after 5

minutes; then add remaining ingredients. Reduce flame and simmer for 15 to 20 more minutes or until thick, stirring frequently.

Step 2: Keeps for 1 to 1 1/2 weeks. Serve with Veggy Wraps (pg.203) or with Fish.

$\longleftrightarrow$

SWEET-AND-HOT WASABI SAUCE™
(Japanese Dip)
(For Asian cooking)

1/2 cup non-alcohol white wine	1 teaspoon garlic, minced
2 tablespoons light soy sauce	1 tablespoon ginger, minced
1/4 cup cilantro, chopped	1 tablespoon dark sesame oil
2 tablespoons red wine vinegar	1 tablespoon light brown sugar
1 tablespoon wasabi paste or horseradish	

Step 1: In a bowl, combine the wine, soy sauce, oil, vinegar and brown sugar in a bowl and mix until the sugar dissolves.

Step 2: Stir in the garlic, ginger and cilantro.

Step 3: Cover and refrigerate. Utilize with Asian dishes. Fish dishes, dress vegetables or green salads.

$\longleftrightarrow$

CURRIED SESAME SAUCE™
East Indian

1/2 cup buttermilk	2 tablespoons Ketchup (pg.109)
1 tablespoon horseradish	1 teaspoon lemon juice
1/2 teaspoon black pepper	
2 teaspoons Sesame Seasoning™ (pg.307)	
1 teaspoon Muhammad's Curry Powder™ (pg.307)	

Step 1: Blend all ingredients together in a bowl and chill.

Step 2: Utilize in a Fish Dish (pg.267).

$\longleftrightarrow$
$\longleftrightarrow$

DIPS, FLAVORED BUTTERS, CONDIMENTS, MARINADES, CHUTNIES & SALSAS

NAVY BEAN DIP™

2 cups navy bean purée

2 tablespoons olive oil

Ground black pepper to taste

3 large garlic cloves, smashed

Salt to taste

Step 1: Sauté garlic in olive oil.

Step 2: Place in blender with navy beans and salt and pepper. Blend till smooth.

← ————————————————————————————— →

NAVY BEAN DIP II™

2 1/2 cups navy bean purée

1/2 small yellow onion, coarsely chopped

2 scallions, chopped

1/4 teaspoon thyme, minced

2 tablespoons olive oil

1/4 teaspoon white pepper

2 jalapeño peppers, roasted, skin & seeds discarded, and finely chopped

2 garlic cloves, minced

2 medium tomatoes, roasted & diced

1/2 cup cilantro, finely chopped

1/4 lime juice

1/2 teaspoon salt

Step 1: Heat olive oil in a skillet over a high flame; sauté onion, garlic, thyme and scallions until golden brown.

Step 2: Place in a bowl with remaining ingredients and mix well. Serve with Pitas (pg.203) or as a dip for crackers (pg.204)

← ————————————————————————————— →

GUACAMOLE™

2 ripe avocados

1 clove garlic, minced

1/2 teaspoon salt

1/4 teaspoon black pepper

3 green chili peppers, roasted, skin & seeds discarded, and finely chopped

5 tablespoons minced onion

3 tablespoons lime juice

Step 1: Peel and seed the avocados. Pureé one in a blender and finely chop the other in a food processor. Mix the two with remaining ingredients.

Step 2: Cover and refrigerate a few hours before serving.

√ Guacamole Sauce™

Blend together *1 hard-boiled egg, peeled & mashed/ 1/2 cup olive oil and 1 tablespoon heavy cream (optional)* fold into mixed ingredients.

← ————————————————————————————— →

FISH SPREAD™

1 1/2 sticks sweet butter

1 tablespoon mashed anchovies

1 teaspoon Worcestershire sauce

1 eight-ounce salmon fillet, steamed 8 minutes & flaked

2 teaspoons lime juice

Step 1: Combine ingredients together in a bowl, cover, and chill. Serve on Whole Wheat Crackers (pg.204)

←——————————————————————————→

LEMON BUTTER SAUCE™

(Serve hot with baked, steamed, boiled or planked fish)

1/2 stick butter, room temp.

1/8 teaspoon white pepper

1 teaspoon lemon juice

1/4 teaspoon finely grated lemon rind

Step 1: Melt butter in a small saucepan over low heat.

Step 2: In a small bowl blend lemon juice, rind and pepper; add melted butter; mix well.

←——————————————————————————→

CLARIFIED BUTTER™
Ghee-Butterfat East Indian

1 1/2 pound unsalted butter, room temp.

Strainer

Several layers of cheesecloth

Sterilized glass jar and lid

Step 1: Melt butter in a large heavy-bottomed saucepan over low heat. After it melts let it cook for 30 minutes without allowing it to boil. The butterfat will separate and ascend, moisture in the butter will crackle as it evaporates, foam will appear on the surface, and the solids will descend to the bottom of the pan. When the descended solids begin to brown, pour off the clear clarified butter into a stainless steel bowl, then pour it through several layers of cheesecloth lining a strainer and into a sterilized glass jar. The cheesecloth filters out impurities, leaving a clear, pale yellow liquid.

Step 2: Allow it to cool, then seal jar; it will cool into a thick, soft yellow paste. It will be good for months.

←——————————————————————————→

PARSLEY BUTTER™

1 stick butter

1/4 teaspoon ground black pepper

Salt to taste

2 tablespoons finely chopped parsley

1 tablespoon fresh lime juice

Step 1: Put the butter , parsley, and pepper in a bowl and blend with a mixer. Slowly add lime juice, then salt to taste. Form into a block or cylinder, wrap in wax paper, chill in refrigerator.

Step 2: Once it is chilled, cut into slices and serve on fish or vegetables.

√ Herb Butter™

Delete the *parsley.* Substitute a combination of herbs. Utilize 1 1/2 teaspoon *chopped chives,* 1/2 teaspoon *thyme* or *tarragon* or *marjoram,* and 1/2 teaspoon chopped *parsley.*

PESTO SAUCE™

1 bunch Italian parsley, stems removed	3 bunch basil, leaf only
10 garlic cloves	8 ounce cream cheese
1/2 cup olive oil	1/3 cup grated Parmesan cheese
Salt to taste	Ground black pepper

Step 1: Chop parsley, basil and garlic in food processor fitted with metal blade, while motor is running, slowly add olive oil till paste is smooth, about 30 seconds, transfer the mixture to a small bowl and set aside.

Step 2: Place the cream cheese, salt, pepper and Parmesan cheese in the food processor and pulse 4 times to blend. Add 5 tablespoons of herb-garlic mixture and process for 2 minutes. If necessary thin the sauce with a little olive oil. Sauce can be stored in refrigerator.

Step 3: Toss with cooked whole wheat pasta or utilize in salmon recipe.

MUSTARD™

2 teaspoons dry mustard	1 teaspoon water
1/2 teaspoon vinegar	

Step 1: Place all ingredients in a bowl and blend well.

DIJON MUSTARD™

1/2 cup dry mustard	2 1/2 tablespoons unbleached flour
1/2 cup white wine vinegar	2 tablespoons brown sugar
1/3 teaspoon salt	Dash white pepper

Step 1: Place dry ingredients in a bowl and mix well; then blend in the vinegar; chill.

√ Herb Mustard™

Add 1 teaspoon each of fresh minced *summer savory, basil, and chives (fresh mint, dill and a 1/2 teaspoon of oregano* can be substituted for any of the herbs).

← ────────────────────────────────────── →

MUSTARD SAUCE™

2 tablespoons dry mustard	1 teaspoon Raw™ sugar
1 teaspoon unbleached flour	1 cup light cream
1 egg yolk	1/2 cup vinegar, heated
1/2 teaspoon salt	1/2 teaspoon white pepper

Step 1: Blend the dry mustard, flour, and 1/4 cup of the cream.

Step 2: Put the remaining 3/4 cup cream in a heavy-bottomed pan. Heat; then stir in the mustard mixture.

Step 3: Beat the egg yolk in a small bowl. Beat in 2 tablespoons of the hot mustard mixture, then stir in the yolk-sauce mixture into the saucepan. Add the sugar, and cook, stirring constantly, until thickened.

Step 4: Stir in the heated vinegar, salt and pepper. Serve on spinach, patties and fish sausage.

√ Honey Mustard Sauce™

Substitute sugar with 1/4 cup *honey.* Add 1/2 teaspoon *turmeric,* 1/2 teaspoon paprika, 1/4 teaspoon *garlic powder* and 1/4 teaspoon *onion powder.* Incorporate honey & spices when the sugar is to be added in the Mustard Sauce recipe above.

← ────────────────────────────────────── →

LIME MUSTARD SAUCE™

2 tablespoons butter	1 tablespoon flour
1 tablespoon Dijon Mustard™ (pg.108)	1 large egg yolk
1 1/2 tablespoons lime juice	1/4 teaspoon salt
3/4 cups milk	
1/8 teaspoons Muhammad's Red Hot Sauce™ (pg.307)	

Step 1: Melt the butter in a small-size saucepan over medium heat. Stir in the flour; cook 3 minutes, but don't brown; add the milk; boil until thick, about 5 minutes; cover; set aside.

Step 2: In a small bowl, beat together egg yolk, lime juice, mustard and hot sauce; stir in 1/4 cup of the hot milk mixture into the egg yolk; then pour the egg yolk mixture back into the saucepan; cook over medium flame, stirring constantly, until thick, for 3 to 5 minutes; don't let boil.

Step 3: Utilize with vegetable dishes, eggs and baked fish.

← ────────────────────────────────────── →

Ketchup™

1 cup tomato strained &pureéd	2 tablespoons honey
2 tablespoons Raw™ sugar	2 tablespoons vinegar
1/2 teaspoon allspice or cloves	1 teaspoon onion, crushed
1/2 teaspoon garlic pureé	1/2 teaspoon black pepper

Step 1: Heat a heavy-bottom saucepan over a medium flame. Add tomato pureé then remaining ingredients. Reduce flame and simmer for 15 to 30 more minutes or until thick.

Step 2: Blend all ingredients in a blender or food processor and pureé.

SPICED Ketchup™

4 tomatoes, diced	1/4 cup water (or less)
1/3 cup Raw™ sugar	1/2 cup red wine vinegar
1/2 teaspoon salt	1/2 cup onion, diced
1/2 teaspoon onion powder	1/4 teaspoon molasses
1/4 teaspoon black pepper	
1/2 teaspoon Muhammad's Chili Powder™(pg.307)	
1/2 teaspoon Muhammad's Red Hot Sauce™(pg.307)	

Step 1: Heat a heavy-bottom saucepan over a medium flame. Add water, diced tomatoes then remaining ingredients. Reduce flame and simmer for 20 to 30 more minutes or until thick.

Step 2: Blend all ingredients in a blender or food processor and pureé. Keeps for 2 weeks.

SUN-DRIED TOMATO Ketchup™

3 tomatoes, diced	6 cloves garlic, minced
1/3 cup maple syrup	1/2 cup red wine vinegar
1/2 teaspoon salt	1/4 cup onion, diced
1 tablespoon Raw™ sugar	1/4 teaspoon white pepper
2 drops of molasses	
3 ounces sun-dried tomatoes (36 dried tomatoes)	
6 cups boiling water, (to soak sun-dried tomatoes in)	

Step 1: Soak the dried tomatoes in the boiling water for 2 minutes; drain; discard soaking water. (If the tomatoes are packed in oil, this step can by skipped.)

Step 2: Heat a heavy-bottom saucepan over a medium flame. Add diced tomatoes then remaining ingredients; cook 10 minutes; reduce flame and simmer for 3 to 5 more minutes or until thick; remove from heat and let cool 5 minutes.

Step 3: Blend all ingredients in a blender or food processor and pureé. Keeps for 2 weeks.

← ─────────────────────────────── →

PLUM-RHUBARB Ketchup™
(For Plantains)

1 cup rhubarb, leaves discarded, diced

1/4 cup Raw™ sugar

1/2 teaspoon salt

1/4 cup raisins

1/4 teaspoon black pepper

3 plums, diced

3/4 cup red wine vinegar

1/2 cup red onion, minced

1 teaspoon molasses

Step 1: Heat a heavy-bottom saucepan over a medium flame. Add diced plums then remaining ingredients. Reduce flame and simmer for 15 to 20 more minutes or until thick.

Step 2: Blend all ingredients in a blender or food processor and pureé.

Step 3:Serve on Plantains (pg.156).

← ─────────────────────────────── →

TARTAR SAUCE I™

3/4 cup Mayonnaise (pg.183)

2 teaspoons minced onions or scallions

1 teaspoon capers (OPTIONAL)

Salt to taste

1 teaspoon minced sweet pickle

1 teaspoon minced parsley

1 tablespoon lemon juice or vinegar

Fresh ground white pepper

Step 1: Place all ingredients in a bowl and blend well; chill.

← ─────────────────────────────── →

TARTAR SAUCE II™

1/2 cup Mayonnaise (pg.183)

2 tablespoons minced onions

1/4 teaspoon lemon juice

2 tablespoons hard-boiled egg, chopped (pg.125)

4 tablespoons minced sweet pickle or sweet pickle relish

1 teaspoon Mustard (pg.108)

1 teaspoon minced parsley

Step 1: Place all ingredients in a bowl and blend well; chill.

← ─────────────────────────────── →

LEMON GARNISH™

1 lemon cut in half   2 pieces 4" x 4" cheese clothes

2 pieces ribbon

Step 1: Wrap each lemon half with a piece of cheese cloth and tie top with a piece of ribbon; set on side of dish for diner to squeeze juice through cloth as needed.

BARBECUE SAUCE™

(For Meatless patties)

2 tablespoons butter   2 tablespoons brown sugar

2 cups strained tomato pureéd   1 small onion, finely chopped

1/2 clove garlic, finely chopped   1/2 cup lime juice

4 teaspoons Worcestershire sauce   1/2 teaspoon salt

1/4 teaspoon black pepper

1/2 teaspoon Muhammad's Red Hot Sauce™ (pg.307)

1/2 teaspoon Muhammad's Chili Powder™ (pg.307)

Step 1: Melt butter in a saucepan and sauté onion and garlic until soft. Mix rest of the ingredients in and bring to a boil, reduce the heat, then simmer 20 minutes, stirring often. Serve on Meat Alternative patties and burgers.

SMOOTH BARBECUE SAUCE™
(SAUCE & MARINADE)

1 cup non-alcohol dry white wine   1 clove garlic, crushed

2 tablespoons butter   1/4 cup olive oil

1 onion, finely chopped   1 teaspoon rosemary, crumbled

1 teaspoon salt   1/8 teaspoon white pepper

Step 1: Combine all ingredients in a heavy-bottom saucepan. Simmer for 30 minutes or until reduced to a smooth sauce. Utilize to marinate fish in.

VEGETABLE MARINADE™

1/4 cup non-alcohol dry white wine   1/4 cup white wine vinegar

1/4 teaspoon dried tarragon   2 cloves garlic, crushed

1/4 teaspoon dried marjoram   1/4 teaspoon dried thyme

1/3 cup extra virgin olive oil   1/2 teaspoon salt

1/4 teaspoon white pepper

Step 1: Place all ingredients in a small saucepan over a high flame; boil for 1 to 3 minutes.

Step 2: Use to marinade heavy vegetables in, inside the refrigerator overnight; drain; serve cold or heated.

FISH MARINADE™

1 3/4 cup Ketchup (pg.109)   2 tablespoons ginger, grated

2 tablespoons lemon juice   2 tablespoons brown sugar

1 1/2 cup light soy sauce   1 small onion, finely chopped

1/2 cup non-alcohol dry red wine

Dash Muhammad's Red Hot Sauce™ (pg.307)

2 cloves garlic, mashed

Step 1: Place all ingredients in a bowl and blend well. Marinate fish in.

SALMON MARINADE™

1/3 cup pineapple juice   1/3 cup light soy sauce

1/4 cup non-alcohol dry white wine

1 tablespoon cilantro, chopped

Dash Muhammad's Red Hot Sauce™ (pg.307)

Step 1: Place all ingredients in a bowl and blend well. Marinate fish in.

FISH BASTING SAUCE™

1/2 stick unsalted butter   1/4 cup lemon juice

1 1/2 tablespoons light soy sauce   1 clove garlic, minced

1/2 cup non-alcohol dry white wine

1 teaspoon lemon zest, grated

3 scallions, both white & green parts, chopped

Step 1: Place all ingredients in a small saucepan over a low flame; cook for 10 to 15 minutes.

Step 2: Use to baste fish with while baking, broiling or grilling fish.

CRÉME FRAÎCHE™

1 cup heavy cream

1/2 cup sour cream or yogurt, sour milk or buttermilk

Step 1: Blend in a glass container.

√ **Firm Créme Fraîche™**

Let blended mixture sit in a warm place for 6 hours and then refrigerate.

CARIBBEAN SALSA™

2 cups tomatoes, cut into 1/4-inch dices

2 tablespoons onions, diced*

1 red bell pepper , cut into 1/4-inch dices

Juice of 2 limes or 1 Seville orange

1 habanero chile, seeded and finely chopped

4 tablespoons basil or mint, julienned

1/2 teaspoon salt

Step 1: Combine ingredients together in a bowl, cover, and chill—if desired.

*Soak the onions in a bowl of hot water for 10 minutes; drain & pat dry with paper towel to take the sharpness or bite out of them.

FRUIT SALSA™

1 granny smith apple, cored & minced

1 onion, minced*

1/4 teaspoon black pepper

1/2 red bell pepper, cut into 1/4-inch dices

1 tablespoon lemon or Seville orange juice

1 green chili pepper, roasted , skin & seeds discarded, and finely chopped

2 tablespoons cilantro, chopped

3 tablespoons extra virgin olive oil

1/2 teaspoon salt

Step 1: Combine ingredients together in a bowl, cover, and chill—if desired.
Step 2: Serve with grilled or broiled fish (pg.269).

*Soak the onions in a bowl of hot water for 10 minutes; drain & pat dry with paper towel to take the sharpness or bite out of them.

SHABAZZ SALSA™

2 large tomatoes, seeded & chopped   3 garlic cloves, minced

1 onion, finely chopped*   Pinch roasted & ground cumin

1 tablespoon non-alcohol dry white wine   1/4 teaspoon black pepper

1/2 teaspoon salt   Pinch of sugar

1/4 cup lime or Seville orange juice

1 teaspoon Muhammad's Chili Powder™ (pg.307)

1 green chili pepper, roasted , skin & seeds discarded, and finely chopped

Step 1: Combine ingredients together in a bowl, cover, and chill—if desired.

Step 2: Serve with grilled, broiled fish (pg.272) or fill a Bread Wrap or Pita (pg.203).

*Soak the onions in a bowl of hot water for 10 minutes; drain & pat dry with paper towel to take the sharpness or bite out of them.

GREEN TOMATILLO SALSA™

1/2 cup cilantro, chopped   2 tablespoons lemon juice

1/2 teaspoon salt

1 bunch scallions, (white and green parts), chopped

1 pound tomatillos, hulled, stemmed and chopped

2 yellow chili peppers, roasted , skin & seeds discarded, and finely chopped

Step 1: Combine ingredients together in a bowl, cover, and chill—if desired.

Step 2: Serve with grilled, broiled fish (pg.272).

*Soak the onions in a bowl of hot water for 10 minutes; drain & pat dry with paper towel to take the sharpness or bite out of them.

MUHAMMAD'S RED TOMATO SALSA™
(For Wraps or Pitas filling)

2 large tomatoes, seeded & diced   2 large tomatoes, seeded & crushed

1/2 cup green or red onions, diced*   3 cloves garlic, roasted & sliced

1/2 teaspoon salt   1 red bell pepper, seeded & diced

1 teaspoon extra virgin olive oil   1/4 teaspoon black pepper

1 teaspoon cumin seed, roasted & ground   2 teaspoons oregano, minced

1/4 teaspoon white pepper

1 tablespoon cilantro, finely chopped

1 teaspoon Muhammad's Red Hot Sauce™ (pg.307)

2 teaspoons lime juice or dry sherry vinegar

1 jalapeño pepper, roasted , skin & seeds discarded, and finely chopped

Step 1: Combine ingredients, except the two crushed tomatoes, together in a bowl and toss well.

Step 2: Place three-quarters of the mixture in a food processor fitted with a steel blade for blending and blend for a few seconds to mash vegetables well.

Step 3: Return the mashed vegetables tot he bowl, add crushed tomatoes, and blend well, cover, and chill—if desired.

Step 4: Use as filler for Veggy Wraps (pg.203) or Pita Breads (pg.203)

*Soak the onions in a bowl of hot water for 10 minutes; drain & pat dry with paper towel to take the sharpness or bite out of them.

TOMATILLO-PAPAYA SALSA™
For Grilled Fish

1 medium papaya, seeded & diced

1/2 cup green or red onions, diced*

2 tablespoons cilantro, finely chopped

4 tomatillos, hulled, stemmed and diced

1 unwaxed cucumber, seeded & diced (unpeeled)

2 green chili peppers, roasted , skin & seeds discarded, and finely chopped

1/4 cup lime or lemon juice

1/4 teaspoon salt

Step 1: Combine ingredients together in a bowl and toss well; cover, and chill—if desired.

Step 2: Use as an accompaniment for a Fish Dish (pg.207)

*Soak the onions in a bowl of hot water for 10 minutes; drain & pat dry with paper towel to take the sharpness or bite out of them.

SWEET & SPICY MANGO CHUTNEY™
Caribbean

5 Haitian mangoes, peeled, pitted & diced

1 1/2 cups white wine vinegar

1 red bell pepper, seeded & julienned

4 teaspoons ginger, finely grated

2 teaspoons cinnamon

2 cups Raw™ sugar

1 cup golden raisins, pureéd

3 large onions, chopped

2 teaspoons lemon peel, finely grated

2 teaspoons garlic powder

2 teaspoons salt

1 teaspoon cardamom seeds, roasted & ground

4 teaspoons coriander seeds, roasted & ground

4 teaspoons Muhammad's Chili Powder™ (pg.307)

1/2 teaspoon Muhammad's Red Hot Sauce™ (pg.307)

Step 1: Heat a heavy-bottom saucepan over a medium flame; add ingredients; reduce flame and simmer 30 minutes or until thick, stirring frequently.

Step 2: Utilize with Oriental vegetable dishes and veggie wraps.

TANGY CARROT CHUTNEY™
Eastern Africa

1/2 pound carrots, finely grated

3 tablespoons Raw™ sugar

1/2 teaspoon ginger, grated

1 1/2 teaspoons cardamom seeds, ground

1/2 teaspoon salt

1/2 teaspoon Muhammad's Chili Powder™ (pg.307)

1/2 cup water

Dash of nutmeg

2 cloves garlic, crushed

1 cup vinegar

Step 1: Heat a heavy-bottom saucepan over a medium flame; add water and sugar; reduce flame and simmer until dissolved, stirring frequently.

Step 2: Add carrots, ginger, garlic, chili and cardamom; simmer for 20 minutes.

Step 3: Add vinegar, nutmeg and salt; simmer until thick.

Step 4: Utilize with East African vegetable and fish dishes.

GREEN CHILE CHUTNEY™

2 cups sugar

1 teaspoon salt

1 tablespoon Mexican oregano, roasted & ground

2 pounds New Mexico green chilies, roasted , seeded and diced

2/3 cups apple cider vinegar or champagne vinegar

Step 1: Combine ingredients together in a bowl.

Step 2: Heat a stainless steel pan over medium heat; add cider vinegar then remaining ingredients; simmer for 10 to 15 minutes.

Step 3: Allow to cool and serve cold with eggs (pg.125) Sautéed Salmon or Trout (pg.282).

MANGO-HABANERO SAUCE™

8 ripe mangoes, peeled and diced

1/2 cup carrot diced

2 orange habanero chilies, seeded & minced

1/2 cup champagne vinegar

1/4 cup sugar

1/4 teaspoon salt

2 tablespoons sesame or peanut oil

1/2 cup onion, diced

1/2 cup Ketchup (pg.109)

Step 1: Heat oil in a heavy-bottomed skillet over medium heat; add mangoes, onion and chilies; cook for 10 minutes or until golden.

Step 2: Deglaze with champagne vinegar; add Ketchup and sugar; lower flame and simmer over low heat for 35 to 45 minutes.

Step 3: Allow to cool.

Step 4: In a blender purée; season with salt; strain through a medium seive. Add water to adjust constituency. Use on seafood or as a barbecue sauce.

TAMARIND CHIPOTLE SAUCE™

6 tablespoons tamarind purée

1/2 cup dark brown sugar

Juice of 1 lime

2 cups chilies In Adobo Sauce™ (pg.307)

Water

2 cloves garlic, roasted and crushed

Step 1: Combine ingredients together in a blender. Purée until smooth, adding enough water until the consistency of a thick sauce is obtained.

Step 2: Serve warm with Sautéed Salmon or Trout (pg.280 &282). Use like Chinese Plum Sauce.

STUFFING FOR FISH

1 teaspoon fresh savory, minced	1/4 cup milk
4 tablespoons butter	1 onion, minced
1/2 teaspoon fresh marjoram, minced	1/2 teaspoon salt
1/4 teaspoon black pepper	
3 cups Whole Wheat Sourdough Bread crumb (pg.189)	

Step 1: Heat a heavy saucepan, over a high flame, add butter, when it sizzles; add onion; sauté 3 minutes or until golden brown; remove from heat; add marjoram, savory, salt and pepper; blend well.
Step 2: Place bread crumbs in a large bowl; add sauteéd onions and seasonings; mix well. Add only enough milk to moisten stuffing lightly. Fills 4 pound fish.

√ Celery Stuffing For Fish
Utilize *1 cup chopped celery* instead of milk.
√ Cheese Stuffing For Fish
Add *1 cup grated Cheddar cheese.* along with bread crumbs.
√ Green Chili Pepper Stuffing For Fish
Utilize *1 green chili pepper, roasted , skin & seeds discarded, and finely chopped* and *1/2 cup minced green bell pepper* instead of milk.

(COMING SOON)
GUEST RECIPE

See your recipe on this page

*(Recipe must conform to the theme of this cookbook)

1. Provide List of Ingredients.

2. Step by Step procedures for preparing and cooking dish.

3. Provide picture of self and/or cooked dish.

4.Send to the Publisher by postal mail or email@:

Attn: Aubrey Muhammad

Muslim Cookbook, Muhammad's Sauces & Seasonings™

600 Fulton Ave. 26F

Hempstead, New York 11550

Phone: 516-483-7673

Email: Muslimcooking@Yahoo.com

3. RICE

BOILED BROWN RICE

2 cups brown rice   1/2 teaspoon salt

1/2 teaspoon olive oil

Step 1: Rinse rise continuously until water is clear, drain water.

Step 2: Bring 5-6 cups water, oil and salt to a boil in a pot. Trickle the rice slowly into the water so that it doesn't cease boiling. Keep the water boiling over low heat. Rice will be done in 45 minutes. Let set till cool.

Step 3:(OPTIONAL):Then, oil a baking dish; pour cooked rice in; evenly distribute 1/4 cup water. Bake 1/2 hour in a preheated 360°F oven, adding water if needed.

⟷

CARIBBEAN YELLOW RICE

2 cups unconverted long-grain rice   2 tablespoons olive oil

3 1/2 cups water   1/2 teaspoon parsley, chopped

1 teaspoon turmeric   2 teaspoons salt

Step 1: In a large bowl wash the rice in several changes of cold water until the water runs clear. Drain off water.

Step 2: In a large heavy-saucepan, heat oil over moderately high heat. Add the rice, sauté, stirring for 2 to 3 minutes. Sauté until rice is well coated and turns lightly brown. Add the water, salt and turmeric and boil, uncovered without stirring. Cook 8 to 10 minutes. Reduce heat to a simmer and add parsley. Cover pan. Cook 15 more minutes.

Step 3: Remove the pan from the heat and let rice stand, covered, for 5 minutes. Fluff the rice with a fork. Serve with fish and vegetables.

⟷

BROWNED RICE

1 cup brown rice   2 tablespoons butter

1/8 teaspoon turmeric   2 cups cold water

1/2 teaspoon salt

Step 1: In a large bowl wash the rice in several changes of cold water until the water runs clear. Drain off water.

Step 2: Melt butter in skillet, add rice and brown. Stir it constantly to keep from burning. Add water and seasonings, cover, let simmer. Allow to steam until the rice is well done. Please don't stir rice while simmering. Add water if needed. Fluff with a fork.

MUSLIM BAKED RICE

4 cups steamed cabbage, roughly chopped

1 1/2 cup cooked brown rice

1 onion, sliced

2 tablespoons corn oil

1 teaspoon Muhammad's Seasoning™ (pg.307)

1/4 teaspoon Muhammad's Red Hot Sauce™ (pg.307)

1/2 red bell pepper, sliced

1/2 green bell pepper, sliced

Step 1: Sauté onion, peppers while sprinkling with seasoning in a large-skillet with corn oil for a few minutes.

Step 2: Combine all ingredients in a buttered baking dish and bake in a 360° oven for 20 minutes. Serve with a fish dish.

LIGHT CURRY RICE

1 cup steamed cabbage, roughly chopped

1 1/2 cup cooked brown rice

1 onion, sliced

2 garlic cloves , chopped

2 tablespoons olive oil

1 tablespoon Muhammad's Mild Curry Seasoning™ (pg. 307)

1/4 teaspoon Muhammad's Red Hot Sauce™ (pg.307)

1 stalk celery, chopped

1 green bell pepper, sliced

Step 1: Sauté onion, peppers, celery and garlic while sprinkling with Curry seasoning in a large-skillet with olive oil for a few minutes.

Step 2: Combine all ingredients in a buttered baking dish and bake in a 360° oven for 20 minutes. Serve with a fish dish.

RICE & CHEESE

4 cups cooked brown rice

1/2 stick butter

Salt to taste

1/2 cup buttered wheat germ

1/2 cup buttered Whole Wheat Cracker crumbs (pg.204)

1/8 teaspoon Muhammad's Red Hot Sauce (pg.307)

1 cup Cheddar cheese, grated

1 cup milk

Step 1: Butter a 1 1/2-quart baking dish.

Step 2: Lay half the rice on bottom of baking dish, spread half the cheese over rice with hot pepper, salt and dot with 2 tablespoons butter.

Step 3: Repeat Step 2.

Step 4: Conclude by pouring the milk evenly over all and sprinkling the top with buttered wheat germ and cracker crumbs. Bake in 350° oven for 30 minutes.

← ——————————————————————————————— →

BROWN RICE CROQUETTES

1/2 cup brown rice	6 tablespoons butter
1 cup milk	2 tablespoon olive oil
2 eggs	
1 1/2 Whole Wheat Bread crumbs (pg.188)	
1/2 teaspoon salt	

Step 1: Trickle the rice and salt into 1/2 cup boiling water. Cover and cook slowly 10 minutes. Add the milk, stir, cover, and cook 35 minutes more.

Step 2: Stir in 1 egg and 2 tablespoons butter.

Step 3: Spread the mixture on a shallow plate, cover with plastic wrap, and refrigerate.

Step 4: Beat the remaining egg in a shallow dish and put the crumbs on a piece of wax paper.

Step 5: Shape the chilled rice mixture into 6 patty or conical shapes. Dip each croquette into the egg and cover with the crumbs.

Step 6: Melt the remaining 4 tablespoons of butter in a skillet with the oil. When hot, fry the croquettes until golden brown. Do not rush in cooking them for the insides will remain cool.

← ——————————————————————————————— →

SAUTÉED RICE

4 cups cooked brown or unconverted rice	1 onion, finely chopped
5 tablespoons olive oil	2 eggs, slightly beaten
3 tablespoons light soy sauce	1/4 teaspoon ground black pepper

Step 1: Make sure rice is hot or heat rice and soy sauce in a casserole in a warm oven till ready to sauté.

Step 2: Heat the oil in a large skillet or wok, sauté onions 1 minute, add (heated) rice, and pepper. Cook over medium-high heat, stirring frequently, for 6 minutes; add the eggs and stir briskly so they cook and break into small bits throughout the rice. As soon as the egg is set, remove and serve.

← ——————————————————————————————— →

ASIAN SAUTÉED RICE

4 cups cooked brown or unconverted rice   1 onion, finely chopped

5 tablespoons corn oil   2 eggs, slightly beaten

3 tablespoons light soy sauce   1/4 teaspoon ground black pepper

1/4 cup celery, chopped fine

1/4 teaspoon Muhammad's Red Hot Sauce™ (pg.307)

Step 1: Make sure rice is hot or heat rice and soy sauce in a casserole in a warm oven till ready to sauté.

Step 2: Heat the oil in a large skillet or wok, add onions, celery, and hot pepper, sauté 1 minute, add (heated) rice, and pepper. Cook over medium-high heat, stirring frequently, for 6 minutes; add the eggs and stir briskly so they cook and break into small bits throughout the rice. As soon as the egg is set, remove and serve.

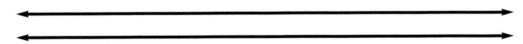

TOASTED RICE

(This gives rice a nutty flavor)

2 cups (uncooked) brown or unconverted rice

Cookie pan

Step 1: Preheat oven to 350°

Step 2: Sprinkle rice evenly across cookie pan.

Step 3: Bake 10 to 15 minutes, or until light-golden brown in a preheated 350°F oven, shaking cookie pan if needed, to ensure even toasting.

Step 4: Toasted rice can be utilized like any other uncooked rice. Store unused portion in an air-tight container.

4. EGGS

INFO ON EGGS

- Eggs are basic, complete and versatile. The recipes in 'Muslim Cooking With Muhammad™' call for "Large" eggs.
- Cold eggs separate best. To separate an egg, crack it with a knife or against the edge of a bowl and split the shell into two parts. Pass the yolk back and forth between the halves of the shell, allowing the white to fall into a bowl underneath.
- Temper the egg yolks. Egg yolks are often added to hot mixtures, frequently to sauces, so that as the heat works on the yolks, it will cause them to thicken a sauce. Yolks should be tempered first so they don't cook prematurely and float, scrambled, in the sauce. To temper them, softly beat the yolks with a whisk in a separate bowl, then add a bit of the hot sauce to them in a thin stream. When this mixture has become warm and thick, you can stir it into the whole potful of simmering liquid. Keep it below the boiling temperature except if the sauce is bound by flour, which prevents curdling.

BASIC WAYS TO COOK AN EGG

- High heat toughens eggs. A golden, tender and well-cooked egg can be produced at low heat.
- It is ideal to let eggs stand at room temperature for a while before cooking them. The will be more tempered so the shells won't crack when hot water touches them. Also pierce the large end of the egg with a needle; this reduces the pressure that often cracks the shell.

$$\longleftrightarrow$$

SOFT-BOILED EGGS

(Although they are called "boiled" eggs, they are actually simmered. The water must completely cover the eggs and should not boil once the eggs have been placed into it.)

Step 1: Bring water to a boil in a saucepan large enough to accommodate the number of eggs you are cooking.

Step 2: Lower the eggs carefully into the water on a spoon and reduce heat so water doesn't boil. If cooking many eggs utilize a wire basket to lower eggs into water. Let the water simmer 3 to 5 minutes, depending on how hard you like your eggs. Remove them immediately when time is up. Soft-boiled eggs should have softly set whites and runny yolks.

MEDIUM-BOILED EGGS

(Coddled or, formally, medium-boiled eggs have fine, firm opaque whites and soft yolks. They can be shelled and utilized in place of poached eggs.)

Step 1: Fill a saucepan with enough water to cover the egg, and heat to a gentle boil.
Step 2: Lower the egg on a tablespoon. Cover the pan, remove from heat, and let stand for 4 to 5 minutes. Depending on how firm you wish it to be.

HARD-BOILED EGGS

Step 1: Fill a saucepan with enough water to cover the egg, and heat to a simmer.
Step 2: Lower the egg on a tablespoon. Cover the pan, allowing 15 to 20 minutes. Stir the eggs carefully with a spoon once or twice during cooking to keep the yolk in the center. High heat or over cooking may give that harmless, unattractive greenish rim that develops around the yolk.
Step 3: Remove from the heat and place the egg in cold water immediately. The egg should have a firm white and yolk.

POACHED EGGS

(A poached egg requires a perfectly fresh egg. It is cooked out of its shell in simmering liquid until its white is opaque and firm and its yolks runny or firm.)

4 eggs, at (room temp.)   1 teaspoon salt

Step 1: Fill a shallow pan 2/3 thirds full of water; add salt; bring the water to a simmer, break each egg, one by one, into a saucer, and slide it gently into the water. Don't crowd the eggs. Spoon simmering water over the eggs for 2 to 3 minutes until they are set; or turn off the heat, cover the pan, and let the eggs stand in the water for 5 to 6 minutes. The eggs are done when the whites become opaque and the yolks lose their shine. Let them set a few minutes longer if you like the yolks firm.
Step 2: Remove one by one with a draining spoon. Practice poaching one egg at a time until you have perfected the technique. Serve on toast.

SHIRRED EGGS

2 eggs   1 1/2 teaspoons butter
1/4 teaspoon parsley, finely chopped   Ground black pepper
Salt to taste

Step 1: Preheat oven to 400°. Butter two shirring (baking) dishes and place them in oven until butter melts. Swirl it to coat bottom and sides of dish.

Step 2: Crack the eggs, put them in the dish, and cover tightly with foil.

Step 3: Bake for 7 to 10 minutes depending on how firm you like the yolk.

Step 4: Remove foil, and season to taste.

√ Shirred Eggs with Whole Wheat Crumbs

Sprinkle 2 tablespoons *Whole Wheat Bread crumbs (pg.188)* over the buttered bottom of the baking shirring dish. Add the eggs, and sprinkle with another 2 tablespoons of *crumbs*.

√ Shirred Eggs with Fish Sausage

For each 2 eggs cook 4 small *Fish Sausages (pg.288)* until done. Drain and place the *fish sausages* around the eggs in the shirring dish.

√ Shirred Eggs Italian Style

Spread 1 tablespoon chopped *cooked spinach (pg.74 & 159)* for each egg on the bottom of the shirring dish. Put the egg on top and sprinkle with 1 tablespoon *grated Parmesan cheese*.

⟵————————————————————⟶

SCRAMBLED EGGS

2 tablespoons olive oil	4 eggs
1 tablespoon butter	1/8 teaspoon ground black pepper
Salt to taste	*(OPTIONAL) 2 tablespoons water

Step 1: Heat olive oil then melt the butter in a heavy-skillet over a low flame.

Step 2: Combine the eggs, salt, pepper, and *(if utilizing) 2 tablespoons water in a bowl. Whisk; pour into skillet, and turn heat to medium-low. Stir the egg mixture, lifting it up and over from the bottom as it gets thick. Stir till desired texture is achieved. The longer they cook the drier they become. We want a soft and creamy texture.

√ Scrambled Eggs with Cream Cheese

Cut 3 ounces *cream cheese* into small pieces then add to the eggs after they begin to thicken in the skillet.

√ Scrambled Eggs with Garlic

Sauté 1 minced *garlic clove* 1/2 chopped *onion* in the oil and butter before adding the eggs.

⟵————————————————————⟶

SOUTHWESTERN EGG SANDWICH

2 tablespoons olive oil	4 eggs
1 tablespoon butter	1/4 teaspoon ground black pepper

1/2 teaspoon salt

1/2 cup green bell pepper, minced

4 slices Basic Whole Wheat Herb Bread, toasted (pg.192)

1/4 green chili pepper, roasted , skin & seeds discarded, and finely chopped

Step 1: Heat olive oil then melt the butter in a heavy-skillet. Combine the eggs, salt and pepper in a bowl. Whisk; pour into skillet, and turn heat low. Stir the egg mixture, lifting it up and over from the bottom once or twice as it gets thick; shift till desired texture is achieved. The longer they cook the drier they become. We want a soft and creamy texture.

Step 2: Arrange on two slices of bread; sprinkle minced green bell & chili pepper over eggs; top with remaining two slices of bread to make sandwiches.

√ Coyote Egg Sandwich with Cream Cheese

Cut 3 ounces *cream cheese* into small pieces then add to the eggs after they begin to thicken in the skillet.

√ Coyote Egg Sandwich with Garlic

Sauté 1 minced *garlic clove* 1/2 chopped *onion* in the oil and butter before adding the eggs.

FRENCH OMELET

Read these instructions before starting to cook. An omelet is creamy scrambled eggs enclosed in an envelope of coagulated egg. Utilize quickness and proper heat. The filling cannot be too liquid.

2 eggs

1 tablespoon olive oil

Salt to taste

Ground black pepper

*(OPTIONAL) Muhammad's Red Hot Sauce™ (pg.307)

*(OPTIONAL) 4 tablespoons filling

1 tablespoon butter

Step 1: Beat the eggs in a bowl until they are slightly blended. Add a pinch of salt and pepper or a dash of Tabasco™.

Step 2:Optional:*If filling is utilized, have it prepared and warm.

Step 2: Heat a 8 inch skillet until hot; add olive oil then butter. As it foams and sizzles, pour in eggs. Wiggle the skillet . Utilizing a fork, pull back a little of the edge of the egg that will have started to curl up and, by tilting the skillet, permit the liquid egg in the center of the pan to run over. Continue to wiggle and fork around the edges. Spread the filling across the center of the omelet.

Step 3: Have a warm plate on stand by. Utilize a spatula or fork and roll one-third of the omelet over onto itself, then out of the skillet onto the plate, propelling it to make the second fold as it drops. Cook till the omelet is firm all through.

√ Cheese Omelet

Spread 1/4 cup freshly *grated Swiss cheese* over the omelet just before folding.

√ Herb Omelet

Add 1 teaspoon *minced parsley,* 1 tablespoon *minced chives,* 1/8 teaspoon *tarragon,* and 1/8 teaspoon *marjoram* , to the egg mixture.

√ Fish Sausage Omelet

Break one *Fish Patti* into small pieces and sprinkle over omelet just before folding.

√ Veggie Omelet

Heat 1/2 cup of Chopped *tomato, onion, pepper,* and a pinch of *hot pepper* then spread over the omelet just before you fold it.

√ Veggie Omelet II

Heat 1/2 cup of Chopped *mixed vegetables* then spread over the omelet just before you fold it.

$\longleftarrow \qquad \longrightarrow$

APPLE OMELET

4 eggs, beaten	2 tablespoons cream
1 cup shredded apple	1/4 cup tomato juice
1/2 teaspoon salt	(OPTIONAL)1/8 teaspoon white pepper

Step 1: Whisk the eggs, then beat in other ingredients.

Step 2: Pour into an oiled baking dish and bake at 350° for 15 minutes, or until golden brown.

$\longleftarrow \qquad \longrightarrow$

STUFFED EGGS

12 eggs, hard-boiled	2 tablespoons Mayonnaise (pg.183)
1 tablespoon minced parsley or herbs	Dash of salt
Dash of ground black pepper	
1 teaspoon Dijon mustard (pg.108) or horseradish	

Step 1: Shell the egg and slice it in half lengthwise. Remove the yolk and mash it with the mayonnaise, mustard, Salt and pepper until it is completely blended and creamy.

Step 2: Utilize a pastry tube to pipe the smooth yolk mixture into the hollow of the egg white. Sprinkle parsley or herbs on top or garnish with a caper or slivers of green or red pepper, slice of olive or pickle.

√ **Cheese-stuffed Eggs**

Utilize 1 1/2 tablespoons *grated Parmesan cheese* instead of the Dijon mustard.

EGGS A LA MODE

2 soft-boiled eggs, shell removed	2 slices Whole Wheat toast (pg.188)
2/3 cup seasoned stewed tomatoes	2 sprigs parsley or watercress

Step 1: Butter a slice of whole wheat toast.

Step 2: Place hot soft-boiled egg on it.

Step 3: Cover each portion with 1/3 cup of stewed tomatoes. Serve on a hot platter garnished with a sprig of parsley.

EGGS AND RICE CASSEROLE

1 cup unconverted rice	1/4 cup green bell pepper, chopped
6 tablespoons butter	2 eggs
1/4 cup minced onion	4 tablespoon tomato pureé
2 cups water	1/8 teaspoon cardamom, ground
1/2 tomato, seeded & chopped	
Salt to taste	Ground black pepper

Step 1: Brown rice in 4 tablespoons butter heated in a skillet over a low flame, adding water and cook until tender.

Step 2: In a skillet over over a medium flame brown onion and pepper in 2 tablespoon butter for 10 minutes.

Step 3: Add to cooked rice.

Step 4: Beat eggs and cook in butter until set, add to rice and blend, add chopped tomato & pureé. Cover pot and steam for 10 minutes. Add salt, cardamom and pepper to taste. Serve with fish.

EGG CHOP SUEY

2 onions, cut wedges	1 green bell pepper, diced
5 stalks celery, cut in 1-inch pieces	2 cups strained tomatoes
3 tablespoons corn oil	1/4 teaspoon ground black pepper
1/4 teaspoon salt	
One 4-Egg cooked French Omelet, cubed (pg.128)	

Step 1: Heat the oil in a covered skillet. Sauté the onion and celery in the oil for 10 minutes, add a tablespoon of water to keep from burning if necessary.

Step 2: Add the green pepper, cook ten more minutes, add the omelet, tomatoes, salt and black pepper. Stir over low heat until heated through. Serve with vegetables.

CHEESE SOUFFLE

5 eggs, separated	1 cup Cheddar cheese
4 tablespoons butter	3 tablespoons unbleached flour
2/3 cup hot milk	
1/2 teaspoon salt	
Dash Muhammad's Red Hot Sauce™ (pg.307)	

Step 1: Preheat oven to 350°.

Step 2: Butter a 1 1/2-quart straight-side souffle' dish.

Step 3: Melt the butter in the top of a double-boiler. Blend in the flour & hot sauce and gradually stir in the hot milk. Cook over hot water, stirring constantly, until thick and smooth. Add the grated cheese and remove from heat.

Step 4: Beat the egg yolks. Add 3 tablespoons of the hot cheese mixture into the egg yolks and then return to the cheese mixture and stir over hot water 1 minute.

Step 5: Remove from heat and let the mixture cool to lukewarm by letting the bowl sit in cold water in sink.

Step 6: Beat the egg whites until stiff but not dry. Stir a fourth of the whites into the cheese sauce, then fold in the remaining whites. Spoon into the souffle' dish. Bake in the middle rack of the oven 30 to 40 minutes, until the center is firm. This souffle' must be brought to the table as soon as it is ready.

√ Spinach Souffle'

Instead of the 1 cup Cheddar cheese, utilize 3/4 cup drained, *finely chopped cooked spinach*, 1/3 cup *grated Swiss cheese* and 1/8 teaspoon *ground black pepper.*

√ Herb Souffle'

Delete the cheese and add 1 1/2 tablespoons *minced onion*, 1 teaspoon *finely chopped basil*, 1 teaspoon *finely chopped tarragon*, 1 tablespoon *finely chopped parsley*, and 1/8 teaspoon *ground black pepper* to the cream sauce base.

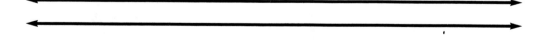

(COMING SOON)
GUEST RECIPE

See your recipe on this page

*(Recipe must conform to the theme of this cookbook)

1. Provide List of Ingredients.

2. Step by Step procedures for preparing and cooking dish.

3. Provide picture of self and/or cooked dish.

4.Send to the Publisher by postal mail or email@:

Attn: Aubrey Muhammad

Muslim Cookbook, Muhammad's Sauces & Seasonings™

600 Fulton Ave. 26F

Hempstead, New York 11550

Phone: 516-483-7673

Email: Muslimcooking@Yahoo.com

5. LAND OF CHEESE

HOMEMADE SOUR MILK

The pasteurized milk available in today's' supermarkets spoils before it turns sour. To "sour" pasteurized milk, for immediate utilization:

Step 1: Add 1 tablespoon white vinegar or lemon juice to 1 cup of milk and let stand at room temperature 10 to 15 minutes.

←——————————————————————————————→

HOMEMADE CREAM CHEESE

Step 1: Set a bottle of fresh cream at room temperature for 2 days. It will "sour".
Step 2: Pour the contents into a fine cheese clothe bag and allow it to drain.
Step 3: When solid, place it in the refrigerator and chill it, forming it into a flat cake or into balls.

←——————————————————————————————→

HOMEMADE COTTAGE CHEESE

Cottage cheese is formed by heating sour milk until the curds coagulate and separate from the liquid part, the whey. We can either allow the milk to turn sour by itself, heat it over low heat to lukewarm, and drain through cheese clothe, or sour the milk by the Homemade method above:

Step 1: Put fresh milk in a saucepan, heat it gently to lukewarm, stirring with a wooden spoon, put into it 2 teaspoons of lemon juice or vinegar per cup of milk. Stir well, until milk is curdled.
Step 2: Strain it through cheese clothe, pressing out whey with wooden spoon to drain the cheese sufficiently.
Step 3: Flavor with a little vegetable water and enrich it by adding chopped chives or parsley and lemon or lime. Store in the refrigerator.

←——————————————————————————————→

CHEESE CROQUETTES

1 cup Parmesan or Cheddar cheese	2 egg whites, stiffly beaten
2 teaspoons whole wheat flour	3/4 cup fine Cracker crumbs (pg.204)
1/2 cup extra virgin olive oil	1/4 teaspoon salt
1/8 teaspoon ground black pepper	
Dash of Muhammad's Red Hot Sauce™ (pg.307)	

Step 1: Combine the cheese, flour, salt, pepper and hot sauce. Utilizing your hands, gently stir in the egg whites.

Step 2: Pat the mixture into small balls and roll them in cracker crumbs until thoroughly coated.

Alternate Step 3:To Fry: Heat the oil in a skillet over medium heat. Put the balls in the pan without crowding them; increase flame to medium-high, turning until all sides become golden brown (uhmn).

Alternate Step 3:To Bake: Arrange on a parchment lined baking sheet 1-inch apart; bake in a preheated 350° oven, turning often until golden brown.

Step 4: Drain on paper towels.

Step 5: Serve as hors d'oeuvre.

REAL CHEESEBURGERS

16 ounce cottage cheese (pg.133)   1 egg, beaten

1 tablespoon parsley, minced   3 tablespoons onion, minced

Extra virgin olive oil

Butter

1 teaspoon Worcestershire Sauce or 1 tablespoon Muhammad's Chili Sauce™ (pg.307)

1 cup fine Whole Wheat Bread crumbs (to coat patties) (pg.188)

3/4 cup Whole Wheat Bread crumbs (pg.188)

Ground black pepper

Step 1: Combine cottage cheese with bread crumbs, egg, onion, parsley, Worcestershire Sauce, salt and pepper.

Step 2: Form into palm size patties and coat with fine bread crumbs.

Step 3: Heat some olive oil in a skillet over a medium flame; add a little butter till it sizzles then sauté the patties until brown on both sides.

Step 4: Serve with a Barbecue Sauce (pg.112), Jalepeño Ketchup (pg.307) , or Mustard Sauce (pg.109) on a bun with lettuce and tomato.

WELSH RAREBIT

1/2 pound sharp Cheddar cheese, diced   4 slices Whole Wheat toast (pg.188)

1 egg, slightly beaten   1 tablespoon butter

1/2 teaspoon dry mustard   Salt to taste

1/2 cup non-alcohol beer or milk

1/8 teaspoon Muhammad's Red Hot Sauce™ (pg.307)

Step 1: Combine the cheese, butter, mustard and hot sauce in a double boiler. Cook over low heat, stirring constantly, until cheese has melted.

Step 2: Beat a little of the hot cheese mixture into the egg, and then return the egg-cheese mixture to the pan.

Step 3: Add salt to taste; add the non-alcohol beer or milk and cook 1 to 2 minutes more, until simmering but not boiling. Serve on the toast.

← →

CHILI WITH CHEESE

1 cup grated sharp Cheddar cheese

2 tablespoons olive oil

1 cup strained tomato purée

2 eggs, beaten

1/8 teaspoon ground black pepper

1 tablespoon Muhammad's Chili Powder™ (pg.307)

1/4 to 1/2 cup milk

2 teaspoons onion, minced

1/4 teaspoon salt

Step 1: Sauté onion in olive oil. Add tomato, milk, chili powder. Simmer, but don't boil, until thick about 15 minutes.

Step 2: Add cheese, eggs, salt and pepper.

Step 3: Serve on Whole Wheat Bread slices toasted (pg.188).

← →

CHILALY

1 tablespoon Olive oil or butter

2 tablespoons onion, finely chopped

2 tablespoons milk or cream

1 egg, slightly beaten

2 tablespoons green bell pepper, finely chopped

1/8 teaspoon Muhammad's Red Hot Sauce™ (pg.307)

4 slices Whole Wheat Herb Bread, toasted (pg.188)

1 1/2 cups grated Cheddar cheese

1/2 cup strained tomato purée

1/4 teaspoon salt

Step 1: Melt the olive oil or butter in a skillet. Sauté the onion and green bell pepper, until golden brown. Add the tomatoes and stir over low heat about 5 to minutes or until thick .

Step 2: Add the salt, hot sauce, and cheese and cook, stirring frequently, until the cheese melts. Stir in the milk or cream mixed with the egg, cook for 1 minute more, and serve on whole wheat toast.

← →

CORN & CHEESE SOUFFLE

2/3 cup grated Cheddar cheese

1 tablespoon olive oil

2 tablespoons butter

2 eggs, separated

1 teaspoon salt

2/3 grated corn from the cob

1 1/3 cup light cream

2 tablespoons minced green bell pepper

3 tablespoons unbleached flour

Step 1: Butter a baking dish.

Step 2: Preheat oven to 400°F.

Step 3: Heat the olive oil in a saucepan and add butter. Sauté the green pepper a few minutes, then add flour. Stir until blended. Add the cream, stirring until thick and smooth. Add the cheese and stir until melted.

Step 4: Remove from heat and add corn and salt.

Step 5: Beat the egg yolks. Add 3 tablespoons of the hot cheese mixture into yolks and then return slowly to the cheese mixture.

Step 6: Let the mixture cool and beat the egg whites stiff but not dry. Fold into the cheese mixture, then pure into buttered baking dish.

Step 7: Place in 400°F oven for a few minutes, then turn the temperature down to 325°. Bake until the center is firm, approximately 30 minutes. Serve immediately, the longer it sets out the more it will deflate.

$\longleftarrow\hspace{6cm}\longrightarrow$

CHEESE STUFFED APPLES

1/2 cup cottage cheese	4 Granny Smith apples, cored
1/3 cup minced raisins or dates	1/4 cup pineapple or lemon juice

Step 1: Combine cheese with raisins or dates; stuff into the centers of cored apples. Cut apples in slices, sprinkle with pineapple or lemon juice and serve as an hors doeuvre on crisp lettuce leaves.

$\longleftarrow\hspace{6cm}\longrightarrow$

STUFFED CELERY

1/3 cup cottage cheese	5 celery stalks
1 tablespoon Mayonnaise (pg.183)	1/2 teaspoon marjoram
1/2 teaspoon salt	
Dash of Muhammad's Red Hot Sauce™ (pg.307)	

Step 1: Blend cheese and mayonnaise, add seasonings and whip until smooth.

Step 2: Fill a pastry bag with mixture and pipe into cuff fill celery stalks. Serve with salads, or cut in 1 1/2-inch pieces as an hors doeuvre.

$\longleftarrow\hspace{6cm}\longrightarrow$

CHEESE-OLIVE TURNOVERS

Basic pastry dough (pg.231)

2/3 cup grated Cheddar cheese

2/3 ripe Black Mediterranean olives, chopped

1/3 cup Muhammad's Complex Chili Sauce™ (pg.307)

Step 1: Prepare one recipe of the basic pastry dough, roll into 2-inch rounds.

Step 2: Mixed grated cheese with olives & chili sauce. Place one teaspoon of filling on center of each pastry round, moisten edges, fold over half and crimp edges together; arrange on cookie sheet. Chill.

Step 3: When ready to serve, bake in a preheated 475°F oven 10 to 12 minutes or until golden brown. Serve immediately as an hors doeurve.

$\longleftrightarrow$

CHEESE BLINTZES

BATTER FOR CREPE

3 eggs, slightly beaten	1/2 cup water
4 tablespoons whole wheat flour	Dash of salt

FILLING

1 pound dry cottage cheese (pg.133)	2 eggs, slightly beaten
2 tablespoons Raw™ sugar	Pinch of cinnamon

Step 1: Dry the cottage cheese in a sieve, pressing it down firmly and letting it stand and drip for an hour.

Step 2: Blend eggs, flour, water and salt to make a thin batter.

Step 3: Heat 1 tablespoons olive oil in a skillet over a low flame. Utilize a multi-folded paper towel to evenly distribute oil to cover surface (be careful not to let hot oil from towel touch your fingers). Pour 3 tablespoons of batter into skillet, turning quickly so that batter covers whole flat surface and forms a thin crepe. Cook until brown on under side only.

Step 4: Blend filling ingredients together. Pour a portion of filling in center of crepe. Roll and fold ends under. Fry again until brown on both sides. Serve with strawberry purée and sour cream.

$\longleftrightarrow$

CREAM CHEESE THINS

1 1/4 cup whole wheat flour, sifted	4 ounces cream cheese
1/2 teaspoon coarse salt	1/2 stick unsalted butter (softened)
1/4 teaspoon cayenne pepper	2 to 3 tablespoons evaporated milk

Step 1: Sift the flour, pepper and salt and utilizing a pastry blender, add the cream cheese and butter, cutting into small pieces. Add enough milk to make into a dough and then wrap it in parchment or wax paper and leave it in the refrigerator overnight.

Step 2: Roll it out the next day on the paper till it is as thin as a quarter and then cut into 1-inch squares, rounds or any shape you prefer; prick tiny holes around centers with a fork.

Step 3: Bake in a preheated 400°F oven for 10 to 15 minutes. Watch closely to see that they don't burn. Serve hot.

PLAIN CHEESE THINS

1/4 pound unsalted-butter (softened)	2 cups grated cheese
1 cup unbleached flour	1/4 tsp. almond flavor (Optional)
1/4 teaspoon cayenne pepper	1/8 teaspoon coarse salt

Step 1: Sift the flour, combine all ingredients cutting with a pastry blender. Make two log-shaped rolls 1 1/2 inches in diameter. Wrap in parchment or wax paper and refrigerate overnight.
Step 2: Preheat oven to 375°F.
Step 3: Slice the dough into penny-thin wafers, prick tiny holes around centers with a fork, arrange on a parchment lined baking sheet and bake 6 to 10 minutes, depending on the thickness of the slices. Observe diligently to make sure they don't burn.

CHEESE SAVORY CUSTARD

2/3 cup heavy cream	2 eggs, slightly beaten
1/2 cup Swiss cheese, finely diced	1/2 teaspoon black pepper, ground
1/2 cup Parmesan cheese, freshly grated	
1/4 teaspoon mace	
1/8 teaspoon Muhammad's Red Hot Sauce™ (pg.307)	

Step 1: Preheat the oven to 450°F.
Step 2: Mix all ingredients together in a bowl. Beat thoroughly and pour into a small casserole or four ramekins.
Step 3: Bake 15 minutes or until golden-brown on top. Serve hot.

WHOLE WHEAT MACARONI AND CHEESE

9 ounces whole wheat macaroni, cooked	1/2 cup grated sharp Cheddar cheese
2 cups Cheese sauce (pg. 97)	
1/2 cup buttered Whole Wheat Bread crumbs (pg.188)	

Step 1: Preheat the oven to 375°F.
Step 2: Butter a 1 1/2-quart casserole. Place the cooked macaroni into the casserole, pour cheese sauce over it, and mix slightly with a wooden spatula. Spread the grated cheese evenly over the top and spread the bread crumbs over the cheese.

Step 3: Bake uncovered, until the top is golden and the sauce is bubbling, approximately 30 minutes.

6. VEGETABLES

GARLIC STUFFED ARTICHOKES

4 large artichokes

1/4 teaspoon salt

1/8 teaspoon pepper

1 cup Whole Wheat Bread crumbs (pg.188)

4 tablespoons extra virgin olive oil (for sautéing)

2 tablespoons extra virgin olive oil (for pouring)

4 cloves garlic, minced

2 tablespoons parsley, chopped

Step 1: Cut off stems of artichokes so they will stand upright. With a knife slice off an inch of the tops of the artichokes. With scissors, snip off the prickly tips of the remaining side leaves. Wash thoroughly and spread the leaves apart.

Step 2: Sauté the garlic, bread crumbs, parsley, salt & pepper with 4 tablespoons olive oil 2 minutes in a skillet. Pour into a bowl, let cool, and mix. With a small spoon, insert some of the stuffing between most of the leaves of artichokes.

Step 3: Place the stuffed- artichokes in a large pot with one inch of water. Pour the remaining 2 table-spoons of olive oil evenly over each stuffed-artichoke. Cover and cook over low heat for 1 hour, or until a leaf can be pulled off easily. As the stuffed-artichokes cook, check the water level and add as needed. Drain well. [See (pg.70) on the art of eating an artichoke.]

←──────────────────────────────→

PLAIN ASPARAGUS

2 bunches asparagus, peeled

2 tablespoons butter

1/4 teaspoon salt

1/2 green bell pepper, sliced

1/4 cup water

1/8 teaspoon black pepper

Step 1: Cut off the tough, woody bottom-ends of asparagus, peel lower half and rinse thoroughly.

Step 2: Place in a pot, add seasonings, cover the pot. Cook on a low flame until tender, begin testing after 4 to 8 minutes. Check the water level and add as needed. Drain and serve.

←──────────────────────────────→

ASPARAGUS WITH CITRUS SAUCE

1 pound asparagus, peeled

2 tablespoons extra virgin olive oil

1/4 teaspoon salt

1/2 cup Muhammad's Citrus Mayonnaise (pg.184)

1/2 teaspoon thyme

Step 1: Cut off the tough, woody bottom-ends of asparagus, peel lower half and rinse thoroughly.

Step 2: In a bowl, whisk together the oil, thyme and salt. Pour over asparagus and set aside.

Step 3: Arrange asparagus in a single layer on a baking sheet. Bake in preheat 450°F oven 7 minutes or until tender, turning once halfway through baking time. Remove asparagus to a serving dish and serve with Muhammad's™ Citrus Mayonnaise.

⟵──────────────────────────────⟶

CORN JAMBOREÉ #1

2 cups corn, cut from cobs   2 onions, chopped

1 clove garlic, sliced   1 green bell pepper, chopped

1 cup tomatoes, chopped   1/8 teaspoon black pepper

3 tablespoons extra virgin olive oil   1 tablespoon unsalted butter

1/4 teaspoon salt

4 cups broccoli flowerets, cut in 3/4-inch dices

1 tablespoon Muhammad's Seasoning™ (pg.307)

1/2 yellow chili pepper, roasted , skin & seeds discarded, and finely chopped

Step 1: Heat oil in a large skillet over a medium flame. Add the onions, garlic, green pepper, yellow chili pepper & seasonings; sauté 2 to 3 minutes; Add corn and tomatoes spreading them evenly over the sautéing vegetables. Cover skillet, lower flame and cook 2 minutes; remove cover; add broccoli and butter; cover skillet; cook 5 to 7 minutes more till broccoli and corn is crisp-tender; pour from skillet, into colander to drain-if necessary, leaving any charred vegetables in skillet-if necessary.

⟵──────────────────────────────⟶

SUNSHINE SURPRISE

1 cup corn, cut from cobs   2 onions, chopped

2 cloves garlic, sliced   2 cups cabbage, roughly chopped

2 tablespoons extra virgin olive oil   1/8 teaspoon black pepper

1/4 teaspoon salt

3 yellow squash, washed, and cut diagonally into 1/2-inch slices

2 tablespoon Muhammad's Lemon Dressing™ (pg.181)

1/2 yellow chili pepper, roasted, skin & seeds discarded, and finely chopped

Step 1: Heat oil in a large skillet over a medium flame. Add the onions, garlic, yellow chili pepper and salt & black pepper; sauté 1 to 2 minutes; arrange squash slices to the bottom of skillet, add corn and cabbage spreading them evenly over the sautéing vegetables; drizzle dressing over all; cover skillet, lower flame and cook 7 to 9 minutes more till cabbage and corn is crisp-tender; pour from skillet, into colander to drain-if necessary, leaving any charred vegetables in skillet-if necessary.

TANGY VEGETABLE MIX

4 cups cabbage, roughly chopped

2 onions, chopped

2 cloves garlic, sliced

1 green bell pepper, chopped

2 tablespoons corn oil

1 teaspoon ginger, finely grated

1/8 teaspoon black pepper

1/2 teaspoon horseradish, finely grated

1/2 tablespoon cilantro, chopped

1/2 tablespoon parsley, chopped

1/4 teaspoon salt

2 carrots, julienned or 2 cups green beans, cut in diagonal slanted slices "French"

1 yellow squash, washed, and cut diagonally into 1/2-inch slices

1 tablespoon Muhammad's Seasoning™ (pg.307)

1/2 yellow chili pepper, roasted, skin & seeds discarded, and finely chopped

Step 1: Heat oil in a large skillet over a medium flame. Add the onions, garlic and yellow chili pepper; cover; roast 2 minutes; arrange squash slices to the bottom of skillet; add carrots or green beans—if using and cabbage spreading them evenly over the roasting vegetables; sprinkle seasoning, ginger, horseradish, cilantro, parsley, salt and black pepper over all; cover skillet, lower flame and cook 7 to 9 minutes more till cabbage and carrots or green beans are crisp-tender; pour from skillet, into colander to drain-if necessary, leaving any charred vegetables in skillet-if necessary.

STRING or GREEN BEANS

1 pound green beans

1 tablespoon butter

1/8 teaspoon salt

1/8 teaspoon fresh black pepper

Step 1: Wash the beans; remove ends; cut in diagonal slanted slices "French".

Step 2: Place them into a large pot of salted boiling water with a drop of oil added and boil them gently until just done and crisp, about 5-8 minutes.

Step 3: Drain the beans and serve with butter, salt and pepper.

√ String Beans au Gratin

Boil beans for only 2 minutes. Drain and mix with 1 1/2 cups *Cheese Sauce (Pg.97)*. Place in buttered casserole, spread *buttered Whole Wheat Bread crumbs (pg.188)* over top and bake, uncovered, in a preheated 400°F oven 20 minutes. Serve hot.

ASIAN SWEET & SOUR GREEN BEANS

3 cups green beans

1 1/2 cup green bell pepper, chopped

1 onion, chopped

3 tablespoons corn oil

1/4 teaspoon salt

1/4 cup Muhammad's Thai Sweet & Sour Sauce (pg.307)

2 yellow squash, washed, and cut diagonally into 1/2-inch slices

1 zucchini, washed, and cut diagonally into 1/2-inch slices

1 clove garlic, sliced

1/8 teaspoon black pepper

Step 1: Wash the beans. Remove ends. Cut in diagonal slanted slices "French".

Step 2: Heat oil in a large skillet over a medium flame. Add the onions, garlic and green peppers. Sauté 2 to 3 minutes. Add green beans spreading them evenly over the sautéing vegetables; cover skillet, lower flame and cook 3 minutes; remove cover and add squash, zucchini, sauce, salt and black pepper; cover; cook 5 more minutes till beans are crisp-tender; pour from skillet, into colander to drain-if necessary, leaving any charred vegetables in skillet-if necessary. Serve with Buttered Rice (pg.121)

√ Asian Sweet & Sour Cabbage

Omit the 1 1/2 cup green pepper. Substitute 3 cups green beans with *3 cups cabbage, roughly chopped* and substitute the squash and zucchini with *3 cups broccoli flowerets, chopped in 3/4-inch pieces.* Proceed with recipe

ASIAN STIR FRIED GREEN BEANS
(FOR VEGETABLE PATTIES & WRAPS)

3 cups green beans or broccoli flowerets

2 cups cabbage, shredded

2 tablespoons chopped parsley

1 teaspoon ginger, finely grated

3 tablespoons corn oil

1/4 teaspoon salt

1/2 jalapeno pepper, roasted , skin & seeds discarded, and finely chopped

1 green bell pepper, chopped

2 onions, chopped

2 cloves garlic, sliced

1 tablespoon, non-alcohol dry sherry

1/8 teaspoon black pepper

Step 1: Wash the beans. Remove ends. Cut in diagonal slanted slices "French". (Or if using broccoli chop in 1/2-inch chunks.)

Step 2: Heat oil in a large skillet over a medium flame. Add the onions, garlic, green peppers, jalapeno pepper, parsley & seasonings. Sauté 2 to 3 minutes. Add green beans or broccoli & cabbage spreading them evenly over the sautéing vegetables, add non-alcohol dry sherry. Cover skillet, lower flame and cook 7 to 10 minutes till beans are crisp-tender; pour from skillet, into colander to drain-if necessary, leaving any charred vegetables in skillet-if necessary. (5 minutes for broccoli.) Use to fill Veggy Patties (pg.203) or Wraps (pg.203)

VEGGY PATTY FILLINGS—CABBAGE
(FOR VEGETABLE PATTIES & WRAPS)

5 cups cabbage, shredded

2 onions, chopped

1 carrot, peeled & juiliened

1 green bell pepper, chopped

2 tomatoes, chopped

1/8 teaspoon black pepper

3 tablespoons extra virgin olive oil

1/4 teaspoon salt

1/2 green chili pepper, roasted , skin & seeds discarded, and finely chopped

Step 1: Heat oil in a large skillet over a medium flame. Add the onions, green peppers, green chili pepper & seasonings. Sauté 2 to 3 minutes. Add carrots, cabbage and tomatoes spreading them evenly over the sautéing vegetables. Cover skillet, lower flame and cook 5 to 8 minutes till cabbage and carrots are crisp-tender; pour from skillet, into colander to drain-if necessary, leaving any charred vegetables in skillet-if necessary.

Step 2: Use to fill Veggy Patties (pg.203) or Wraps (pg.203)

VEGGY PATTY & WRAPS FILLINGS—MIXED VEGETABLE
(FOR VEGETABLE PATTIES & WRAPS)

3 cups cabbage, shredded

2 onions, chopped

2 cloves garlic, sliced

1 green bell pepper, chopped

2 tomatoes, chopped

1/8 teaspoon black pepper

3 tablespoons extra virgin olive oil

2 cups corn, cut from cobs

1/4 teaspoon salt

2 cups cauliflower flowerets, cut in 1/4-inch dices

4 tablespoons Muhammad's Thai Sweet & Sour Sauce™ (pg.307)

1/2 yellow chili pepper, roasted , skin & seeds discarded, and finely chopped

Step 1: Heat oil in a large skillet over a medium flame. Add the onions, garlic, green pepper, red chili pepper & seasonings. Sauté 2 to 3 minutes. Add cauliflower, corn, cabbage and tomatoes spreading them evenly over the sautéing vegetables; add sauce. Cover skillet, lower flame and cook 5 to 8 minutes till cabbage and carrots are crisp-tender; pour from skillet, into colander to drain-if necessary, leaving any charred vegetables in skillet-if necessary.

Step 2: Use to fill Veggy Patties (pg.203) or Wraps (pg.203)

ASIAN STIR-FRIED CAULIFLOWER

1 carrot, peeled and sliced

1/2 cup tomato pureé

1 tomato, chopped

1 onion, chopped

2 cloves garlic, sliced

1 teaspoon ginger, finely grated

1 to 2 tablespoons non-alcohol dry sherry

2 tablespoons parsley, minced

1/2 teaspoon salt

1/4 teaspoon black pepper

2 tablespoons corn oil

4 cups cauliflower flowerets, cut in 1/2-inch chunks

1 red chili pepper, roasted , skin & seeds discarded, and finely chopped

Step 1: Heat oil in a large skillet over a medium flame. Add the onions, garlic, ginger, red chili pepper, parsley, salt & black pepper. Sauté 2 to 3 minutes. Add cauliflower & chopped tomato & tomato pureé spreading them evenly over the sautéing vegetables, add non-alcohol dry sherry.

Step 2: Cover skillet, lower flame and cook 6 to 9 minutes till cauliflower is crisp-tender; pour from skillet, into colander to drain-if necessary, leaving any charred vegetables in skillet-if necessary.

Step 3: Use to fill Veggy Patties (pg.203) or Wraps (pg.203)

√ Asian Stir-Fried Cauliflower & Broccoli

Omit 1 cup cauliflower, add *2 cups broccoli, cut in 1/2-inch chunks* along with cauliflower.

←——————————————————————————→

ROASTED BEETS

2 to 4 small beets

aluminum foil

DRESSING INGREDIENTS

2 tablespoons red wine vinegar

4 tablespoons extra virgin olive oil

1 teaspoon chopped parsley

1/8 teaspoon salt

1/4 teaspoon black pepper

Step 1: Wash beets. Leave whole with skins still on. Cut off stems. Place in aluminum foil; Spurt some of the dressing mix over beets; loosely seal or leave foil opened if you like tough skins.

Step 2: Roast small beets in a preheated 375°F oven for 30 minutes. For larger beets lower heat to 350°F and bake longer for 1 to 1 1/2 hour. If the skins are tough & unattractive, peel, discard and serve beets hot.

←——————————————————————————→

BROCCOLI & CHEESE

1 pound broccoli flowerets

1/4 cup mozzarella cheese, shredded

1 teaspoon chopped parsley

Slice of lemon

1/4 teaspoon salt

1/8 teaspoon pepper

1/2 tablespoon extra virgin olive oil

Step 1: Steam broccoli for 4 to 5 minutes.

Step 2: Place in baking dish coated with 1/2 tablespoon olive oil. Sprinkle shredded mozzarella cheese, then the parsley, over broccoli. Add salt pepper and a spurt of lemon juice.

Step 3: Bake in a 400°F oven until cheese is melted and starts to turn golden brown.

BROCCOLI & MARINARA SAUCE

1 pound broccoli flowerets	1 large onion, chopped
1/2 green bell pepper, chopped	1 garlic clove, minced
1 cup strained tomatoes	1/8 teaspoon black pepper
1/4 cup extra virgin olive oil	
1/2 teaspoon Muhammad's Seasoning™ (pg.307)	
1/8 teaspoon Muhammad's Red Hot Sauce™ (pg.307)	

Step 1: Heat oil in a large skillet over a medium flame. Sauté onion, green bell pepper and garlic for 2 minutes.

Step 2: Add Seasonings, broccoli & tomato sauce; lower flame, cover and cook 5 to 7 more minutes till broccoli is crisp-tender. Lift out of skillet with a slotted spoon, to drain. Serve with whole wheat toast and butter.

BROCCOLI, THAI

1 onion, chopped	1 cup strained tomato pureé
Juice of 1 lemon	1/2 green bell pepper, chopped
1 clove garlic, sliced	1/4 teaspoon black pepper
1/2 teaspoon salt	
2 tablespoons corn oil	
6 cups broccoli flowerets, cut in 3/4-inch chunks	
3 tablespoons Muhammad's Thai Sweet & Sour Sauce™ (pg.307)	
1/2 yellow chili pepper, roasted , skin & seeds discarded, and finely chopped	

Step 1: Sprinkle lemon juice over broccoli; drain.

Step 2: Mix Thai Sauce and tomato pureé.

Step 3: Heat oil in a large skillet over a medium flame. Add the onions, garlic, yellow chili pepper and salt & black pepper. Sauté 2 to 3 minutes. Add broccoli, green bell pepper and spreading them evenly over the sautéing vegetables, add Thai sauce & tomato pureé mixture. Cover skillet, lower flame and cook 5 to 8 minutes till broccoli is crisp-tender; pour from skillet, into colander to drain-if necessary, leaving any charred vegetables in skillet-if necessary.

Step 4: Serve with Fish Dish (pg.267)

√ Cauliflower & Broccoli, Thai

Omit 3 cups broccoli, add *3 cups cauliflower, cut in 1/2-inch chunks* along with broccoli.

←――――――――――――――――――――――――――――――――→

CABBAGE

1/2 head of cabbage, roughly chopped	1 onion, chopped
4 tablespoons extra virgin olive oil	1/2 green bell pepper, chopped
1/8 teaspoon Hungarian paprika	1/8 teaspoon turmeric
1/8 teaspoon salt	1/4 teaspoon black pepper

Step 1: Heat oil in a large skillet over a medium flame. Sauté onion, green pepper and seasonings 2 minutes. Add cabbage; lower flame, cover and cook 5-7 minutes until cabbage is crisp-tender, add some water if needed during cooking; pour from skillet, into colander to drain-if necessary, leaving any charred vegetables in skillet-if necessary.

√ Basic Cabbage

See *Steaming Vegetables Section,* (Pg.72)

←――――――――――――――――――――――――――――――――→

GARAM MASALA CABBAGE

ROAST

2 onions, chopped	3 cloves garlic, sliced
1 red bell pepper, sliced	1/2 green bell pepper
1/2 teaspoon salt	1/4 teaspoon black pepper
2 tablespoons corn oil	
1 tablespoon butter	

1/2 teaspoon Muhammad's Garam Masala™ (pg.307)

1 Serano pepper, roasted , skin & seeds discarded, and finely chopped

STEAM

6 cups cabbage, cut in 2-inch pieces

Step 1:To Roast Vegetables: Coat a baking sheet with corn oil & butter; arrange onion, garlic, green & red bell peppers and Serano pepper on sheet; sprinkle with Garam Masala, salt and pepper. Bake in a preheated 400°F for 15 minutes or until golden browned.

Step 2:To Steam: Meanwhile boil 1-inch of water with a little oil and salt in the bottom section of a double steamer over a medium flame, place cabbage in top basket; Cover, turn down flame to low and steam a few minutes or until done; pour from skillet, into colander to drain-if necessary, leaving any charred vegetables in skillet-if necessary. Mix with roasted vegetables on a warm platter. Serve hot.

BROCCOLI & CAULIFLOWER

ROAST

1 onion, chopped

1 green bell pepper, sliced

1/2 teaspoon salt

1 teaspoon Muhammad's Seasoning™ (pg.307)

1/8 teaspoon Muhammad's Garam Masala Seasoning™ (pg.307)

2 cloves garlic, sliced

2 tablespoons corn oil

SAUTÉ & STEAM

3 cups cauliflower flowerets

2 tablespoons corn oil

1 green chili pepper, roasted , skin & seeds discarded, and finely chopped

3 cups broccoli flowerets

Step 1:To Roast Vegetables: Coat a baking sheet with corn oil; arrange onion, garlic and green bell pepper on sheet; sprinkle with seasonings, salt and pepper. Bake in a preheated 400°F for 15 minutes or until golden browned.

Step 2:To Sauté & Steam: Meanwhile heat oil in a skillet over a medium flame, sauté cauliflower, for 3 minutes; add broccoli, and chili. Cover skillet, turn down flame to low and steam a few minutes or until done; pour from skillet, into colander to drain-if necessary, leaving any charred vegetables in skillet-if necessary. Mix with roasted vegetables on a warm platter. Serve hot.

CARROTS

1 pound or bunch of carrots

1/8 teaspoon salt

1 tablespoon butter

1/8 teaspoon black pepper

Step 1: Clean, peel and diagonal slice carrots.

Alternate Step 2:To Boil: Cook them, immersed, in about 2 inches of boiling water until they are crisp-tender, about 10 to 12 minutes; drain.

Alternate Step 2:To Steam: Place in the top-portion of a steamer set over bottom-portion of steamer filled with 1-inch water, dash of salt and a few drops of oil; bring bottom-portion to a rolling boil over a medium flame and steam vegetables until they are crisp-tender, about 8 to 10 minutes; drain. Serve hot with butter, salt and pepper.

√ **Basic Carrots**

See *Steaming Vegetables Section*, (Pg.72)

√ **Puréed Carrots**

Strain carrots through a Foley™ mill, or purée them in a food processor. Season and add a *dash of mace*. Reheat and serve.

←——————————————————————————————————→

CANDIED CARROTS

1 pound or bunch of carrots	5 tablespoons butter
1/4 cup brown or Raw™ sugar	1/2 teaspoon mace
1/8 teaspoon salt	1 teaspoon vanilla or amaretto flavoring

Step 1: Clean, peel and diagonal slice carrots.

Step 2:To Steam: Place in the top-portion of a steamer set over bottom-portion of steamer filled with 1-inch water, dash of salt and a few drops of oil; bring bottom-portion to a rolling boil over a medium flame and steam vegetables until they are crisp-tender, about 8 to 10 minutes; drain.

Step 3: Add ingredients to pot and continue cooking until the syrup thickens and carrots are glazed. Serve hot.

←——————————————————————————————————→

CARROT CLOUD

1 pound or bunch of carrots	1 stick of butter
1 1/2 tablespoon unbleached flour	1/2 cup brown or Raw™ sugar
1/2 teaspoon mace	
1 orange, juiced & rind, finely grated	

Step 1: Clean, peel and diagonal slice carrots.

Step 2:To Steam: Place in the top-portion of a steamer set over bottom-portion of steamer filled with 1-inch water, dash of salt and a few drops of oil; bring bottom-portion to a rolling boil over a medium flame and steam vegetables until they are crisp-tender, about 8 to 10 minutes; drain.

Step 3: Mash and beat with an egg beater until fluffy.

Step 4: Place sugar, flour and orange juice in a pan and over a medium flame continue to stir until it begins to simmer. Lower the flame and continue to cook for 5 minutes. Remove from flame, add butter.

Step 5: Add grated orange rind to carrots, blend well and add syrup slowly folding a little at a time into the carrots.

Step 6: Pour carrot mixture into a buttered 1 1/2 quart baking dish and bake in a preheated 400° F oven for 30 minutes. (uhmm)

←——————————————————————————————————→

CREAMED CAULIFLOWER AU GRATIN

1 head of cauliflower	1 1/2 cups White Sauce (pg.97)
1/8 teaspoon salt	1/2 cup Cheddar or Parmesan, grated
1/8 teaspoon white pepper	

Step 1: Separate and clean cauliflower flowerets.

Step 2:To Steam: Place in the top-portion of a steamer set over bottom-portion of steamer filled with 1-inch water, dash of salt and a few drops of oil; bring bottom-portion to a rolling boil over a medium flame and steam vegetables until they are crisp-tender, about 8 to 10 minutes; drain.

Step 3: Arrange steamed flowerets in a baking dish. Cover with White sauce. Spread cheese evenly over top and season with salt & pepper.

Step 4: Bake in a preheated 400°F oven until bubbly throughout and golden brown on top, about 15 to 20 minutes.

CAULIFLOWER AND PEPPERS

1 head of cauliflower	1/2 green bell pepper, sliced
2 tablespoons butter, melted	1/2 red bell pepper, sliced
2 tablespoons extra virgin olive oil	1/8 teaspoon paprika
1/2 teaspoon salt	
1/4 teaspoon black pepper	
1/2 green chili pepper, roasted , skin & seeds discarded, and finely chopped	

Step 1: Separate and clean cauliflower flowerets.

Step 2: Arrange in pot in an upright position, stem parts down. Sprinkle spices over top, lay peppers in this arrangement. Pour butter and olive oil over top. Don't add water.

Step 3: Cover tightly and cook over a low flame until crisp-tender. Start checking for doneness after 7 to 10 minutes. Please do not over cook. Lift out of skillet with a slotted spoon, to drain.

BRAISED CELERY

1 pound celery	2 tablespoons butter
Vegetable Stock (pg.81)	1/8 teaspoon salt
1/4 teaspoon black pepper	

Step 1: Wash the celery, cut off leaves and wide pale bottoms. Cut the stalks in diagonal slices 3 inches long.

Step 2: Heat butter in a skillet over a medium flame; sauté celery slices 5 minutes. Add 1/2 inch of stock; cover, reduce flame and cook over low heat until the celery is crisp-tender, about 10 to 15 minutes. Place celery in a serving dish.

Step 3: Rapidly boil the remaining liquid in the pan until it has reduced to a few tablespoons. Pour over celery and serve.

√ Braised Celery au Gratin

Place the *braised celery* in a baking dish and pour a little of the cooking liquid over it. Sprinkle 1/2 *cup freshly grated Parmesan cheese* over top and place under the broiler flame until the cheese has melted.

←——————————————————————————————→

LONG ISLAND CORN ON THE COB

6 ears of Golden corn	4 tablespoons cold butter

SPICE & HERB MIXTURE

1/2 teaspoon parsley, chopped	1/8 teaspoon oregano
1/4 teaspoon salt	1/4 teaspoon black pepper
1/4 teaspoon red pepper flakes	
1/4 teaspoon thyme	

(Optional: try a variety of herb mixes, 1/8 teaspoon each of cilantro, marjoram, tarragon, or chives)

Step 1: Husk the corn and place each ear on foil or parchment paper, coat each ear of corn with butter and sprinkle on spice & herb mixture; wrap ears of corn in foil.

Alternate Step 2:To Bake: Bake in a preheated 400°F oven for 25 minutes.

Alternate Step 2:To Grill: Roast the foil-wrapped (do not grill parchment paper) corn on a grill or over hot coals, for 25 minutes, turning once half way during the roasting.

√ Indian Corn On The Cob

Omit butter & spice mixture and use *2 tablespoons Garam Masala II (pg.307)* blended with *1 tablespoon lemon or lime juice.*

√ Moroccan Corn On The Cob

Omit spice mixture and use *2 tablespoons Moroccan Mint Blend(pg.307).*

←——————————————————————————————→

BAKED-STUFFED EGGPLANT

2 Eggplant	1 onion, chopped fine
1 cup tomatoes, chopped or pureé	2 tablespoons grated cheese
1 cup Whole Wheat Bread crumb (pg.188)	1 clove garlic, chopped

4 tablespoons butter	1 egg, well beaten
1 tablespoon chopped parsley	1/8 teaspoon salt
1/8 teaspoon black pepper	Dash of cinnamon

Step 1: Place the Eggplant in a large pot filled with boiling salted water and boil for 12 to 15 minutes; drain, then cut in half lengthwise. Remove the pulp gently without breaking the sensitive skin. Chop the pulp, including the seeds, and mix in the bread crumbs; set aside.

Step 2: Melt the butter in a skillet. Add the onion, garlic, tomato & parsley and cook a few minutes; add to the eggplant pulp mixture; add salt & pepper. Stir in the beaten egg and toss to mix thoroughly.

Step 3: Carefully put the eggplant shells (skins) in a well buttered round baking dish to cover the bottom and sides. Spoon the eggplant pulp mixture into the dish, sprinkle grated cheese & cinnamon over top.

Step 4: Bake in a preheated 375°F oven for 35-40 minutes.

Step 5: Unmold and serve hot with a rice or fish dish or cold with a salad

⟵⟶

GOLDEN EGGPLANT

1 medium eggplant	4 tablespoons butter
1 egg, beaten well	1/4 teaspoon Hungarian paprika
1/4 extra virgin olive oil	1/8 teaspoon black pepper
1/8 teaspoon salt	
1 cup Whole Wheat Herb Bread crumbs, toasted (pg.192)	

Step 1: Wash, peel and slice eggplant into 1/2 inch thick pieces.

Step 2: Let drain on paper towels for 30 minutes; pat dry.

Step 3: Dip eggplant slices in egg, then dip in bread crumbs, coat well, shake off excess crumbs.

Step 4: Heat butter, until it sizzles, in a large skillet over a medium flame; sauté coated Eggplant slices until browned on both sides.

Step 5: Remove from skillet and arrange in a pan, add seasonings, cover and steam in a preheated 350°F oven for 20 minutes.

⟵⟶

ROASTED GARLIC

4 whole heads of garlic	4 tablespoons extra virgin olive oil
1/2 tablespoon parsley, chopped	1/4 teaspoon black pepper
1/4 teaspoon salt	

Step 1: Position each garlic head on its side and cut 1/2 inch off straight across the top. Peel off the papery skin. Put the heads in a small baking dish. Pour the olive oil over the garlic, cover with foil and

place in a preheated 350°F oven for 30 minutes.

Step 2: Remove foil, turn garlic over, and cook 30 minutes longer. Sprinkle with parsley & pepper.

←——————————————————————————————→

OKRA

1 pound okra	5 tablespoons butter
1/8 teaspoon salt	1/8 teaspoon black pepper

Step 1: Clean and cut off the stems of okra.

Step 2: Drop them in a large pot of boiling water for 1 minute; drain.

Step 3: Melt the butter, until it sizzles, in a skillet over a medium flame; sauté the okra for 3 minutes, shifting the pan frequently to coat the okra with butter. Lift out of skillet with a slotted spoon, to drain. Season with salt & pepper and serve hot.

√ Okra with Whole Wheat Bread Crumbs

Drop the okra into boiling water and cook for 3 minutes. Drain. Sauté *3/4 cup freshly made whole wheat Herb bread crumbs (pg.192)* in the butter until browned. Add okra, salt & pepper, and toss together for one minute.

←——————————————————————————————→

SAUTÉED OKRA

(Have two skillets, one with a lid, ready for this recipe.)

1 1/2 pound okra	2 onions, chopped
1 green bell pepper, chopped	2 cloves garlic, minced
1/2 cup strained tomato pureé	4 tablespoons butter
1 tablespoon unbleached flour	1/8 teaspoon black pepper
1/8 teaspoon salt	

1/4 teaspoon Muhammad's Seasoning™ (pg.307)

1/2 yellow chili pepper, roasted , skin & seeds discarded, and finely chopped

Step 1: Clean and cut okra into 1/2 inch pieces. Sprinkle with seasonings & flour.

Step 2: Melt half the butter (2 tablespoons), until it sizzles, in skillet, add okra and sauté on a low flame until tender about 2 minutes, shaking the pan often to coat the okra with butter & to keep from browning, cut off flame.

Step 3: In the other skillet, over a medium flame, add rest of butter (2 tablespoons), until it sizzles, and sauté vegetables for about 5 minutes. Add tomato pureé, cover, reduce flame to low, steam for 5 minutes.

Step 4: Pour okra into steaming vegetables and continue steaming for 5 more minutes. Lift out of skillet with a slotted spoon, to drain. Serve hot.

BAKED OKRA

(Have a skillet and a roaster-with lid ready for this recipe.)

1 pound okra,

3 onions, chopped

1 cup strained tomato pureé

Dash of cinnamon

1/8 teaspoon black pepper

1 red chili pepper, roasted , skin & seeds discarded, and finely chopped

1 green bell pepper, chopped

1 garlic clove, chopped

4 tablespoons butter

1/8 teaspoon salt

Step 1: Clean okra, cut off stem, arrange in roaster with red chili pepper and have ready for sauteed vegetables.

Step 2: Melt the butter, until it sizzles, in skillet over medium flame, sauté onions, pepper & garlic until golden light-brown, add tomato pureé. Continue cooking for 5 minutes.

Step 3: Pour over okra in prepared roaster, season, cover and cook in a preheated 350°F oven until okra is done.

ROASTED ONIONS & HERBS

(Have a skillet and·10-inch earthenware dish or casserole ready for this recipe.)

3 yellow onions, peeled & halved

2 tablespoons extra virgin olive oil

2 tablespoons butter

1/8 teaspoon salt

1/8 teaspoon black pepper

1 clove garlic, chopped

4 fresh sage sprigs

6 thyme sprigs

1 cup non-alcohol white wine

2 fresh rosemary sprigs

Step 1: In a large skillet, heat butter and oil, over a medium-high flame. Add onions, cut-side down, and sauté, shifting around skillet to ensure even cooking, until browned, about 10 minutes.

Step 2: Turn over on curved-side, add garlic and cook 3 more minutes.

Step 3: Line bottom of baking dish with sage, rosemary and thyme sprigs. Arrange onions, browned side up, on herbs. Pour in non-alcohol wine. Sprinkle with salt & pepper. Cover with aluminum foil. Bake in a preheated 375°F oven 45 minutes to 1 hour or until soft enough to pierce with a knife. Serve hot.

GLAZED BABY WHITE ONIONS

1 pound baby white onions

5 tablespoons unsalted butter

1 1/2 tablespoons honey

1/8 teaspoon salt

Step 1: Drop the onions into a pot of boiling water and boil for 5 minutes; drain and peel.

Step 2: Melt the butter in a skillet over a medium flame and stir in the honey; add the onions and cook for 8 minutes or until onions are golden brown, shaking pan often to coat the onions with the glaze. Lift out of skillet with a slotted spoon, to drain.

Step 3: Season with salt and serve with vegetables or rice.

←──────────────────────────────────→

ONION RINGS

2 large onions, in 1/4 inch slices	2 eggs, well beaten
2/3 cup whole wheat flour	Corn oil for deep frying
1/8 teaspoon salt	
1/2 teaspoon Muhammad's Seasoning™ (pg.307)	

Step 1: Separate the onion slices into rings.

Step 2: Mix Muhammad's seasoning and beaten eggs together in a bowl. Soak the onions rings in this mixture. In a separate bowl mix the flour with salt, and dip the rings into this mixture, coating them all over.

Alternate Step 3:To Deep Fry: Heat oil to 370°F and deep-fry the rings several at a time until golden on both sides. Pat free of oil with paper towels, place in a warmed baking dish while frying the rest. Serve with fish.

Alternate Step 3:To Bake: Arrange on two parchment lined baking sheets 1-inch apart; bake in a pre-heated 350° oven, until golden brown. Pat free of oil with paper towels; serve in a warm baking dish with fish.

←──────────────────────────────────→

GREEN PEAS WITH TOMATOES

1 pound of peas	2 tomatoes, chopped
1 onion, chopped	1 garlic clove, chopped
1/2 green bell pepper	4 tablespoons butter
1/8 teaspoon cinnamon	
1/8 teaspoon salt	
1/4 cup Whole Wheat Bread crumbs, toasted (pg.188)	
1/4 teaspoon Muhammad's Seasoning™ (pg.307)	

Step 1: Melt the butter in a large skillet over medium flame, add onion, garlic and pepper. Sauté until golden light-brown; add tomato, toasted crumbs, seasonings and a few spurts of water if needed, mix well. Add peas and seasonings, cover and simmer on a low flame. For young peas start checking for tenderness after 6 minutes or up to 20 minutes for older peas. Lift out of skillet with a slotted spoon, to

drain. Serve hot with rice..

GREEN PEAS AND CARROTS

1 pound peas	1/2 bunch carrots, thin diagonal slices
1 green bell pepper, sliced	2 onions, chopped large pieces
4 tablespoons unsalted butter	1/8 teaspoon black pepper
1/8 teaspoon salt	
1/8 teaspoon cardamom seeds, roasted & ground	

Step 1: Melt butter, until it sizzles, in a large skillet over medium flame, add onion & pepper. Sauté 2 minutes; add carrots, peas & seasonings and add a few spurts of water if needed, mix well. Cover and reduce flame to low and simmer. After ten minutes start checking for tenderness in young peas & carrots or up to 20 minutes for older peas. Lift out of skillet with a slotted spoon, to drain. Serve hot.

STUFFED PEPPERS
(IMPORTANT: Read entire recipe before proceeding)

3 large green bell peppers, halved & seeded	1 onion, finely chopped
1 cup Whole Wheat Bread crumbs (pg.188)	1 cup Cheddar cheese, grated
1 cup cooked Rice (pg.121)	3 tablespoons extra virgin olive oil
2 tomatoes, peeled & coarsely chopped	1/4 teaspoon salt
2 tablespoons parsley, minced	1/2 teaspoon savory, crumbled
1/4 teaspoon black pepper	
1 green chili pepper, roasted , skin & seeds discarded, and finely chopped	

Step 1: Oil a large shallow baking dish that has the room to fit the 6 pepper-halves in a single layer.
Step 2: Cook the bell peppers in boiling water for 1 minute; drain and set aside.
Step 3: Heat oil in skillet sauté onion until golden brown.
Step 4: Transfer onions to a bowl, add cooked rice, green chili pepper, cheese, tomatoes, parsley, savory, and salt & pepper, and mix well; loosely fill each pepper half with some of the mixture. Sprinkle the tops with the bread crumbs.
Step 5: Bake in a 350°F preheated oven for 30 to 40 minutes or until crumbs are lightly browned.

PLANTAINS

Choose plantains referred to as 'yellow plantains' or 'sweet plantains' also so-called "cooking plantains". They are very large, yellow and firm. A Caribbean grocery store or farmers market will be able to show you how to choose ripe plantains. Two renditions of how to cook them are presented here. The first is a boiling or steaming method the second a traditional fry method.

BOILED OR STEAMED PLANTAINS

4 large ripe plantains	Juice from 2 limes
2 cups water	1/8 teaspoon salt
3 tablespoons butter	1/8 teaspoon black pepper

BOIL METHOD

Step 1: Peel & diagonal slice plantains into thirds (about 3 inches) and cut each piece in half lengthwise.

Step 2: In a shallow saucepan bring water and lime juice to boil over a high flame and cook 10 to 12 minutes until tender when pierced with a fork.

Step 3: Remove from water, drain, place on a warm platter, season with salt & pepper and butter.

STEAMING METHOD

Step 1: Peel & diagonal slice plantains into thirds (about 3 inches) and cut each piece in half lengthwise.

Step 2: In a steamer bring water and lime juice to boil over a medium flame and cook 12 to 15 minutes until tender when pierced with a fork.

Step 3: Remove from steamer, drain, place on a warm platter, season with salt & pepper and butter.

CARIBBEAN FRIED PLANTAINS

2 ripe plantains	3 tablespoons corn oil
1 tablespoon extra virgin olive oil	Slices of lime
2 tablespoons unsalted butter	1/4 teaspoon black pepper
Plum-Rhubarb Ketchup (pg.111)	1/2 cup whole wheat flour
1/4 teaspoon salt	

Step 1: Peel & diagonal slice plantains to form oblong sizes 1/4 inch thick. Spurt juice of one slice of lime over plantains; dredge plantains in flour.

Step 2: Heat corn & olive oil in a large skillet over a medium flame; add butter; when the butter begins to sizzle, place plantains in hot oil/butter; cover; cook plantains 2 to 3 minutes or until golden brown ; uncover; turn over and allow to brown further, about 2 to 3 minutes or until golden brown.

Step 3: Drain on paper towels, then serve on a warm platter with salt, pepper, Plum-Rhubarb Ketchup & slices of lime as garnish. Or serve with another flavored Ketchup (pg.111)

SPICED BAKED POTATOES

6 large red potatoes   Extra virgin olive oil

6 tablespoons butter   aluminum foil

6 large bay leaves

HERB & SPICE MIXTURE

Dash of Muhammad's™ Seasoning (pg.307)   1/2 teaspoon red pepper flakes

1/2 teaspoon oregano   1/2 teaspoon thyme

1 teaspoon parsley, finely chopped   1/2 teaspoon salt

1/2 teaspoon black pepper

Step 1: Thoroughly scrub potatoes with a vegetable brush; coat each one with olive oil; place them slightly apart from each other on a bed made from the bay leaves on piece of aluminum foil atop a baking sheet and sprinkle herb & spice mixture on each side and make a mound of herb mixture atop each potato.

Step 2: Place an oven-proof bowl half-full with boiled water on lower oven rack; place baking sheet on top oven rack and baked in a preheated 450°F oven for 1 hour for large potatoes; 50 minutes for medium; and 45 for small potatoes. Remove from oven; scrap off bay leaves, charred herb & spice mixture and discard; reserve 1 tablespoon of toasted herbs which haven't been charred and place in a warmed platter.

Step 3: Pierce baked potatoes apart with knife while they are very hot and add 1 tablespoon of butter to inside of potato; sprinkle some of the toasted herbs equally over each potato.

√ Crusty Baked Red Potatoes

For a thick, crackly potato skin, allow them to bake 2 hours for large, 1 1/2 hours for medium. Most of the herbs will be charred, but overall the potatoes will be flavored well.

√ Stuffed & Spiced Baked Potatoes

Cut the baked potato in half lengthwise and scoop out the white pulp, leaving the skins intact. Beat until fluffy, adding 2 to 4 *tablespoons milk or cream* per potato, 1 *tablespoon butter*, and an additional 1/8 *teaspoon herb & spice mixture*. Refill the skin shells and sprinkle 2 *Tablespoons grated cheese* over tops. If the potatoes are at room temperature, reheat them in a 400°F oven for 20 minutes. If chilled, reheat them for 30 minutes.

MASHED BAKED POTATOES

BAKED POTATOES

6 large Idaho potatoes

12 bay leaves

corn oil

aluminum foil

HERB & SPICE MIXTURE

Dash of Muhammad's Seasoning™ (pg.307)

1/2 teaspoon oregano

1/2 teaspoon basil, finely chopped

1 tablespoon parsley, finely chopped

1/4 teaspoon dill

1/4 teaspoon coriander seeds, ground

1/2 tablespoon rosemary

1/2 tablespoon thyme

1/2 tablespoon chives, finely chopped

MASHED POTATO INGREDIENTS

1/2 to 2/3 cup sour cream

1/2 teaspoon parsley, finely chopped

1/4 teaspoon black pepper

1 green chili pepper, roasted , skin & seeds discarded, and finely chopped

2 tablespoons butter (optional)

1/2 teaspoon salt

Step 1:For The Baked Potatoes: Thoroughly scrub potatoes with a vegetable brush; coat each one with corn oil; place them slightly apart from each other on a bed made from the bay leaves on piece of aluminum foil atop a baking sheet and sprinkle herb & spice mixture on each side and make a mound of herb mixture atop each potato.

Step 2:For The Baked Potatoes: Place an oven-proof bowl half-full with boiled water on lower oven rack; place baking sheet on top oven rack and baked in a preheated 450°F oven for 1 hour for large potatoes; 50 minutes for medium; and 45 for small potatoes. Remove from oven; scrap off bay leaves, charred herb & spice mixture and discard; reserve 1 tablespoon of toasted herbs which haven't been charred and sprinkle in a bowl with potatoes and mash (do not mash until smooth but until rustic); discard skins—if desired.

Step 3:For The Mashed Potato Ingredients: Add sour cream, butter-if using, green chili, parsley, salt and pepper and whip until just incorporated, but not smooth. Serve on a warm platter with a Fish Dish.

√ Mashed Baked Red Potatoes

Substitute the 6 large Idaho potatoes with *6 large Red potatoes.*

√ Mashed Navy Bean & Baked Potatoes

Add *2 cups thick navy bean pureé* to mashed potatoes in bowl and use an additional *1/2 cup sour cream.*

SAUTÉED SPINACH

1 package spinach

1 garlic clove, sliced thin

1/8 teaspoon salt

Slice of lemon 1/8 teaspoon butter

4 tablespoons extra virgin olive oil

1/2 teaspoon chopped parsley

1/8 teaspoon black pepper

Step 1: Rinse spinach thoroughly, let drain in a colander, pat dry as much as possible with a towel.

Step 2: Heat 4 tablespoons of olive oil in a large skillet over medium heat. Sauté garlic until light-golden. Turn up flame to high, add spinach and parsley (be careful of splattering water from wet spinach when it hits hot oil) cover and cook 3 minutes, turn heat to medium, cook 1 to 2 minutes more, for 5 minutes total.

Step 3: Lift out of skillet with a slotted spoon, to drain. Serve on a warm platter with a splash of lemon juice, salt & pepper.

√ Oriental Sautéed Spinach

Sprinkle *1 teaspoon superfine sugar* over spinach after placing in skillet. And proceed with recipe.

CREAMED SPINACH

1 package spinach

1/4 cup shallots, minced

1 cup buttermilk

1/8 teaspoon salt

2 tablespoon extra virgin olive oil

1 tablespoon unbleached flour

Pinch of mace

1/8 teaspoon black pepper

Step 1: Rinse spinach thoroughly, let drain in a colander.

Step 2:To Steam: Place in the top-portion of a steamer set over bottom-portion of steamer filled with 1-inch water, dash of salt and a few drops of oil; bring bottom-portion to a rolling boil over a medium flame and steam spinach until they are crisp-tender, about 3 minutes; drain.

Step 3: Heat 2 tablespoons of olive oil in a large skillet over medium heat. Sauté shallots 2 minutes.

Step 4: Add steamed spinach. Combine flour & buttermilk then pour into skillet, add seasonings and cook a few minutes.

BAKED SQUASH & NAVY BEANS

2 yellow squash, well-scrubbed

4 large plum tomatoes, finely chopped

4 cloves garlic, minced

2 medium zucchini, well-scrubbed

2 cups cooked Navy Beans (pg.70)

1 tablespoon oregano

3 tablespoon extra virgin olive oil

5 ounces shredded mozzarella (Optional)

1/4 teaspoon salt

1/4 teaspoon black pepper

1 tablespoon coriander seeds, roasted & ground

2/3 cup Whole Wheat bread crumbs (pg.188)

Step 1: Wash and cut squash & zucchini diagonally into 3/4-inch chunks.

Step 2: In a large bowl combine zucchini, squash, navy beans, tomatoes, garlic, coriander, oregano, olive oil, salt, pepper and if utilizing cheese, mix well.

Step 3: Transfer to a well greased, 1 1/2 quart baking dish.

Step 4: Bake in a preheated 350°F for 40 minutes.

Step 5: Remove from oven. Sprinkle bread crumbs on top.

Step 6: Return to top rack of oven and bake until zucchini is tender and bread crumbs are golden brown, about 15 minutes. Serve hot.

SAUTÉED SUMMER SQUASH

1 pound summer squash

3 tablespoons butter

1/8 teaspoon salt

1/8 teaspoon black pepper

Step 1: Wash, peel and cut squash diagonally into 3/4-inch dices.

Step 2: Melt butter, until it sizzles, in a skillet over a low flame, sauté squash about 8 minutes. Lift out of skillet with a slotted spoon, to drain. Season to taste.

SUMMER SQUASH

1 pound squash

2 onions, chopped

1 tablespoon chopped parsley

2 tablespoons extra virgin olive oil

1/8 teaspoon Hungarian paprika

1/8 turmeric

1/8 teaspoon salt

1/8 teaspoon black pepper

Step 1: Wash, peel and cut squash diagonally into 1/2-inch dices.

Step 2: Heat oil in a skillet over a medium flame, sauté onions for one minute, add squash, parsley and seasonings. Cover skillet, turn down flame to low and steam a few minutes, and shake skillet once and a while to toss ingredients around until done. Lift out of skillet with a slotted spoon, to drain. Serve hot.

ZUCCHINI PATTIES

3 medium zucchini, well-scrubbed

1 onion

3 eggs, slightly beaten

3 ounces Cheddar cheese, grated

2 tablespoons extra virgin olive oil

1/8 teaspoon black pepper

1 cup Whole Wheat Herb Bread crumbs (pg.188)

1 clove garlic, finely chopped

1/8 teaspoon salt

Step 1: Grate zucchini, with skin left on, and onion and remove excess liquid by squeezing or a strainer.

Step 2: In another bowl, add eggs; add cheese, garlic, seasonings, zucchini & onion mixture and bread crumbs. Mix well.

Step 3: Heat oil in a large skillet over medium-high flame.

Step 4: Place heaping tablespoons of mixture into skillet; flatten into patties with back of spoon. Cook until golden brown, turn and continue cooking until both sides are golden brown. Lift out of skillet with a slotted spoon, to drain. Serve hot.

BROILED TOMATOES & CHEESE

4 large tomatoes

1 clove garlic, minced

1 teaspoon salt

1 teaspoon fresh oregano

1 teaspoon fresh marjoram

1 cup Whole Wheat Herb Bread Crumbs, buttered (pg.192)

1/2 cup Parmesan cheese, grated

1/4 teaspoon black pepper

1/4 teaspoon fresh rosemary

Step 1: Cut the tomatoes in half and arrange then cut side up in a buttered 1 1/2 quart baking dish.

Step 2: Combine the remaining ingredients and sprinkle evenly over tomatoes.

Step 3: Broil under the broiler, until the crumbs are golden brown and the tomatoes are heated. Please do not over cook or the texture and shape of tomatoes will wimp. Serve with fish.

WHITE TURNIPS

2 pounds white turnips

1 tablespoon parsley, chopped

1/2 teaspoon salt

2 to 4 tablespoons butter

1/4 teaspoon black pepper

Step 1: Peel turnips and cut into quarters, in a bowl toss with parsley.

Step 2:To Steam: Place in the top-portion of a steamer set over bottom-portion of steamer filled with 1-inch water, dash of salt and a few drops of oil; bring bottom-portion to a rolling boil over a medium flame and steam vegetables until they are crisp-tender when pierced with a knife, about 8 to 10 minutes; drain. Serve hot with butter, salt and pepper.

√ **Mashed Turnips**

After steaming, mash with a fork, then add *1/2 to 2/3 cup of heated-heavy cream/ 2 tablespoons soft-ened butter/ 1 teaspoon grated lemon rind/ 1 tablespoon Herbes De Provence II (pg.94)/ 1/2 teaspoon salt and 1/4 teaspoon black pepper.* Beat with an electric beater until smooth.

VERSATILE VEGETABLES
THE STAPLE FOR MOST MAIN DISHES
(Have a steamer and skillet ready for this recipe.)

4 cups string beans	4 carrots
4 red potatoes, frenched cut (Optional)	1 red bell pepper, sliced
1 green bell pepper, sliced	8 radishes, sliced
2 onions, chopped	1 tablespoon parsley, chopped
4 cloves garlic sliced	
3 tablespoons extra virgin olive oil	
1 red chili pepper, roasted , skin & seeds discarded, and finely chopped	

Step 1: Wash all vegetables. French cut string beans into 1 inch pieces. Peel carrots & diagonal cut in 1/4 inch slices.

Step 2:To Steam: Place carrots, string beans, radishes and if utilizing potatoes in the top-portion of a steamer set over bottom-portion of steamer filled with 1-inch water, dash of salt and a few drops of oil; bring bottom-portion to a rolling boil over a medium flame and steam vegetables until they are crisp-tender when pierced with a knife, about 8 to 10 minutes; drain; transfer to a large bowl; add red chili pepper.

Step 3:To Sauté: Heat oil in a large skillet over high flame; sauté onions, garlic and parsley for 2 to 3 minutes or until light brown, add bell peppers and sauté for 2 more minutes. Transfer to bowl with steamed vegetables. Toss everything together in bowl.

√ **We Can:**

√ Serve HOT by adding *butter* and mixing with *brown rice.*

√ Serve HOT by adding *butter* and mixing in *1 tablespoon Herbes De Provence II (pg.94)* along with the parsley during **Step 3**.

√ Add to a multiple of baked fish dishes.

√ Serve COLD by adding *quartered tomatoes* and a *dressing.* (SEE SALAD DRESSINGS pg.181)

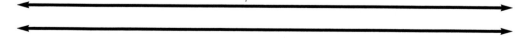

7. SALADS & SALAD DRESSINGS

INFO ON SALADS:

The Most Honorable Elijah Muhammad says don't make a whole meal from the salad. Utilize it as an accompaniment. We eat a small salad near the beginning of our meal as a traditional appetizer, and/or a full salad midway, and a fruit bowl near the end of our meal.

CLASSIFICATION OF SALAD INGREDIENTS:

A WIDE VARIETY OF SALAD GREENS

Greens are the foundation for salads. The most preferable are the deep-green leaf type, for they contain an abundance of chlorophyll, vitamins and minerals. The lighter color green leaves are mainly composed of water. All ingredients should be thoroughly washed and/or scrubbed well before utilizing.

ICEBERG LETTUCE: Compact, all-purpose and crisp. But, due to the fact that it is not dark green to the core, it is not highly nutritional.

BUTTER or BOSTON LETTUCE: Its head is loose and has large, dark green, soft leaves and a tender heart. Its delicate flavor is best complimented with a light dressing.

BIB LETTUCE: Smaller than a Boston lettuce, yet similar in texture and is shaped like a green rose. Their cup shaped leaves make excellent salad shapes.

LEAF or GARDEN LETTUCE: Long, loose, deep-green leaves with rust-colored crimpled edges. Excellent by itself with a light dressing of lemon and herbs. The leaves go in any salad.

RED-LEAF LETTUCE: A loose-leaf garden variety with leaves tinged in red. They look and tastes good in any kind of mixed green salad.

ESCAROLE: A broad-leafed endive, dark-green, sharp in taste. It can be a little tough on the outside, though the heart is always tender. Best utilized when chopped with other greens.

CHICORY: Also known as endive, has flat green spiky leaves that have a mild to pleasing bitter taste and is very decorative.

WATERCRESS: Dark-green, the small flat leaves have a peppery taste that mixes well with other greens. Like a basis for a salad, in tossed green salad, finger salad, garnish, chopped in sandwiches, or with citrus fruits like oranges and grapefruit. It is vital from a nutritional viewpoint.

BELGIAN ENDIVE: The thin, long blanched leaves add a contrast of color, texture, and a slightly bitter taste in a mixed salad. The crisp leaves, left whole or broken into rustic pieces, hold their shape. A salad can be made of just endives, beets and olives with a spurt of vinaigrette.

SPINACH: Wash well and utilize occasionally. It is best when the leaves are young, in a tossed salad composed of a chopped hard-cooked egg.

ROMAINE: Deep-green, large spearlike leaves that are utilized as a base, a garnish, served alone or in a tossed green salad. It has a crunchy, sharper taste than leaf lettuce. When young   the tender heart can be served whole, though frequently the leaves are torn into bite-size pieces; romaine holds up well to an assertive dressing.

CHINESE CABBAGE: Has long, tight head and pale-green wide leaves with a white center section and mild to strong flavor. The firm white center is often cut out and steamed as a vegetable. The flavor is mild cabbagy. Does well with a lemon dressing.

ARUGOLA or ROCKET: A couple of arugola leaves add a dominate flavor to a green salad.

GREEN CABBAGE: Often mixed with green salad, raw vegetables, fruits, slaws, or served alone.

CELERY TOPS or BEET TOPS: Use when young and tender as an addition to green salads, potato salad and vegetable salads.

NASTURTIUM LEAVES: Of the pungent juice and long-spurred, usually yellow, orange, or red irregular flower, used as a green background decoration for fruit salads.

SWISS CHARD: When very young use in a green salad.

SALAD COMPANIONS

Are the small and decorative garnish additions to the main dish. They consist of sprigs of herbs like thyme, parsley, dill, sage, watercress, etc., or radish roses and other shaped-hard vegetables. A refresher like little lettuce cups filled with fruit or vegetable salad, or small molded gelatin salads. Limit the use of dressings and depending on the place of the salad in the meal it ought to be appealing. Use alone or in combination to give variety in contrast, taste, texture and color to a mixed green salad. What we do choose to include make sure it is just a very light and delicate accent.

Raw Vegetables:

AVOCADO: Peel just before serving, then slice, chunk or dice. When storing the unused portion, rub exposed inner flesh with lemon juice, keep the seed or stone in the center, wrap with plastic wrap, and refrigerate.

BABY ZUCCHINI: Just scrub well, do not peel, and cut into thin slices.

CARROTS: Peel, then grate or julienne or make in to curls for a garnish, or make diagonal slices with a potato peeler.

CELERY: Use the inner tender stalks (the leaves are to pronounced for a mixed salad). Slice, julienne or dice.

CUCUMBERS: Scrub well. Leave unpeeled and score, or semipeeled, if tender and young. Dice or cut into slivers.

SWEET RED or GREEN PEPPERS: Scrape out seeds and remove inner ribs, then slice into rings, julienne or dice.

JERUSALEM ARTICHOKES: Peel, then dice, cut into slivers or julienne.

FENNEL: The bulb is julienned or chopped and some of the feathery green once and a while can be used. The flavor is strong, use sparingly.

RADISHES: Scrub well, slice grate or shape into roses.

SCALLIONS or SPRING ONIONS: Diagonal chop, using most of the green if tender.

TOMATOES: If the skins are tough, score, then drop into a pot of boiling water for 45 seconds to allow skin to peel easily, then gently squeeze the seeds out, slice or cut into wedges. Leave cherry tomatoes whole or halve them.

Raw Fruits:

APPLE: Peel or leave unpeeled and dice or slice into 1/16ths.

GRAPEFRUIT: Peel while whole and separate by segments.

PEAR: Peel or leave unpeeled and dice or slice into 1/16ths. Excellent in a winter salad with slightly bitter greens.

ORANGE: Peel whole and separate by segments or cut across into slices.

Fresh Herbs:

Toss these fresh herbs on a green salad or mixed in with the dressing: *chives, parsley, thyme, tarragon, basil, summer savory* (good with cooked vegetables), *dill* (good with cucumbers),*chervil, marjoram, cilantro, or a little oregano or rosemary.*

PARSLEY: Sprigs are usually a garnish, though Italian-flat parsley can be minced or chopped and served in green salads, in sandwiches or on hor dóeuvres. Chew on a few leaves after a meal to refreshen breath.

MINT LEAVES: Used as garnish for accompaniment salad, main dishes, desserts or cocktails. Chew on a few leaves after a meal to refreshen breath.

GARNISH or APPETIZER COMPLEMENTS

OLIVES: Green or black Mediterranean, ripe can be stuffed with celery, carrot sticks, pimentos or cream cheese. Pit and slice. Roll in olive oil to bring back gleam. Put a few in a green salad; put plenty in a composed salad made of tomato slices, string beans and Muhammad's Lemon Dressing™ (pg.181), where they are left whole.

PIMIENTO: Put some in a composed salad, sliced or chopped.

CAPERS: A pickled flower bud of this plant, used as a pungent condiment in sauces, relishes, and various other dishes. Drain and rinse if very salty. Use sparingly in small pieces or mashed into the dressing. The flavor can be overwhelming.

RADISH ROSES: Cut off root and stem ends. Cut lengthwise slits through top of radish, but leave the bottom uncut. With tip of knife, press into open petals. let set in ice water until the petals unfold.

RADISH ACCORDIONS: Cut off root and stem ends. Make slits horizontally, almost through radish, and set in ice water until radish expands.

COTTAGE CHEESE: Good for a lunch salad, arranged on top in attractive mounds or scoops and sprinkled with chopped scallions, chives and dusted with paprika.

CREAM CHEESE BALLS: Prepare like cottage cheese.

CHEESE FRUITS: Cheese Apples: Tint cream cheese with red vegetable coloring. Shape into miniature apples and insert a few cloves to represent blossom and stem ends. Cheese Pears : Utilize pale-green coloring and shape into pears. Cheese Oranges: Utilize orange coloring for carrots. Cheese Bananas: Utilize yellow coloring and shape into bananas. The coloring can be brushed on cream cheese instead of incorporating in. A little turmeric can be used instead of yellow coloring, egg yolk hard-cooked and grated instead of orange coloring and sieved or strained spinach instead of green coloring, if you prefer.

FRENCH-CUT TOMATOES: Slice very thin vertically from stem to blossom end to form wedges.

TOMATO FLOWERS: Use small, firm tomatoes. Peel or leave unpeeled. With a small knife, divide each tomato into eights, cutting almost through to the base. Spread into a petalled shape and stuff with cream cheese mixture, deviled egg or mixture of avocado saturated in lemon juice. Garnish with black Mediterranean olives and serve on lettuce leaves.

CELERY CURLS: Cut large stalks into 2-inch pieces. Make lengthwise slits, very close to each other, from each end of the pieces, leaving 1/2 inch uncut in the center. Soak 1 hour in ice water until the slit ends form into curls.

HARD-BOILED EGGS: quartered or chopped eggs are more appropriate to a substantial salad, but when grated they can be formed into a Mimosa effect, having globular heads of small flowers with protruding stamens, to the green salad.

CARROT CURLS: Peel (room temperature) large carrots. Then thinly scrape carrot with vegetable peeler. Fasten with toothpick, soak in ice water until the curl is set.

BEETS: Cook beets, then dice or julienne, add to green salad. Goes well with an endive, chicory and parsley salad.

FRINGED CUCUMBERS: Carrots, radishes or beets are scored lengthwise with a fork, then sliced vertically.

NAVY BEANS: Cooked, scatter one tablespoon per serving in a large salad.

CROUTONS: Must be fresh. Good for contrasting texture in a salad. Use the garlic & herb croutons to enhance the flavor to salad. (See 8.BREADS pg.188)

←—————————————————————————————————————→

TOSSED & COMPOSED GREEN SALADS

GREEN SALAD should glitter and be composed of dirt-free, chill crisp greens, fresh oil, light touch of vinegar and/or fresh lemon juice, salt, black pepper, and a variety of herbs & spices like mustard, herbs, and aromatics as accents. There are plenty of ways to vary your dressings with herbs, garlic, cheese, etc. (See SALAD DRESSINGS pg.180).

Green salads should be dressed lightly just before serving or made available at table for self service. Most greens should be bite size, about a square inch, torn by hand instead of chopped, with the smaller leaves or the heart simply pulled apart, though the shape left intact. Sauté to light brown onions and garlic, but scallions & chives are milder and more subtle.

Some Ideas to vary our tossed green salads
- When using left-over vegetables, like snow peas, carrots, string beans or beets, add them to salad greens before tossing.
- Blue cheese crumbled over greens just before serving taste great.
- Grated red cabbage, carrots, raw beets, young turnips, thinly sliced green or sweet red peppers, or cucumbers. Toss in along with dressing.
- String beans are all purpose topping for green salads.
- Slices of peeled avocado (saturated with lemon juice) alternated with wedges of tomato can be arranged on tossed salad after dressing has been mixed into salad.
- Scatter 1/2 cup of whole wheat croutons throughout salad.
- Top with sliced hard-cooked egg or thin slices of radish.

←—————————————————————————————————————→

COMPOSED SALAD is one that has been symmetrically arranged, the ingredients systematically combined and placed on a platter or plate. Imaginatively construct ingredients to contrast colors and textures in a circle on a plate or an oval on a platter. Example: On a bed of watercress form a circle of sliced tomatoes alternated with slices of cucumber with chopped parsley sprinkled on top, place a few halved hard-boiled eggs, sprinkled with black pepper and a small bunch of cooked string beans with a few slivers of sauteed garlic on top.

With a composed salad be creative, but basically the three main ingredients should each make up about 1/3rd of the salad, and the salad should be large enough to have about 1 cup per person being served.

Some Ideas to vary our composed salads
- Diced cooked potatoes, cooked leeks, slices of fish sausage links (See 16 FISH pg.267), & halved hard-boiled eggs (pg.125).
- Cold cooked brown rice, sliced sweet onions, cucumber, & steamed and flaked whiting-served cold.
- Red Delicious apple wedges-sprinkled with nutmeg, Belgian endive & soft cream cheese.
- Asparagus, papaya slices, & grapefruit sections.
- Black olives, artichoke hearts, Raw snow peas & cilantro.

STANDARD TOSSED & COMPOSED GREEN SALAD RECIPES

SPRING SALAD BOWL

1 cup water cress, chopped	2 cups lettuce, bite-size pieces
1 cup young radishes, sliced thin	1/2 cup red or green onions, sliced
2 cups tomato wedges	2 cucumbers, sliced
1 cup carrots, thin diagonal slices	French Dressing II (See pg.182)

Step 1: Combine all ingredients in a large salad bowl and pour the dressing evenly over all.

CAESAR SALAD

4 small heads romaine lettuce	1/2 cup Parmesan cheese, grated
1 egg, Soft-Boiled (pg.125)	1 to 2 anchovy fillets
6 tablespoons olive oil	2 teaspoons Dijon Mustard (pg.108)
3 tablespoons lemon juice	1/2 teaspoon black pepper
1/8 teaspoon salt	
1 1/2 cups Herb & Garlic Whole Wheat Croutons (pg.202)	

Step 1: Trim the heads of lettuce to the hearts and leave whole, rinse in cold water and dry thoroughly.
Step 2: In a bowl, mash the anchovies; mix in the olive oil & lemon juice, whisking briskly; add mustard, egg and blend.
Step 3: Place the lettuce in a salad bowl, pour the dressing over, and toss the salad gently until the dressing has been incorporated, using your hands is the best way to incorporate mixture. Add the remaining ingredients, toss slightly and serve.

√ Quick & Easy Caesar Salad

Place some *greens* in a bowl, then add *1 cup Herb & Garlic Whole Wheat Croutons (pg.202)*. In a small bowl mash a *few anchovies* and blend with *dressing* and pour over greens and toss well.

⟵———————————————————————⟶

CARROT RAISIN SALAD

1 1/2 cup carrots, finely shredded   1/2 cup golden raisins

1/4 cup fresh lime juice   1/4 cup Mayonnaise (pg.183)

Lettuce leaves

Step 1: Soak raisins in lemon juice until raisins are swollen, mix with carrots, blend in mayonnaise and serve on beds of lettuce leaves.

⟵———————————————————————⟶

CHILDREN'S CARROT RAISIN SALAD

3 cups carrots, finely shredded   3/4 cup celery, thin diagonal sliced

1/4 cup red onion, thinly sliced   1/3 cup golden raisins, chopped

1/2 cup apple, julienned   1/2 cup Mayonnaise (pg.183)

1/8 teaspoon salt   1/8 teaspoon black pepper

Step 1: In a large bowl combine all ingredients, and chill before serving.

⟵———————————————————————⟶

SUMMER SALAD

2 cups cabbage, finely shredded   2 cups plum tomatoes, sliced

1/8 teaspoon black pepper   1/4 cup red onion, sliced

Muhammad's™ Lemon dressing (pg.181)

2 cucumbers, peeled, seeded & cut into 1-inch pieces

Step 1: In a large bowl combine all ingredients, and chill before serving.

⟵———————————————————————⟶

BEET & ARUGULA SALAD

3 cups baby arugula leaves   4 baby beets, sliced lengthwise

1 orange, peeled, seeded & diced

Dash of salt

1/4 cup Muhammad's™ Citrus Mayonnaise (pg.184)

Step 1: In a salad bowl combine all ingredients, and chill before serving.

← ──────────────────────────────→

ITALIAN OLIVES

3 tomatoes, peeled & diced   2 cups olives

2 cups steamed string beans, french cut   2 clove garlic, crushed

1 lemon wedge   1/4 teaspoon basil

Olive oil for soaking   1/8 teaspoon oregano

1/8 teaspoon black pepper   1/2 teaspoon parsley

Salt to taste

Step 1: Marinate olives and garlic in olive oil over night.

Step 2: Make a composed or tossed salad of tomatoes, string beans, marinated olives.

Step 3: Sprinkle seasonings and squeeze juice from lemon wedge over salad.

← ──────────────────────────────→

CARROT & TURNIP SALAD

3 cups peeled & finely shredded turnips   3 cups peeled & finely shredded carrots

1/2 cup celery, sliced thin   Lettuce-heart cups

Water cress, for garnish   French Dressing II (pg.182)

Step 1: Combine turnips, carrots & celery.

Step 2: Serve the mixture in lettuce-heart cups garnished with water cress. Serve with dressing.

← ──────────────────────────────→

CUCUMBER SALAD

2 cups celery, coarsely shredded   1/2 cup green onions, chopped

Lettuce hearts   tomato slices, chilled

Dash of paprika

Mayonnaise or Sour Cream Dressing (pg.183 or 186)

3 cucumbers, peeled, seeded & cut into 1-inch pieces

Step 1: Arrange lettuce hearts and a few tomato slices on a platter.

Step 2: In a bowl mix cucumber, celery, onions with a little dressing.

Step 3: Place a large spoonful of this mixture on the tomato slices. Sprinkle paprika on top.

← ──────────────────────────────→

CUCUMBER SALAD #2

1/2 head lettuce, coarsely shredded

1/2 cup green bell peppers, sliced

1/2 cup red bell peppers, sliced

Tropical Dressing or Thousand Island dressing (pg.185)

3 cucumbers, peeled, seeded & cut into 2-inch pieces

Step 1: Arrange lettuce, cucumber and peppers slices on a platter. Drizzle dressing on top.

RAW CHEF'S SALAD

1 small head iceberg lettuce

1 stalk celery, julienned

1/2 cup Swiss cheese, thin strips

1 teaspoon parsley, chopped

Dash of paprika

1/2 teaspoon black pepper

1 cup French or Russian Dressing (pg.182,185)

1/2 green chili pepper, roasted , skin & seeds discarded, and minced

10 radishes, trimmed, sliced

3 cups peeled tomato wedges

3 hard-boiled eggs, quartered (pg.126)

1/8 teaspoon salt

Step 1: Core the lettuce and reserve four outside leaves for the bed in which to place the salad. Arrange them around the edges of a salad bowl.

Step 2: Tear the rest of the lettuce into bite-size pieces, put in bowl, and toss with the radishes, green chili, celery and half the dressing.

Step 3: Place the tomato wedges around the inside edges of the lettuce. Sprinkle the cheese over the lettuce and vegetables.

Step 4: Arrange the hard-boiled eggs between the tomato wedges. Sprinkle seasonings over the salad. Spoon the remaining dressing over the salad.

CAULIFLOWER & CABBAGE SLAW

4 cups cabbage, shredded

2 cups peeled & grated carrots

1 red onion, chopped

3 cups cauliflower, in 1/2-inch pieces

1 zucchini, diced

1/4 cup fresh parsley, chopped

DRESSING

1/4 cup white wine vinegar or lemon juice

1/2 teaspoon dried Mexican oregano

1/4 teaspoon salt

1/4 cup olive oil

1/2 teaspoon black pepper

1/4 teaspoon dried cilantro

Step 1: In a salad bowl add the cabbage, carrots, cauliflower, onions, zucchini & parsley, toss gently.

Step 2: Whisk together the dressing ingredients and pour over the slaw and toss gently.

Step 3: Cover and refrigerate overnight to marinate & soften the hard vegetables. Toss gently again before serving.

← ─────────────────────────────────── →

LONG ISLAND COLESLAW

10 cups cabbage, shredded

1/4 onions, chopped

3/4 cup chopped green pepper

1/2 cup lemon juice

1/2 teaspoon salt

1/2 teaspoon black pepper

1/2 red chili pepper, roasted , skin & seeds discarded, and minced

1 1/2 carrots, shredded

3/4 cup chopped red sweet pepper

1 cup Mayonnaise (See pg.183)

1/2 cup golden raisins (Optional)

1/2 cup honey (Optional)

Step 1: Steam cabbage & carrots 2 minutes. Drain and thoroughly pat dry.

Step 2: In a salad bowl combine steamed cabbage, carrots, onions & peppers. If using raisins, soak them in lemon juice until plump and combine with vegetables.

Step 3: In a bowl, whisk together mayonnaise, honey (if using instead of raisins), lemon juice, salt and pepper, and pour over vegetable mixture. Toss well and serve.

← ─────────────────────────────────── →

VEGETABLES SALADS

VEGETABLES SALADS should include crisp, cooked vegetables and be balanced in proportion to their flavor, where one vegetable doesn't overwhelm the salad. Vegetables should be briefly steamed about 2 to 4 minutes, depending on how hard they are, and drained, then pat dry or cooled dry. Some skin left on vegetables is attractive and adds flavor, but tough and waxed skins should be avoided. Leftover vegetables should be used immediately before they develop the refrigerator-wilted look or get soggy.

Individual cooked vegetables, like string beans, cauliflower flowerets, broccoli flowerets, asparagus, beets, and yellow squash & zucchini are excellent by themselves with just our favorite dressing and some chopped parsley or scallions and chives, served on cups of lettuce or a bed of water cress.

Some Ideas to vary our vegetable salads
- Broccoli & cauliflower flowerets, and slices of green & red peppers.
- Steamed & sliced zucchini and yellow squash, cucumber slices, and green pepper slices.
- Steamed string beans, shredded beets, steamed red potatoes and celery slices.
- Steamed cabbage, green pepper slices, cucumber slices and onions (with

Muhammad's™ lemon dressing).
• Zucchini & eggplant slices, sautéed in olive oil, and skinned & diced tomatoes.

←——————————————————————————————→

VEGETABLE SALAD RECIPES

STUFFED TOMATO SALAD

4 large tomatoes

2 cups favorite fish or vegetable mix

4 lettuce leaves

Salad dressing or cream cheese, topping

Step 1: In a pot of boiling water, briefly dip tomatoes in for 45 seconds, to loosen skins, peel and chill. Cut out cone-shaped center. Scrape out remaining pulp and turn upside-down to drain.

Step 2: Place each tomato on a lettuce leaf and fill with favorite fish or vegetable mixture-which salad dressing has been incorporated.

Step 3: Place the cone-shaped core tops on to resemble hats, with a cream cheese ball.

←——————————————————————————————→

CAULIFLOWER, ZUCCHINI & TOMATO SALAD

3 cups cauliflower, in 1/2 in pieces

2 tomatoes

1/2 teaspoon chopped parsley

1/8 teaspoon salt

3 zucchini, scrubbed well

2 tablespoons finely chopped onion

French Dressing II (pg.182)

1/4 teaspoon black pepper

Step 1: Place whole zucchini in a large pot of boiling water for 3 minutes. Add cauliflower and cook 4 more minutes, and then add whole tomatoes and continue cooking for 45 seconds.

Step 2: Remove all from pot and drain cauliflower. Peel tomatoes & chop. Trim away ends of zucchini and slice into 1/4- slices.

Step 3: Combine all the ingredients in a bowl and toss well. Chill and serve.

←——————————————————————————————→

MAIN-COURSE SALAD RECIPES

EGG SALAD

8 hard-boiled eggs, diced

2/3 cup Mayonnaise (pg.183)

2 1/2 tablespoon lime juice

1 tablespoon parsley or dill, minced

Dark-green leaf lettuce

1/2 green pepper, finely chopped

1 tablespoon chives, minced

8 sprigs watercress, garnish

1/8 teaspoon white pepper   1/8 teaspoon Hungarian paprika

1/4 teaspoon salt

1/2 yellow chili pepper, roasted , skin & seeds discarded, and minced

Step 1: Arrange 4 crisp outer leaves of lettuce on each salad plate and put 1/2 cup of shredded lettuce on top.

Step 2: Combine the mayonnaise, lime juice, chives, parsley or dill, salt and white pepper. Mix well. Add green pepper, yellow chili and eggs; gently toss to mix.

Step 3: Place a portion of egg salad on each lettuce bed. Sprinkle with paprika and garnish with 2 sprigs watercress each. Chill and serve.

← ——————————————————————————— →

CAULIFLOWER SALAD

5 hard-boiled eggs, diced (pg.125)   1 stalk celery, finely chopped

1/2 cup Mayonnaise (pg.183)   3/4 green pepper, finely chopped

1 tablespoon lime juice (optional)   2 tomatoes, seeded & diced

2 tablespoons parsley or dill, minced   8 sprigs watercress, garnish

1/8 teaspoon black pepper   Iceberg lettuce

1/4 teaspoon salt

1 teaspoon Muhammad's Garam Masala (pg.307)

1 cucumber, peeled, seeded & cut into 1/4-inch dices

1 small head cauliflower, cut in 1/2 inch pieces

1 green chili pepper, roasted, skin & seeds discarded, and finely chopped

Step 1: Arrange 4 crisp outer leaves of lettuce on each salad plate and put 1/2 cup of shredded lettuce on top.

Step 2: Steam cauliflower for 6 minutes or until crisp-tender; drain. In a bowl gently fold with eggs, green bell pepper, celery, green chili pepper, cucumber and tomatoes.

Step 3: Combine the mayonnaise, Garam Masala, lime juice, parsley or dill, salt and black pepper; mix well; add to cauliflower mixture; gently toss to mix.

Step 4: Place a portion of cauliflower salad on each lettuce bed. Garnish with 2 sprigs water cress each. Chill and serve.

← ——————————————————————————— →

SALMON SALAD

1 1/2 cup steamed or canned salmon, flaked   1/2 cup Mayonnaise (pg.183)

1/2 cup celery, finely chopped   1 head Boston lettuce, shredded

1 tablespoon parsley, minced   3 tablespoons lemon or juice

1 teaspoons capers   1/8 teaspoon salt

1/4 teaspoon white pepper

1/8 teaspoon Muhammad's Red Hot Sauce™ (pg.307)

Step 1: On four salad plates make a bed of shredded lettuce.

Step 2: In a bowl combine the salmon, celery, capers, hot sauce, mayonnaise, lemon juice, salt & white pepper. Toss until well mixed.

Step 3: Place a portion of the salmon salad on each lettuce bed. Sprinkle with parsley. Chill and serve.

$\longleftrightarrow$

NAVY BEAN SALAD

2 cups cooked navy beans	2 cloves sautéed garlic, chopped
4 radishes, sliced	3 tablespoons chopped parsley
3 leaves basil, chopped	3 tablespoon olive oil
1 tablespoon vinegar	1/8 black pepper
1/8 teaspoon salt	
1/4 teaspoon Muhammad's Chili Powder™ (pg.307)	

Step 1: Drain the navy beans, reserving 1 tablespoon of their cooking liquid.

Step 2: Add the liquid to the garlic, olive oil, vinegar, chili powder, salt and pepper and mix well. Pour over the navy beans, toss with the radishes, and sprinkle basil and parsley over the top.

$\longleftrightarrow$

FRUIT SALADS

FRUIT SALADS are healthy and a treat at the same. Pick a favorite fruit and utilize fresh fruits. Arrangement of the choice of fruits depends on individual's taste. Preferred fruits choices are the fruits in season and ripened in the sun. (See "What chefs buy" pg.37). The quickest way to ripen fruit is to place it in a loosely sealed brown paper bag and store at room temperature. Combine many different fruits with certain vitamins and fiber types we need.

FRUIT should be prepared in large bite-size, orderly cubes, slices, balls or wedges. Toss on as a garnish a few grapes, raisins, cherries, berries or some bright jelly or conserve (see FRUIT DRESSINGS pgs.183). When fruit is pared delay oxidation by coating with acid fruit juice—citrus, pineapple. Refrigerate cut fruit and don't mix until ready to serve.

Various ingredients to add to fruit salad or as garnish
- Sweet dried fruits
- Raisins
- Candied peel

- Sliced kumquats
- Crystallized or plain ginger
- Chopped dates
- Shredded rind of lemon, lime or orange
- Mint candies—cinnamon, spearmint, peppermint, & various fruit flavors
- Celery
- Cucumber
- Mild cheese
- Cottage cheese
- Water cress
- Sprigs of mint
- Pimento

Suggested mixed combinations of raw fruits
- Mango, cantaloupe & kiwi
- Pitted cherries, pear-halves , watercress
- Apple & mint
- Banana & raisins or dates
- Pear-halves & cream cheese
- Orange & banana
- Orange & red onion
- Orange & persimmon
- Orange & figs
- Cantaloupe rings with raspberries in center
- Avocado & citrus fruit
- Pineapple, strawberry & kiwi
- Pineapple & cream cheese
- Pineapple & date
- Pineapple & mint
- Watermelon & black grapes

Apples & oranges are basic ingredients. The orange is versatile and can be prepared in many shapes—whole, sliced, cubed, skinned sections, or small wedges sliced across the sections from the core outwardly.

$\longleftrightarrow$

FRUIT SALAD RECIPES

FRUIT BOWLS

√ In a salad bowl sprinkle cinnamon and a dash of nutmeg on cut up apples and bananas and combine with orange slices, pear halves, mango chunks, cantaloupe balls, grapes and a lemon wedge.

√ In a salad bowl combine 2 papaya's cubed (reserve seeds of one papaya for topping), 2 kiwi's sliced, 2 peaches sliced, dressed with reserved seeds of papaya, 2 teaspoons corn oil, 2 teaspoons lime juice, and 2 teaspoons honey blended together. Garnish with sprigs of mint.

√ In a salad bowl combine 2 cups pineapple cubes, 2 cups cantaloupe balls, 2 cups avocado slices, 1 cup strawberry-halves, & Lime wedge.

√ In a salad bowl combine 3 cups large watermelon chunks, 1 cup kiwi quartered, 1/2 cup black grapes, sprig of mint.

←————————————————————————————————→

FRUIT SALAD COMBOS

MANDARIN SALAD

√ Make a bed of shredded lettuce or watercress and arrange on it: 2/3 cup Mandarin orange slices, a few slices of thin red onion rings, dressed with Apple Honey Dressing (pg.183).

←————————————————————————————————→

FRUIT & CREAM CHEESE BALLS

1/4 cup finely minced parsley	Lettuce leaves or water cress
8 ounces cream cheese	
Apple Honey Dressing (pg.183)	
8 peach-halves or pear-halves or thick pineapple rings	

Step 1: Shape cream cheese into eight balls, then roll balls in parsley.
Step 2: Arrange lettuce or water cress on a cold platter and place choice of fruit on top. Put a cream cheese ball in each hollow.
Step 3: Serve Fruit Salad Dressing in a separate dish.

←————————————————————————————————→

MUHAMMAD'S™ FRUIT & YOGURT

1 cup banana slices	1/2 cup orange wedges
1 cup honey dew melon balls	1 cup pineapple cubes
1/2 cup strawberry halves	4 peach halves

1/4 cup black cherry halves

2 cups yogurt

Dash of cinnamon (powdered)

4 whole sticks of cinnamon

1/4 cup red raspberries

1/2 teaspoon vanilla flavor

4 sprigs of mint, as garnish

Step 1: Arrange banana slices in a fan-shape circle on a platter. Position the peach halves at 12,3,6 & 9 o'clock of the banana circle, fill them with black cherries & red raspberries, arrange orange wedges & strawberry halves, randomly place the honeydew melon balls and pineapple cubes.

Step 2: In a small bowl blend yogurt & vanilla flavoring, insert 1 sprig of mint in cinnamon stick and place in yogurt as garnish. Set bowl next to platter as dressing.

Step 3: Arrange the other 3 sprigs of mint & 3 sticks of cinnamon using the same technique as garnish on platter. Sprinkle bananas with cinnamon (powdered).

⟵⟶

SALAD DRESSINGS

Dressed For Success

Always strive to minimize the amount of dressing. Too much dressing robs us of the healthy benefit of a salad, saturates & droops them, takes away the texture and overwhelms the taste.

A simple ratio for dressing per single serving (two cups greens) of salad is: 1 tablespoon vinaigrette or 1 1/2 tablespoons of thick mayonnaise-type dressing.

1 cup of mayonnaise will moisten 4 cups of flaked whiting or salmon.

Salad Dressing Ingredients:

LEMON: Yellow aromatic rind and juicy, acid pulp.Is less assertive than vinegar and is loaded with valuable Vitamin C. Blend with oil, honey or simply spurt on salad.

PINEAPPLE: A tropical tangy sweet juice that adds a tropical twist to dressings.

VINEGAR: Red wine & balsamic vinegar is strong; white wine & tarragon are lighter. Japanese rice vinegar are good on fruits.

OLIVE OIL: Buy quality oils. Olive oil is healthy and adds great taste. Best for green salads. (See 'THE SUPREME OIL" Pg.46).

CORN OIL: Best for Fruit salad dressing because it has neutral flavor.

MAYONNAISE: Its best to use homemade mayonnaise instead of the soybean oil loaded commercial brands. Its a basic sauce and adds body to dressings. (See "Homemade Mayonnaise" Pg.183).

HERBS & SPICES: Should be used to enhance and not overwhelm the flavor of dressing.

Try a few herb mixes (pg.94)

SWEETENERS: SWEETENERS basically go with fruit dressing.

←——————————————————————→

SALAD DRESSING RECIPES

HERB DRESSING™
For Salad & Vegetables

2/3 cup olive oil

1 clove crushed garlic

1/2 teaspoon dry mustard

1/4 teaspoon oregano

1/2 teaspoon salt

1/3 cup red wine vinegar

1 sprig fresh thyme, for garnish

1/4 teaspoon basil leaves

1/4 teaspoon crushed red pepper

1/2 teaspoon black pepper

Step 1: Combine all ingredients in a tall olive oil bottle.

Step 2: Chill to blend flavors. Then shake before serving.

√ Dijon Mustard Herb Dressing™

Omit garlic, and crushed red pepper. Add *1 tablespoon Dijon mustard, 1/2 teaspoon tarragon, 1/4 teaspoon of each basil, oregano, and thyme.*

←——————————————————————→

MUHAMMAD'S LEMON DRESSING™

(For Salad & Vegetables)

1 cup olive oil

1/2 teaspoon chives

1/4 teaspoon marjoram

1/2 teaspoon black pepper

1/2 teaspoon salt

1/4 teaspoon Muhammad's Red Hot Sauce™ (pg.307)

Juice from 2 lemons

1/2 teaspoon thyme

1/4 teaspoon oregano

Step 1: Combine all ingredients in a tall olive oil bottle.

Step 2: Chill to blend flavors. Then shake before serving.

←——————————————————————→

VINAIGRETTE™

(For Salad & Vegetables)

6 tablespoons vinegar

1 cup olive oil

181

2/3 teaspoon salt   1/2 teaspoon black pepper

Combine all ingredients in a tall olive oil bottle. Chill to blend flavors. Then shake before serving.

√ Mustard Dressing™

Add *3 tablespoons Dijon mustard, thin slice of onion, one crushed garlic clove*. Blend well.

√ Herb Vinaigrette™

Add *1 tablespoon chopped parsley, basil, tarragon & chervil.*

√ Blue Cheese Dressing™

Add *6 tablespoons crumbled blue cheese.* Blend well.

FRENCH DRESSING™

2 teaspoons dry mustard   1 cup olive oil

1/2 cup white wine vinegar   1/2 teaspoon garlic powder

1/2 teaspoon salt   1/4 teaspoon white pepper

Step 1: Combine all ingredients in a tall olive oil bottle. Chill to blend flavors. Then shake before serving.

FRENCH DRESSING II™

1/4 cup red wine vinegar   4 tablespoons minced onion

1 teaspoon Dijon mustard (pg.108)   1/2 cup corn oil

2 tablespoons sugar or honey   1 teaspoon Worcestershire sauce

1/2 teaspoon salt

1/4 teaspoon paprika

1/4 cup Muhammad's Chili Sauce™ (pg.307)

Step 1: Combine all ingredients in a tall olive oil bottle. Chill to blend flavors. Then shake before serving.

GARLIC HONEY VINAIGRETTE™

2/3 cup honey   1 cup apple cider vinegar

1/4 cup olive oil   2 tablespoons minced parsley

7 cloves crushed garlic   1/2 teaspoon black pepper

1/2 teaspoon salt

Step 1: Combine all ingredients in a tall olive oil bottle. Chill to blend flavors. Then shake before serving.

TROPICAL DRESSING™

1/8 cup honey

1/8 cup corn oil

1/4 cup pineapple juice or pureé

1/2 teaspoon salt

1/4 teaspoon Muhammad's Red Hot Sauce™ (pg.307)

1/2 cup apple cider vinegar

1 teaspoon minced cilantro

1/2 teaspoon black pepper

Step 1: Combine all ingredients in a tall olive oil bottle. Chill to blend flavors. Then shake before serving.

APPLE HONEY DRESSING™
For Fruit Salads

2/3 cup honey

1/4 cup finely grated lemon rind

Dash of salt

1/2 cup apple juice

Dash of cinnamon

Dash of nutmeg

Step 1: Combine all ingredients in a tall olive oil bottle. Chill to blend flavors. Then shake before serving.

KEY LIME DRESSING™
For Fruit Salads

1/4 cup key lime juice

1/4 teaspoon black pepper

1 tablespoon Raw sugar or honey

1/4 teaspoon Muhammad's Red Hot Sauce™ (pg.307)

1/2 cup corn oil

Dash of salt

Step 2: Combine all ingredients in a tall olive oil bottle. Chill to blend flavors. Then shake before serving.

MAYONNAISE™
(PURCHASE A HAND BLENDER, IF JUST TO MAKE THIS MAYONNAISE)

1 egg yolk (room temp.)   3/4 cup olive oil

Pinch dry mustard   1 tablespoon lemon juice

1/2 teaspoon salt

Dash of Muhammad's Red Hot Sauce (pg.307)

Step 1: Put the yolk, mustard, salt, hot sauce and olive oil in a 2-cup tall glass. The oil will rise to the top, the yolk will sink to the bottom.

Step 2: Immerse the hand blender blade through the oil until it is at the bottom of the glass in the yolk. Gently begin blending yolk part keeping the blade at bottom of cup, increase blender speed & blend until yolk thickens, then slowly raise blender up to incorporate the oil into a creamy thick foam. Then at the last moment of blending add lemon juice; chill.

√ **Practice this blending technique** with *1 or 2 yolks, 3/4 cup corn oil and 1 tablespoon vinegar* until you perfect getting the right consistency. REMEMBER TO ALLOW THE YOLK TO THICKEN DURING BLENDING BEFORE *SLOWLY* RAISING THE HAND BLENDER BLADE INTO THE OIL (FLOATING ABOVE) TO INCORPORATE INTO A THICK CREAMY FOAM. THEN AT THE LAST MOMENT OF BLENDING ADD VINEGAR AND ADDITIONAL INGREDIENTS.

√ **Mustard Mayonnaise™**

Add *1 additional teaspoon dry mustard* to ingredients before blending. (or *2 teaspoons dry mustard* if you like it stronger.)

√ **Mild Mayonnaise™**

Add *1/2 teaspoon honey* along with lemon juice during last moment of blending. Omit pinch of dry mustard & dash of hot sauce.

√ **Muhammad's Citrus Mayonnaise™**

Add *2 teaspoons orange peel zest, 2 tablespoons reduced orange juice (6 tablespoons reduced to 2 tablespoons in saucepan over low heat), 1/2 teaspoon tarragon*, &   an additional *1/8 teaspoon Muhammad's Red Hot Sauce™ (pg.307)*   along with lemon juice during last moment of blending.

√ **Moroccan Mayonnaise™**

Add *1 tablespoon horseradish, 1 tablespoon Moroccan Mint Blend (pg.95)*, and an additional *tablespoon lemon juice* along with lemon juice during last moment of blending. Use with Salads (pg.163).

Basil Mayonnaise™

Add *1 cup fresh basil leaves, minced & 1 bunch scallions-white part only, minced* along with lemon juice during last moment of blending.

Jalapeño Mayonnaise™

Add *3 jalapeño peppers, roasted , skin & seeds discarded, and pureéd/ 2 teaspoons fresh Mexican oregano leaves, minced & 3 tablespoons fresh cilantro, minced* along with lemon juice during last moment of blending.

Sun-Dried Tomato Mayonnaise™

Add *7 sun-dried tomatoes, which have been soaked in hot water 5 minutes, drained & chopped/ 1 tablespoon parsley, chopped/ 1 clove garlic, minced & 1/4 teaspoon saffron, soaked in hot water for 5 minutes* along with lemon juice during last moment of blending.

⟷

RUSSIAN DRESSING I™

1 cup Mayonnaise (pg.183)   2 tablespoons chives, finely chopped
1 teaspoon pimiento, minced
1/4 cup Muhammad's Chili Sauce™ (pg.307)

Step 1: Mix all ingredients together in a bowl.
Step 2: Chill in refrigerator for several hours. Serve chilled.
Step 3: Utilize with baked and Grilled Salmon (pg.272), vegetables or as a salad dressing.

⟷

THOUSAND ISLAND DRESSING™

1 cup Mayonnaise (pg.183)   1 tablespoon pickle relish
1/4 cup Ketchup (pg.109)
1/2 cup Muhammad's Chili Sauce™ (pg.307)

Step1: Blend ingredients together.

⟷

THOUSAND ISLAND DRESSING II™

1 cup Mayonnaise (pg.183)   2 tablespoons parsley, chopped
1 tablespoon green bell pepper, minced   1 teaspoon pimiento, chopped
1/2 teaspoon Worcestershire sauce
3 tablespoons Muhammad's Chili Sauce™ (pg.307)
1 medium tomato, peeled, seeded & chopped
1 large hard-boiled egg, peeled and chopped (pg.126)

Step 1: Place all ingredients in a bowl and blend well; chill.

LONG-ISLAND DRESSING™

(For Salad, Vegetables)

1/3 cup corn oil

2 teaspoons Worcestershire sauce

2 tablespoons orange juice

1 tablespoon lime juice

1/4 teaspoon salt

1 teaspoon onion powder

1/2 teaspoon dry mustard

2 teaspoons minced parsley

1/2 teaspoon paprika

1/4 teaspoon black pepper

Step 1: Combine all ingredients in a tall olive oil bottle. Chill to blend flavors. Then shake before serving.

SOUR-CREAM DRESSING™

(For Vegetables Salad & Fruit Salads)

1 cup sour cream

Dash dry mustard

1/4 teaspoon salt

1/8 teaspoon Muhammad's Red Hot Sauce™ (pg.307)

1 tablespoon Raw™ sugar (for fruit salad) or 1 teaspoon Raw™ sugar (for green salad)

1/4 cup Key lime juice

1/4 teaspoon white pepper

Step 1: Combine all ingredients in a small bowl and blend well. Chill.

ASIATIC DRESSING™

1/2 cup peanut or corn oil

1 tablespoon lime zest

1 tablespoon light soy sauce

1/2 teaspoon salt

1 tablespoon Tahini (pg.94)

1/2 teaspoon Muhammad's Hot Chili Paste™ (pg.307)

1/4 cup lime juice

1 clove garlic

1 tablespoon white wine vinegar

Step 1: Place lime zest, sesame seeds, and garlic in a food processor; pulse a few times until finely chopped; add remaining ingredients and process until creamy.

Step 2: Chill in refrigerator for several hours. Return to room temperature before serving.

Step 3: Utilize with Oriental baked and grilled fish or as a pasta dressing.

JAPANESE HORSERADISH DRESSING™

Japanese

1/4 teaspoon wasabi (Japanese horseradish)   1/8 teaspoon garlic powder

1 cup yogurt or sour cream   1/4 teaspoon paprika

1 tablespoon tarragon vinegar   1 tablespoon dill, chopped

1 tablespoon chives, chopped   1 tablespoon sugar

3/4 teaspoon Herbes De Provence (pg.94)

Step 1: Combine all ingredients in a small bowl and blend well. Chill.

HORSERADISH DRESSING™

1/3 cup red wine vinegar   1/4 cup light soy sauce

1/4 cup Raw™ sugar   1 tablespoon horseradish, grated

1/2 cup olive oil

Dash Muhammad's Red Hot Sauce™ (pg.307)

Step 1: Mix all ingredients together in a bowl.

Step 2: Chill in refrigerator for several hours. Return to room temperature before serving.

Step 3: Utilize with baked and grilled fish, vegetables or as a salad dressing.

RED BELL PEPPER DRESSING™

1/3 cup extra virgin olive oil   1/4 cup lemon juice

1/2 green onion, minced   2 tablespoons white wine vinegar

1 clove garlic, minced

2 large red bell peppers, roasted, skin & seeds discarded, and chopped

Step 1: Place ingredients in a food processor; pulse a few times until finely chopped; then process until creamy.

Step 2: Chill in refrigerator for several hours. Return to room temperature before serving.

Step 3: Utilize with fish salad or as a pasta dressing.

---

8. BREADS

INFO ON BREAD

Traditionally breads have been overkneaded and underrisen. Just simply knead until all the flour is absorbed and ingredients are incorporated, just a few minutes. The Honorable Elijah Muhammad says let the dough rise, punch it down, add more yeast if you want and rise again, punch it down again add more flour and yeast again if you desire. (Put the dough on your time.) Place in buttered pans or coat with soft butter then shape and roll in navy bean meal or flour and place on baking sheets and rise again till double in bulk and bake till toasty brown about 40 minutes. Then bake again. Remove from oven, cool and do not serve bread until 24 hours have lapse. Even then, toast again a few minutes.

$$\longleftrightarrow$$

BREAD & ROLL RECIPES

WHOLE WHEAT BREAD
(Have a 4 3/4-quart and a 7 3/4-quart stainless steel bowls ready)

1 package yeast

4 1/4 cups whole wheat flour‡

2 tablespoons extra virgin olive oil

1 teaspoon butter, softened (optional)

4 tablespoons navy bean meal or corn meal

1 3/4 cups warm water

2 tablespoons Raw™ sugar

1 teaspoon salt

Step 1: In a large cup dissolve the yeast in the warm water, add sugar & oil, let sit for 10 minutes. Pour flour and salt in 4 3/4-quart bowl.

Step 2: Pour yeast mixture into flour and with a strong wooden mixing spoon, mix ingredients until incorporated then knead in the bowl with your hands for a few minutes until smooth and satiny.

Step 3: Cover with 7 3/4-quart bowl to form a dome or cover with plastic wrap. Let rise 1 to 2 hours at room temperature.

Step 4: Remove cover and punch down, Cover with 7 3/4-quart bowl to form a dome or cover with plastic wrap. Let rise 1 to 2 more hours at room temperature.

Step 5: Remove cover and punch down knead for a few seconds, form into an oval loaf, coat with butter-if desired, dust loaf all over with navy bean meal or corn meal (to prevent loaf from sticking to pan), Place in a 8" x 4" loaf pan. Or omit dusting with meal and place oval loaf in a buttered loaf pan.

Step 6: Cover with 7 3/4-bowl or plastic wrap and allow to rise until double in bulk, about 30 minutes or until loaf rises 1 or 2 inches above pan rim.

Step 7: Uncover and place in a cold oven. For a "Traditional Loaf" Turn on heat to 350°F and bake until toasty brown about 45 minutes. Cool on a rack. Brush off excess meal. For a "HOW TO EAT TO LIVE™" loaf, bake for at total of 90 minutes or more.

‡ Decrease or increase the amount of flour depending on whether you want a moister or lighter loaf of bread.

(After a few times of making this nutritional loaf of bread you will discover whether to let it rise for shorter or longer periods of time or bake it at a higher or lower temperature or vary the time of baking to your desire.)

$$\longleftrightarrow$$

SOURDOUGH WHOLE WHEAT BREAD
(Have a 4 3/4-quart and a 7 3/4-quart stainless steel bowls ready)

1 package yeast	1 3/4 cups warm water
4 1/4 cups whole wheat flour‡	3 tablespoons Raw™ sugar
4 tablespoons navy bean meal or corn meal	1 teaspoon salt
1 teaspoon butter, softened(optional)	

Step 1: In a large cup dissolve the yeast in the warm water, add sugar, let sit for 10 minutes. Pour flour and salt in 4 3/4-quart bowl.

Step 2: Pour yeast mixture into flour and with a strong wooden mixing spoon, mix ingredients until incorporated then knead in the bowl with your hands for a few minutes until smooth and satiny.

Step 3: Cover with 7 3/4-quart bowl to form a dome or cover with plastic wrap. Let rise 6 hours at room temperature.

Step 4: Remove cover and punch down knead for a few seconds, form into an oval loaf, coat with butter-if desired, dust loaf all over with navy bean meal or corn meal (to prevent loaf from sticking to pan), Place in a 8" x 4" loaf pan. Or omit dusting with meal and place oval loaf in a buttered loaf pan.

Step 5: Cover with 7 3/4-bowl or plastic wrap and allow to rise about 30 minutes or until loaf rises 1-inch above pan rim. This dough may not rise as high as normal due to the longer fermentation process. (It will stretch-rise like a biscuit in the cold then heated oven).

Step 6: Uncover and place in a cold oven. For a "Traditional Loaf" Turn on heat to 350°F and bake until toasty brown about 45 minutes. Cool on a rack. Brush off excess meal. For a "HOW TO EAT TO LIVE™" loaf, bake for at total of 90 minutes or more.

‡ Decrease or increase the amount of flour depending on whether you want a moister or lighter loaf of bread.

(After a few times of making this flavorous loaf of bread you will discover whether to let it rise for shorter or longer periods of time or bake it at a higher or lower temperature or vary the time of baking to your desire.)

←――――――――――――――――――――――――――――――――――→

BASIC WHEAT BREAD

(Have a 4 3/4-quart and a 7 3/4-quart stainless steel bowls ready)

1 package yeast   1 3/4 cups warm water

3 1/2 cups whole wheat flour‡   3/4 cup unbleached flour‡

2 tablespoons sweetener*   1 teaspoon salt

1 teaspoon butter, softened(optional)

4 tablespoons navy bean meal or corn meal

Step 1: In a large cup dissolve the yeast in the warm water, add sweetener*, let sit for 10 minutes. Pour flour and salt in 4 3/4-quart bowl.

Step 2: Pour yeast mixture into flour and with a strong wooden mixing spoon, mix ingredients until incorporated then knead in the bowl with your hands for a few minutes until smooth and satiny.

Step 3: Cover with 7 3/4-quart bowl to form a dome or cover with plastic wrap. Let rise 1 to 2 hours at room temperature.

Step 4: Remove cover and punch down, Cover with 7 3/4-quart bowl to form a dome or cover with plastic wrap. Let rise 1 to 2 more hours at room temperature.

Step 5: Remove cover and punch down and knead for a few seconds, form into an oval loaf, coat with butter-if desired, dust loaf all over with navy bean meal or corn meal (to prevent loaf from sticking to pan), Place in a 9" x 5" loaf pan. Or omit dusting with meal and place oval loaf in a buttered loaf pan.

Step 6: Cover with 7 3/4-bowl or plastic wrap and allow to rise until double in bulk, about 30 minutes or until loaf rises 1 or 2 inches above pan rim.

Step 7: Uncover and place in a cold oven. For a "Traditional Loaf" Turn on heat to 350°F and bake until toasty brown about 45 minutes. Cool on a rack. Brush off excess meal. For a "HOW TO EAT TO LIVE™" loaf, bake for at total of 90 minutes or more.

* Sweeteners can be brown sugar, Raw™ sugar, honey, molasses, raisins or pure maple syrup.

‡ Decrease or increase the amount of flour depending on whether you want a moister or lighter loaf of bread. The unbleached flour makes this loaf more flexible in handling and is a good loaf to practice with until the best consistency is perfected.

(After a few times of making this loaf of bread, which is the least-nutritional of the wheats, you will discover whether to let it rise for shorter or longer periods of time or bake it at a higher or lower temperature or vary the time of baking to your desire.)

←――――――――――――――――――――――――――――――――――→

WHOLE WHEAT OAT BREAD

(Have a 4 3/4-quart and a 7 3/4-quart stainless steel bowls ready)

3 cups whole wheat flour, sifted‡	1 3/4 cup warm water
1 1/4 cups rolled oats‡	1 package yeast
1 teaspoon salt	2 tablespoons honey or molasses
2 tablespoons rolled oats, for topping	
4 tablespoons navy bean meal or corn meal, for dusting	

Step 1: In a large cup dissolve the yeast in the warm water, add honey or molasses, let sit for 10 minutes. Combine sifted flour, oats and salt in 4 3/4-quart bowl.

Step 2: Pour yeast mixture into flour and with a strong wooden mixing spoon, mix ingredients until incorporated then knead in the bowl with your hands for a few minutes until smooth and satiny.

Step 3: Cover with 7 3/4-quart bowl to form a dome or cover with plastic wrap. Let rise 1 to 2 hours at room temperature.

Step 4: Remove cover and punch down and knead for a few seconds, form into an oval loaf, dust loaf all over with navy bean meal or corn meal (to prevent loaf from sticking to pan). Sprinkle top with chaff reserved from sifting. Place in a 8" x 4" loaf pan. Or omit dusting with meal and place oval loaf in a buttered loaf pan and sprinkle top with 2 tablespoons rolled oats.

Step 5: Cover with 7 3/4-bowl or plastic wrap and allow to rise until double in bulk, about 30 minutes or until loaf rises 1 or 2 inches above pan rim.

Step 6: Uncover and place in a cold oven. For a "Traditional Loaf" Turn on heat to 350°F and bake until toasty brown about 45 minutes. Cool on a rack. Brush off excess meal. For a "HOW TO EAT TO LIVE™" loaf, bake for at total of 90 minutes or more.

‡ Decrease or increase the amount of flour or oats depending on whether you want a moister or lighter loaf of bread.

(After a few times of making this loaf of bread, which is less-nutritional than the whole wheat loaf, you will discover whether to let it rise for shorter or longer periods of time or bake it at a higher or lower temperature or vary the time of baking to your desire.) (It is less-nutritional because some of the chaff which is left in sieve after sifting is the vitamin rich germ or so-called cracked wheat.)

$\longleftrightarrow$

(SIFTED) WHOLE WHEAT BREAD

(Have a 4 3/4-quart and a 7 3/4-quart stainless steel bowls ready)

1 3/4 cup warm water	1 package yeast
1 teaspoon extra virgin olive oil	2 tablespoons sweetener*
1 teaspoon salt	
1 teaspoon butter, softened(optional)	

4 tablespoons navy bean meal or corn meal

4 1/2 cups whole wheat flour, sifted‡, (sifted chaff reserved for topping)

Step 1: In a large cup dissolve the yeast in the warm water, add sweetener* & oil, let sit for 10 minutes. Pour sifted flour and salt in 4 3/4-quart bowl.

Step 2: Pour yeast mixture into flour and with a strong wooden mixing spoon, mix ingredients until incorporated then knead in the bowl with your hands for a few minutes until smooth and satiny.

Step 3: Cover with 7 3/4-quart bowl to form a dome or cover with plastic wrap. Let rise 1 to 2 hours at room temperature.

Step 4: Remove cover and punch down, Cover with 7 3/4-quart bowl to form a dome or cover with plastic wrap. Let rise 1 to 2 more hours at room temperature.

Step 5: Remove cover and punch down and knead for a few seconds, form into an oval loaf, coat with butter-if desired, dust loaf all over with navy bean meal or corn meal (to prevent loaf from sticking to pan). Sprinkle top with chaff reserved from sifting. Place in a 8" x 4" loaf pan. Or omit dusting with meal and place oval loaf in a buttered loaf pan and sprinkle top with chaff reserved from sifting.

Step 6: Cover with 7 3/4-bowl or plastic wrap and allow to rise until double in bulk, about 30 minutes or until loaf rises 1 or 2 inches above pan rim.

Step 7: Uncover and place in a cold oven. For a "Traditional Loaf" Turn on heat to 350°F and bake until toasty brown about 45 minutes. Cool on a rack. Brush off excess meal. For a "HOW TO EAT TO LIVE™" loaf, bake for at total of 90 minutes or more.

* Sweeteners can be brown sugar, Raw™ sugar, honey, molasses, raisins or pure maple syrup.

‡ Decrease or increase the amount of flour depending on whether you want a moister or lighter loaf of bread. The sifted flour makes this loaf more flexible in handling and is a good loaf to practice with until the best consistency is perfected.

(After a few times of making this loaf of bread, which is less-nutritional than the whole wheat loaf, you will discover whether to let it rise for shorter or longer periods of time or bake it at a higher or lower temperature or vary the time of baking to your desire.) (It is less-nutritional because some of the chaff which is left in sieve after sifting is the vitamin rich germ or so-called cracked wheat. Be sure to utilize it by sprinkling over the top of loaf before baking).

$\longleftrightarrow$

BASIC WHOLE WHEAT HERB BREAD

(Have a 4 3/4-quart and a 7 3/4-quart stainless steel bowls ready)

1 3/4 cup warm water	1 package yeast
1 teaspoon extra virgin olive oil	2 tablespoons sweetener*
1 teaspoon salt	
1 teaspoon butter, softened(optional)	
1 tablespoon rosemary leaf, finely chopped	

1/4 tablespoon sage leaf, finely chopped

1/8 tablespoon marjoram leaf, finely chopped

4 tablespoons navy bean meal or corn meal

4 1/2 cups whole wheat flour, sifted‡, (sifted chaff reserved for topping)

Step 1: In a large cup dissolve the yeast in the warm water, add sweetener* & oil, let sit for 10 minutes. Pour sifted flour, herbs and salt in 4 3/4-quart bowl.

Step 2: Pour yeast mixture into flour and with a strong wooden mixing spoon, mix ingredients until incorporated then knead in the bowl with your hands for a few minutes until smooth and satiny.

Step 3: Cover with 7 3/4-quart bowl to form a dome or cover with plastic wrap. Let rise 1 to 2 hours at room temperature.

Step 4: Remove cover and punch down, Cover with 7 3/4-quart bowl to form a dome or cover with plastic wrap. Let rise 1 to 2 more hours at room temperature.

Step 5: Remove cover and punch down and knead for a few seconds, form into an oval loaf, coat with butter-if desired, dust loaf all over with navy bean meal or corn meal (to prevent loaf from sticking to pan). Sprinkle top with chaff reserved from sifting. Place in a 8" x 4" loaf pan. Or omit dusting with meal and place oval loaf in a buttered loaf pan and sprinkle top with chaff reserved from sifting.

Step 6: Cover with 7 3/4-bowl or plastic wrap and allow to rise until double in bulk, about 30 minutes or until loaf rises 1 or 2 inches above pan rim.

Step 7: Uncover and place in a cold oven. For a "Traditional Loaf" Turn on heat to 350°F and bake until toasty brown about 45 minutes. Cool on a rack. Brush off excess meal. For a "HOW TO EAT TO LIVE™" loaf, bake for at total of 90 minutes or more.

* Sweeteners can be brown sugar, Raw™ sugar, honey, molasses, raisins or pure maple syrup.

‡ Decrease or increase the amount of flour depending on whether you want a moister or lighter loaf of bread.

(After a few times of making this loaf of bread, which is less-nutritional than the whole wheat loaf, you will discover whether to let it rise for shorter or longer periods of time or bake it at a higher or lower temperature or vary the time of baking to your desire.) (It is less-nutritional because some of the chaff which is left in sieve after sifting is the vitamin rich germ or so-called cracked wheat. Be sure to utilize it by sprinkling over the top of loaf before baking).

←――――――――――――――――――――――――――→

VARIOUS WHOLE WHEAT BREADS

√ HERB BREAD

•One recipe of Whole Wheat bread dough (See pg.188).

•Omit 2 tablespoons of water from recipe.

•In **Step 2** add *1 egg & 1 to 1 1/2 tablespoons* of a combination of: *Thyme, chives, rosemary and parsley.*
PROCEED WITH RECIPE.

√ HERB & RAISIN BREAD

•One recipe of Whole Wheat bread dough (See pg.188).
•Omit 2 tablespoons of water from recipe.
•Use *1/4 cup raisins & 1 tablespoon honey* as the sweetener in recipe.
•In **Step 2** add *1 egg & 1 to 1 1/2 tablespoons* of a combination of: *Tarragon & marjoram.*
PROCEED WITH RECIPE.

√ GOLDEN RAISIN & FENNEL BREAD

•One recipe of Whole Wheat bread dough (See pg.188).
•Omit 2 tablespoons of water from recipe.
•Use *1/4 cup Golden raisins & 1 tablespoon brown sugar* as the sweetener in recipe.
•In **Step 2** add *1 egg & 1 to 1 1/2 tablespoons of fennel.*
PROCEED WITH RECIPE.

√ CARROT BREAD

•One recipe of Whole Wheat bread dough (See pg.188).
•Omit 2 tablespoons of water from recipe.
•Omit 1/2 cup of whole wheat flour from recipe.
•Use *2 tablespoons Honey* as the sweetener in recipe.
•In **Step 2** add *2 finely grated or minced carrots* and a *pinch of mace.*
PROCEED WITH RECIPE.

√ BANANA BREAD

•One recipe of Whole Wheat bread dough (See pg.188).
•Omit 2 tablespoons of water from recipe.
•In **Step 2** add *1 cup of mashed bananas* and a *pinch of mace.*
PROCEED WITH RECIPE.

√ CRUSTY LOAF

√ For a CRUSTY LOAF of bread place a pan of *hot water* on a rack in the oven while the bread is baking.

√ For a HARD-CRISP CRUST, brush the bread with *cold water* several times while the bread is baking.

√ For a SOFT CRUST, brush the bread with *melted butter* or *milk* before baking. Or brush with *corn oil* while still hot from baking.

√ For a GOLDEN-GLAZED CRUST mix an *egg yolk* and *1 tablespoon milk* and brush the bread with mixture before baking.

←————————————————————————————————→

WHOLE WHEAT FRENCH BREAD

1 3/4 cup warm water	1 package yeast
1 teaspoon salt	2 tablespoons sweetener*
1 teaspoon butter, softened(optional)	
4 tablespoons navy bean meal or corn meal	
4 1/2 cups whole wheat flour, sifted‡, (sifted chaff reserved for topping)	

Step 1: In a large cup dissolve the yeast in the warm water, add sweetener* & oil, let sit for 10 minutes. Pour sifted flour and salt in 4 3/4-quart bowl.

Step 2: Pour yeast mixture into flour and with a strong wooden mixing spoon, mix ingredients until incorporated then knead in the bowl with your hands for a few minutes until smooth and satiny.

Step 3: Cover with 7 3/4-quart bowl to form a dome or cover with plastic wrap. Let rise 1 to 2 hours at room temperature.

Step 4: Remove cover and punch down, Cover with 7 3/4-quart bowl to form a dome or cover with plastic wrap. Let rise 1 to 2 more hours at room temperature.

Step 5: Remove cover and punch down and knead for a few seconds, split dough into two equal parts, on a lightly oiled board shape by rolling and stretching into two long, cylindrical 15-inch loaves, coat with butter-if desired, heavily dust with meal or flour and place on a baking sheet and with a serrated knife make 1/4-inch deep diagonal slits 3 inches apart across the top of loaves.

Step 6: Cover with plastic wrap and let rise again until almost double in bulk.

Step 7: Uncover and place in a cold oven. For a "Traditional Loaf" Turn on heat to 350°F and bake until toasty brown about 30 to 40 minutes. Cool on a rack. Brush off excess meal. For a "HOW TO EAT TO LIVE™" loaf, bake for at total of 60 minutes or more.

√ Herb French Bread

Use one recipe of Whole Wheat-Herb bread dough (See pg.192) Proceed as above.

←————————————————————————————————→

GARLIC & HERB FRENCH BREAD
(Have a 4 3/4-quart and a 7 3/4-quart stainless steel bowls ready)

1 3/4 cup warm water

1 package yeast

1 teaspoon extra virgin olive oil

2 tablespoons honey or Raw™ sugar

1 teaspoon salt

1 teaspoon butter, softened(optional)

1 tablespoon rosemary leaf, finely chopped

1/4 tablespoon sage leaf, finely chopped

1/8 tablespoon marjoram leaf, finely chopped

4 tablespoons navy bean meal or corn meal

4 1/2 cups whole wheat flour, sifted‡, (sifted chaff reserved for topping)

TOPPING

2 minced garlic cloves

1 tablespoon extra virgin olive oil

Step 1: In a large cup dissolve the yeast in the warm water, add honey or sugar & oil, let sit for 10 minutes. Pour sifted flour, herbs and salt in 4 3/4-quart bowl.

Step 2: Pour yeast mixture into flour and with a strong wooden mixing spoon, mix ingredients until incorporated then knead in the bowl with your hands for a few minutes until smooth and satiny.

Step 3: Cover with 7 3/4-quart bowl to form a dome or cover with plastic wrap. Let rise 1 to 2 hours at room temperature.

Step 4: Remove cover and punch down, Cover with 7 3/4-quart bowl to form a dome or cover with plastic wrap. Let rise 1 to 2 more hours at room temperature.

Step 5: Remove cover and punch down and knead for a few seconds, split dough into two equal parts, on a lightly oiled board shape by rolling and stretching into two long, cylindrical 15-inch loaves, coat with butter-if desired, heavily dust with meal or flour and place on a baking sheet and with a serrated knife make 1/2-inch deep diagonal slits 3 inches apart across the top of loaves. Place some of the garlic & olive oil mixture in the slits on top of loaf.

Step 6: Cover with plastic wrap and let rise again until double in bulk.

Step 7: Uncover and place in a cold oven. For a "Traditional Loaf" Turn on heat to 350°F and bake until toasty brown about 30 to 40 minutes. Cool on a rack. Brush off excess meal. For a "HOW TO EAT TO LIVE™" loaf, bake for at total of 60 minutes or more.

‡ Decrease or increase the amount of flour depending on whether you want a moister or lighter loaf of bread.
(After a few times of making this loaf of bread, you will discover whether to let it rise for shorter or longer periods of time or bake it at a higher or lower temperature or vary the time of baking to your desire.)

√**Onion Garlic & Herb French Bread**

Add *1 onion, finely chopped & roasted* along with garlic and olive oil to topping mixture.

WHOLE WHEAT BURGER & FRANKFURTER BUNS
(Have a 4 3/4-quart and a 7 3/4-quart stainless steel bowls ready)

1 3/4 cup warm water	1 package yeast
1 teaspoon salt	2 tablespoons honey
4 tablespoons milk, for brushing	
4 1/2 cups whole wheat flour, sifted‡, (sifted chaff reserved for topping)	

Step 1: In a large cup dissolve the yeast in the warm water, add honey, let sit for 10 minutes. Pour sifted flour and salt in 4 3/4-quart bowl.

Step 2: Pour yeast mixture into flour and with a strong wooden mixing spoon, mix ingredients until incorporated then knead in the bowl with your hands for a few minutes until smooth and satiny.

Step 3: Cover with 7 3/4-quart bowl to form a dome or cover with plastic wrap. Let rise 30 minutes at room temperature.

Alternate Step 4:For Burger Buns: Remove cover and punch down and knead for a few seconds, using your hands, divide the dough into 6 pieces, on a lightly oiled board, form each into a burger bun (flat disc) shape. Brush tops with milk and arrange on baking sheet. Sprinkle top with chaff reserved from sifting.

Alternate Step 4:For Frankfurter Buns: Remove cover and punch down and knead for a few seconds, using your hands, divide the dough into 6 pieces, on a lightly oiled board, form each into a Frankfurter bun (cigar) shape. Brush tops with milk and arrange on baking sheet. Sprinkle top with chaff reserved from sifting.

Step 5: Cover with plastic wrap and allow to rise until double in bulk, about 30 minutes.

Step 6: Uncover and place in a cold oven. For a "Traditional Bun" Turn on heat to 350°F and bake until toasty brown about 20 to 25 minutes. Cool on a rack. For a "HOW TO EAT TO LIVE™" loaf, bake for at total of 40 minutes or more.

* Sweeteners can be brown sugar, Raw™ sugar, honey, molasses, raisins or pure maple syrup.

‡ Decrease or increase the amount of flour depending on whether you want a moister or lighter loaf of bread.

√ **Onion Buns**

Combine *1 onion, finely chopped & roasted in 2 tablespoons olive* and *1 clove garlic, minced* into a topping mixture and spread about 2 teaspoons of the mixture over the center of each bun in **Step 4;** PROCEED WITH RECIPE.

STANDARD HOT ROLLS

(Have a 4 3/4-quart and a 7 3/4-quart stainless steel bowls ready)

2 packages of yeast	1/4 cup hot water
2 eggs, slightly beaten	1 teaspoon salt
1 cup milk (room temp.)	2 tablespoons honey or molasses
1/4 cup corn oil or butter (softened)	
4 tablespoons navy bean meal or corn meal	
5 cups whole wheat flour, sifted, (sifted chaff reserved for topping)	

Step 1: In a large cup dissolve the yeast in the milk & hot water, add honey or molasses & oil or butter, let sit for 10 minutes. Pour 4 cups of sifted flour and salt in 4 3/4-quart bowl.

Step 2: Pour yeast mixture and eggs into flour and with a strong wooden mixing spoon, mix ingredients until incorporated.

Step 3: Cover with 7 3/4-quart bowl to form a dome or cover with plastic wrap. Let rise 20 minutes or until double in bulk at room temperature.

Step 4: Remove cover and punch down, add remaining cup of flour and knead for a few minutes, form, on a lightly oiled board, into a dozen one square inch pieces or shapes (See following suggestions in "Various Shaped Rolls").

Step 5: Dust pieces all over with navy bean meal or corn meal (to prevent rolls from sticking to pan). Sprinkle top with chaff reserved from sifting. Place on a baking sheet. Or omit dusting with meal and place pieces on a buttered baking sheet and sprinkle top with chaff reserved from sifting.

Step 6: Cover with plastic wrap and allow to rise until double in bulk, about 20 to 30 minutes.

Step 7: Uncover and place in a preheated 400°F oven and bake until toasty brown about 15 minutes. Cool on a rack. Brush off excess meal. For "HOW TO EAT TO LIVE™" rolls, bake for at total of 30 minutes or more.

VARIOUS SHAPED ROLLS

(When arranging these rolls on a baking sheet you can dust them with meal or the 'chaff reserved from sifting' or omit and simply coat the rolls with butter and line the baking sheet with parchment paper or butter the baking sheet before placing rolls on.)

Crescents—Using a rolling pin, roll out the dough for Standard Hot Rolls into a circular shape about 1/4 inch thick. Cut in pie-slice shaped pieces. Brush with *melted butter* and roll up, beginning at wide end. Curve into Crescents, arrange on buttered baking sheet. PROCEED from **Step 6** above. (There is no need to dust these with flour or meal).

Bowknot or Twists—Using your hands, roll the dough for Standard Hot Rolls to 1/2-inch thickness. Cut in pieces 8" long. Tie in knots or twist them, dust all over with meal, arrange on baking sheet.

PROCEED from **Step 6** above.

Burger Rolls—Using your hands, divide the dough for Standard Hot Rolls into 6 pieces, on a lightly oiled board, form each into a burger bun (flat disc) shape. Brush tops with milk and dust all over with meal, arrange on baking sheet. PROCEED from **Step 6** above.

Frankfurter Rolls—Using your hands, divide the dough for Standard Hot Rolls into 6 pieces, on a lightly oiled board, form each into a Frankfurter bun (cigar) shape. Brush tops with milk and dust all over with meal, arrange on baking sheet. PROCEED from **Step 6** above.

Clover Leaf Rolls—Shape the dough for Standard Hot Rolls 1-inch balls, arrange three balls together and squeeze the tops closely to each other, place the three ball clusters in each section of a buttered muffin tin, with the squeezed together areas at bottom of tin section. PROCEED from **Step 6** above.

Parker House Rolls—Using a rolling pin roll out the dough for Standard Hot Rolls until it is 1/3-inch thick. Brush with melted butter. Cut with 3-inch biscuit cutter or oval Parker House cutter. Fold each round or oval in half and lightly seal edges. Arrange 1-inch apart on a buttered baking sheet. PRO-CEED from **Step 6** above.

$$\longleftrightarrow$$

WHOLE WHEAT EGG ROLLS
(Have a 4 3/4-quart and a 7 3/4-quart stainless steel bowls ready)

1 package yeast	1 cup milk
3 eggs, beaten	1/3 cup hot water
1/2 cup sweetener*	1 teaspoon salt
1/2 cup corn oil	

5 1/2 cups whole wheat pastry flour or whole wheat flour, sifted, (sifted chaff reserved—for dusting)

Step 1: In a large cup dissolve the yeast in the milk & hot water, add sweetener & oil, let sit for 10 minutes. Pour 4 cups of flour and salt in 4 3/4-quart bowl.

Step 2: Pour yeast mixture and eggs into flour and with a strong wooden mixing spoon, mix ingredients until incorporated.

Step 3: Cover with 7 3/4-quart bowl to form a dome or cover with plastic wrap. Let rise 20 minutes or until double in bulk at room temperature.

Step 4: Remove cover and punch down, add remaining 1 1/2 cup of flour and knead for a few minutes, form, on a lightly oiled board, into a dozen square pieces or roll shapes.

Step 5: Brush with melted butter and place pieces on a buttered baking sheet or dust with reserved chaff and arrange on baking sheet.

Step 6: Cover with plastic wrap and allow to rise until double in bulk, about 20 to 30 minutes.

Step 7: Uncover and place in a cold oven, turn on heat to 350°F and bake until toasty golden brown about 20 to 30 minutes. Cool on a rack. For "HOW TO EAT TO LIVE™" rolls, bake for at total of 40 minutes or more.

* Sweeteners can be brown sugar, Raw™ sugar, honey, molasses, raisins or pure maple syrup.
(•When arranging these rolls on a baking sheet you can dust them with meal or the 'chaff reserved from sifting' or omit and simply butter the baking sheet before placing rolls on.)

⬅——————————————➡

ARABIC COFFEE BREAD

(Have a 4 3/4-quart and a 7 3/4-quart stainless steel bowls ready)

1 package yeast	1 cup lukewarm milk
2 eggs, beaten	1/3 cup molasses
1 teaspoon salt	
1/2 stick butter (room temp.)	
4 cups whole wheat flour, sifted, (sifted chaff reserved for topping)	

TOPPING

1/2 cup whole wheat bread crumbs	1 tablespoon cinnamon
2 tablespoons melted butter	2 tablespoons Raw™ sugar

Step 1: In a large cup dissolve the yeast in the milk & molasses, let sit for 5 minutes, add butter & eggs.

Step 2: Pour in 4 3/4 quart bowl, add flour and salt and with a strong wooden mixing spoon, mix ingredients until incorporated.

Step 3: Cover with 7 3/4-quart bowl to form a dome or cover with plastic wrap. Let rise 20 minutes or until double in bulk at room temperature.

Step 4: Remove cover and stir down with spoon and beat thoroughly.

Step 5: Spoon into a buttered 8" x 4" loaf pan.

Step 6: Mix the topping ingredients together and sprinkle them on the batter.

Step 7: Cover with buttered plastic wrap and allow to rise until double in bulk, about 20 to 30 minutes.

Step 8: Uncover and place in a preheated 350°F oven and bake until toasty golden brown about 40 to 50 minutes. Cool on a rack.

⬅——————————————➡

CROSS BUNS

(Have a 4 3/4-quart and a 7 3/4-quart stainless steel bowls ready
and read entire recipe before proceeding.)

3 1/4 cups whole wheat flour, sifted	1 cup lukewarm milk

1/2 stick butter (room temp.)   1 package yeast

1 whole egg, beaten   2 tablespoons sweetener*

1 teaspoon salt   1 teaspoon cinnamon

1/2 cup raisins or currants, chopped

GLAZE & TOPPING

• 1 egg yolk, beaten (to coat with before baking)

• Mix 3/4 cup confectioner's sugar, 1 teaspoon vanilla & 3 to 4 teaspoons warm water.

Step 1: In a large cup dissolve the yeast in the milk & sweetener, let sit for 5 minutes, add butter & beaten whole egg.

Step 2: Pour in 4 3/4 quart bowl, add 2 cups flour and salt and with a strong wooden mixing spoon, mix ingredients until incorporated.

Step 3: Cover with 7 3/4-quart bowl to form a dome or cover with plastic wrap. Let rise 20 minutes or until double in bulk at room temperature.

Step 4: Remove cover and stir down with spoon, add fruit, remaining flour, cinnamon and beat thoroughly.

Step 5: Again, cover with 7 3/4-quart bowl to form a dome or cover with plastic wrap. Let rise 20 minutes or until double in bulk at room temperature.

Step 6: Remove cover, stir down with spoon and knead for a few minutes, on a lightly oiled board form into a dozen square pieces or roll shapes.

Step 7: Place on buttered baking sheet.

Step 8: Brush tops with egg yolk (for glaze).

Step 9: Place in a preheated 350°F oven and bake until toasty golden brown about 20 to 30 minutes.

Step 10: For Glaze: Make a cross on top of each roll with tip of a metal spoon, using confectioner's sugar glaze mixture. Cool on a rack.

* Sweeteners can be honey, molasses or pure maple syrup.

←——————————————————————→

CINNAMON ROLLS

(Have a 4 3/4-quart and a 7 3/4-quart stainless steel bowls ready
and read entire recipe before proceeding.)

4 1/2 cups whole wheat flour, sifted   1 cup lukewarm milk

1 package yeast   3/4 cup Raw™ sugar

2 tablespoons butter (room temp.)   1/2 cup raisins

1 teaspoon salt 1 tablespoon cinnamon

2 eggs, beaten

•Milk (to coat before baking)

•Mix 3/4 cup confectioner's sugar, 1 teaspoon vanilla & 3 to 4 teaspoons warm water.

Step 1: In a large cup dissolve the yeast & sugar in the milk, let sit for 5 minutes.

Step 2: Pour in 4 3/4 quart bowl, add eggs, butter, cinnamon, 3 cups flour and salt and with a strong wooden mixing spoon, mix ingredients until incorporated.

Step 3: Cover with 7 3/4-quart bowl to form a dome or cover with plastic wrap. Let rise 20 minutes or until double in bulk at room temperature.

Step 4: Remove cover and stir down with spoon, add raisins, remaining flour and beat thoroughly.

Step 5: Knead for a few minutes, on a lightly floured board form into 16 pieces, roll each about 8 inches long and wind it into a coil.

Step 6: Arrange in two buttered 9-inch cake pans, cover with buttered plastic wrap. Let rise 20 minutes or until double in bulk at room temperature.

Step 7: Brush tops with milk.

Step 8: Place in a preheated 375°F oven and bake until toasty golden brown about 20 to 30 minutes.

Step 9: For Glaze:Spread a thin layer of the confectioner's sugar glaze mixture immediately after removing from oven.

Step 10: Cool on a rack.

WHOLE WHEAT CROUTONS

(For use in soups and salads)

√ Sautéed Whole Wheat Croutons

Step 1: Cut slices of Whole Wheat Bread (pg.188) in even cubes, removing the crusts.

Step 2: Sauté in pan with butter, turning to golden brown on all sides. Drain on paper towels.

√ Baked Whole Wheat Croutons

Step 1: Lightly butter slices of Whole Wheat Bread (pg.188) on both sides, then cut in cubes, removing the crusts.

Step 2: Bake on a baking sheet in a preheated 350°F oven, turning a few times until evenly brown.

√ Herb & Garlic Whole Wheat Croutons

Use slices of Whole Wheat Herb Bread (pg.192). Add a minced clove garlic to the butter when you sauté or butter the herb bread. Prepare by sauté or baking procedures above.

√ Whole Wheat Carrot Croutons

Use slices of Whole Wheat Carrot Bread (pg.194). Prepare by sauté or baking procedures above.

PITA BREAD™
Arabian "Khubz"

3 cups whole wheat flour, sifted‡	1 1/2 cup lukewarm water
1 1/2 teaspoons dry yeast	1/2 tablespoon extra virgin olive oil
1/2 tablespoon salt	

Step 1: In a 3-quart stainless steel bowl, sprinkle the yeast over the warm water; stir to Dissolve; Mix in 1 1/2 cups flour and stir for a minute; let this sponge sit for 10 minutes, or as long as 2 hours.

Step 2: Sprinkle the salt over the sponge and add olive oil and remaining flour and knead until elastic and smooth; cover with 4 3/4-quart stainless steel bowl; let rise until double in bulk, about 1/2 to 1 1/2 hours.

Alternate Step 3:For Commercial Bakery: The dough can be punched down again and wrapped in a plastic bag, with room to expand, and secured at opening of bag. Then, from day to day cut off pieces, allow to room temperature, then proceed to bake. The dough can be stored for up to 7 days, it will be well fermented also, adding better flavor.

Alternate Step 3: Punch down dough and divide into 8 pieces and flatten each with lightly floured hands; with a rolling pin, roll out each piece to a disc 8 to 9 inches in diameter and less than 1/4 inch thick. Cover laid out until ready to bake; do not stack.

Step 4: Place 2 disc on a heated baking sheet or heated unglazed quarry tiles and bake in a preheated 450°F oven 2 to 3 minutes, or until they "balloon".

Step 5: Wrap the baked pitas together in a large clothe to keep them soft and warm, while the remaining ones or baked.

‡ Decrease or increase the amount of flour depending on whether you want a moister or lighter pita. (After a few times of making the pitas you will discover whether to let it "balloon" for shorter or longer periods of time or bake it at a higher or lower temperature or vary the time of baking to your desire. The pitas that "balloon" well can be cut across the top and used in an envelope dough style with the precooked or prepared ingredients stuffed inside them. If, for what ever reason, the pitas don't "ballon" evenly. These can be used for "wraps".)

←——————————————————————————————————→

VEGGY WRAP BREADS™

1 1/4 cups whole wheat flour, sifted‡	3/4 cup lukewarm water
3/4 cup unbleached flour	3 tablespoons extra virgin olive oil
1/2 tablespoon salt	1 1/2 teaspoon light brown sugar
1 teaspoon baking powder	1/2 teaspoon baking soda

Step 1: In a 3-quart stainless steel bowl, combine flours, salt, baking soda & powder; make a well in the

middle; put olive oil, sugar and water in the well; stir water until sugar is dissolved; fold flour and moist ingredients until dough forms into a ball; knead until elastic and smooth.

Step 2: Divide the dough into 4 pieces; roll each into a disc; place on a lightly floured baking sheet; cover with plastic wrap; allow to rest for 30 minutes, or up to 1 hour.

Step 3: Working with one piece at a time, flatten each with lightly floured hands; with a rolling pin, roll out each piece to a disc 8 to 9 inches in diameter and less than 1/4 inch thick. Cover laid out until ready to bake; do not stack.

Step 4: Heat a skillet over a low flame; cook a wrap 2 to 3 minutes on each side.

Step 5: Stack the wraps together in a large clothe to keep them soft and warm, while the remaining ones are cooked.

‡ Decrease or increase the amount of flour depending on whether you want a moister or lighter wrap. (After a few times of making the wraps you will discover whether to let it brown for shorter or longer periods of time or cook it at a higher or lower temperature or vary the time of resting to your desire. Wrap your favorite vegetables or salads in these wraps.)

←—————————————————————————————→

CRACKERS™
Eastern Crackers

1 1/2 cups whole wheat flour, sifted‡	3/4 cup warm water
3/4 teaspoons salt	
1 tablespoon extra virgin olive oil (optional)	

OPTIONAL TOPPINGS

Grated Parmesan or Cheddar	Sunflower seeds, crushed
Cayenne pepper (Thai)	Sesame seeds
Cumin seeds	Coarse salt

Step 1: In a food processor, add flour and salt and process for a few seconds to blend. While the motor is running, add the water steadily until the dough forms into a ball, about 10 seconds. If too moist add a little more flour; if too dry add a little more water and process until a ball of dough forms. Once the ball of dough forms process for 1 minute longer.

Step 2: Place the dough on a lightly floured surface and knead a half-minute. Cover and let sit for a half-hour.

Step 3: Divide the dough into 4 pieces. Handle one piece at a time, leaving the remaining ones covered. On a lightly floured surface with lightly floured hands, flatten into a disc. Then with a rolling pin roll it out to a thin rectangle. Carefully lift the dough with two spatulas and place on a parchment lined baking sheet. Sprinkle on a topping, if desired. Cut into square crackers with a pizza cutter or knife. Spray the dough lightly with a water from a clean water sprayer.

Step 4: Bake in a 450°F to 500°F preheated oven; begin to check on them after 2 to 3 minutes. (Crackers brown from underneath.) The thinner ones will be done quicker than the thicker ones. Cook until golden brown about a total of 5 minutes. Let cool.

Step 5: Repeat steps for remaining dough.

‡ Decrease or increase the amount of flour depending on whether you want a firmer or crisper cracker. (After a few times of making the crackers you will discover whether to let it bake for shorter or longer periods of time or bake it at a higher or lower temperature or vary the time of baking to your desire.)

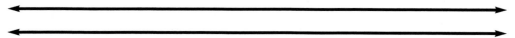

9. CAKES & MUFFINS

POINTERS ON CAKE BAKING:

A cake should be tender with a light texture.

The ingredients should be premeasured and brought to room temperature, especially the butter and eggs—If the eggs are required to be separated do so while they are cold then let sit to room temp.

Butter, which contributes to flavor, and sugar when creamed together should be light in color and fluffy to give cake a fine texture. This is usually the first ingredients in bowl.

Use medium mixing speed since high speed will heat the ingredients too quickly.

Add eggs along with flavoring next. The mixed dry ingredients should be incorporated next. It is VERY IMPORTANT to allow the whole wheat flour to rest at this point for 10 to 20 minutes to absorb the moist ingredients. If egg whites are used fold them in last.

Butter and dust pans with flour. Pans can additionally be lined with cooking parchment or wax paper. The pans should be filled with batter no more than two-thirds full. Bake cakes in center of oven with 1-inch space between pans. If you have a small oven rotate pans around every 10 minutes.

Begin testing for doneness 5 to 10 minutes before the specified baking time has elapsed. Test for doneness by inserting a toothpick in center of cake. If it comes out clean and dry, with no crumbs or batter clinging to it, the cake is done.

Remove from oven. Let them cool and shrink in their pans for 5 to 10 minutes, then turn them out on a wire rack that allow air to circulate underneath.

Allow to fully cool before frosting.

$\longleftrightarrow$

CAKE RECIPES

BANANA CAKE

2 cups whole wheat flour, sifted	1 stick butter
1 1/2 cup Raw™ sugar	1 cup mashed bananas
2 eggs (room temp.)	1 teaspoon vanilla
1/2 cup sour milk (pg.132)	1/8 teaspoon cinnamon
1 teaspoon baking soda	1/2 teaspoon salt
1/8 teaspoon mace	

Step 1: Butter, dust with flour and line with parchment a 9-inch square cake pans.

Step 2: In a 4 3/4-quart stainless steel bowl, Cream butter and sugar, add eggs one at a time, blend in, banana, vanilla & sour milk.

Step 3: In another bowl resift together the flour, cinnamon, salt & baking soda. Add gradually to moist mixture, blend well until fluffy. We can add more milk if necessary, to obtain the proper consistency.

Step 4: Pour in the prepared loaf pan.

Step 5: Bake 40 to 50 minutes in a preheated 350°F oven; test for doneness with a toothpick until it comes out clean.

Step 6: Cool cakes on wire rack 10 minutes before removing from pans, then cool completely on wire racks.

Step 7: Split the cake and fill with *Banana Cream Filling* (pg.223) Frost with *Banana Frosting* (pg.220). Sprinkle mace over top of frosted cake.

⟵⟶

LUSCIOUS CHOCOLATE CAKE

4 tablespoons cocoa	2 eggs, separated
1 1/4 cup Raw™ sugar	1 cup whole wheat flour, sifted
3/4 cups milk	1 stick butter, (room temp.)
1 teaspoon vanilla	1/2 teaspoon baking powder
1/2 teaspoon salt	1/2 teaspoon baking soda

Step 1: Butter, dust with flour and line with parchment two 8-inch round cake pans.

Step 2: In a 4 3/4-quart stainless steel bowl, Cream butter and 1 cup of the sugar, add eggs yolks one at a time, blend in cocoa, vanilla & milk.

Step 3: In another bowl resift together the flour, salt, baking powder & baking soda. Add gradually to moist chocolate mixture, blend well.

Step 4: Beat the egg whites separately until they are foamy, slowly add the remaining 1/4 cup sugar, and continue to beat until tips can be formed when whisk is pulled out of whites. Fold the whites into the batter.

Step 5: Divide the batter evenly between the prepared cake pans.

Step 6: Bake 30 to 40 minutes in a preheated 350°F oven; test for doneness with a toothpick until it comes out clean.

Step 7: Cool cakes on wire rack 10 minutes before removing from pans, then cool completely on wire racks.

Step 8: Frost with *Chocolate Frosting* (pg.219) or *Fudge Frosting* (pg.220).

⟵⟶

GOLDEN CAKE
(an excellent birthday cake)

2 cups fine cake flour	1 stick unsalted butter (room temp.)
1 cup Raw™ sugar	5 egg yolks
1 whole egg	1/2 cup milk
2 teaspoons vanilla extract	2 1/2 teaspoons baking powder
1/2 teaspoon salt	

Step 1: Butter, dust with flour and line with parchment two 8-inch round cake pans.

Step 2: In a 4 3/4-quart stainless steel bowl, Cream butter and sugar, add egg yolks and beat well. Blend in whole egg, vanilla & milk.

Step 3: In another bowl resift together the flour, salt, & baking powder. Add gradually to moist mixture, blend well.

Step 4: Divide the batter evenly between the prepared cake pans.

Step 5: Bake 20 to 30 minutes in a preheated 350°F oven; test for doneness with a toothpick until it comes out clean.

Step 6: Cool cakes on wire rack 10 minutes before removing from pans, then cool completely on wire racks.

Step 7: Frost with *Mango Frosting* (pg.220) or *Light Frosting* (pg.222).

WHOLE WHEAT BROWNIES

1 cup whole wheat flour	2 cups Raw™ sugar
3/4 cup cocoa powder	1/4 teaspoon salt
1 stick butter (room temp.)	1/4 cup corn oil
3 large eggs	1 teaspoon vanilla extract
1/2 teaspoon almond extract	

Step 1: Butter, dust with flour and line with parchment a 9-inch square cake pan.

Step 2: In a 4 3/4-quart stainless steel bowl, Cream butter and sugar, add, eggs and beat well. Blend in, cocoa, extracts & oil.

Step 3: In another bowl sift together the flour & salt. Add gradually to moist mixture, blend well.

Step 4: Pour in the prepared cake pan.

Step 5: Bake 30 to 40 minutes in a preheated 350°F oven; test for doneness with a toothpick until it comes out clean. You'll need to adapt the baking time whether the brownies come out too fudgey, or too dry.

Step 6: Cool cakes on wire rack 10 minutes before removing from pan, then cool completely on wire rack.

Step 7: Frost in thin strings across tops with *Cream Cheese Frosting* (pg.221) or for Double Chocolatey taste *Chocolate Frosting* (pg.219).

POUND CAKE

1/4 cup milk	2 sticks unsalted butter (room temp.)
2 cups whole wheat flour, sifted	1 2/3 cup Raw™ sugar
5 eggs	1/2 teaspoon salt

3/4 teaspoon mace

Step 1: Butter, dust with flour and line with parchment a 9 x 5-inch loaf pan.

Step 2: In a 4 3/4-quart stainless steel bowl, Cream butter and sugar, add, eggs one at a time and beat well.

Step 3: In another bowl resift together the flour, mace & salt. Add gradually to moist mixture, blend well. Add milk, adjusting the amount to obtain desired consistency.

Step 4: Pour in the prepared loaf pan.

Step 5: Bake 1 hour 15 minutes to 1 hour 40 minutes in a preheated 325°F oven; test for doneness with a toothpick until it comes out clean. You'll need to adapt the baking time wether the cake comes out too gooey, or too dry

Step 6: Cool cakes on wire rack 10 minutes before removing from pan, then cool completely on wire rack.

CARROT CAKE DELIGHT

1 cup carrots, puréed

5 eggs, separated

1 teaspoon vanilla

1/4 teaspoon salt

1 cup Raw™ sugar

1 cup cream, whipped

Pinch nutmeg

Step 1: Butter, dust with flour and line with parchment a 9-inch springform pan.

Step 2: In a 4 3/4-quart stainless steel bowl, mix 5 egg yolks, sugar and salt and beat lightly blend in, carrot purée & vanilla.

Step 3: In another bowl beat the egg whites until tips can be formed when whisk is pulled out of whites. Fold the whites into the batter.

Step 4: Pour in the prepared 9-inch springform pan. Sprinkle nutmeg over top.

Step 5: Bake 40 to 50 minutes in a preheated 400°F oven; test for doneness with a toothpick until it comes out clean.

Step 6: Cool cakes on wire rack 10 minutes before removing from pans, then cool completely on wire racks.

Step 7: Serve with a spoonful of whipped cream placed on top of each slice.

CHEESE CAKE

FILLING

16 ounces cream cheese (room temp.)

1/4 cup white flour

1/2 cup Raw™ sugar

1 cup heavy sweet cream

4 eggs, separated (room temp.)

1 teaspoon vanilla

1/4 teaspoon salt   1 tablespoon lemon juice

CRUST

1/2 stick unsalted butter (room temp.)   1/2 teaspoon mace

1/2 teaspoon cinnamon

1/4 cups light-brown sugar

10 "shortbreads" cookies, broken into 1" bits (pg.228)

Step 1: Crust:Place the shortbread cookies in a food processor fitted with the metal chopping blade. Process until they form crumbs. In a bowl combine the crumbs, butter, cinnamon, mace, and light brown sugar, mix well. Press into the bottom of a 9-inch springform pan. Bake 8 to 10 minutes in a pre-heated 350°F oven, then set on a wire rack and cool.

Step 2:To make filling: Change oven temperature to 325°F. In a 4 3/4 quart stainless steel bowl beat the 4 egg yolks well, add flour, 1/4 cup of the Raw™ sugar, sweet heavy cream, vanilla, lemon juice & salt and blend, add cream cheese and beat well until smooth.

Step 3: Beat the egg whites separately until they are foamy, slowly add the remaining 1/4 cup Raw™ sugar, and continue to beat until tips can be formed when whisk is pulled out of whites. Fold the whites into the cream cheese mixture. Pour the filling into the crumb crust and smooth top.

Step 4: Bake for 1 to 1 1/2 hour, or until set in the center and then turn off the oven with out opening the door (TRY with door OPEN to). Allow the cake to cool in the oven for 2 hours. Remove the cake from oven, allow to fully cool on a rack. Cover then chill in the refrigerator for a minimum of 8 hours. Serve sliced.

FRUIT & WHITE CHOCOLATE CHEESE CAKE

FILLING

2 1/2 pounds cream cheese (room temp.)   8 ounces white chocolate, chopped

1/4 cup heavy cream   3 eggs (room temp.)

1 cup Raw™ sugar

CRUST

2 tablespoons Raw™ sugar

11 whole chocolate graham crackers(1/3 lb)

1/2 stick unsalted butter (room temp.)

RASPBERRY, RED CURRANT COULIS

1 pint raspberries   1/2 cup superfine sugar

1 pint red currants   1 teaspoon lemon juice

1 teaspoon almond extract

GARNISH

1/2 pint raspberries   White chocolate curls or shavings

Step 1:Crust: Break chocolate graham crackers into 1" pieces, place in a food processor fitted with the metal chopping blade. Process until they form crumbs. In a bowl combine the crumbs, butter and Raw™ sugar, mix well. Press into the bottom of a 10-inch springform pan. Bake 8 to 10 minutes in a preheated 350°F oven, then set on a wire rack and cool.

Step 2:To make filling: In a small saucepan, melt the white chocolate with the cream over a low-flame, stirring frequently until smooth. Set aside to cool.

Step 3: In a 4 3/4 quart stainless steel bowl beat the cream cheese and 1 cup Raw™ sugar well. Beat in the eggs one at a time;continue mixing for 3 minutes. Pour in the cooled white chocolate mixture. Gently mix until smooth. Pour the filling into the crumb crust and smooth top.

Step 4: Bake for 1 hour, or until set in the center and then turn off the oven with out opening the door (TRY with door OPEN to). Allow the cake to cool in the oven for 2 hours. Remove the cake from oven, allow to fully cool on a rack. Cover then chill in the refrigerator for a minimum of 8 hours.

Step 5:To make Raspberry & Red Currant Coulis: Place raspberries and red currants in a bowl. Sprinkle the superfine sugar, lemon juice and almond extract on top;. Mash with a fork, then push through a fine mesh sieve, discarding the seeds. Or place all ingredients in a Foley™ mill with a fine strain and process.

Step 6:Garnish: Before serving, uncover the cheesecake. Garnish the top of the cheesecake with white chocolate curls or shavings. Arrange the 1/2 pint raspberries all over the white chocolate garnish. Cut the cake into slices and serve with the Raspberry & Red Currant Coulis swirled on each serving plate.

$$\longleftrightarrow$$

HONEY CAKE

3 1/3 cups whole wheat flour, sifted	1 cup boiled gourmet coffee
1 cup Raw™ sugar	3 eggs, well beaten
1 cup honey	2 tablespoons corn oil
2 teaspoons baking powder	1 teaspoon baking soda
1 teaspoon each cinnamon, ginger & mace	1/4 teaspoon salt
Confectioner's sugar, for dusting	

Step 1: Butter and dust with flour a tube pan.

Step 2: In a 4 3/4-quart stainless steel bowl add eggs, and beat in sugar.

Step 3: In another bowl mix honey, cooled-coffee, and corn oil. Add to egg mixture.

Step 4: In another bowl resift together flour, spices, salt, baking soda & powder. Add gradually to moist mixture, blend well until fluffy. We can add a little milk if necessary, to obtain the proper consistency.

Step 5: Pour in the prepared tube pan.

Step 6: Bake 40 to 50 minutes in a preheated 350°F oven; test for doneness with a clean knife until it comes out clean.

Step 7: Cool cakes on wire rack 10 minutes before removing from pan, then cool completely on wire racks. Dust top of cake with confectioner's sugar.

MUFFINS

INFO ON MUFFINS

Muffins are a science in themselves. Most people are use to the extra-large ones at the donut shop which are laborious to eat due to its dryness, which the donut shop hopes will encourage you to order a large coffee. The dough should be only slightly beaten and left rough looking almost resembling a stiff cookie dough than like the smooth and super thick glutinous looking batter generally made today. Due to the high absorbability of whole wheat flour decrease or increase the amount of flour depending on whether you want a moister or lighter muffin. Any fruit ingredients, especially blueberries, utilized should be frozen so when the muffins bake the fruit will retain its form and texture and won't resemble runny thick greyish-blue hue sauce scattered throughout the muffins. The muffin should be styled like a nice little tender tea cake. After 5 minutes of cooling coat the tops of muffins with one of the excellent glazes and crispy sugar coatings presented. We will enjoy a true muffin.

STANDARD MUFFINS

1 3/4 cups whole wheat flour, sifted	1 egg (room temp.)
1 tablespoon baking powder	1 teaspoon mace
1/2 teaspoon salt	1/4 cup melted butter
6 tablespoons Raw™ sugar	

1 cup sour cream or (1 cup evaporated milk and 1 teaspoon finely grated lime peel)

Step 1: Preheat oven to 350°F. Butter 2 muffin pans.

Step 2: Sift flour, mace, baking powder and salt into a bowl.

Step 3: In another bowl, beat egg, add sugar and continue beating until fluffy, gradually add melted butter then gradually add sour cream or evaporated milk & lime peel stirring till smooth. Pour into sifted dry ingredients.

Step 4: With a wooden spoon, gently fold the dry and moist ingredients together only enough to dampen the flour; for about 30 seconds; the batter should not be smooth.

Step 5: With a 2-ounce or 1/4 cup ice cream scoop, spoon into muffin pans, filling each cup about three-fourth full.

Step 6: Bake for about 25 to 30 minutes; test for doneness with a toothpick until it comes out clean.

Step 7: Cool muffins on wire rack 5 minutes before removing from pans, then cool completely on wire racks.

BLUEBERRY MUFFINS

1 3/4 cups whole wheat flour, sifted

1 tablespoon baking powder

1/2 teaspoon salt

1/2 cup Raw™ sugar

1 egg (room temp.)

1 cup sour cream

1/4 cup melted butter

1 cup frozen small blueberries

TOPPINGS
(two alternatives)

(#1 LEMON)

1/4 cup lemon juice

1 teaspoon finely grated lemon zest

1/4 cup superfine sugar

1/2 cup superfine sugar, for dipping

(#2 CINNAMON)

1/4 stick butter

Pinch of mace

1/2 teaspoon cinnamon

1/2 cup superfine sugar, for dipping

Step 1: Preheat oven to 350°F. Butter 2 muffin pans.

Step 2: Sift flour, baking powder and salt into a bowl. Mix frozen blueberries in.

Step 3: In another bowl, beat egg, add sugar and continue beating until fluffy, gradually add melted butter then gradually add sour cream stirring till smooth. Pour into flour & blueberry mixture.

Step 4: With a wooden spoon, gently fold the dry and moist ingredients together only enough to dampen the flour; for about 30 seconds; the batter should not be smooth.

Step 5: With a 2-ounce or 1/4 cup ice cream scoop, spoon into muffin pans, filling each cup about three-fourth full.

Step 6: Bake for about 25 to 30 minutes; test for doneness with a toothpick until it comes out clean.

Step 7: Cool muffins on wire rack 5 minutes before removing from pans, then coat with one of the toppings.

Alternate Step 8:To make #1 Lemon Topping: In a small sauce pan on low flame heat lemon juice and1/4 cup superfine sugar until it reduces to 1/4 cup liquid. Mix lemon zest into bowl of dipping sugar. Brush tops of muffins with liquid then dip tops into bowl of lemon zest & sugar until coated. Cool coated muffins completely on wire racks.

Alternate Step 8:To make #2 Cinnamon Topping: In a small sauce pan on low flame heat butter until melted. Mix cinnamon into bowl of dipping sugar. Dip tops of muffins in butter then dip tops into bowl of cinnamon & sugar until coated. Sprinkle the pinch of mace over muffins. Cool coated muffins completely on wire racks.

√ Red Currant Muffins with Ginger Topping.

For Muffins:Substitute *1 cup frozen red currants* for the 1 cup frozen blueberries.

For #1 Lemon Topping:Substitute *1 teaspoon finely grated ginger* for the 1 teaspoon finely grated lemon zest.

Or For #2 Cinnamon Topping:Substitute *1 teaspoon finely grated ginger* for the 1/2 teaspoon cinnamon.

√ Pineapple Muffins with Ginger Topping.

For Muffins:Substitute *1 cup diced & frozen pineapples* for the 1 cup frozen blueberries.

For #1 Lemon Topping:Substitute *1 teaspoon finely grated ginger* for the 1 teaspoon finely grated lemon zest.

Or For #2 Cinnamon Topping:Substitute *1 teaspoon finely grated ginger* for the 1/2 teaspoon cinnamon.

√ Cranberry Muffins with Orange Topping.

For Muffins:Substitute *1 cup frozen cranberries* for the 1 cup frozen blueberries.

For #1 Lemon Topping:Substitute *1 teaspoon finely grated orange zest* for the 1 teaspoon finely grated lemon zest.

Or For #2 Cinnamon Topping:Substitute *1 teaspoon finely grated orange zest* for the 1/2 teaspoon cinnamon.

√ Rhubarb Oatmeal Muffins with Orange Topping.

For Muffins:Substitute *1/2 cup diced, frozen strawberries & 1/2 cup diced & frozen rhubarb* for the 1 cup frozen blueberries. Substitute *1 cup rolled oats* for 1 cup of the whole wheat flour.

For #1 Lemon Topping:Substitute *1 teaspoon finely grated orange zest* for the 1 teaspoon finely grated lemon zest.

Or For #2 Cinnamon Topping:Substitute *1 teaspoon finely grated orange zest* for the 1/2 teaspoon cinnamon.

CHOCOLATE LATTÉ MUFFINS

1 cup whole wheat flour, sifted	3/4 cup Raw™ sugar
3 tablespoons unsweetened cocoa powder	2 teaspoons baking powder
Pinch of salt	3/4 cup buttermilk
1 teaspoon freeze-dried coffee granules	1/2 stick butter, melted
1 egg (room temp.)	1/2 teaspoon vanilla

3/4 cup chopped bittersweet chocolate

GLAZE

1/2 cup confectioner's sugar   1 to 2 teaspoons brewed coffee

Step 1: Preheat oven to 350°F. Butter 2 muffin pans.

Step 2: Sift flour, cocoa powder, baking powder and salt into a bowl. Mix coarsely chopped bittersweet chocolate in.

Step 3: In another bowl, beat egg, add Raw™ sugar and continue beating until fluffy, gradually add melted butter. In a small bowl, stir together buttermilk, vanilla and coffee granules until coffee granules dissolves then gradually add to egg mixture stirring till smooth. Pour into flour mixture.

Step 4: With a wooden spoon, gently fold the dry and moist ingredients together only enough to dampen the flour; for about 30 seconds; the batter should not be smooth.

Step 5: With a 2-ounce or 1/4 cup ice cream scoop, spoon into muffin pans, filling each cup about three-fourth full. Makes about 9 muffins.

Step 6: Bake for about 25 to 30 minutes; test for doneness with a toothpick until it comes out clean.

Step 7: Cool muffins on wire rack 5 minutes before removing from pans, then coat with glaze.

Step 8:To Make Glaze: In a small bowl stir together brewed coffee and confectioner's sugar to make thick liquid mixture. Drizzle over hot muffins and set aside until glaze is firm. Cool glazed muffins completely on wire racks.

←——————————————————————————————→

POPOVERS

2/3 cup whole wheat flour, sifted   2 eggs (room temp.)

1/3 cup unbleached flour   1 cup milk

1 tablespoon melted butter   1 teaspoon vanilla (Optional)

1/4 teaspoon salt

Step 1: Place all ingredients in a bowl and stir, without over beating.

Step 2: Half-fill buttered muffin tins. Makes about 10 popovers.

Step 3: Place in a COLD oven, set temperature to 450°F. Bake for 15 minutes, then reduce temperature to 350°F and bake for another 15 to 20 minutes. Its done when crisp outside and tender and moist inside.

←——————————————————————————————→

CURRANT CREAM SCONE

1 1/2 cup whole wheat flour, sifted   1/2 cup unbleached flour

5 tablespoons butter, frozen   1 cup black currants

1 cup cream*   3 tablespoons Raw™ sugar

1 tablespoon baking powder   1 /2 teaspoon salt

GLAZE

4 tablespoons cream   4 tablespoons sugar

Step 1: Preheat oven to 425°F.

Step 2: In a food processor, place flour, salt, baking powder and pulse a few times to mix. Add frozen butter and pulse 10 to 12 times until the mixture resembles coarse meal. Add currants and pulse 2 or 3 times to mix. Pour into a large bowl.

Step 3: Add cream to flour mixture and with a wooden spoon, gently fold the dry and moist ingredients together only enough to dampen the flour; for about 30 seconds; the batter should not be smooth. Turn out onto a lightly floured board and knead for about a minute. Place in a 8" round-cake pan and press down until it forms a smooth top and is shaped like the round pan. Turn back out to board and cut into 8 wedges.

Step 4: Arrange on a parchment lined or plain cookie sheet.

Step 5:For Glazing: Brush tops of SCONE with cream for glazing and sprinkle sugar on tops.

Step 6: Place in oven and bake for 10 to 12 minutes. Cool SCONE completely on wire racks. Serve with butter & honey or maple syrup.

*The cream can be substituted with sour cream or evaporated milk or a combination of them.

√ Raspberry SCONE with Ginger Glaze.

For SCONE:Substitute *1/2 cup chopped raspberries & 1/2 cup red currants* for the 1 cup black currants.

For Glaze:Add *1 teaspoon finely grated ginger* to the 4 tablespoons of sugar.

√ Banana SCONE with Cinnamon Glaze.

For SCONE:Substitute *1 cup diced & floured bananas* for the 1 cup black currants. Add *1 teaspoon vanilla extract* along with cream.

For Glaze:Add *1/2 teaspoon cinnamon* to the 4 tablespoons of sugar.

√ Raisin SCONE with Cinnamon Glaze.

For SCONE:Substitute *1 cup raisins* for the 1 cup black currants.

For Glaze:Add *1/2 teaspoon cinnamon* to the 4 tablespoons of sugar.

CUPCAKES

1 1/4 cups whole wheat cake flour, sifted   5 tablespoons butter (room temp.)

1 cup Raw™ sugar   2 eggs (room temp.)

2/3 cup milk

2 teaspoons baking powder

1/4 teaspoon mace

1/4 teaspoon salt

Step 1: Preheat oven to 350°F.

Step 2: Butter muffin tins for 12 cupcakes or line them with fluted paper cup.

Step 3: In a bowl cream the butter, gradually add sugar, and beat until light and fluffy. Stir in the eggs one at a time and beat well.

Step 4: Sift the flour, baking powder, mace and salt together. Add to the first mixture, then stir in the milk and beat until well combined and add more or less milk to get right consistency. Spoon into tins, filling each cup about two-thirds full.

Step 5: Bake for 15 to 17 minutes; test for doneness with a toothpick until it comes out clean.

Step 6: Cool on wire rack 5 minutes before removing from pans, then frost with *Chocolate Frosting*. (pg.219), or *Banana Frosting* (pg.220).

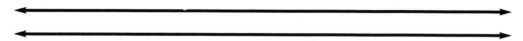

10. FROSTINGS & FILLINGS

POINTERS ON FROSTINGS & FILLINGS

•To thicken an *uncooked* frosting which has become too thin: stir in some powdered sugar.

•To thicken an *cooked* frosting which has become too thin: put it in the top of a double boiler and beat over hot water until it thicken to right consistency.

•To thin any frosting which has become too thick, very gradually beat in a few drops of hot water until proper consistency is acquired.

•When melting chocolate in the top of a double-boiler be sure to not allow any steam or a drop of water to touch chocolate, if about a teaspoon accumulates it will clump up and not get smooth, which is referred to as being "seized". To bring a seized chocolate back to a smooth consistency add about 1/4 cup water and proceed. Melting chocolate can be better achieved by using a large glass bowl and set it on top of a much smaller opening pot with 1 inch of water simmering on a low flame.

•Before frosting a cake, arrange 4-inch wide strips of aluminum foil around edge of serving plate so the cake's center will lay on plate center and the cakes' edges will lay on foil to catch any excess frosting that may drip down. After frosting remove strips of foil by slowly pulling out.

FROSTING RECIPES

BASIC CONFECTIONER'S FROSTING

3 cups confectioner's sugar	3 to 4 tablespoons hot water

Step 1: Place 3 tablespoons hot water in a bowl and thoroughly beat in the sugar until very creamy; add more hot water if necessary.

√ Alternative Flavors

Substitute *3 to 4 tablespoons of hot coffee, lemon juice, Key lime juice or orange juice* for the hot water.

Or substitute 1 1/2 teaspoon of vanilla, mint or almond extract for the hot water.

CREAM CONFECTIONER'S FROSTING

3/4 stick unsalted butter	3 cups confectioner's sugar
2 tablespoons cream	1/8 teaspoon salt

Step 1: In a bowl cream the butter and salt together, then beat in the sugar; add the cream and beat well

until creamy and smooth.

√ Alternative Colors

Tint with a few drops of vegetable coloring.

⟷

CREAMY CHOCOLATE FROSTING

2 ounces unsweetened chocolate | 2 cups confectioner's sugar
1 tablespoon butter | 1/3 cup cream, whipped
1 teaspoon vanilla

Step 1: Melt the chocolate and butter together in a glass bowl over simmering water.
Step 2: Cool to lukewarm, then stir in the whipped cream, vanilla and sugar; beat until creamy.
Step 3: Let cool.

⟷

DEEP CHOCOLATE FROSTING

3 ounces unsweetened chocolate | 3 cups confectioner's sugar
3 tablespoons butter | 1 tablespoon cocoa powder
1 1/2 teaspoon vanilla | 1/2 cup milk

Step 1: Melt the chocolate, cocoa powder and butter together in a glass bowl over simmering water.
Step 2: Cool to lukewarm, then beat in the milk, vanilla and sugar; beat until thickened.
Step 3: Let cool.

⟷

CHOCOLATE FROSTING

6 tablespoons cocoa powder | 3 tablespoons butter
2 cups confectioner's sugar | 1 teaspoon vanilla
1/3 cup milk

Step 1: In a bowl beat butter, add cocoa & continue beating while adding vanilla, milk and sugar; beat until smooth and creamy.

⟷

CREAM FROSTING
(For Chocolate Cake)

2 ounces cream cheese, softened | 3 cups confectioner's sugar
1/2 stick butter | 4 tablespoons milk

1 teaspoon vanilla extract

1/2 teaspoon almond extract

1/8 teaspoon salt

Step 1: In a bowl cream the butter, cream cheese, extracts, milk and salt together, then beat in the sugar; beat well until creamy and smooth.

BANANA FROSTING
(For Banana Cake)

1 ripe banana, mashed

1/2 stick butter

2 cups confectioner's sugar

1/2 teaspoon almond extract

Step 1: In a bowl cream the butter, banana, and extract together, then beat in the sugar; beat well until creamy and smooth.

√ Mango Frosting

Substitute *1/2 cup mashed & well drained mango* for banana.

MAPLE FUDGE FROSTING

2 ounces unsweetened chocolate, cut in bits

1 1/2 cups Raw™ sugar

1/2 stick butter

1 tablespoon pure maple syrup

1/2 cup milk

1 teaspoon vanilla

1/4 teaspoon salt

Step 1: Stir together all the ingredients except the vanilla in a heavy-bottomed sauce pan. Heat over a medium flame until it comes to a rolling boil and cook, stirring constantly, for 1 minute; cool.

Step 2: Add the vanilla and beat until thick.

VANILLA FUDGE FROSTING
(We'll need a candy thermometer)

1 1/2 cups Raw™ sugar

1/2 cup milk

1 tablespoon butter

1 teaspoon vanilla extract

1/8 teaspoon salt

1 vanilla pod, split and deseeded

Step 1: Stir together the sugar, milk and salt in a heavy-bottomed pan; add vanilla pod; bring to the boiling point over a medium flame, then cook without stirring until the mixture reaches 234°F.

Step 2: Let cool, discard vanilla pod, then beat until thick enough to spread.

Step 3: Add the vanilla extract; beat until creamy.

CARAMEL FROSTING

1 stick unsalted butter   1/2 cup dark-brown sugar
1/4 cup milk   2 cups confectioner's sugar

Step 1: Melt the butter and brown sugar in a heavy-bottomed pan over medium heat until the sugar is dissolved; add the milk and blend; cool.
Step 2: Then beat in the confectioner's sugar until thick and creamy.

MAPLE FROSTING

1 1/2 cups maple syrup   1/4 superfine sugar
2 egg whites (room temp.)   1/4 teaspoon cream of tartar
Pinch of salt

Step 1: Combine all the ingredients together in a glass bowl over simmering water. Beat until it stands in stiff peaks, 5 to 7 minutes.
Step 2: Let cool.

CREAM CHEESE FROSTING I

4 ounces cream cheese (room temp.)   2 cups confectioner's sugar
1 teaspoon vanilla   1/8 teaspoon salt

Step 1: In a bowl, beat all the ingredients together until creamy and light.

CREAM CHEESE FROSTING II
(We'll need a candy thermometer)

1 cup Raw™ sugar   8 ounces cream cheese, cold
1/4 cup fruit juice   1 egg yolk

Step 1: Boil the sugar and juice without stirring in a heavy-bottomed pan until the mixture reaches 240°F.
Step 2: While the sugar syrup is cooking, beat the egg yolk well.
Step 3: Slowly pour the 240°F syrup over the beaten yolk, beating constantly.
Step 4: Beat in 1 ounce pieces of the cold cream cheese until it is all incorporated. Continue to beat

until the frosting is of spreading consistency.

BUTTER ALMOND FROSTING

4 cups confectioner's sugar   1 stick butter (room temp.)

1 teaspoon almond extract   3 tablespoons milk

Step 1: In a bowl, beat together butter, sugar, almond and milk until smooth and creamy.

LIGHT FROSTING

1 1/2 cups superfine sugar   2 egg whites (room temp.)

2 teaspoons vanilla   1/8 teaspoon salt

1/4 cup water

Step 1: Combine together water, sugar, egg whites, & salt in a glass bowl over simmering water. Beat with mixer until it stands in stiff peaks, 5 to 7 minutes. Remove from the heat and continue to beat until thick enough to spread.

Step 2: Add the vanilla before spreading.

√ Citrus Frosting

Omit the vanilla and substitute *1/4 cup lemon & lime or orange juice* for the water. Add *1 teaspoon finely grated lemon or orange rind* before spreading.

Note: Keep refrigerated if not utilizing within a few hours for it will dry out.

GLAZE

2 cups confectioner's sugar   hot water

Step 1: In a bowl add hot water very gradually to the sugar and beat constantly until the glaze is syrupy.

Step 2: Pour it over cake and allow it to dribble down the sides. Or pour in a stream over muffins, rolls and other small cakes.

√ Flavored Glazes

Utilize *hot lemon juice, Key lime juice, orange juice, strong coffee* instead of the hot water.

STRAWBERRY GLAZE

222

1 small jar strawberry preserves

Step 1: In a heavy-bottomed pan melt the strawberry preserves over low heat until liquid.
Step 2: Strain through a fine strainer and spread on the cake.

√ Apricot Glaze

Utilize *1 small jar apricot preserves* instead of the strawberry preserves.

⟵──────────────────────────────⟶
⟵──────────────────────────────⟶

FILLINGS

CUSTARD CREAM FILLING

1 cup milk	1/2 cup Raw™ sugar
3 tablespoons unbleached flour	2 egg yolks, slightly beaten
1/8 teaspoon salt	
2 teaspoons vanilla extract or 2 vanilla pods, split & deseeded	

Step 1: In a heavy-bottomed pan scald milk over low flame, if utilizing vanilla pods place in with milk.
Step 2: In a bowl mix together the sugar, flour and salt, then stir in the hot milk (discard vanilla pods), and beat well. Pour back into the pan and stir vigorously over low heat for 4 to 5 minutes, until thick and smooth.
Step 3: Pour a tablespoon of the hot mixture into a bowl with the egg yolks and lightly beat a few times. Add this to the pan and cook for a few minutes more.
Step 4: Cool, stirring occasionally, then add the vanilla extract if utilizing instead of pods.

√ Mango Custard Cream Filling

Omit the vanilla. Add an additional *tablespoon unbleached flour.* Stir a *pureéd mango* into a cooled & especially thick filling.

√ Banana Custard Cream Filling

Omit the vanilla. Mash *1 large banana* and beat until smooth, add *2 tablespoons lemon juice,* and stir the mixture into the cooled filling.

√ Chocolate Custard Cream Filling

Melt *2 ounces unsweetened chocolate* in the milk and utilize *1 cup Raw™ sugar* instead of 1/2 cup.

⟵──────────────────────────────⟶

LEMON FILLING

1 cup Raw™ sugar

2 1/2 tablespoons unbleached flour

1 egg, slightly beaten

Grated rind of 2 lemons

1/4 lemon juice

1 tablespoon butter

Step 1: Combine all the ingredients together in a heavy-bottomed pan. Cook over medium flame, stirring vigorously, until thick and smooth.

Step 2: Cool filling before spreading between layers of cake.

ORANGE FILLING

3/4 cup Raw™ sugar

1/4 cup unbleached flour

1 tablespoon lemon juice

Grated rind of 1 orange

2 egg yolks, slightly beaten

Pinch of salt

Step 1: Combine all the ingredients together in a heavy-bottomed pan. Cook over medium flame, stirring vigorously, until thick and smooth.

Step 2: Cool filling before spreading between layers of cake.

BUTTERSCOTCH FILLING

1/4 cup Raw™ sugar

2 tablespoons butter

1 cup milk

1/2 teaspoon vanilla

1/4 cup dark-brown sugar

2 eggs, slightly beaten

3 tablespoons unbleached flour

1/2 teaspoon salt

Step 1: Combine the butter, Raw™ & dark-brown sugar in a heavy-bottomed pan. Cook over a low flame, stirring constantly, until blended well. Add 1/2 cup of the milk and continue cooking until blended.

Step 2: Mix the flour & salt with remaining 1/2 cup of milk, add to the first mixture, and cook, stirring vigorously, until thickened.

Step 3: Pour a tablespoon of the hot mixture into a bowl with the egg yolks and lightly beat a few times. Add this to the pan and cook for a few minutes more.

Step 4: Cool, stirring occasionally, then add the vanilla extract. Spread between layers of cake.

FRENCH CREAM FILLING

1 cup heavy cream

1/4 cup confectioner's sugar

1 egg white

1 teaspoon vanilla extract

1/8 teaspoon salt

Step 1: Beat the egg white with a hand mixer until foamy, then add salt and keep beating until firm but not dry peaks form.

Step 2: In another bowl beat the cream until it forms soft peaks, then slowly beat in the sugar and vanilla extract.

Step 3: Fold the two mixtures together. Spread between layers of cake.

√ **French Mocha Filling**

Substitute *2 teaspoons instant coffee* for the vanilla extract.

√ **French Fruit Filling**

Utilize *1/3 cup confectioner's sugar* instead of 1/4 cup and fold in *1/2 cup mashed strawberries* or *bananas* or *blueberries* or *raspberries* or *cherries* at the end.

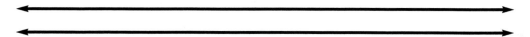

11. COOKIES

INFO ON COOKIES

Due to the high absorbability of whole wheat flour, decrease the amount of flour if you desire a more crisp richer traditional cookie or increase the amount of flour if you desire a more cake-like or lighter cookie.

(After a few times of making these nutritional cookies you will discover whether to let the dough rest for shorter or longer periods of time or bake it at a higher or lower temperature or vary the duration of baking to your desire.)

$$\longleftrightarrow$$

COOKIE RECIPES

CITRUS SUNSHINE'S
Featured in Domino® Sugar's **"MOST ORIGINAL COOKIE" CONTEST**

1 1/4 cup whole wheat flour, sifted	1 stick butter (room temp.)
1/4 cup Domino® light-brown sugar	1 egg (room temp.)
1/2 cup Domino® granulated sugar	1 teaspoon grated lemon peel
1/4 teaspoon baking powder	2 teaspoons grated orange peel
1/8 teaspoon salt	

Step 1: In a bowl, beat egg, sugars & butter.

Step 2: In another bowl sift together flour, baking powder & salt. Add lemon and orange peel, mix well. Pour into moist mixture and fold until well blended. Let rest 10 minutes.

Step 3: Place in refrigerator until chilled.

Step 4: Preheat oven to 350°F.

Step 5: Drop by teaspoons onto ungreased cookie sheet, lined with parchment paper, about one-inch apart, press tops down even with a cold tablespoon.

Step 6: Bake for 8 to 11 minutes until the edges are lightly browned.

Step 7: Cool on rack. Makes about 40 cookies.

$$\longleftrightarrow$$

CHOCOLATE CHIP COOKIES

1 3/4 cup whole wheat flour, sifted	2 eggs (room temp.)
1 cup light-brown or Raw™ sugar	1 teaspoon vanilla extract
1 1/4 cups semi-sweet chocolate chips, cold	1 stick butter (room temp.)
1 teaspoon salt	1 teaspoon baking powder

Step 1: In a bowl, beat eggs, sugar, butter & vanilla.

Step 2: In another bowl sift together flour, baking powder & salt. Pour into moist mixture and fold well until blended. Add cold chocolate chips, mix well. Let rest 10 minutes.

Step 3: Place in refrigerator until chilled.

Step 4: Preheat oven to 350°F.

Step 5: Arrange by a level size 40, 3/4 oz. capacity disher (small ice cream scoop) onto ungreased cookie sheet, lined with parchment paper, about one-inch apart, press tops down even with a cold tablespoon.

Step 6: Bake for 8 to 10 minutes until the edges are lightly browned.

Step 7: Cool on rack. Makes about 12 cookies.

√ Oatmeal Chocolate Chip Cookies

Add *1/2 cup oatmeal* to flour.

CHOCOLATE LATTÉ COOKIES

2 cups whole wheat flour, sifted	2 sticks butter (room temp.)
1 1/2 cup light-brown or Raw™ sugar	2 eggs (room temp.)
2 cups semi-sweet chocolate chips, cold	1 1/2 teaspoon vanilla
1 1/2 teaspoons cinnamon	1 teaspoon baking powder
2 tablespoons strong coffee	

Step 1: In a bowl, beat eggs, sugar, butter, coffee & vanilla.

Step 2: In another bowl sift together flour, baking powder, cinnamon & salt. Pour into moist mixture and fold well until blended. Add cold chocolate chips, mix well. Let rest 10 minutes.

Step 3: Place in refrigerator until chilled.

Step 4: Preheat oven to 350°F.

Step 5: Arrange by a level size 40, 3/4 oz. capacity disher (small ice cream scoop) onto ungreased cookie sheet, lined with parchment paper, about two-inches apart, press tops down even with a cold tablespoon.

Step 6: Bake for 8 to 12 minutes until the edges are browned.

Step 7: Cool on rack. Makes about 25 cookies.

GINGERSNAPS

1 1/2 cups whole wheat flour, sifted	1/2 cup molasses
1/2 stick butter (room temp.)	3/4 teaspoon salt
1/4 teaspoon baking powder	
1 to 2 tablespoons ginger, finely grated & dried	

Step 1: In a bowl, stir together molasses & butter.

Step 2: In another bowl sift together flour, baking powder & salt. Add grated ginger, mix well. Pour into moist mixture and mix until well blended. Let rest 10 minutes.

Step 3: Place in refrigerator until chilled.

Step 4: Preheat oven to 350°F.

Step 5: Using a rolling pin, roll the dough out onto a board as thin as possible. Cut into 1 1/2-inch rounds with a small cutter. Arrange on ungreased cookie sheet, lined with parchment paper, about one-inch apart.

Step 6: Bake for 5 to 6 minutes until the dry and crisp.

Step 7: Cool on rack. Makes about 40 cookies.

$\longleftrightarrow$

SHORTBREADS

What Ed Norton on the "Honeymooners™" called a short-cookie.

1 1/2 cup whole wheat flour, sifted	1/2 cup confectioner's sugar
1/2 cup unbleached flour, sifted	2 tablespoons Raw™ sugar
2 sticks butter, softened	1/4 teaspoon baking powder
1 teaspoon vanilla extract	1/4 teaspoon salt

Step 1: In a bowl, cream together butter, vanilla and sugars.

Step 2: In another bowl sift together flours, baking powder & salt. Pour into first mixture and knead lightly until dough just holds together. Let rest 10 minutes.

Step 3: Place in refrigerator until chilled.

Step 4: Preheat oven to 350°F.

Step 5: Arrange by a level size 40, 3/4 oz. capacity disher (small ice cream scoop) onto ungreased cookie sheet, lined with parchment paper, about one-inch apart, press tops down even with a cold tablespoon, prick each cookie with a fork or form 3 ridges.

Step 6: Bake for 18 to 22 minutes or until the edges are lightly browned.

Step 7: Cool on rack. Makes about 20 cookies.

√ **Cinnamon Shortbreads**

Add *1 teaspoon of cinnamon* to flour.

√ **Spiced Shortbreads**

Add *1/2 teaspoon nutmeg, 1/2 teaspoon mace* to flour.

$\longleftrightarrow$

CRISPY CHOCOLATE COOKIES

2 ounces unsweetened chocolate	2 cups whole wheat flour, sifted

1 1/2 sticks butter	3/4 teaspoon vanilla extract
1 cup Raw™ sugar	1 egg (room temp.)
2 tablespoons milk	1/4 teaspoon salt

Step 1: Preheat oven to 375°F.

Step 2: Melt the chocolate in a glass bowl over simmering water; set aside.

Step 3: Cream the butter, add sugar, continue beating while adding egg, chocolate, vanilla, salt and milk. Add flour and stir gently.

Step 4: Arrange on ungreased cookie sheet, lined with parchment paper, about one-inch apart.

Step 5: Bake for 8 to 11 minutes or until crisp.

Step 6: Cool on rack. Makes about 40 cookies.

SUNFLOWER OATMEAL COOKIES™

2 cups rolled oats	1 1/4 cup whole wheat flour, sifted
1 cup sunflower seeds, roasted & mashed	2 eggs (room temp.)
1 cup Raw™ sugar	1 cup light brown sugar
1 teaspoon vanilla extract	1 teaspoon baking soda
2 sticks butter (room temp.)	1/2 teaspoon salt
1 teaspoon baking powder	Milk as needed

Step 1: In a bowl, beat eggs, sugars, butter & vanilla.

Step 2: In another bowl sift together flour, oats, baking soda, baking powder & salt. Pour into moist mixture and fold well until blended. Add mashed sunflower seeds, mix well; add any milk to gain the right consistency of the batter. Let rest 10 minutes.

Step 3: Place in refrigerator until chilled.

Step 4: Preheat oven to 350°F.

Step 5: Arrange by a level size 40, 3/4 oz. capacity disher (small ice cream scoop) onto ungreased cookie sheet, lined with parchment paper, about one-inch apart, press tops down even with a cold tablespoon.

Step 6: Bake for 8 to 12 minutes until the edges are lightly browned.

Step 7: Cool on rack. Makes about 20 cookies.

√ **Sunflower Oatmeal Chocolate Chip Cookies™**

Add *1/2 cup semi-sweetened chocolate chips* to flour.

AUBREY'S™ VANILLA WAFER COOKIES

3 3/4 cup whole wheat flour, sifted	6 extra large eggs (room temp.)

3 cups Raw™ sugar

3 tablespoons vanilla extract

2 cups unbleached flour

3 sticks butter (room temp.)

1 teaspoon salt

1 teaspoon almond extract

1 teaspoon baking powder

Step 1: In a bowl, beat eggs, sugar, butter, vanilla and almond.

Step 2: In another bowl sift together flours, baking powder & salt. Pour into moist mixture and fold well until blended; mix well. Let rest 10 minutes.

Step 3: Place in refrigerator until chilled.

Step 4: Preheat oven to 350°F.

Step 5: Arrange by a level size 40, 3/4 oz. capacity disher (small ice cream scoop) onto ungreased cookie sheet, lined with parchment paper, about one-inch apart, press tops down even with a cold tablespoon.

Step 6: Bake for 8 to 10 minutes until the edges are lightly browned.

Step 7: Cool on rack. Makes about 45 cookies.

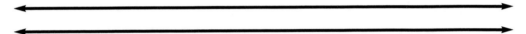

12. PIES, CRUST, PASTRIES & DESSERTS

CRUST

BASIC WHOLE WHEAT PIECRUST
(PIE SHELL)

1 cup whole wheat flour, sifted	1/2 stick butter, cold
1 egg, beaten	2-4 tablespoons ice water
2 tablespoons Raw™ sugar	1/4 teaspoon salt

Step 1: Combine flour, sugar and salt in a bowl. With a pastry blender cut in butter until mixture resembles coarse crumbs. Add beaten egg and water a little at a time, mixing lightly until pastry just holds together. Chill dough in refrigerator for 1 hour.

Step 2: Roll dough on lightly floured board into a circle 2 inches larger in diameter than pie pan.

Step 3: Use a spatula to help lift the dough and fold it loosely in half, then in quarters. Ease dough in the center of the pan. Open up the dough and press it lightly into the pan to fit. Trim the edges and flute. Fill and bake according to the pie recipe.

Or for a Baked Crust:prick the bottom with a fork and place foil over dough and place 3 cups of beans (Reserved for this purpose of preventing the crust from swelling) on top of foil and bake in a 425°F oven 10 to 12 minutes. When utilizing a springform pan, only remove sides when tart is ready to serve.

$$\longleftrightarrow$$

BASIC WHOLE WHEAT PIECRUST
(TWO-CRUST PIE)

2 cups whole wheat flour, sifted	1 stick butter, cold
2 eggs, beaten	4 tablespoons ice water
4 tablespoons Raw™ sugar	1/2 teaspoon salt

Step 1: Combine flour, sugar and salt in a bowl. With a pastry blender cut in butter until mixture resembles coarse crumbs. Add beaten eggs and water a little at a time, mixing lightly until pastry just holds together. Divide dough in half. Flatten each half with palm of your hand to form a disk. Wrap both disks in wax paper & chill dough in refrigerator for 1 hour.

Step 2: Roll one dough on lightly floured board into a circle 2 inches larger in diameter than pie pan.

Step 3: Use a spatula to help lift the dough and fold it loosely in half, then in quarters. Ease dough in the center of the pan. Open up the dough and press it lightly into the pan to fit.

Step 4: Repeat the rolling process of step 2 with the second disk to make the top crust

Step 5: Fill the pie generously, then put on top crust and make slits with a knife or prick with a fork to make vents in it. Or make strips with the top crust dough and lay in a lattice pattern. Flute or crimp the edges. Bake according to the pie recipe.

VEGGIE PATTY PASTRY™

2 cups whole wheat flour sifted	2/3 cup butter
1/2 teaspoon baking powder	1/3 cup ice water
1 teaspoon salt	

Step 1: Sift the flour, baking powder and salt in a bowl. Cut in 1/3 cup of the butter with a pastry blender until mixture resembles coarse crumbs. Sprinkle the ice water a little at a time, mixing lightly until pastry just holds together.

Step 2: Roll out the dough into a rectangle. Dot with half of the remaining butter, then roll up the dough like a jelly roll. Roll out again until 1/4 inch thick and dot with the last half of the remaining butter. Roll up the dough and repeat once more. Chill dough in refrigerator for 1/2 hour.

Step 3: Roll dough on lightly floured board into a rectangle and cut into squares or ovals.

Step 4: Place filling in center of squares or ovals and fold edges together to form a patty and crimp edges. Cut vents in pastry and bake according to the patty recipe.

TART PASTRY

3/4 cup whole wheat flour, sifted	1 egg yolk, cold
1/4 cup unbleached flour	2 tablespoons ice water
6 tablespoons butter, cold & chopped	1/4 teaspoon salt

Step 1: Combine flours and salt in a bowl. With a pastry blender cut in butter until mixture resembles coarse crumbs.

Step 2: In another bowl mix egg yolk and water, add to flour mixture mixing lightly until pastry just holds together. Divide dough in half. Flatten each half with palm of your hand to form a disk. Wrap both disks in wax paper & chill dough in refrigerator for 1 hour.

Step 3: Roll one dough on lightly floured board into a circle 2 inches larger in diameter than pie pan. Save the other for another use.

Step 4: Use a spatula to help lift the dough and fold it loosely in half, then in quarters. Ease dough in the center of the pan. Open up the dough and press it lightly into the pan to fit. Trim the edges. Fill and bake according to the pie recipe.

Or for a Prebaked Crust:prick the bottom with a fork and place foil over dough and place 3 cups of beans (Reserved for this purpose of preventing the crust from swelling) on top of foil and bake in a 425°F oven 10 to 12 minutes. When utilizing a springform pan, only remove sides when tart is ready to serve.

FLAKY TART PASTRY

3/4 cup whole wheat flour, sifted

1/4 cup unbleached flour

2 teaspoons baking powder

1/2 cup corn oil

1/4 cup milk or sour cream

1/4 teaspoon salt

Step 1: Combine flours, baking soda and salt in a bowl.

Step 2: In another bowl mix corn oil and milk or sour cream, add to flour mixture, with a pastry blender cut until mixture resembles coarse crumbs, mixing lightly until pastry just holds together. Divide dough in half. Flatten each half with palm of your hand to form a disk. Wrap both disks in wax paper & chill dough in refrigerator for 1 hour.

Step 3: Roll one dough on lightly floured board into a circle 2 inches larger in diameter than pie pan. Save the other for another use.

Step 4: Use a spatula to help lift the dough and fold it loosely in half, then in quarters. Ease dough in the center of the pan. Open up the dough and press it lightly into the pan to fit. Trim the edges. Fill and bake according to the pie recipe.

Or for a Prebaked Crust:prick the bottom with a fork and place foil over dough and place 3 cups of beans (Reserved for this purpose of preventing the crust from swelling) on top of foil and bake in a 400°F oven 10 to 12 minutes. When utilizing a springform pan, only remove sides when tart is ready to serve.

FLAKY PIE CRUST
[For TWO-CRUST PIE, double the ingredients and follow the instructions for
BASIC PIE CRUST (TWO-CRUST PIE) (pg.231)]

3/4 cup whole wheat flour, sifted

1 egg, beaten

1 tablespoon Raw™ sugar

1/8 teaspoon salt

1/2 stick butter, in bits, cold

2 tablespoons ice water

1/4 teaspoon baking powder

Step 1: Combine flour, baking powder, sugar and salt in a bowl. With a pastry blender cut in butter until mixture resembles coarse crumbs. Add beaten egg and water a little at a time, mixing lightly until pastry just holds together. Chill dough in refrigerator for 1 hour.

Step 2: Roll dough on lightly floured board into a circle 2 inches larger in diameter than pie pan.

Step 3: Use a spatula to help lift the dough and fold it loosely in half, then in quarters. Ease dough in the center of the pan. Open up the dough and press it lightly into the pan to fit. Trim the edges and flute. Fill and bake according to the pie recipe.

√ Light & Flaky Pie Crust

Substitute *1/4 cup unbleached flour* for 1/4 cup of the whole wheat flour and proceed with recipe.

← ─────────────────────────────────── →

RICH & FLAKY PIE CRUST

[For TWO-CRUST PIE, double the ingredients and follow the instructions for
BASIC PIE CRUST (TWO-CRUST PIE) (pg.231)]

1 1/4 cup whole wheat flour, sifted	1 stick butter, in bits, cold
2 tablespoon Raw™ sugar	4-6 tablespoons ice water
1/2 teaspoon salt	

Step 1: Combine flour, sugar and salt in a bowl. With a pastry blender cut in butter until mixture resembles coarse crumbs. Add water, mixing lightly until pastry just holds together. Chill dough in refrigerator for 1 hour.

Step 2: Roll dough on lightly floured board into a circle 2 inches larger in diameter than pie pan.

Step 3: Use a spatula to help lift the dough and fold it loosely in half, then in quarters. Ease dough in the center of the pan. Open up the dough and press it lightly into the pan to fit. Trim the edges and flute. Fill and bake according to the pie recipe.

√ Super Rich & Flaky Pie Crust

Substitute water with *1/4 cup sour cream.*

√ Lightly Rich & Flaky Pie Crust

Substitute *1/4 cup unbleached flour* for 1/4 cup of the whole wheat flour and proceed with recipe.

← ─────────────────────────────────── →

SPICED RICH & FLAKY PIE CRUST

(FOR BEAN PIE)

[For TWO-CRUST PIE, double the ingredients and follow the instructions for
BASIC PIE CRUST (TWO-CRUST PIE) (pg.231)]

1 1/4 cup whole wheat flour, sifted	1 stick butter, in bits, cold
2 tablespoon Raw™ sugar	4-6 tablespoons ice water
1/2 teaspoon salt	1 teaspoon ginger
1/2 teaspoon cinnamon	1/4 teaspoon mace
Pinch of allspice or cloves	

Step 1: Combine flour, spices, sugar and salt in a bowl. With a pastry blender cut in butter until mixture resembles coarse crumbs. Add water, mixing lightly until pastry just holds together. Chill dough in refrigerator for 1 hour.

Step 2: Roll dough on lightly floured board into a circle 2 inches larger in diameter than pie pan.

Step 3: Use a spatula to help lift the dough and fold it loosely in half, then in quarters. Ease dough in the center of the pan. Open up the dough and press it lightly into the pan to fit. Trim the edges and flute. Fill and bake according to the pie recipe.

√ **Super Rich Spiced & Flaky Pie Crust**

Substitute half of the water with *1/4 cup sour cream.*

√ **Super Rich Spiced & Flaky Oatmeal Pie Crust**

Substitute half of the water with *1/4 cup sour cream.* Substitute *3/4 cups rolled oats* for 3/4 cup of the whole wheat flour and proceed with recipe.

√ **Lightly Rich Spiced & Flaky Pie Crust**

Substitute *1/4 cup unbleached flour* for 1/4 cup of the whole wheat flour and proceed with recipe.

√ **Supreme Pie Crust**

Substitute the 1 teaspoon ginger with *1 teaspoon mace.*

⟵─────────────────────────────────⟶

SHORTCRUST PIE CRUST

[For TWO-CRUST PIE, double the ingredients and follow the instructions for
BASIC PIE CRUST (TWO-CRUST PIE) (pg.231)]

1 cup whole wheat flour, sifted	1/2 stick butter, in bits, cold
1 teaspoon confectioner's sugar	4-6 tablespoons ice water
1 tablespoon Raw™ sugar	1/8 teaspoon salt

Step 1: Combine flour, sugar and salt in a bowl. With a pastry blender cut in butter until mixture resembles coarse crumbs. Add water a little at a time, mixing lightly until pastry just holds together. Chill dough in refrigerator for 1 hour.

Step 2: Roll dough on lightly floured board into a circle 2 inches larger in diameter than pie pan.

Step 3: Use a spatula to help lift the dough and fold it loosely in half, then in quarters. Ease dough in the center of the pan. Open up the dough and press it lightly into the pan to fit. Trim the edges and flute. Fill and bake according to the pie recipe.

√ **Light Shortcrust Pie Crust**

Substitute *1/4 cup unbleached flour* for 1/4 cup of the whole wheat flour and proceed with recipe.

⟵─────────────────────────────────⟶

BASIC CRUMB CRUST

1 1/2 cups graham cracker, fine crumbs	1/3 cup butter, melted
2 tablespoons Raw™ sugar	

Step 1: Break graham crackers into 1" pieces, place in a food processor fitted with the metal chopping

blade. Process until they form crumbs.

Step 2: In a bowl combine the crumbs, butter and Raw™ sugar, mix well. Press & pat into the bottom of a pie pan or springform pan.

Step 3:For a Prebaked Crust: Bake 8 to 10 minutes in a preheated 350°F oven, then set on a wire rack and cool. Or fill unbaked as instructed in the filling recipe.

√ Cookie Crumb Crust

Substitute one of the following type cookies:*chocolate graham crackers, gingersnaps,* (pg.227) *vanilla wafers* (pg.229), *shortbread* (pg.228), *oatmeal raisin* (pg.229) *or chocolate cookies* (pg.229) for the 1 1/2 cup graham crackers and proceed with recipe.

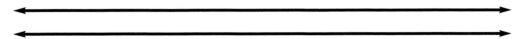

TOP CRUST & TOPPINGS FOR PIES & COBBLERS

Tips On Whipping Meringue:

• Use a stainless-steel or copper bowl and make sure to use clean bowls and utensils that do not have any residue from the other ingredients of the baked goods because egg whites don't whip properly if they come into contact with fat.

• Place bowl in a pan that has hot water in it to keep the bowl and egg whites warm as they are beaten. Or place bowl in sink that has the hot water slightly running so that the hot water comes into contact with the bottom of bowl.

• Start beating egg whites with beater on low-speed for a minute or two then increase to medium-speed and whip until the soft peaks form. This stage is reached when the revolving beater blades form curving lines in the egg whites. Beat egg whites until they form a peak when we pull the beater blades or whip out of them.

• When adding sugar, do so just as the whites reach the soft peak stage. Add 1 tablespoon of superfine sugar every 1/2 minute until dissolved. When adding confectioner's sugar fold it in after the superfine sugar has been incorporated.

• A soft meringue has 1 1/2 to 2 tablespoons of sugar added per egg white and bakes quickly in a 325°F oven until the top becomes golden brown.

• Store a soft meringue in refrigerator.

• A hard meringue has 4 tablespoons of sugar added per egg white and bakes slowly in a 225°F oven until the moisture evaporates out and it becomes dry & crisp. Remove from oven and the interior will become firm after it cools down.

• A hard meringue will become soft if stored in a humid place. Keep in a clean metal tin for a few days or freeze for longer storage to keep well.

• Serve meringue topped or crusted goods preferably the same day.

MERINGUE TOPPINGS & CRUST

TOASTED MERINGUE

4 egg whites (room temp.)   6 tablespoons superfine sugar
1/2 teaspoon vanilla   1/4 teaspoon salt

Step 1: Place the egg whites in a stainless-steel bowl and place the bowl in a pan that has hot water in it. Start beating egg whites with beater on low-speed for a minute or two then increase to medium-speed and add vanilla and salt.
Step 2: Remove bowl from hot water.
Step 3: Whip egg whites until the soft peaks start to form. Add 1 tablespoon of sugar every 30 seconds until dissolved and beat until meringue is stiff and shiny.
Step 4: Spread the meringue over a filled pie shell until it touches the inner edges of the crust.
Step 5: Place the pie under the broiler for a minute and let the meringue turn light-golden brown.

$\longleftrightarrow$

SOFT MERINGUE

4 egg whites (room temp.)   6 tablespoons superfine sugar
1/2 teaspoon vanilla   1/4 teaspoon salt

Step 1: Place the egg whites in a stainless-steel bowl and place the bowl in a pan that has hot water in it. Start beating egg whites with beater on low-speed for a minute or two then increase to medium-speed and add vanilla and salt.
Step 2: Remove bowl from hot water.
Step 3: Whip egg whites until the soft peaks start to form. Add 1 tablespoon of sugar every 30 seconds until dissolved and beat until meringue is stiff and shiny.
Step 4: Spread the meringue over a filled pie shell until it touches the inner edges of the crust.
Step 5: Place the pie in a preheated 325°F oven for a few minutes or until the top becomes golden brown.

$\longleftrightarrow$

HARD MERINGUE

4 egg whites (room temp.)   1 cup superfine sugar
1/2 teaspoon vanilla   1/4 teaspoon salt

Step 1: Place the egg whites in a stainless-steel bowl and place the bowl in a pan that has hot water in it. Start beating egg whites with beater on low-speed for a minute or two then increase to medium-speed and add vanilla and salt.

Step 2: Remove bowl from hot water.

Step 3: Whip egg whites until the soft peaks start to form. Add 1 tablespoon of sugar every 30 seconds until dissolved and beat until meringue is stiff and shiny.

Step 4: Spread the meringue over a filled pie shell until it touches the inner edges of the crust.

Step 5: Place the pie in a preheated 225°F oven and bake slowly until the moisture evaporates out and it becomes dry & crisp. Remove from oven and the interior will become firm after it cools down.

$$\longleftrightarrow$$

MERINGUE PIECRUST

4 egg whites	1 cup superfine sugar
1/8 teaspoon peppermint extract	1/4 teaspoon salt

Step 1: Place the egg whites in a stainless-steel bowl and place the bowl in a pan that has hot water in it. Start beating egg whites with beater on low-speed for a minute or two then increase to medium-speed and add peppermint and salt.

Step 2: Remove bowl from hot water.

Step 3: Whip egg whites until the soft peaks start to form. Add 1 tablespoon of sugar every 30 seconds until dissolved and beat until meringue is stiff and shiny.

Step 4: Spread the meringue into an ungreased 9-inch glass pie pan to form the shape of a crust.

Step 5: Place the pie in a preheated 350°F oven and bake slowly until the moisture evaporates out, about 35 to 40 minutes and it becomes dry & crisp. Remove from oven and cool on a wire rack.

$$\longleftrightarrow$$

TOPPING CRUST
(FOR FRUIT COBBLERS)

1 1/2 cup whole wheat flour, sifted	1 stick unsalted butter
1 egg, slightly beaten	1 tablespoon Raw™ sugar
1 to 3 tablespoons ice water	1/4 teaspoon mace
1/8 teaspoon baking powder	1/8 teaspoon salt

Step 1: Combine flour, sugar, baking powder, mace and salt in a bowl. With a pastry blender cut in butter until mixture resembles coarse crumbs. Add beaten egg and water a little at a time, mixing lightly until pastry just holds together. Flatten with palm of your hand to form a disk. Wrap disk in wax paper & chill dough in refrigerator for 1 hour.

Step 2: Roll dough on lightly floured board into a rectangle. Make strips with the dough and lay in a lattice pattern over filled pie shell. Flute or crimp the edges. Bake according to the pie recipe.

$$\longleftrightarrow$$

CLEAR GLAZE

(FOR FRUIT TARTS)

1 to 2 tablespoons water

1 tablespoon lemon juice

1 cup apricot or strawberry jam or preserves

Step 1: In a small sauce pan melt jam or preserves, lemon juice and water until pouring consistency is achieved.

Step 2: Strain. Let cool a bit, then spread over a fruit-filled tart.

√ Red Currant Glaze

Melt *1 cup red currant jelly & 2 teaspoons water* over low heat, stirring and cooking for just a minute after melting. Let cool a bit, then spread over a fruit-filled tart.

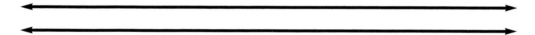

CLOUDY GLAZE

(FOR PIECRUST)

1/2 cup confectioner's sugar   1 tablespoon water

Step 1: In a small bowl mix the sugar with the water and spread it on a hot baked pie just after it is removed from the oven.

PIES
• To avoid any bacteria in eggs that might cause food-borne illness, make sure the temperature of custards used as pie fillings registers 160°F on an instant-read thermometer.
• Before baking pies, make sure to place a cookie sheet or foil under it to catch any drippings while the pies are baking.
• The pie crust in the pie recipes are suggested. A few can be varied to find the ones we like.

ORIGINAL BEAN PIE

2 cups navy beans, strained & cooled   4 ounces or 1/3 can evaporated milk

1/2 stick butter, (room temp)   2 eggs (room temp.)

3/4 cup Raw™ sugar   1 tablespoon vanilla extract

1 1/2 teaspoon cinnamon

Supreme Pie crust for 9-inch pie shell (pg.235)

239

Step 1: In a small bowl whip the butter and spice together.

Step 2: In another bowl lightly mix the sugar and beans. Slowly add eggs & vanilla, continue beating while adding milk then add butter.

Step 3: Pour into the prepared 9-inch crust, which can be a Prebaked Crust or refrigerated. Set aside a few minutes to settle filling and allow crust to slightly absorb some filling.

Step 4: Bake in a preheated 350°F oven for 1 hour 10 minutes or a 330°F oven for 1 hour 30 minutes. The pie is done when the center of the pie no longer has a puddle of moisture when we tap the sides of the pie with a spatula.

Step 5: Place the pie under the broiler flame to toast the top, if desired.

Step 6: Remove from oven and cool on rack.

NOTE:While perfecting pie making, vary the baking temperature and time until we get the right stiffness of the filling and a deep-brown toasted top.

APPLE PIE

3 large Granny Smith apples   1/2 cup Raw™ sugar

1 tablespoon lemon juice   1 tablespoon tapioca (Kosher)

1 teaspoon grated lemon peel   3/4 teaspoon cinnamon

1/4 teaspoon mace   1/4 cup raisins, chopped

2 tablespoons butter, (room temp.)   1/2 cup sour cream

3 Macintosh apples

Light & Flaky Pie Crust for 9-inch two-crust pie (pg.233)

Step 1: Peel, core, and slice the apples into eights, toss together in a bowl with water and the lemon juice.

Step 2: Roll out slightly less than half the pastry dough and line a 9-inch pie pan.

Step 3: In a bowl mix the sugar, tapioca, lemon peel, mace & cinnamon. Drain the slice apples, and toss them in sugar mixture, then put all this into the lined pan and dot with butter and pour sour cream over all.

Step 4: Roll out the top crust and drape it over the pie, crimping the edges to seal them and cut several vents in the top.

Step 5: Bake in a 450°F preheated oven for 10 minutes, then lower heat to 350°F and continue baking for a further 30 to 40 minutes or until the pie filling begins bubbling out or the crust is golden brown. Remove from oven. Can be served warm or cold.

SQUASH PIE

2 cups winter squash, cooked & puréed

1 cup Raw™ sugar

1 teaspoon cinnamon

1/2 teaspoon almond flavor

Spiced Rich & Flaky Pie crust for 9-inch pie shell (pg.234)

1 cup heavy cream

3 egg yolks, slightly beaten

1/2 teaspoon mace

Step 1: In a small bowl lightly whip the cream and spices together.

Step 2: In another bowl lightly mix the sugar and squash. Slowly add eggs & almond, continue beating while adding cream.

Step 3: Pour into the prepared 9-inch crust, which can be a Prebaked Crust or refrigerated. Set aside a few minutes to settle filling and allow crust to slightly absorb some filling.

Step 4: Bake in a preheated 425°F oven for 10 minutes, then reduce temperature to 350°F and bake for 45 minutes to 1 hour more or until brown. The pie is done when the center of the pie no longer has a puddle of moisture when we tap the sides of the pie with a spatula.

Step 5: Place the pie under the broiler flame to toast the top, if desired.

Step 6: Remove from oven and cool on rack.

NOTE:While perfecting pie making, vary the baking temperature and time until we get the right stiffness of the filling and a deep-brown toasted top.

PEACH PIE

1 cup Raw™ sugar

1/2 teaspoon vanilla extract

1 teaspoon grated lemon peel (optional)

2 tablespoons butter, (room temp.)

1/4 teaspoon mace

4 tablespoons unbleached flour

1/2 teaspoon cinnamon

Lightly Rich Spiced & Flaky Pie Crust for 9-inch two-crust pie (pg.235)

4 cups peaches, (do not peel) sliced into 8ths with red inner-core trimmed

Step 1: Place peaches in a bowl.

Step 2: Roll out slightly less than half the pastry dough and line a 9-inch pie pan.

Step 3: In a bowl mix the sugar, flour, vanilla, mace, cinnamon and lemon peel if using. Add the sliced peaches, and toss them in sugar mixture, then put all this into the lined pan and dot with butter.

Step 4: Roll out the top crust and drape it over the pie, crimping the edges to seal them and cut several vents in the top.

Step 5: Bake in a 450°F preheated oven for 10 minutes, then lower heat to 350°F and continue baking for a further 30 to 40 minutes or until the pie filling begins bubbling out or the crust is golden brown. Remove from oven. Can be served warm or cold.

BLUEBERRY PIE

4 cups fresh or frozen blueberries   1 cup Raw™ sugar

3 tablespoons unbleached flour   2 tablespoons butter

1/2 teaspoon cinnamon   1/8 teaspoon mace

1/8 teaspoon salt

Super Rich Spiced & Flaky Oatmeal Pie Crust for 9-inch two-crust pie (pg.235)

Step 1: Wash fresh blueberries. Use frozen ones right out the bag, if using.

Step 2: Roll out slightly less than half the pastry dough and line a 9-inch pie pan.

Step 3: In a bowl mix the sugar, flour, mace, cinnamon and salt. Add the blueberries, and toss them in sugar mixture, then put all this into the lined pan and dot with butter.

Step 4: Roll out the top crust and drape it over the pie, crimping the edges to seal them and cut several vents in the top.

Step 5: Bake in a 450°F preheated oven for 10 minutes, then lower heat to 350°F and continue baking for a further 30 to 40 minutes or until the pie filling begins bubbling out or the crust is golden brown. Remove from oven. Can be served warm or cold.

←——————————————————————————→

CHERRY TREE-HOUSE PIE®

4 cups fresh sour cherries, pitted   1 cup Raw™ sugar

2 tablespoons unbleached flour   1 teaspoon vanilla

1/8 teaspoon salt

1/8 teaspoon cinnamon

Light & Flaky Pie Crust for 9-inch two-crust pie (pg.235)

Step 1: Wash the cherries.

Step 2: Roll out slightly less than half the pastry dough and line a 9-inch pie pan.

Step 3: In a bowl mix the sugar, flour, cinnamon and salt. Add the cherries, and toss them in sugar mixture, then put all this into the lined pan.

Step 4: Roll out the top crust and cut into stripes and make into a lattice top over the pie. Crimp the edges.

Step 5: Bake in a 450°F preheated oven for 10 minutes, then lower heat to 350°F and continue baking for a further 30 to 40 minutes or until the pie filling begins bubbling out or the crust is golden brown. Remove from oven. Can be served warm or cold.

←——————————————————————————→

PEAR PIE

FILLING

6 ripe pears, peeled, cored and quartered

1/4 teaspoon ginger

1 teaspoon grated Key lime zest

Basic Crumb Crust (pg.236), using ginger snaps

1/2 cup maple syrup

3 tablespoons Key lime Juice

CRUMB TOPPING

1/2 cup whole wheat flour, sifted

1/2 teaspoon mace

1/2 cup Raw™ sugar

1/3 cup butter (room temp.)

CREAM TOPPING

1/2 cup sour cream

2 tablespoons light-brown sugar

Step 1: For The Filling:Slice quartered pears in half to make large chunks; arrange in the prepared ginger snap crumb crust. Sprinkle the ginger & lime zest over top, then pour lime juice and maple syrup over all. Set aside a few minutes to settle filling and allow crust to slightly absorb some filling.

Step 2: For The Topping:In a bowl mix the flour, Raw™ sugar & mace with the butter until mixture resembles crumbs. Sprinkle over top of filling

Step 3: Bake in a preheated 400°F oven for 40 to 45 minutes. The pie is done when the pears are tender.

Step 4: For The Cream Topping:Remove from oven and cool on rack. Serve warm topped with a scoop of sour cream and a sprinkle of light-brown sugar.

$$\longleftrightarrow$$

RED POTATO PIE

2 cups red potatoes, baked and mashed*

6 ounces or 1/2 can evaporated milk

1 cup light-brown or Raw™ sugar

1 teaspoon vanilla extract

Dash cinnamon

Basic Whole Wheat Pie crust for 9-inch pie shell (pg.231)

1/2 stick butter

2 eggs (room temp.)

1 tablespoon unbleached flour

1/2 teaspoon mace

Step 1: In a small bowl whip the butter, mace and cinnamon together.

Step 2: In another bowl lightly mix the sugar, flour and skinned & chilled baked red potatoes. Slowly add eggs & vanilla, continue beating while adding milk then add butter.

Step 3: Pour into the prepared 9-inch crust, which can be a Prebaked Crust or refrigerated. Set aside a few minutes to settle filling and allow crust to slightly absorb some filling.

Step 4: Bake in a 425°F preheated oven for 10 minutes, then lower heat to 330°F and continue baking for a further 40 to 50 minutes. The pie is done when the center of the pie no longer has a puddle of moisture when we tap the sides of the pie with a spatula.

Step 5: Place the pie under the broiler flame to toast the top, if desired.

Step 6: Remove from oven and cool on rack. Top with whipped cream or Soft Meringue (pg.237).

NOTE:While perfecting pie making, vary the baking temperature and time until we get the right stiffness of the filling and a deep-brown toasted top.

* Bake 2 large red potatoes in a 400°F oven for one hour. Allow to cool. Then refrigerate.

←——————————————————————————→

CHEDDAR CHEESE PIE

1 1/2 cups grated sharp Cheddar cheese	4 eggs, slightly beaten
2 cups heavy cream, slightly whipped	2 tablespoons Raw™ sugar
1/8 teaspoon salt	
1/8 teaspoon Muhammad's Red Hot Sauce™ (pg.307)	
Tart Pastry for 9-inch pie shell (pg.232)	

Step 1: Sprinkle the cheese evenly over the bottom of the prepared 9-inch crust, which can be a Prebaked Crust or refrigerated.

Step 2: In a bowl add the eggs, and whip in the cream, sugar, salt and pepper, continue beating until blended. Pour over the cheese in the pie shell. Set aside a few minutes to settle filling and allow crust to slightly absorb some filling.

Step 3: Bake in a preheated 425°F oven for 10 minutes, then reduce temperature to 330°F and bake for 35 minutes to 45 minutes more or until brown. The pie is done when the center of the pie no longer has a puddle of moisture when we tap the sides of the pie with a spatula.

Step 4: Place the pie under the broiler flame to toast the top, if desired.

Step 5: Remove from oven and cool on rack.

NOTE:While perfecting pie making, vary the baking temperature and time until we get the right stiffness of the filling and a deep-brown toasted top.

←——————————————————————————→

LEMON MERINGUE PIE

FILLING

Grated rind of 2 lemons	Juice of 2 lemons
3/4 cups Raw™ sugar	3 tablespoons cornstarch
3 egg yolks	

MERINGUE

6 egg whites	1 tablespoon lemon juice
1/8 teaspoon salt	1/2 cup superfine sugar
Pinch cream of tartar	1/2 teaspoon vanilla

CRUST
Basic Crumb Crust (pg.236), using graham crackers. (Prebaked)

Step 1:For The Filling: In a double boiler mix the Raw™ sugar, lemon rind, egg yolks and juice of 2 lemons. Cook, stirring frequently, until the mixture has the consistency of thick pudding and starts to leave the sides. Let is set aside a few minutes to cool, pour into the prebaked graham cracker crumb crust. Set aside a few minutes to settle filling and allow crust to slightly absorb some filling.

Step 2:For The Meringue: Combine egg whites with salt, cream of tartar, 1 tablespoon lemon juice and vanilla extract, beating until soft peaks form. Beat in 1 tablespoon of sugar every 30 seconds until incorporated and whites are stiff. Spread on top of filling, covering edges. Swirl with spatula, pulling up to make points.

Step 3: Bake in a preheated 355°F oven for 12 minutes or until the meringue is golden brown

Step 4: Remove from oven and cool on rack.

NOTE:While perfecting pie making, vary the time until we get the right stiffness of the filling.

$\longleftrightarrow$

FLORIDA'S KEY LIME PIE

3/4 cup Key lime juice, about 16 limes	1 tablespoon grated Key lime zest
1 (14-ounce) can sweetened condensed milk	4 eggs, separated
5 tablespoons superfine sugar	
Basic Whole Wheat Pie crust for 9-inch pie shell (pg.231) (Prebaked)	

Step 1:For The Filling: In a saucepan over a medium-low flame, cook the lime juice & egg yolks a few minutes, stirring frequently, (do not over cook or yolks will toughen) add the milk and lime zest and continue stirring until the mixture has the consistency of thick pudding and starts to leave the sides. Let is set aside a few minutes to cool, pour into the prebaked crust. Set aside a few minutes to settle filling and allow crust to slightly absorb some filling.

Step 2:For The Meringue: In a stainless-steel bowl, beat egg whites until soft peaks form. Beat in 1 tablespoon of sugar every 30 seconds until incorporated and whites are stiff. Spread on top of filling, covering edges. Swirl with spatula, pulling up to make points.

Step 3: Bake in a preheated 325°F oven for 25 minutes or until the meringue is golden brown

Step 4: Remove from oven and cool on rack. Chill before serving

NOTE:While perfecting pie making, vary the time until we get the right stiffness of the filling.

$\longleftrightarrow$

BANANA CUSTARD PIE

CUSTARD

2 cups milk

2/3 cups Raw™ sugar

1/4 teaspoon salt

1 tablespoon cornstarch

2 teaspoons vanilla extract

4 egg yolks, slightly beaten

4 tablespoons unbleached flour

MERINGUE

4 egg whites

1/3 cup superfine sugar

Pinch of mace

1/2 teaspoon almond extract

Pinch salt

CRUST

2 bananas, sliced

Pinch of cinnamon

Basic Crumb Crust (pg.236), using vanilla wafers (Prebaked)

Step 1:For The Crust: Line a 9-inch pie pan with the crumb crust mixture and Bake 8 to 10 minutes in a preheated 350°F oven, then set on a wire rack and cool.

Step 2:For The Custard: In a bowl combine the Raw™ sugar, flour, cornstarch, salt and egg yolks and blend gently.

Step 3: In a saucepan over a medium-low flame, scald the milk (heat to the point where tiny bubbles begin to form, just before it begins to boil) and slowly add to the yolk mixture in bowl, stirring constantly. Pour ingredients of bowl back into saucepan and continue cooking, stirring frequently, until the mixture has the consistency of thick pudding. Pour into a bowl, stir in vanilla. Cover entire top surface with plastic wrap (to prevent skin from forming). Place in refrigerator to chill.

Step 4: Shortly before serving, arrange sliced bananas to cover the bottom and sides of crust and sprinkle with cinnamon. Add the chilled custard into the prebaked crust, spreading it evenly with spatula.

Step 5:For The Meringue: In a stainless-steel bowl, beat egg whites, almond, and salt until soft peaks form. Beat in 1 tablespoon of sugar every 30 seconds until incorporated and whites are stiff. Spread on top of filling, covering edges. Swirl with spatula, pulling up to make points, then sprinkle topping with mace.

Step 6: Place under broiler flame until the meringue is golden brown.

Step 7: Slice and serve.

NOTE:While perfecting pie making, vary the cooking time of the custard until we get the right stiffness.

BASIC DESSERT SOUFFLÉ

1 cup milk	3 eggs, separated
2 tablespoons Raw™ sugar	3 tablespoons superfine sugar
3 tablespoons unbleached flour	2 teaspoons vanilla extract
Granulated sugar for sprinkling	Butter for coating soufflé dish

Step 1: Butter a 1 1/2-quart soufflé dish and sprinkle it with granulated sugar.

Step 2: Scald the milk in a saucepan (heat to the point where tiny bubbles begin to form, just before it begins to boil).

Step 3: In a bowl beat the egg yolks and 2 tablespoons Raw™ sugar until thick and blended, then stir in the flour and vanilla.

Step 4: Pour a little of the scalded milk into yolk mixture, whisk it in, then pour the rest of the milk in. Then return all to the saucepan, bring to a boil stirring constantly for 2 to 3 minutes; remove from the flame and set aside.

Step 5: Put the egg whites in a stainless-steel bowl and whip until foamy. Slowly add the 3 tablespoons superfine sugar and whip until whites are stiff and glossy but not dry.

Step 6: Whisk a third of the whites into the sauce to lighten it, then fold in the remaining whites. Spoon into the buttered soufflé dish and bake for 40 to 45 minutes in a preheated 400°F oven. Serve immediately.

CHOCOLATE SOUFFLÉ

1 1/2 ounces unsweetened chocolate	3 eggs, separated
3/4 cup milk	2 tablespoons Raw™ sugar
2 tablespoons butter	3 tablespoon superfine sugar
1 teaspoon vanilla	2 tablespoons unbleached flour
1/8 teaspoon almond extract	1/8 teaspoon salt
Granulated sugar for sprinkling	Butter for coating soufflé dish

Step 1: Butter a 1 1/2-quart soufflé dish and sprinkle it with granulated sugar.

Step 2: Place the chocolate, 2 tablespoons of the Raw™ sugar, and 2 tablespoons hot water in a small saucepan and heat slowly, stirring frequently, until the chocolate is smooth; remove from the flame and set aside.

Step 3: In a skillet over a low flame, melt the butter, then add flour and salt and cook stirring constantly for a few minutes, gradually add milk. Cook to the boiling point, stirring constantly until thick. Blend in the chocolate mixture.

Step 4: In another bowl, beat the egg yolks well. Stir a few tablespoons of the heated sauce into the yolks, then add the yolks to the remaining sauce. Stir in the almond & vanilla, then set aside to cool.

Step 5: Whip the egg whites, slowly adding the 3 tablespoons superfine sugar and continue whipping until we have a glossy finish. Stir a third of the whites into the chocolate mixture, then fold in the remaining whites. Spoon into the buttered soufflé dish and bake for 35 to 40 minutes in a preheated 325°F oven.

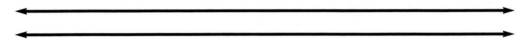

13. FRUIT DESSERTS

MANGO SOUFFLÉ

3/4 cup mango, drained & puréed

1 tablespoon Key lime juice

Granulated sugar for sprinkling

1/8 teaspoon salt

3 egg whites

1/4 cup Raw™ sugar

Butter for coating soufflé dish

Step 1: Butter a 1 1/2-quart soufflé dish and sprinkle it with granulated sugar.

Step 2: In a small saucepan and slowly heat mango purée, add lime juice, Raw™ sugar and salt, stirring frequently, until blended and smooth; remove from the flame and set aside.

Step 3: Whip the egg whites until they develop soft-peaks. Stir a third of the whites into the mango mixture, then fold in the remaining whites. Spoon into the buttered soufflé dish and bake for 20 to 25 minutes in a preheated 375°F oven.

←——————————————————————————→

BANANA PUDDING

CUSTARD

1/2 cup Raw™ sugar

4 egg yolks, slightly beaten

1 teaspoon vanilla

1/4 teaspoon salt

1/3 cup unbleached flour

2 cups scalded milk

2 cups milk

LAYERED CRUST

20 to 30 small vanilla wafers (pg.229)

1/4 teaspoon cinnamon

6 bananas

MERINGUE

4 egg whites

Pinch mace

6 tablespoons superfine sugar

Step 1:For The Custard: Combine sugar, flour and salt in a double boiler. Add 2 cups scalded milk and stir well. then stir in remaining milk. Stir yolks into mixture and continue cooking, stirring frequently, until the mixture has the consistency of thick pudding and pulls away from the sides. Pour into a bowl, stir in vanilla. Cover entire top surface with plastic wrap (to prevent skin from forming). Place in refrigerator to chill.

Step 2:Layered Arrangement: Place a layer of vanilla wafers in a glass baking dish. Slice some bananas over wafers and sprinkle with half the cinnamon. Pour half the custard over bananas. Top with another layer of vanilla wafers. Slice some bananas over wafers and sprinkle with the remaining half of cinnamon. Pour the remaining half of custard over bananas.

Step 3:For The Meringue: In a stainless-steel bowl, beat egg whites, until soft peaks form. Beat in 1 tablespoon of sugar every 30 seconds until incorporated and whites are stiff. Spread on top of filling, covering edges. Swirl with spatula, pulling up to make points, then sprinkle topping with mace.

Step 4: Bake in a 425°F preheated oven 5 to 7 minutes, or until top is golden brown. Serve warm or cold.

VERY BERRY SALAD
Also called $20 Salad
(Handle the berries very lightly so as to not bruise them.)

2 pints strawberries, hulled & halved	1 pint red currants
1 pint blueberries	1 pint blackberries
1 pint raspberries	2 tablespoons pineapple juice
2 tablespoons orange juice	2 tablespoons orange zest, finely grated
3 tablespoons mint leaves , chopped	10 mint sprigs
1 cup Citrus Chantilly (pg.254)	

Step 1: In a large bowl, place the strawberries, red currants, blueberries, blackberries and raspberries.

Step 2: In a small bowl mix pineapple juice, orange juice, orange zest and chopped mint together. Lightly toss with the berries. Allow to sit an hour at room temperature before serving.

Step 3: Spoon berries into serving bowl. Garnish with mint sprigs. Top each serving with a heaping spoonful of Citrus Chantilly.

APPLESAUCE
(Utilize Reinette apples, or others which collapse when cooked)

6 medium apples, cored, peeled & quartered	1/2 cup water or pineapple juice
1/4 cup Raw™ sugar	3/4 teaspoon cinnamon
1/8 teaspoon ground ginger or mace	1 tablespoon lime juice
1/8 teaspoon salt	

Step 1: In a large pot, over a medium flame, combine the water (or pineapple juice), sugar and apples. Stir in seasonings cover and cook for about five minutes. Uncover and begin stirring & mashing apples with a wooden spatula, making sure the mixture does not stick. Frequently stir until apples are thick purée and the liquid is absorbed, which, depending on the collapsibility of the type of apples, should take about 25 to 30 minutes.

Step 2: Stir in the lemon juice and serve warm or cold.

←——————————————————————————————————————→

VERY BERRY PARFAIT

(We will need six 12-ounce parfait glasses, tall tumblers or a mold)

BERRY MIX

1/2 pint red currants   1/2 pint blackberries

1 pint blueberries   1 pint raspberries

2 cups heavy cream, whipped

1 pint strawberries, hulled & cut into 1/2" pieces

SAUCE

1 pint strawberries, hulled & chopped   1/4 cup pineapple juice

1 cinnamon stick, whole

GARNISH

1 tablespoon lemon zest, finely grated   6 mint sprigs

6 individual blackberries   6 individual raspberries

Pinch of ground cinnamon

Step 1: Place the 1/2" pieces of strawberries, red currants, raspberries, blackberries and blueberries in a large bowl.

Step 2:For The Sauce: Place the chopped strawberries, pineapple and stick of cinnamon in a heavy saucepan. Cook over a low-flame, stirring frequently, for 10 minutes. Remove from heat, discard cinnamon stick, cool sauce to room temperature, then purée in a blender until very smooth. Toss 1 cup of the sauce with the 1/2" pieces of strawberries, red currants, raspberries, blackberries and blueberries in the large bowl. Save the remaining sauce in refrigerator for another recipe.

Step 3:To Assemble The Parfaits: In six glasses, place 1/4 cup berries in the bottom of each glass. Top with 1/4 whipped cream. Next, add another 1/4 cup berries, followed by another 1/4 cup whipped cream. Finish with 1/2 cup berries. Dollop each with 1 tablespoon Whipped cream.

Step 4:For The Garnish: Garnish each with a few sprinkles of lemon zest, ground cinnamon, an individual raspberry, blackberry, and a sprig of mint.

Step 5: Refrigerate for 2 hours before serving.

√ **Strawberry Banana Parfait**

FOR THE BERRY MIX: Use an additional *1 pint strawberries - hulled & cut into 1/2" pieces* and use *4 cups 1/2" thick sliced & quartered bananas.* Omit the blackberries, raspberries, blueberries and red currants.

FOR THE GARNISH: Use an additional *6 raspberries* instead of the 6 blackberries.

√ Cherry Tree-House Parfait

FOR THE BERRY MIX: Use *4 cups mangos - cut in 1/2" cubes, 2 cups 1/2" thick sliced & quartered bananas, and 2 cups black cherries - pitted & halved.* Instead of the strawberries, blackberries, raspberries, blueberries and red currants.

FOR THE SAUCE: Use *2 cups crushed pineapples* instead of the 1 pint strawberries, hulled & chopped.

FOR THE GARNISH: Use *12 black cherries - pitted & halved* instead of the 6 blackberries & 6 raspberries. Use *1 tablespoon lime zest - finely grated* instead of the 1 tablespoon lemon zest, finely grated.

√ Strawberry Banana Kiwi Parfait

FOR THE BERRY MIX: Use *3 cups 1/2" thick sliced & quartered bananas, and 3 cups kiwis - cut in 1/2" cubes* instead of the blackberries, raspberries, blueberries and red currants.

FOR THE GARNISH: Use an additional *6 raspberries* instead of the 6 blackberries.

$\longleftrightarrow$

APPLE CRISP

FILLING

4 cups Granny Smith apples, cored, peeled & sliced

3 cups Macintosh apples, cored, peeled & sliced

TOPPING

1 cup Raw™ sugar	1 stick butter, in small pieces
3/4 cup whole wheat flour, sifted	2/3 teaspoon cinnamon
1/4 teaspoon mace	1/2 teaspoon lemon rind, finely grated

Step 1:For The Filling: Place sliced apples in a buttered 1 1/2-quart baking dish.

Step 2:For The Topping: Mix the topping ingredients in a bowl until it resembles coarse crumbs. Sprinkle it over the apples.

Step 3: Bake in a 350°F preheated oven 30 to 45 minutes or until crust is browned. Serve topped with ice cream, if desired.

√ Apple Banana Crisp

FOR THE FILLING: Add *4 bananas - thickly sliced* and use only 2 cups of the Granny Smith apples and 2 cups of the Macintosh apples.

FOR THE TOPPING:Add *1 cup rolled oats* and use only 1/2 cup whole wheat flour, sifted.

$\longleftrightarrow$

VERY BERRY CRISP

FILLING

1 pint blueberries

1 pint raspberries

1/2 pint red currants

1/4 cup pineapple juice

TOPPING

1 cup rolled oats

1/2 teaspoon cinnamon

1 cup Raw™ sugar

1/2 cup whole wheat flour, sifted

1 stick butter, cut in small pieces

1/2 teaspoon lemon rind, finely grated

Step 1:For The Filling: Very gently toss the blueberries, raspberries and red currants in the pineapple juice. Spoon into a buttered 1 1/2-quart baking dish.

Step 2:For The Topping: Mix the topping ingredients in a bowl until it resembles coarse crumbs. Sprinkle it over the apples.

Step 3: Bake in a 350°F preheated oven 25 to 35 minutes or until crust is browned. Serve topped with ice cream, if desired.

⟵——————————————————————————⟶

APPLE BROWN BETTY

Juice & grated peel of 1 lemon

1 cup light-brown sugar

1/2 teaspoon mace

1/4 teaspoon ground cloves

3 Macintosh apples, cored, peeled & sliced

2 cups Whole Wheat Bread crumbs (pg.188)

3 Granny Smith apples, cored, peeled & sliced

1/2 stick melted butter

1 teaspoon cinnamon

Step 1: In a bowl, mix the sliced apples with lemon juice and peel.

Step 2: In another bowl, mix the light-brown sugar with the cinnamon, mace and cloves.

Step 3: In another bowl, toss the melted butter with the bread crumbs. Spread about a 2/3 cup of the crumbs in a buttered 1 1/2-quart baking dish, then spread half the apple mixture over the crumbs, then a layer of 1/2 cup sugar & spice mixture. Then spread another 2/3 cup of crumbs over sugar mixture, spread the remaining half of apple mixture over crumbs, spread the remaining 1/2 cup sugar mixture over apples and spread the final 2/3 cup of crumbs on top.

Step 4: Cover dish with foil and bake in a preheated 350°F for 20 minutes. Uncover and continue baking for another 25 to 30 minutes or until the top is crisp. Serve hot topped with a dollop of Citrus Chantilly (pg.254).

√ Peach Brown Betty

Substitute *6 ripe peaches - unpeeled & sliced into 1/2" wedges* for the 6 Granny Smith apples. Substitute *2 teaspoons ground ginger* for the ground cloves, cinnamon & mace. Substitute *1/8 cup water* for the lemon juice and peel. Adjust the amount of water depending on how moist the peaches are.

CITRUS CHANTILLY CREAM

(The suggested serving size for this tangy topping is:
ONE HEAPING TABLESPOON per dessert serving)

1 cup freshly squeezed orange juice   1 cup heavy cream

Step 1: In a small saucepan bring orange juice to a boil, reduce flame and simmer for about 20 minutes, swirling the pan frequently until the juice has reduced to 2 tablespoons of a very thick syrup. Set aside to cool.

Step 2: In a bowl, over another bowl of ice, whip the heavy cream with beaters until it holds soft peaks, do not beat until thick like butter. Gently fold the orange sauce into the whipped cream with a rubber spatula. Store in refrigerator.

√ Key Lime Chantilly Cream

Substitute *1/2 cup key lime juice* for the 1 cup orange juice and reduce sauce to 1 1/2 tablespoon instead of 2 tablespoons.

√ Whipped Evaporated Milk

Pour a *can of evaporated milk* in a bowl then place in freezer until the edges start forming into ice crystals, then whip well, until soft peaks form. Do not beat until thick like butter.

14. FOREIGN DISHES

CHINESE FRIED RICE

4 cups cooked brown or unconverted rice

5 tablespoons corn oil

1/2 teaspoon non-alcohol dry sherry

1 green bell pepper, chopped

1 scallion, finely chopped

2 eggs, slightly beaten

1/4 teaspoon ground black pepper

Step 1: Make sure rice is hot or heat rice and dry sherry in a casserole in a warm oven till ready to fry.

Step 2: Heat the oil in a large skillet or wok, scramble eggs for a minute; add scallions, sauté 1 minute, add (heated) rice, and green bell pepper. Cook over medium-high heat, stirring frequently, for 6 minutes. Remove and serve.

INDIAN RICE

1 cup brown rice

2 cloves garlic, chopped

1/4 teaspoon parsley, minced

3 tablespoons olive oil

1/2 teaspoon Muhammad's Garam Masala™ (pg.307)

1/2 yellow chili pepper, roasted, skin & seeds discarded, and minced

1 onion, chopped

Salt to taste

1 teaspoon paprika

Step 1: In a pot, boil 3 cups of water, add salt, paprika, Garam Masala, 1 tablespoon olive oil and brown rice. Bring water back to a rolling boil, reduce flame, cover and simmer for 40 minutes. Set aside to cool.

Step 2: In a skillet over a high flame, sautée the onions and garlic in 2 tablespoons olive oil until light brown. Combine with cooked rice and yellow chili pepper.

Step 3: Spoon into a buttered 1 1/2-quart baking dish and bake in a preheated 375°F for 20 minutes. Serve with fish or vegetable dish.

BROCCOLI, ITALIAN STYLE

6 cups broccoli flowerets

1/2 cup shredded mozzarella cheese

2 tablespoons olive oil

Salt to taste

4 garlic cloves, minced

1/2 teaspoon chopped parsley

Spurt of lemon juice

Black pepper to taste

Step 1: In a steamer, steam broccoli for 3 minutes. Then place in a lightly oiled baking dish.

Step 2: In a small skillet sautée garlic cloves until light-golden brown. Pour over broccoli. Sprinkle with cheese, lemon juice, salt & pepper.

Step 3: Bake in a preheated 375°F oven 10 to 13 minutes until cheese melts.

ITALIAN VEGETABLE LASAGNA

1 cup chopped onion

1/2 cup peeled & finely chopped carrots

2 1/2 cups strained tomato purée

1/2 teaspoon black pepper

1 1/2 cups mozzarella cheese, shredded

2 tablespoons Parmesan cheese, grated

1 green chili pepper, roasted , skin & seeds discarded, and minced

2 tablespoons chopped Italian parsley or fresh basil

1 tablespoon of a mixture of chopped thyme, rosemary & oregano (optional)

3 cups packed, washed, trimmed and coarsely chopped spinach (opt. dash lemon juice)

1/2 cup Whole Wheat Herb Bread crumbs (pg.192)

6 whole wheat lasagna noodles, cooked & drained

3 garlic cloves, chopped

2 tablespoons olive oil

1/2 teaspoon salt

1 cup ricotta cheese

Step 1:For The Spinach Mixture: Heat the olive oil in a skillet, over a medium flame. Add the onion, then carrot and cook for 4 minutes. Add garlic and sauté 1 minute more, until light-golden. Turn up flame to high, then add bread crumb and spinach (be careful of splattering water from wet spinach when it hits hot oil) cover and cook 2 minutes, turn heat back to medium, cook 2 minutes more, or until spinach starts to wilt. Season with salt and pepper; mix in green chili. Lift out of skillet with a slotted spoon, to drain.

Step 2:For The Ricotta Pureé: Combine 1 tablespoon of the Parmesan, ricotta and 2 tablespoons parsley or (optional 1 tablespoon herbs) and pureé until smooth.

Step 3:To Assemble The Lasagna: Drizzle 1/2 cup tomato pureé over the bottom of a 9"x13" baking dish. Cover with 2 lasagna noodles. Evenly spread the spinach mixture over the noodles and sprinkle with 1/4 cup of the mozzarella and top with 2 more lasagna noodles. Cover the noodles with the ricotta pureé and sprinkle with 1/4 cup of the mozzarella. Top with the last 2 noodles. Pour the remaining 2 cups of tomato pureé on top and finish by sprinkling with the remaining mozzarella and Parmesan.

Step 4:Cover the dish with foil and bake in a preheated 375°F oven for 30 minutes. Uncover and bake 20 minutes longer or until hot and bubbling. Let cool a few minutes before serving.

MEDITERRANEAN TOAST

4 tablespoons Tomato Sauce (pg.98)

2 tablespoons grated Mozzeralla cheese

2 4"x4" 1-inch thick slices Sourdough Whole Wheat Bread (pg.189)

Step 1: Place 2 slices of bread in a baking dish. Spread 2 tablespoons of tomato sauce on each slice, then 1 tablespoon of cheese on top. Cover with foil.

Step 2: Place in preheated 350° oven for 15 minutes. Remove foil, then place under the broiler flame to toast the top until cheese is golden-browned.

$$\longleftrightarrow$$

FISH AND NAVY BEAN SAMOSAS
(EASTERN INDIAN)

SPICED FISH FILLING

1/3 cup grated carrot

1 teaspoon ginger, finely grated

1/2 cup onion, chopped

1 teaspoon cumin seeds, roasted & ground

1/2 teaspoon coriander, roasted & ground

1/4 teaspoon black pepper

1 cup cooked navy bean, pureé (pg.70)

1/2 green chili pepper, roasted , skin & seeds discarded, and minced

[1/2 pound Whiting or salmon fillet, steamed 8 minutes, skin removed & flaked (pg.276)]

1 scallion, thinly sliced

1 teaspoon garlic, minced

1 tablespoon corn oil

1/2 teaspoon salt

1 teaspoon water

DOUGH

2 cups whole wheat flour, sifted

1/2 cup cold water

1 teaspoon Raw™ sugar

5 tablespoons melted butter

1/2 teaspoon salt

RAITA

1/2 cup sour cream

1/2 teaspoon coriander, roasted & ground

1 teaspoon cumin seeds, roasted & ground

1 tablespoon cilantro leaves, finely chopped

1/2 large tomato, seeded and finely diced

1 small cucumber, peeled, seeded, cut in 1/4-inch dices

1/2 green chili pepper, roasted , skin & seeds discarded, and minced

1/2 teaspoon honey

1/3 teaspoon salt

1 teaspoon salt, for cucumber coating

DEEP-FRYING

Corn oil

Step 1:For The Dough: Combine the flour, sugar, salt and melted butter in a bowl; using a pastry blender blend the butter into flour until the mixture resembles coarse meal. Sprinkle the water over flour and , using fingers, work in until we have a soft dough. Knead a few minutes until smooth on a lightly floured surface. Divide the dough into 6 pieces. Roll each into a ball, then flatten into a disc. Wrap in plastic wrap, and refrigerate for 30 minutes.

Step 2:For The Raita: Meanwhile place cucumber in a strainer, sprinkle salt over to coat, toss well, and let stand for 15 minutes. Then rinse off salt, and pat dry with paper towels. In a bowl, combine the cucumber with all the remaining raita ingredients. Stir to mix well, and refrigerate.

Step 3:For The Fish Filling: Heat oil in a heavy skillet over a medium flame; add onions, garlic and ginger; sauté for 2 minutes; stir navy bean pureé, green chili, cumin, coriander, fish and 1 teaspoon water and stir combine. Remove skillet from heat and stir in the grated carrot and scallion. Season with salt and black pepper; cover; set aside to cool.

Step 4:To Assemble The Samosas: Work with one piece of the dough at a time, keeping the remaining refrigerated. On a lightly floured or oiled work surface, roll one portion of dough into an 8-inch circle, lift dough, dust with flour, as needed, and rotate to prevent from sticking. Cut the circle in half. Moisten the straight edge of one semicircle with a thin coat of water and roll it up into a cone, overlapping the cut edges. Press the seam to seal. Hold the cone in one hand with the open end up and fill it with 2 tablespoons of the filling. Moisten the inside edges of the open end with water and pinch together to seal. (or press down until shaped into a disk, which resembles a hockey puck.) Repeat with the second semicircle. Place the samosas on a dish and cover with clean towel to prevent them from drying out while we assemble the remaining samosas in the same fashion.

Step 5: Preheat the oven to 225°F.

Step 6:To Deep Fry The Samosas: Heat 2 to 3 inches of corn oil in a deep heavy saucepan or deep fryer, over a medium flame 350°F. Add a few samosas at a time, (Do not crowd skillet), and cook, turning once or twice, until they are brown, about 4 to 6 minutes. Drain; transfer to a paper towel lined platter to drain well; keep them warm in the 225°F oven while the remaining ones are being cooked.

Alternate Step 6:Bake Method: Arrange samosas on an oiled cookie sheet. Bake in a 425°F preheated oven 10 to 15 minutes or until golden brown. Turn once while baking then, brush the top of each samosas with milk once or twice while baking.

Step 7: Serve the samosas hot with the Raita or Tahini Sauce With Herbs (pg.102) on the side.

*Note: Divide the roasted green chili pepper, roasted coriander and roasted cumin amongst the fish filling and Raita.

RED SNAPPER, MEDITERRANEAN STYLE

4 cloves garlic, peeled, roasted & sliced
1 anchovy fillet, finely chopped

1 tomato, diced
1 tablespoon olive oil

1/2 tablespoon sherry vinegar

2 tablespoons fresh tarragon or basil

1/2 teaspoon salt

1/4 teaspoon black pepper

2 tablespoons Kalamata olives, pitted & coarsely chopped

1 tablespoon capers, drained & coarsely chopped

(1 one-pound red snapper, gutted and scaled , head* left on, gills removed, tails and fins trimmed)

1/2 red chili pepper, roasted , skin & seeds discarded, and minced

1 tablespoon unsalted butter, melted

1 fifteen-inch square of parchment

Step 1: In a bowl, combine the tomato, garlic, olive oil, vinegar, capers, olives, anchovy, red chili and tarragon or basil; set aside.

Step 2: Wipe fish with a damp cloth inside and out until there is no trace of blood remaining. Sprinkle fish inside and out with salt and pepper.

Step 3: Coat parchment completely with 1 tablespoon melted butter and place seasoned fish in center of parchment; spoon the tomato mixture over the fish; fold long edge of parchment over filling, fold forward a few times, pressing to crease, sealing the edge. Double fold the ends of packet. Arrange on baking sheet.

Step 4: Bake in a preheated 425°F oven 20 minutes, until the sealed parchment inflates and turns light brown. When serving open them carefully or serve on a warm platter. Serve with a rice dish (pg.121) and Plantains (pg.156).

*The head may be removed or wrapped in a shred of parchment paper if an eye staring back up at you while eating isn't appealing.

SAUTEÉD RED SNAPPER, CANTONESE STYLE™

1 1/2 pound red snapper fillets

2 tablespoons ginger, finely grated

1 1/2 tablespoons corn oil

2 tablespoons light soy sauce

1/2 teaspoon salt

4 sprigs cilantro, for garnish

2 scallions, chopped

3 tablespoons cilantro, chopped

1 teaspoon sesame oil

1 teaspoon non-alcohol dry sherry

1/8 teaspoon white pepper

Step 1: Wipe fillets with a damp cloth. Cut into 1-inch cubes. Sprinkle with white pepper and salt.

Step 2: Heat corn & sesame oil in a heavy skillet over a medium-high flame; add cubed fish, scallion, ginger; sauteé a minute; add cilantro, soy sauce, and sherry; cover; reduce flame to simmer gently for 10 minutes; drain if needed.

Step 3: Arrange cooked fish on a warm platter; garnish with cilantro. Serve with rice.

NAVY BEAN & SPINACH SOUP™
Iranian

2 cups navy beans

2 onions, finely chopped

2 tablespoons olive oil

1/2 teaspoon salt

1/4 teaspoon black pepper

1/2 teaspoon cumin seeds, roasted & ground

1 teaspoon coriander seeds, roasted & ground

1/2 teaspoon Muhammad's Chili Powder™ (pg.307)

1 pound spinach, thoroughly rinsed & chopped

1/4 cup rice, rinsed

1 teaspoon turmeric

1/4 cup lemon juice

Step 1: Rinse and sort beans. Cover beans with water and let soak overnight or boil 2 minutes, cover and let set 1 hour before going to next step. Then drain beans and rinse thoroughly, until water runs clear.

Step 2: Place in a large pot with water. Bring to a boil over high heat, immediately turn down heat. Then after they boil for a few minutes, drain again and replace with fresh boiling water.

Step 3: After 15 minutes add rice, turmeric, cumin, coriander, chili powder and black pepper. Simmer for a total 1 hour or until tender.

Step 4: Meanwhile heat olive oil in a skillet over high flame and sauté onions until golden brown. Add onions and spinach in the last 10 minutes of cooking. It is ready when beans are easily mashed. Stir in lemon juice and salt. Add more boiling water if needed.

Step 5: If you like, serve with Garlic toast (pg.195) and cheese. Soup will naturally thicken immediately after its done, just add boiling water.

15. MEAT ALTERNATIVES, QUICHES, ETC.

MEAT ALTERNATIVES

NAVY BEAN PATTIES

3 cups navy beans, cooked & pureéd   1 large onion, chopped

1 egg, slightly beaten   1/2 teaspoon salt

Corn oil as needed

1 1/2 tablespoons Muhammad's Seasoning™ (pg.307)

1 cup Whole Wheat Herb Bread crumbs (pg.192)

Step 1: In a bowl lightly mix ingredients until they are a very loose consistency, then form into half-inch thick patties. (If mixture is too moist add more bread crumb and lessen egg quantity next time. If too dry vice versa).

Alternate Step 2:Fry Method: Over medium heat in a heavy skillet, heat oil. Add a few patties at a time to oil. (Do not crowd skillet) Cook 4 minutes on each side until golden brown.

Alternate Step 2:Bake Method: Arrange patties on an oiled cookie sheet. Bake in a 425°F preheated oven 15 to 20 minutes or until golden brown. Turn once while baking then, brush the top of each patty with milk once or twice while baking.

Step 3: Serve hot with mustard sauce (pg.109) or tomato sauce (pg.98) or applesauce (pg.250).

←──────────────────────────────→

CARROT LOAF

1 cup carrot, peeled & grated   1 onion, minced

1/2 cup celery, thinly sliced   2 eggs, slightly beaten

2 tablespoons parsley, chopped   2 tablespoons sour cream

1/2 teaspoon black pepper   1 teaspoon salt

3 tablespoons butter

4 sprigs parsley, for garnish

2 tablespoons Whole Wheat Herb Bread crumbs (pg.192)

1/2 cup buttered Whole Wheat Bread crumbs (pg.188)

Step 1: In a bowl combine and lightly mix eggs, sour cream, carrots, onion, celery, parsley, 2 tablespoons whole wheat herb bread crumbs, salt & pepper.

Step 2: Butter a loaf pan with 1 tablespoon of the butter and sprinkle the 1/2 cup whole wheat bread crumbs in pan. Spoon in the carrot mixture and dot with remaining 2 tablespoon butter. Cover with foil.

Step 3: Bake in a 350°F preheated oven for 30 minutes. Uncover and continue baking 5 to 10 more minutes or until golden brown. Remove from oven and invert over a serving dish. Turn out the loaf and serve warm with Tomato Sauce (pg.98) or Applesauce (pg.250) Garnish with parsley sprigs.

←————————————————————————→

BROWN RICE BURGERS

BURGER PATTIES

4 cups Browned Rice, (pg.121)   1 green bell pepper, finely chopped

1 zucchini, finely chopped   1 yellow squash, finely chopped

1 onion, finely chopped   4 to 6 eggs, slightly beaten

Corn oil for cooking   Salt to taste

2 tablespoons olive oil

1/4 cup Muhammad's Thai Steak Sauce™ (pg.307)

1/4 cup Barbeque Sauce™ (pg.112)

1/2 to 1 cup Whole Wheat Herb Bread crumbs (pg.192)

1 teaspoon Muhammad's Hot Cajun Seasoning™ (pg.307)

BUN & GARNISHES

Burger Buns, toasted (pg.197)   Slices of cheese

Lettuce, shredded

tomato slices

Mustard (pg.108), Ketchup (pg.109), or Mayonnaise (pg.183)

Step 1: Over medium-high heat in a heavy skillet, heat olive oil, sauté the squash, zucchini, onion and green pepper, add Cajun Seasoning & salt and cook for 5 to 10 minutes or until translucent. Drain well.

Step 2: In a large bowl lightly mix the sautéed vegetables with the rice, add bread crumbs, Strong-Island Sauce and eggs until mixture is just held together enough to be formable. (If mixture is too moist add more bread crumb and lessen egg quantity next time. If too dry vice versa).

Alternate Step 3:Fry Method: Over medium heat in a heavy skillet, heat some corn oil. Shape the mixture into patties and add a few at a time to oil. (Do not crowd skillet) Cook thoroughly on each side until nicely browned. Or chop up into bits to make a Sloppy Joe™ or put a slice of cheese on top of each patty and let it melt.

Alternate Step 3:Bake Method: Arrange patties on an oiled cookie sheet. Bake in a 350°F preheated oven 15 to 20 minutes or until golden brown. Turn once while baking then, brush the top of each patty with milk once or twice while baking.

Step 4: Place on Burger Bun prepared with garnishes.

←————————————————————————→

NAVY BEAN BURGERS

BURGER PATTIES

2 cups cooked navy beans, drained well   1/2 cup rolled oats

1/2 cups Browned rice, (pg.121)

1 onion, finely chopped

2 cloves garlic, minced

1/2 cup cilantro, chopped

Corn oil for cooking

1/2 teaspoon cumin seeds, roasted & ground

1 green bell pepper, drained & finely chopped

1 teaspoon Muhammad's Chili Powder™ (pg.307)

1/2 teaspoon oregano

1 egg, slightly beaten (optional)

1 teaspoon salt

BUN & GARNISHES

Burger Buns, toasted (pg.197)

Lettuce, shredded

tomato slices

Thinly sliced olives (optional)

Mustard (pg.108), Ketchup (pg.109), or Mayonnaise (pg.183)

Slices of cheese

Slices of Dill pickle (optional)

Step 1: In a bowl lightly mix ingredients until they are a very loose consistency, then form into half-inch thick patties. (If mixture is too moist add more rolled oats and lessen egg quantity next time. If too dry vice versa).

Alternate Step 2:Fry Method: Over medium heat in a heavy skillet, heat oil. Add a few patties at a time to oil. (Do not crowd skillet) Cook 4 minutes on each side until golden brown. Or chop up into bits to make a Sloppy Joe™ or put a slice of cheese on top of each patty and let it melt.

Alternate Step 2:Bake Method: Arrange patties on an oiled cookie sheet. Bake in a 350°F preheated oven 15 to 20 minutes or until golden brown. Turn once while baking then, brush the top of each patty with milk once or twice while baking.

Step 3: Place on Burger Bun prepared with garnishes.

⬅━━━━━━━━━━━━━━━━━━━━━━━━━━➡

SUNFLOWER-RICE BURGERS

BURGER PATTIES

1 cup sunflower seeds, hulled & roasted

2 cups Brown rice, (pg.121)

1/2 cup carrot, finely grated

1 egg, slightly beaten (optional)

1 tomato, chopped

Corn oil for cooking

1/4 cup green bell pepper, drained & finely chopped

1 clove garlic

1 tablespoon basil, chopped

1/2 cup onion, finely chopped

1 tablespoon tarragon, chopped

1 teaspoon salt

BUN & GARNISHES

Burger Buns, toasted (pg.197)

Slices of cheese

Lettuce, shredded

Slices of Dill pickle (optional)

tomato slices

Thinly sliced olives (optional)

Muhammad's Chili Sauce™ (pg.307),Mustard (pg.108), Ketchup (pg.109), Mayonnaise (pg.183) or Muhammad's Thai Steak Sauce™ (pg.307)

Step 1: In a food processor, chop the tarragon, basil and garlic; add the sunflower seeds and rice, and coarsely chop.

Step 2: In a bowl lightly mix ingredients until they are a very loose consistency, then form into half-inch thick patties. (If mixture is too moist add more rice and lessen egg quantity next time. If too dry vice versa).

Alternate Step 3:Fry Method: Over medium heat in a heavy skillet, heat oil. Add a few patties at a time to oil. (Do not crowd skillet) Cook 4 minutes on each side until golden brown. Or chop up into bits to make a Sloppy Joe™ or put a slice of cheese on top of each patty and let it melt.

Alternate Step 3:Bake Method: Arrange patties on an oiled cookie sheet. Bake in a 350°F preheated oven 15 to 20 minutes or until golden brown. Turn once while baking then, brush the top of each patty with milk once or twice while baking.

Step 4: Place on Burger Bun prepared with garnishes.

NAVY BEAN ROAST

2 cups navy bean, cooked & pureéd

1 onion, minced

1/2 cup green bell pepper, finely chopped

2 tablespoons chopped parsley

2 cloves garlic, chopped

1/4 cup celery, chopped

2 eggs, slightly beaten

2 tablespoons butter

2 tablespoons olive oil

1/2 teaspoon salt

1/2 to 1 cup Whole Wheat Herb Bread crumbs (pg.192)

1 teaspoon Muhammad's Hot Cajun Seasoning™ (pg.307)

GARNISH

Paprika

4 sprigs curly parsley

Step 1: Over medium-high heat in a heavy skillet, heat olive oil, sauté the onion, green pepper, garlic and celery, add Cajun Seasoning & salt and cook for 5 to 10 minutes or until translucent. Drain well.

Step 2: In a bowl combine and lightly mix eggs, beans, parsley, whole wheat herb bread crumbs, an sauteéd vegetables.

Step 3: Coat a shallow baking dish with the butter. Spoon in the bean mixture and pat into shape, sprinkle top with paprika.

Step 4: Bake in a 350°F preheated oven for 15 to 25 minutes or until golden brown. Remove from oven and serve warm with Tomato Sauce (pg.98) or Ketchup (pg.109) Garnish with parsley sprigs.

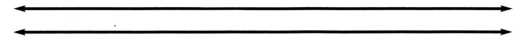

QUICHES

CHEESE & EGG QUICHE

1 cup Swiss cheese, grated	1/8 teaspoon mace
1/8 teaspoon black pepper	
1/2 teaspoon salt	
Dash Muhammad's Red Hot Sauce™ (pg.307)	

FILLING

2 onions, thinly sliced	3 tablespoons butter

CUSTARD

3/4 cup half & half	4 eggs
1 1/4 cup milk (optional 'Low-Fat')	

CRUST

1 Flaky Tart Pastry (pg.232),(Prebaked)

Step 1:For The Filling: Sauté the onions in butter. Sprinkle evenly over bottom of Prebaked crust.

Step 2: Sprinkle the cheese over the onions. Sprinkle with salt, black & hot sauce.

Step 3:For The Custard: In a bowl beat the eggs, add the milk and half & half. Mix thoroughly. Pour over the cheese. Sprinkle with mace.

Step 4: Bake in a preheated 375°F oven for 35 to 40 minutes or until a knife blade comes out clean after inserting.

√ **Broccoli Quiche**

Add *2 cups broccoli floweretts-Sauteéd* along with the onions.

√ **Asparagus & Dill Quiche**

Omit the Swiss cheese and substitute *2 cups chopped Asparagus-Sauteéd* instead of the onions. Add *1 teaspoon freshly chopped dill* along with Asparagus.

√ **Spinach & Feta Quiche**

Substitute *1 cup Feta cheese-diced* for the Swiss cheese and substitute *2 cups spinach-Sauteéd with 2 tablespoons freshly chopped parsley and a squirt of lemon juice* instead of the onions. Top with *2 to 3 tablespoons freshly grated Parmesan or Romano cheese.*

16. MUHAMMAD'S WORLD OF FISH

INFO ON FISH

•Fish are born and live in the water of life.

•When eating fish, we should confine our fish-eating to those fish weighing between one to ten pounds. If it weighs more than ten pounds it is too hard on our digestive system.

•Fish is a better food, if you eat the better fish. The flesh of fish comes out of another world. All of our food in the way of meat should come from the sea, ocean, river or lakes.

•We should eat no meat at all. Of the meats, fish is the least detrimental to our health.

SOME POINTERS ON SHOPPING FOR & STORING FISH

•Fish must look wholesome and alive, with red gills, clear eyes and firm to the touch, unbruised flesh; your finger should not leave a dent after pressing flesh. Steaks and fillets should gleam, without any hints of browning.

•The smell of the fish is a quick indicator to whether it is good or not. Take a whiff if the odor is off don't purchase it. If it smells bad it can't taste good.

•Under no circumstances should prewrapped "fresh" fish be purchased; there is no way to inspect its freshness.

•Do not purchase fish that isn't kept COLD; fish must be kept on ice.

The above tips are more important than whether the fish is labeled "previously frozen" of "fresh". Some boats clean and freeze the fish within hours of the catch; when thawed, this fish is usually in better condition than "fresh" fish that has spent several days in the hold of a ship before reaching the dock.

The better-quality fish has been frozen or kept on ice until it reaches the consumer. It will remain that way for about 3 days if kept in the refrigerator vegetable bin still-wrapped, buried in ice and the smell reduced by placing a piece of smashed garlic clove in the bin. Or freeze it for longer storage.

Cooked, left over fish should be stored in tightly sealed container and placed in refrigerator as soon as we realize it is to be left over.

SOME POINTERS ON NEUTRALIZING FISH ODORS

Fish odor on our hands is minimized by chilling our hands in cold water before touching raw fish.

To cleanse hands AFTER cooking fish, follow these four steps:

1. Don't use soap initially.

2. Rub hands well with a squashed lemon half or moistened salt.

3. Rinse well with warm-hot water.

4. Finally, wash hands with soapy water that has some lemon juice squeezed into it.

To neutralize natural odors on dishes and cooking utensils, rinse off thoroughly and cleanse with soapy water that has the juice of a lemon squeezed into it.

To Reduce Natural Frying Odors, Remember This Simple Point:

•Never permit heated fat to smoke. It will not absorb most of the natural odors.

HOW TO FILLET A FISH

PROCEED WITH A SHARP FILLET KNIFE TO:
1. Cut down through the flesh along the back from the tail to just behind the head.
2. Cut down the backbone just above the collarbone.
3. Turn the knife flat and cut the flesh along the backbone to the tail; the blade runs along the rib bones and the fillet comes off in one piece.
4. Turn the fish over and repeat the same procedure for the other side.
   If we wish to skin the fillets, then continue with step 5;
5. Lay the fillet flat on a cutting board, skin side down.
6. Grasp tail end with fingers; cut through the flesh to the skin (approximately 1/2-inch from the end of the fillet).
7. Flatten the blade on the skin and cut the flesh away by pushing the knife forward; the fillet is now skinned.
8. We should always hold the free end of the skin firmly with our fingers.
9. Wipe the fillet with a damp cloth only; do not wash.

METHODS FOR COOKING FISH

BAKE

Baking is the proffered way to cook fish, especially whole fish such as red snapper or sea trout. Follow these procedures for the best baked fish:

* When washing fish, dip it quickly in cold, salted water; wipe dry with paper towels.
* If marinating, place raw fish in a zip lock™ bag, pour flavored liquid over raw fish and seal allow to rest in refrigerator a few hours to overnight.
* If it is to be filled or stuffed, only fill cavity 2/3rds full. Seal by closing with either skewers, toothpicks or lace with white thread.

* Place fish in shallow baking dish over a layer of buttered parchment paper.
* Roast the fish, uncovered in a preheated 425°F oven for about 10 minutes per inch of thick ness, measure at the thickest point. If not marinated, baste while roasting. Because overbaking dries out natural juices and flavors. Partially cooked vegetables added to the dish will brown nicely and absorb some of the fish juices.
* Serve immediately from the oven; standing cooked fish becomes soggy.

STEAM

Fish is succulent and delicate when steamed. During steaming it won't become dried and shriveled because the juices and flavor remain in the fish when it is cooked over hot moisture that is sealed in a steamer. A steamer should be invested in to easily cook fish and vegetables. Follow these procedures for the best steamed fish:

1. Wipe fish with a damp cloth.
2. Fill bottom portion of steamer with 2 inches of water. Water may be seasoned with lemon juice, vinegar, garlic, onion, cloves, parsley or celery or any herbs so that the flavors blend well and saturate the fish and cuts down on fishy odors in the house.
3. Thinly coat the inside of steamer basket with oil.
4. When water begins to boil, place fish in oiled basket.
5. Steam fish approximately 6 for thin fish and 10 minutes for thick fish, or until flaky.
6. Salt fish only after steaming.
7. Serve steamed fish with accompaniment; or flaked as required by recipe.

BROIL

Fish can be broiled as a fillet, thick-steak, split or kept whole and dressed. It should be served hot and not overcooked.

Thin fillets are placed on the broiler rack 2-inches from the flame and thick split fish and 1-inch steaks are placed on the broiler rack 6-inches from the flame.

The backbone should be left intact on split fish to retain the flavor and juices. The whole dressed fish is prepared as for baking.

Fish, properly broiled, should be juicy and a light-golden brown.

Follow these procedures for the best broiled fish:

1. Preheat broiling compartment and pan at least 10 minutes.

2. If fish must be washed, do so quickly in cold salted water.

3. Dust fish lightly with unbleached flour, if preferred.

4. Brush top of fish with butter and seasonings. For whole fish, brush entire fish.

5. Brush broiling pan with oil.

6. Place fish on pan and position the distance from flame as directed.

7. Thin fillets will be done in 3 or 4 minutes; do not turn fillets and split fish during broiling period; baste as directed; or season at the end of broiling time, if preferred.

8. Thick fillets or steaks take 8 to 10 minutes per inch of thickness. Half way through broiling period, turn over and broil other side. Baste after turning and season at end of broiling time, if preferred.

9. Serve immediately from broiler.

BOIL

It should be called simmering because when a fish is cooked in hot water it should only be gently heated with herbs or in a broth, or if it is to be served with a wonderful sauce (See Fish Sauce (pg.101)]. Steaks and fillets are boiled to make Court Bouillon (pg.81). Fish trimmings, vegetables and herbs are boiled to make Fish Stock (pg.81). Hints to effectively boil fish:

• Wipe fish clean with damp cloth.
• Secure fish in a cheesecloth, except for fish trimmings to make Fish Stock.
• Bring water to a rapid boil; place fish in water and lower flame to a gentle simmer. Cooking time accordingly to recipe.
• Drain; then prepare and serve as desired.

PLANK
To bake or broil and serve fish on a plank.

A whole planked fish should be served with a few favorite vegetables and garnished.

To plank whole fish or steaks:
1. Use a 1 1/2-inch thick wooden plank made from well-seasoned oak, hickory or ash.
2. Place plank in a oven and heat for 10 minutes.
3. Remove hot plank from oven; butter or oil liberally.
4. Arrange whole fish or steak in center of the plank.
5. Proceed as instructed in recipe. Place partially steamed vegetables around fish and garnish; return to oven to bake or to broiler to broil and baste, if preferred.
6. Serve hot on plank at table.

SAUTÉ

Sautéing is a great way to cook fish fillets of all sizes and cuts-like cubes and strips, small whole fish and not-too-thick steaks. Instructions for Sautéing:

1. Wipe fish with damp cloth.
2. Heat a little olive oil and butter in a heavy skillet over medium-high flame.
3. Dredge the fish in flour flavored with herbs and spices as specified in recipe.
4. Place fish in skillet, for thick steaks (add any liquid sauces, fish or vegetable stock) cook, for a total of 7 to 8 minutes per inch of thickness, turning once, until browned.
5. Place fish in skillet, for cut fish (add any liquid sauces, fish or vegetable stock) cook, for a total of 3 to 4 minutes, turning frequently, until browned.
6. Serve fish hot from skillet, with the liquid, which can be further heated until reduced to form a gravy.

FRY
(Not Preferred)

This quick way of cooking fish seals in the juices of the fish and creates a crust.
To fry fillets, steaks, dressed fish, split or cut into strips:

1. Wipe fish with damp cloth.
2. Sprinkle fish with seasoning, then dip into egg or milk batter, then in flour or bread crumbs.
3. Heat 1/2-inch deep layer of oil in a skillet over a medium-high flame. Do not allow oil to smoke.
4. Fry fish 3 minutes or until golden brown. Turn fish carefully with spatula; continue cooking for 3 more minutes or until browned.
5. Drain well and place on paper towels to absorb excess oil. Garnish and serve hot.

DEEP FRY
(Not Preferred)

This is another quick way of cooking fish that seals in the juices of the fish and creates a crust.
To fry fillets or very small whole fish especially porgies:

1. Wipe fish with damp cloth.
2. Sprinkle fish with seasoning, then dip into egg or milk batter, then in flour or bread crumbs. Place one layer only of coated fillets in wire basket.

3. Heat 6-inch deep layer of oil to 350°F to 380°F in a heavy pot over a medium-high flame. Do not allow oil to smoke.

4. Fry fish 3 minutes or until golden brown. Turn fish carefully with spatula; continue cooking for 3 more minutes or until browned.

5. Drain well and place on paper towels to absorb excess oil. Garnish and serve hot.

GRILL

Salmon or Red Snapper cut into 1" to 2" cubes and alternately arranged with chunks of vegetables on skewers called kabobs or salmon steaks are favorites cooked by this technique.

1. Wipe fish with damp cloth.

2. Marinate or season fish and brush with oil. Arrange cuts for kabobs according to recipe.

3. Heat the grill good and hot.

4. Lay fish on grill and cook for 10 to 12 minutes for kabobs and 8 to 10 minutes per inch of thickness for steaks, turn fish halfway through cooking time.

5. Serve hot with accompaniment and garnish.

⟵——————————————————⟶

FISH RECIPES

PACIFIC BAKE SALMON

1 1/2 lbs red salmon fillet, steamed 10 minutes, skin removed & flaked (pg.269)

1/2 green chili pepper, roasted , skin & seeds discarded, and minced

2/3 cup Whole Wheat Herb Bread crumb (pg.192)

1 teaspoon Muhammad's Seasoning™ (pg.307)

1 teaspoon coriander seeds, roasted & ground

1 cup Mayonnaise (pg.183)

3/4 cup onion, chopped	1/2 cup green bell pepper, chopped
1/2 cup celery, chopped	1 clove garlic, minced
2 eggs, slightly beaten	1 teaspoon paprika

Dash of mace Salt & black pepper to taste

Step 1: In a bowl lightly mix ingredients until they are a very loose consistency.

Step 2: Coat a baking dish with butter. Spoon in the mixture and pat into shape.

Step 3: Bake in a 350°F preheated oven for 40 minutes. Serve warm with Tomato Sauce (pg.98) Garnish with a few sprigs of cilantro.

⟵——————————————————⟶

WHITING LOAF

1 1/2 lbs Whiting fillet, steamed 8 minutes, skin removed & flaked (pg.276)

1/2 yellow chili pepper, roasted , skin & seeds discarded, and minced

1/3 to 2/3 cup Whole Wheat Herb Bread crumb, toasted (pg.192)

1 teaspoon Muhammad's Pepper Fish Seasoning™ (pg.307)

1 stick butter

1 tablespoon olive oil	Few sprigs of parsley
2 cups onion, chopped	1 green bell pepper, chopped
1 1/2 cup celery, chopped	1 clove garlic, minced
2 eggs, slightly beaten	Salt & black pepper to taste

Step 1: In a large skillet, over a medium-high flame, heat butter and sauté onion, celery, peppers, garlic, seasoning, salt & black pepper.

Step 2: In a bowl lightly mix all ingredients until they are a very loose consistency. Adjust amount of bread crumbs until mixture is formable.

Step 3: Coat a loaf pan with olive oil. Spoon in the mixture and pat into the shape of a loaf.

Step 4: Bake in a 400˚F preheated oven for 20 minutes or until browned. Serve hot with Tomato Sauce (pg.98) Garnish with a few sprigs of Parsley.

◄──────────────────────────────────►

WHITING BAKE, INDIAN STYLE

1 1/2 lbs Whiting fillet, steamed 8 minutes, skin removed & flaked (pg.276)

1/2 red chili pepper, roasted, skin & seeds discarded, and minced

1/2 to 2/3 cup Whole Wheat Bread crumbs, toasted (pg.188)

3/4 teaspoon Garam Masala™ Seasoning (pg.307)

1/2 cup Mayonnaise

1 tablespoon olive oil	Few sprigs of parsley, for garnish
1/2 cup onion, chopped	1 green bell pepper, chopped
1/2 cup celery, chopped	1 red bell pepper, chopped
2 eggs yolks, slightly beaten	Salt & black pepper to taste
1 teaspoon lime juice	2 tablespoons butter
1 tablespoon parsley, minced	

Step 1: In a large skillet, over a medium-high flame, heat butter and sauté onion, celery,bell peppers, seasoning, salt & black pepper.

Step 2: In a bowl lightly mix all ingredients until they are a very loose consistency. Adjust amount of bread crumbs until mixture is formable.

Step 3: Coat a baking dish with olive oil. Spoon in the mixture and pat into shape.

Step 4: Bake in a 350°F preheated oven for 30 to 40 minutes or until browned. Serve hot with Tomato Sauce (pg.98) Garnish with a few sprigs of Parsley.

SAUTÉED PORGY

4 porgies

1 garlic clove, minced

4 tablespoons olive oil

1 lemon or lime

1 teaspoon salt

4 sprigs of parsley for garnish

1/2 cup whole wheat flour

1/2 teaspoon marjoram, finely chopped

1/4 teaspoon chives, finely chopped

1 tablespoon butter

1 teaspoon black pepper

Step 1: Wipe porgies with a damp cloth.

Step 2: In a bowl combine the flour salt and pepper, and dredge the fish.

Step 3: Heat the olive oil in a large skillet over a high flame, and brown the fish quickly on both sides. Turn the flame to medium, add garlic, marjoram and chives, and cook 10 to 15 minutes. Remove to a warm platter.

Step 4: Squeeze the juice of half the lemon or lime into the skillet with the butter, scrape up the browned bits, and pour the juices over the fish on platter. Slice the other half of the lemon or lime and garnish the fish with them and sprigs of parsley. Serve with rice dish (pg.121).

SAVORY CARRIBEAN BAKED SNAPPER

2 eight-ounce red snapper fillets

2 garlic cloves, sliced

1 teaspoon thyme leaves, finely chopped

1 tablespoon olive oil

1/4 teaspoon salt

1/2 carrot, julienned

2 sprigs thyme for garnish

1/2 teaspoon Herb Fish Seasoning™ (pg.307)

1 onion, sliced

1 teaspoon chives, finely chopped

1 lime, juiced

1 tablespoon butter

1/4 teaspoon black pepper

Step 1: Wipe fillets with a damp cloth. Squirt 1/4 of the lime juice on fillets and sprinkle the seasoning on both sides of fillet.

Step 2: Coat a 2-quart baking dish with olive oil and place fillets in center, skin-side facing up. Arrange onion, garlic and carrot around fillets and dot vegetables with butter.

Step 3: Blend 1/4 of the lime juice with the thyme leaves & chives and sprinkle over fillets. Sprinkle salt & pepper over all.

Step 4: Bake in a preheated 400°F oven for 20 minutes. Basting with the remaining lime juice half way through the baking time. Serve with a rice dish (pg.121).

SPICED SNAPPER IN PARCHMENT

2 eight-ounce red snapper fillets

1 small onion, sliced

1/4 cup basil, julienned

2 fifteen-inch squares of parchment

4 tomatoes-on the vine, sliced

2 garlic cloves, minced

3 tablespoons olive oil

COMBINED SEASONING MIX

1/2 teaspoon oregano, finely chopped

1 teaspoons salt

2 tablespoons Muhammad's Seasoning™ (pg.307)

1/2 teaspoon thyme, finely chopped

Step 1: Wipe fillets with a damp cloth. Coat each fillet with 1 tablespoon olive oil and sprinkle one teaspoon combined seasoning mix on both sides of fillet.

Step 2: Coat each parchment completely with 1 tablespoon olive oil and place seasoned fillets in center of parchment, skin-side facing down. Sprinkle each with 1 tablespoon seasoning mix, then half of the onion, garlic, basil and tomato. Fold long edge of parchment over filling, fold forward a few times, pressing to crease, sealing the edge. Double fold the ends of packet. Arrange on baking sheet.

Step 3: Bake in a preheated 425°F oven 12 to 15 minutes, until the sealed parchment inflates and turns light brown. When serving open them carefully. Serve with a rice dish (pg.121) and Plantains (pg.156).

SWEET & SOUR WHITING, THAI STYLE

(A minimum of one hour before beginning this recipe marinate the fillets
with the sweet & sour sauce, in a plastic bag, in the refrigerator.)

2 whiting fillets

1 onion, sliced

1 stalk celery, thinly sliced

1/4 teaspoon salt

1 1/3 tablespoons corn oil

1/4 cup Muhammad's Thai Sweet & Sour Sauce™ (pg.307)

1 lime, juiced

2 garlic cloves, sliced

1 green bell pepper, sliced

1/4 teaspoon black pepper

Step 1: Wipe fillets with a damp cloth. In a plastic bag, marinate the fillets in the sweet & sour sauce, in the refrigerator for a minimum of 1 hour.

Step 2: Coat a 2-quart baking dish with corn oil and remove fillets from bag and drain off most of the excess sweet & sour sauce, place fillets in center of baking dish, skin-side facing up. Arrange onion, garlic, green pepper and celery around fillets and drizzle 1/3 tablespoon oil over them.

Step 3: Sprinkle 1/2 of the lime juice over fillets. Sprinkle salt & pepper over all.

Step 4: Bake in a preheated 400°F oven for 20 minutes. Basting with the remaining lime juice half way through the baking time. Serve with a rice dish (pg.121).

FISH BAKED SABEA ARABIAN STYLE

3 whiting fillets	4 carrots, julienned
1 onion, sliced	1/4 cup olive oil
1/4 teaspoon dill	1/4 teaspoon fennel
2 egg yolks, beaten	Juice of 1 lemon
1/2 teaspoon salt	1/2 teaspoon black pepper

Step 1: Wipe fillets with a damp cloth. Place in a baking dish; arrange onion and carrots on top & around fillets; pour olive oil all over; sprinkle with fennel, dill, salt & pepper.

Step 2: Bake in a preheated 375°F oven for 25 minutes or until fillets flakes easily. When done, pour liquid from around fish into saucepan; place saucepan over low heat; gradually stir in egg yolks; continue stirring 3 minutes or until sauce thickens.

Step 3: Arrange fillets on preheated platter. Pour hot sauce over fillets. Serve with Rice (pg.121).

WHITING & CHEESE

4 whiting fillets	1 onion, sliced
2 tablespoons lime juice	2 stalks celery, chopped
4 tablespoons butter	1/3 cup grated Cheddar cheese
1 cup rich milk	1 cup water
2 tablespoons white flour	1/4 white pepper
1/8 teaspoon black pepper	8 sprigs of cilantro, for garnish
1 teaspoon salt	
1/4 teaspoon Worcestershire sauce	

Step 1: Wipe fillets with a damp cloth; place in a baking dish; sprinkle with lime juice, 1/2 salt & black pepper. Arrange onion and celery over top of fillets; pour water in dish.

Step 2: Bake in a preheated 350°F oven for 10 minutes.

Step 3: Meanwhile, in a saucepan over a low flame, melt butter; add flour; blend well; when smooth, gradually add milk, stirring constantly until thickened (5 minutes); add remaining salt, white pepper, Worcestershire sauce and 4 tablespoons cheese; blend well. Pour sauce over fillets; sprinkle with remaining cheese; bake 10 minutes longer or until fish flakes easily.

Step 4: Arrange each fillet on a warm plate. Garnish with 2 sprigs of cilantro.

WHITING ESCOVICHÉ

2 eight-ounce whiting fillets

1 clove garlic, chopped

1/2 green bell pepper, cut in strips

1/2 tablespoon fresh parsley, minced

1 lemon, sliced, for garnish

1/4 teaspoon black pepper

4 sprigs cilantro, for garnish

1/2 red chili pepper, roasted , skin & seeds discarded, and finely chopped

1/2 teaspoon Muhammad's Pepper Fish Seasoning™ (pg.307)

1 onion, sliced

1/2 red bell pepper, cut in strips

1 lemon, juiced

1 tablespoon butter

1 teaspoon olive oil

1 teaspoon salt

Step 1: Wipe fillets with a damp cloth; sprinkle with Pepper Seasoning, arrange in the center of a buttered baking dish, skin-side facing up. Surround with red chili, red & green bell peppers, onion, garlic and parsley. Drizzle fillets with 1/2 of lemon juice. Sprinkle vegetables with olive oil. Sprinkle salt & black pepper over all.

Step 2: Bake in a 400°F oven for 15 to 20 minutes. Basting with the remaining lemon juice half way through the baking time. Garnish with sprigs of cilantro. Serve with a rice dish (pg.121).

⟵────────────────────────────────────⟶

FISH & TOMATOES

(A minimum of one hour before beginning this recipe, soak the fillets
in the marinate, in a plastic bag, in the refrigerator.)

3 six-ounce whiting fillets

1 onion, chopped

1 bay leaf

1/2 cup water

1 teaspoon parsley

6 sprigs cilantro, for garnish

1/2 cup Whole Wheat Cracker crumbs (pg.204)

1/2 cup Muhammad's Herb Fish & Vegetable Marinade (pg.307)

2 large ripe tomatoes, halved

1/2 teaspoon basil, minced

2 tablespoons olive oil

1/2 teaspoon salt, divided

Step 1: Wipe fillet with a damp cloth. Sear the thickness part. In a plastic bag, soak the fillets in the marinade, in the refrigerator for a minimum of 1 hour.

Step 2: Meanwhile:In skillet over a high flame, heat olive oil and sauté onion a few minutes; add bay leaf, basil, parsley, pepper and 1/2 salt; simmer 2 more minutes.

Step 3: Remove fillets from bag and drain off most of the excess marinade; arrange fillets in a baking dish, skin-side facing up; pour sautéed onions over fillets; arrange tomato halves around fillets; add 1/2 cup water.

Step 4:Bake in a preheated 350°F oven 30 minutes. A few minutes before taken from oven, sprinkle cracker crumbs and remaining half of salt over tomatoes. Remove from oven and garnish with sprigs of cilantro.

←————————————————————————————————→

WHITING CREOLE

4 whiting fillets, steamed 8 minutes & cut into 1-inch cubes

2 cups cooked, brown rice

CREOLE SAUCE-BASIC

2 onions, chopped

1 chili pepper, deseeded & minced

2 tablespoons olive oil

1/2 teaspoon parsley

Pinch baking soda

1/2 teaspoon Lemon Herb Mix™ (pg.307)

1 green bell pepper, chopped

1 1/2 cup strained tomato pureé

1/2 teaspoon salt

Step 1: For The Creole Sauce: Heat oil in a skillet, over a medium-high flame, add onions and green pepper. Cook, stirring, for 1 minute. Add chili pepper, tomatoes, baking soda, Lemon Herb Mix. Simmer for 15 minutes. Add parsley and salt. Cook 15 to 30 more minutes until thick.

Step 2: Arrange cubed whiting and rice on a warm platter. Pour sauce over all. Toss lightly and serve with salad (pg.165)

←————————————————————————————————→

STUFFED & BAKED SNAPPER

1 whole red snapper, 2 to 3 pounds

1 stalk celery, chopped

1/2 teaspoon rosemary, finely chopped

1/2 teaspoon salt

1/2 teaspoon black pepper

2 tablespoons Muhammad's Grape Juice™ (pg.295)

1 cup Whole Wheat Sourdough Bread crumb (pg.189)

4 scallions, chopped

6 tablespoons butter

2 sprigs of parsley for garnish

Step 1: In a skillet, over a medium-high flame, heat 5 tablespoons butter and sauté the scallions and celery for 6 minutes. Add the crumbs, rosemary, salt and pepper and Sauté a few more minutes.

Step 2: Wipe fish with a damp cloth. Fill the cavity of the fish with the stuffing and sew up the opening (with white thread) or secure with skewers. Brush the fish with 1/2 tablespoon butter. Place in a 1 1/2 quart baking dish.

Step 3: Bake in a preheated 400°F oven for 30 minutes, basting with 1/2 tablespoon butter and grape juice twice during baking time. Remove from oven garnish with sprigs of parsley. Serve with rice (pg.121)

GRILLED SNAPPER KABOBS
(or BROIL)

KABOBS

2 red snapper fillets, cut into 2" pieces   8 small tomatoes

4 to 6 fresh whole rosemary (herb) sticks

2 tablespoons olive oil

1/2 teaspoon Muhammad's Pepper Fish Seasoning™ (pg.307)

BAKED VEGETABLES

1 yellow squash   1 zucchini

1/2 egg plant, thinly sliced   3 small tomatoes, quartered

1 tablespoon olive oil

SAUTEÉD VEGETABLES

1 onion, chopped   1 red bell pepper, chopped

1 garlic clove, sliced   1/4 teaspoon salt

1/4 teaspoon fresh fennel, finely chopped

2 tablespoons olive oil

1/4 red chili pepper, roasted , skin & seeds discarded, and finely chopped

DRESSING

2 tablespoons Thousand Island Dressing (pg.185)

ACCOMPANIMENT

2 cups cooked brown rice (pg.121)

GARNISH

8 sprigs parsley

Step 1:For Sauteéd Vegetables: Heat 2 tablespoons olive oil in a heavy skillet over a high flame. Add onion, red pepper, garlic, chili pepper, fennel and salt until golden.

Step 2:For Baked Vegetables: Wash, and cut squash & zucchini with skins left on, diagonally into 1/2-inch slices. In a bowl combine with eggplant slices, 3 small tomato wedges sauteéd vegetables and toss with tropical dressing. Arrange in a 2 quart baking dish coated with 1 tablespoon olive oil.

Step 3: Bake in a preheated 350°F 20 to 30 minutes or until vegetables ar tender-crisp.

Step 4:For The Kabobs: Utilizing the rosemary sticks as skewers, alternate fish pieces and small tomatoes on sticks, brush with olive oil and sprinkle with Pepper seasoning.

Step 5:For Grilling: Heat the grill good and hot. Lay kabobs on grill and cook for 10 to 12 minutes, turn kabobs halfway through cooking time.

Alternative Step 5:For Broiling:Preheat broiling compartment and pan at least 10 minutes.

Step 6: Brush broiling pan with oil.

Step 7: Place fish on pan and position 4 inches from flame. Broil 8 to 10 minutes. Half way through broiling period, turn over and broil other side. Serve with vegetables, brown rice and garnish with sprigs of parsley.

BROILED RED SALMON

2 salmon steaks, 1 inch thick   4 tablespoon butter, melted

Juice of 1 lemon   Lemon wedges

1/2 teaspoon salt

1 tablespoon Muhammad's Herb Fish Seasoning™ (pg.307)

Step 1: Preheat broiling compartment and pan at least 10 minutes.

Step 2: Wipe steaks with a damp cloth. Brush steaks with 2 tablespoons butter. Mix 2 tablespoons of butter with salt, seasoning and lemon juice.

Step 3: Brush broiling pan with oil. Place fish on pan and position 6 inches from flame. Broil 5 minutes on each side. For the last minutes of cooking baste with seasoned butter.

Step 4: Serve immediately from broiler with accumulated pan juices and surround with lemon wedges.

POACHED SALMON

4 six-ounce salmon fillets   1 teaspoon grated lemon zest

2 tablespoons butter   2 tablespoons lemon juice

1/2 cup water   12 sprigs parsley, for garnish

1 stalk of celery, thinly sliced   1 carrot, thinly sliced

1/2 teaspoon salt

1/4 teaspoon black pepper

1/2 Muhammad's White Grape Juice™ (pg.295) or non-alcohol white wine

Step 1: In a large deep skillet or dutch oven, combine the water, grape juice, lemon juice, lemon zest, celery, carrot, salt and pepper. Bring to boil and cook, covered for 2 minutes.

Step 2: Add the salmon and simmer, covered for 7 to 8 minutes. Transfer the fillets to 4 dinner plates.

Step 3: Use a slotted spoon to lift the carrots and celery from the broth and arrange in equal portions over the fillets.

Step 4: While the remaining broth is boiling, add the butter to it, cook until it's slightly thickened, about 4 minutes and spoon over salmon and vegetables. Garnish each plate with 3 sprigs of parsley. Serve with Sauteéd rice (pg.123) and cauliflower.

$\longleftrightarrow$

SWEET & SOUR SALMON, THAI STYLE

(A minimum of one hour before beginning this recipe marinate the fillets
with the sweet & sour sauce, in a plastic bag, in the refrigerator.)

2 8-ounce red salmon fillet

1 carrot, peeled & juliened

1 red bell pepper, sliced

1/4 teaspoon salt

1 1/3 tablespoons corn oil

1/2 cup Muhammad's Thai Sweet & Sour Sauce™ (pg.307)

2 tablespoons pineapple juice

2 garlic cloves, sliced

1 green bell pepper, sliced

1/4 teaspoon black pepper

Step 1: Wipe fillet with a damp cloth. Sear the thickness part. In a plastic bag, marinate the fillets in the sweet & sour sauce, in the refrigerator for a minimum of 1 hour.

Step 2: Coat a 2-quart baking dish with 1 tablespoon corn oil and remove fillets from bag and drain off most of the excess sweet & sour sauce, place fillets in center of baking dish, skin-side facing up. Arrange carrot, garlic, and green & red pepper around fillets and drizzle 1/3 tablespoon oil over them.

Step 3: Sprinkle 1/2 of the pineapple juice over fillets. Sprinkle salt & pepper over all.

Step 4: Bake in a preheated 400°F oven for 20 minutes. Basting with the remaining pineapple juice half way through the baking time. Serve with a rice dish (pg.121).

$\longleftrightarrow$

SALMON PATTIES

1 1/2 pounds salmon fillet, skin removed and cut into 1/4-inch pieces

1/4 cup Whole Wheat Bread crumbs (pg.188)

1/4 cup Whole Wheat Cracker crumbs (pg.204)

1/8 teaspoon Muhammad's Red Hot Sauce (pg.307)

1/4 cup Mayonnaise (pg.183)

1 1/2 tablespoons shallots, chopped

2 tablespoons cilantro, chopped

1 teaspoon fennel

2 tablespoons lime juice

3/4 teaspoon salt

1/4 cup green bell pepper, chopped

3 tablespoons olive oil

1 teaspoon lime zest

Step 1: In a bowl lightly mix together the salmon, bread crumb, fennel, cilantro, hot sauce, lime zest, lime juice, green pepper, mayonnaise and salt.

Step 2: Form into 8 patties. Roll in cracker crumbs.

Step 3: Heat olive oil in a large skillet over medium-high flame. Add 4 salmon patties and cook 4 minutes, or until golden brown. Carefully turn over with a spatula and cook another 4 to 5 minutes or until golden brown. Remove and keep warm in a warm baking dish. Add remaining tablespoon of olive oil and cook the 4 remaining patties. Serve with Raita (pg.103) and Salad (pg.165).

⬅————————————————➡

STRIPED BASS

1 pound sea bass fillet

1 pound fresh tomatoes, diced

2 onions, chopped

3 tablespoon unbleached flour

2 tablespoons olive oil

1/2 cup non-alcohol white wine

1 teaspoon salt

4 sprigs cilantro, for garnish

2 teaspoons Muhammad's Fragrant Spice Rub™ (pg.307)

Step 1: Combine the flour, spice rub, and salt on a platter. Wipe the fillet with a damp cloth. Dredge the sea bass in the mixture, and reserve remaining flour for the sauce.

Step 2: Heat olive oil in a large skillet over a medium-high flame. Place the fillet skin-side up in the skillet and cook for 4 minutes, or until golden brown. Turn with a spatula and cook another 4 minutes. Transfer to a platter.

Step 3: Add the onion, wine, and tomatoes to the skillet and cook for 2 minutes or until sauce is slightly thickened, stirring quickly. Lay the fish (skin-side down) on top of the mixture. Reduce heat, cover and cook another 5 to 7 minutes, or until fish is cooked.

Step 4: Serve the fillet on a platter with the sauce spooned around it and garnish with sprigs of cilantro. Serve with rice (pg.121).

⬅————————————————➡

BAKED BREAD CRUMB-COATED TROUT

4 six-ounce trout fillets

3 tablespoons butter

1 teaspoon salt

1 1/2 cups fine, Whole Wheat Herb Bread crumbs (pg.188)

1 cup Muhammad's Thai Sweet & Sour Sauce & Fish Marinade™ (pg.307)

Step 1: Wipe fillets with a damp cloth. Sear the thickness parts. In a plastic bag, marinate the fillets in the sweet & sour marinade, in the refrigerator for a minimum of 1 hour.

Step 2: Coat a 2-quart baking dish with butter and remove fillets from bag and drain off most of the excess sweet & sour marinade, roll in the bread crumbs and shake loose any excess. Place fillets in baking dish. Bake in a 400°F preheated oven for 15 to 18 minutes.

Step 3: Serve with Rice (pg.121) and Vegetables (pg.140).

SAUTEÉD TROUT

4 six-ounce trout fillets

6 tablespoons butter

2 tablespoon lime juice

1 lime cut into wedges, for garnish

1 teaspoon salt

1 tablespoon Muhammad's Cajun Spice Seasoning™(pg.307)

1/2 tablespoon of each: rosemary, chives, tarragon, parsley

4 tablespoons unbleached flour

3 tablespoons olive oil

12 sprigs of parsley, for garnish

Step 1: Combine the flour, fish seasoning, and salt on a platter. Wipe the fillets with a damp cloth. Dredge the fillets in the mixture.

Step 2: Heat olive oil and 3 tablespoons of the butter in a large skillet over a medium-high flame. Place the fillet skin-side up in the skillet and cook for 3 minutes, or until golden brown. Turn with a spatula and cook another 3 minutes. Transfer to a platter.

Step 3: Add the remaining butter, lime juice, and herbs to the skillet and cook for 2 minutes or until gravy is slightly thickened, stirring quickly.

Step 4: Serve the fillet on a platter with the gravy spooned on it and garnish with sprigs of parsley and wedges of lime. Serve with rice (pg.121).

SAUTEÉD WHITING

1 pound whiting fillets

1 onion, chopped

1 tablespoon chopped chives

1 teaspoon salt

6 sprigs cilantro, for garnish

1 tablespoon Muhammad's Cajun Spice Seasoning™ (pg.307)

6 tablespoons butter

1/4 teaspoon dill

1 bay leaf

1/4 teaspoon marjoram

Step 1: Wipe fillets with a damp cloth. Cut into 1-inch cubes. Sprinkle with Fish seasoning and salt.

Step 2: Heat 2 tablespoons butter in a heavy skillet over a medium-high flame; add cubed fish, bay leaf; cover; reduce flame to simmer gently for 10 minutes.

Step 3: Meanwhile in another skillet heat remaining butter over a medium-high flame; add onions, dill, chives and marjoram, sauté until golden brown.

Step 4: Arrange cooked fish on a warm platter; pour sauteéd onion & herbs over fish; garnish with cilantro.

FISH FRY

8 six-ounce whiting fillets

1 tablespoon salt

8 Whole Wheat Sub Rolls (pg.198)

Slices of tomato

1 lime, cut in wedges

Tartar Sauce (pg.111) or Muhammad's Red Hot Sauce™ (pg.307)

2 tablespoons Muhammad's Seasoning™ (pg.307)

1 cup Whole Wheat Herb Bread, finely crumbed (pg.192)

Corn oil

Shredded lettuce

Sprigs of parsley, for garnish

Step 1: Combine the fine bread crumbs, seasoning, and salt on a platter. Wipe the fillets with a damp cloth. Dredge the fillets in the mixture.

Step 2: Heat corn oil in a large skillet over a medium-high flame. Place the fillet skin-side up in the skillet and cook for 3 minutes, or until golden brown. Turn with a spatula and cook another 3 minutes; drain on paper towels.

Step 3: Serve the fillet on a platter in sub rolls with lettuce, tomato & sauce and garnish with sprigs of parsley and wedges of lime. Serve with Real French Fries (Version II) and Ketchup (pg.109).

GOLDEN FRIED FISH

8 whiting fillets

1 cup whole wheat flour, sifted

Sprigs of parsley, for garnish

1 lemon, cut in wedges

2 tablespoons milk

Tartar Sauce (pg.111) or Muhammad's Red Hot Sauce™ (pg.307)

2 tablespoons Muhammad's Cajun Seasoning™ (pg.307)

Corn oil

1 tablespoon salt

5 eggs, slightly beaten

Step 1: Combine the flour, fish seasoning, and salt on a platter. Wipe the fillets with a damp cloth. Combine eggs and milk on a platter. Dredge the fillets in the egg mixture, then dredge in the flour mixture.

Step 2: Heat corn oil in a large skillet over a medium-high flame. Place the fillet skin-side up in the skillet and cook for 3 minutes, or until golden brown. Turn with a spatula and cook another 3 minutes; drain on paper towels.

Step 3: Serve the fillets on a platter & garnish with sprigs of parsley and wedges of lime. Serve with Real French Fries (Version II) and Ketchup (pg.109).

BASIC STUFFED FISH

4 whole fish

1 stalk celery, chopped

1 stick butter

1/2 teaspoon salt

2 cup Whole Wheat Herb Bread crumb, toasted (pg.192)

1 tablespoon Herb Fish Seasoning™ (pg.307)

1 onion, chopped

1 green bell pepper, chopped

12 sprigs of parsley for garnish

Step 1: In a skillet, over a medium-high flame, heat 5 tablespoons butter and sauté the onions, green pepper, seasoning, salt and celery for 6 minutes. Add the crumbs, and loosely form into stuffing mix.

Step 2: Wipe fish with a damp cloth. Fill the cavity of the fish with the stuffing and sew up the opening (with white thread) or secure with skewers. Brush each fish with 1/2 tablespoon butter. Place in a 3 quart baking dish or one large enough to hold them.

Step 3: Bake in a preheated 400°F oven for 30 minutes, basting with remaining butter twice during baking time. Remove from oven garnish with sprigs of parsley. Serve with rice (pg.121) and Vegetables (pg.140).

WHITING STUFFED CABBAGE

1 cup onion, chopped

1 cup green bell pepper, chopped

2 teaspoons salt

12 sprigs of parsley, for garnish

1 pound whiting fillets, steamed 8 minutes, skin removed & flaked (pg.269)

1/8 teaspoon Muhammad's Red Hot Sauce™ (pg.307)

2 teaspoons Muhammad's Lemon Herb Seasoning™ (pg.307)

1 head cabbage

1 teaspoon Hungarian paprika

Olive oil

Step 1: Remove outer tough cabbage leaves and discard. Remove about 8 to 10 inner light-green leaves, chopped up the rest and boil all, in a large pot of water for 15 minutes.

Step 2: In a skillet heat some olive oil over a high flame and sauté onion, green pepper, lemon seasoning, 1 teaspoon salt & hot sauce a few minutes.

Step 3: Coat a baking pan with olive oil. Lay open 1 or 2 cabbage leaves, put in some fish, small portion of the chopped cabbage, and sautéed onion mixture. Wrap cabbage leaves around the ingredients. Repeat this step for remaining ingredients. Arrange the rolls, seam side down in baking pan. Sprinkle with salt & paprika.

Step 4: Bake in a 350°F preheated oven for 10 minutes. Serve warm with accompaniment. Garnish with a few sprigs of Parsley.

STUFFED GREEN PEPPERS

1 cup onion, chopped

4 green bell peppers

2 teaspoons salt

1 cup diced tomatoes, for topping

10 sprigs of parsley, for garnish

1 green chili pepper, roasted , skin & seeds discarded, and minced

4 whiting fillets, steamed 8 minutes, skin removed & flaked (pg.269)

1 teaspoon Muhammad's Lemon Herb Seasoning™ (pg.307)

2 teaspoons Muhammad's Pepper Fish Seasoning™ (pg.307)

2 cups brown rice, cooked

1 stick butter

Olive oil

1/2 cup water

Step 1: In a skillet over medium-high flame, heat butter and sauté onion, Lemon seasoning and rice a few minutes, add flaked fish, fish seasoning and 1/2 cup water, cut off flame and let set for 5 minutes.

Step 2: Cut off tops & ribs of green peppers and deseed. Stuff cavities with fish & rice mixture and top with 1/4 cup diced tomatoes each.

Step 3: Coat a baking dish with olive oil and arrange peppers in it. Place in a preheated 350°F oven and bake for 5 to 10 minutes. Serve hot with Yogurt Sauce (pg.100)

←——————————————————————→

HICKORY GRILL BAKE

8 whiting fillets

2 limes, thinly sliced

1 tablespoon chives, finely chopped

1 teaspoon black pepper

4 tablespoons butter, melted

1 clove garlic, minced

2 teaspoons salt

Step 1:For Grill: Heat coals in a grill with a cover.

Step 2: Arrange slices of lime in the bottom of a shallow baking pan; Wipe fillets with a damp cloth. Sprinkle fillets with salt and pepper, arrange in a single layer over slices of lime. Place remaining lime slices on top of fillets.

Step 3: Combine butter, garlic and chives; pour over fillets.

Step 4: Add hickory to coals in the red glowing stage of burning (after flames have ceased).

Step 5: Place baking pan atop grill, close hood and cook 25 to 30 minutes, or until fillets flake easily, basting frequently. Remove from grill and serve on a warm platter with Grilled Corn on the Cob (pg.151).

←——————————————————————→

WHITING SALAD

2 six-ounce whiting fillets

2 tablespoons olive oil

2 stalks celery, chopped

3/4 cup Horseradish mayonnaise (pg.184)

1 small head of Romaine lettuce leaves

1/2 teaspoon salt

1/4 teaspoon white pepper

1 small bowl of a combination of arugula & Belgian endive

1 cucumber, peeled, seeded, cut in 1/4-inch dices

1/2 teaspoon Muhammad's Cajun Seasoning or Herb Fish Seasoning™ (pg.307)

10 stuffed green olives*, chopped

1/8 teaspoon thyme

12 sprigs parsley

Step 1: Wipe fillets with a damp cloth. Cut into 1-inch cubes. Sprinkle with Fish seasoning.

Step 2: Heat 2 tablespoons olive oil in a heavy skillet over a medium-high flame; add cubed fish, sauté for a few minutes, until fish flakes easily. Drain on paper towels and set aside to cool.

Step 3: In a bowl, mix cucumber, mayonnaise, celery, olives, thyme, salt & pepper. Gently fold in sautéed fish.

Step 4: Line a pre-chilled salad bowl with romaine lettuce leaves, arugula and Belgian endive leaves; arrange whiting mixture over greens; garnish with sprigs of parsley. Serve cold with extra helping of mayonnaise at side.

*Or 4 tablespoons pitted, chopped Kalamata (Greece) black olives & 2 tablespoons chopped pimiento.

⟵——————————————————————————————⟶

MUHAMMAD'S WHITING EGG SALAD

6 hard-boiled eggs (pg.125)

1 tablespoon green bell pepper, minced

1 teaspoon lime juice

1/2 teaspoon black pepper

2 large tomatoes, quartered

Crisp red leaf lettuce leaves

12 sprigs parsley, for garnish

1 tablespoon pimiento, chopped

10 Kalamata (Greece) black olives, pitted & halved

1 green chili pepper, roasted , skin & seeds discarded, and minced

1 eight-ounce whiting fillet, steamed 8 minutes, skin removed & flaked (pg.269)

1 stalk celery, minced

1 1/2 tablespoon Mayonnaise* (pg.183)

1/4 teaspoon mustard powder

1/4 teaspoon salt

2/3 red bell pepper, cut in rings

2/3 yellow bell pepper, cut in rings

Step 1: In a bowl mix lime juice, mustard, and mayonnaise, blend well.

Step 2: Cut eggs in half lengthwise; remove yolks; mash and mix with mayonnaise; add chili pepper, celery, minced green bell pepper, salt, black pepper; fold in flaked whiting.

Step 3: Fill whites of eggs with fish mixture.

Step 4: Arrange lettuce leaves on prechilled platter; place filled eggs in center; border platter with tomato quarters, black olives, pimiento and alternate yellow & red pepper rings. Garnish with sprigs of parsley. Serve cold with extra helping of mayonnaise at side.

*OPTIONAL Delete lime juice and mustard. Add 1 teaspoon Dijon mustard (pg.108) to mayonnaise.

FETTICINI & FISH SALAD

1/3 cup Mayonnaise (pg.183)

1 stalk celery, chopped

1 small onion, chopped

1/2 teaspoon salt

1/4 teaspoon black pepper

1 green chili pepper, roasted , skin & seeds discarded, and finely chopped

3 cups whiting fillet, steamed 8 minutes, skin removed & flaked (pg.269)

3 cups cooked whole wheat fetticini or macaroni

1 teaspoon Dijon mustard (pg.108)

1/2 green bell pepper, chopped

2 tablespoons Sweet Relish (Version II)

Step 1: In a bowl combine mayonnaise, mustard, sweet relish, salt & black pepper; blend well. Add celery, onion, green bell pepper, chili pepper; blend well. Gently fold in fetticini & flaked fish; mix lightly.

Step 2: Chill and serve.

SOUSED FISH

BROILED FISH

6 whiting fillets, broiled (pg.269)

SAUCE

3 onions, chopped

4 medium carrots, chopped

3 bay leaves

2/3 cup cider vinegar

1 cup water

1/4 teaspoon black pepper

2 green chili peppers, roasted , skin & seeds discarded, and finely chopped

4 green bell peppers, chopped

1/2 teaspoon dry mustard

1/4 cup olive oil

1 teaspoon salt

12 sprigs parsley, for garnish

Step 1:For The Sauce: Heat oil in a heavy saucepan over a high flame and sauté onion & green bell peppers until golden; add water and remaining ingredients for the sauce; reduce flame and simmer, covered, 20 minutes.

Step 2:For The Broiled Fish: Meantime, prepare fillets as instructed in (pg.269). Arrange fillets on plates.

Step 3: Pour the hot sauce over the fillets or pureé the sauce first in a blender. Garnish with sprigs of parsley. Serve hot or cold.

$\longleftrightarrow$

FISH SAUSAGE

2 eggs, slightly beaten   1/4 teaspoon black pepper

1/2 teaspoon salt

1 1/2 tablespoon fresh oregano, minced or 3/4 tablespoon powdered oregano

2 tablespoons fresh sage, minced or 1 tablespoon powdered sage

2 cups Whole Wheat Herb Bread crumbs* (pg.192)

2 green chili peppers, roasted, skin & seeds discarded, and finely chopped

1 pound whiting fillets, steamed 8 minutes, skin removed & flaked (pg.269)

Corn oil, for deep frying

Step 1: In a bowl lightly mix bread crumbs, peppers, spices & herbs, fish and eggs; form into patties or links.

Step 2:Fry Method: Heat corn oil in a deep fryer on medium heat. Fry patties or links a few minutes on each side or until golden brown. Drain on paper towels. Serve with scrambled eggs (pg.127) or in a sandwich.

Step 3:Baking Method: Place patties or links, one inch apart, on an oiled baking sheet. Bake in a 400°F preheated oven for 8 to 12 minutes, turning once half-way through baking time, or until golden brown. Drain on paper towels, if needed. Serve with scrambled eggs (pg.127) or in a sandwich.

*Add more bread crumbs if mixture is too moist. If too dry, vice versa.

√Herb Sausage
Instead of the sage, use *1 tablespoon ground* spices & herbs combined: *all spice, Hungarian paprika, bay leaf powder & thyme.*
√ Herb Sausage II
Instead of the sage, use *2 tablespoons fresh rosemary, minced.*

$\longleftrightarrow$

WHITING CAKES

2 eggs slightly beaten   3/4 cup chopped onions

1 green bell pepper, chopped   1/2 teaspoon salt

1/4 teaspoon black pepper

Corn oil

1 cup Whole Wheat Sourdough Bread crumbs* (pg.189)

1 pound whiting fillets, steamed 8 minutes, skin removed & flaked (pg.269)

Step 1: In a bowl lightly mix bread crumbs, onions, green bell pepper, salt, black pepper, whiting, and eggs; form into patties.

Step 2:Fry Method: Heat corn oil in a heavy skillet on medium heat. Fry patties a few minutes on each side or until golden brown. Drain on paper towels. Serve with Rice dish (pg.121) or in a sandwich.

Step 3:Baking Method: Place patties, one inch apart, on an oiled baking sheet. Bake in a 400°F pre-heated oven for 8 to 12 minutes, turning once half-way through baking time, or until golden brown. Drain on paper towels, if needed. Serve with Rice dish (pg.121) or in a sandwich.

*Add more bread crumbs if mixture is too moist. If too dry, vice versa.

WHITING POT PIE

1 pound whiting fillets	4 carrots, peeled & sliced
1 cup green peas	1 onion, chopped
1 green bell pepper, chopped	2 tablespoons white flour
1/2 stick butter, (room temp.)	1 1/2 cups water, boiling
1/2 teaspoon salt	
1/4 teaspoon white pepper	

1 recipe Lightly Rich & Flaky Pie Crust (pg.235)

1/2 teaspoon Muhammad's Fish Herb Seasoning™ (pg.307)

1 red chili pepper, roasted , skin & seeds discarded, and finely chopped

Step 1: Wipe fillets with a damp cloth. Cut into 1-inch cubes. Sprinkle with Fish seasoning.

Step 2: In a large skillet over a medium flame, heat butter until it sizzles, add onions, carrots, green peas, green bell pepper, increase flame to high and sauté for 3 minutes; add boiling water, flour, fish, salt and pepper; lightly stir, cook for 2 more minutes or until thick soup consistency.

Step 3: Place fish mixture into a deep pie dish or shallow casserole.

Step 4: Roll out the pastry slightly bigger than pie dish or casserole and drape over top; crimp the edges and cut a few small vents on top. Bake in a preheated 425°F oven for about 20 minutes, until bubbling and top is browned.

GOLDEN BREADED WHITING

4 eight-ounce whiting fillets	1 teaspoon garlic powder
1/2 cup grated Parmesan cheese	1 teaspoon salt
1/4 teaspoon black pepper	1 tablespoon butter
2 tablespoons olive oil	
2 cups Whole Wheat Herb Bread crumbs (pg.192)	

Step 1: Combine the bread crumbs, garlic powder, cheese, black pepper and salt on a platter. Wipe the fillets with a damp cloth; slightly coat fillets with olive oil. Dredge the fillets in the crumb mixture and shake loose any excess..

Step 2: Coat a 2-quart baking dish with butter; Place fillets in baking dish. Bake in a 400°F preheated oven for 15 to 18 minutes.

Step 3: Serve with Rice (pg.121) and Vegetables (pg.140).

WHITING SCALLOPED AU GRATIN

1 pound whiting fillets

1 cup grated Cheddar cheese

1/2 green bell pepper, minced

1/2 stick butter, (room temp.)

1/2 teaspoon salt

1/4 teaspoon white pepper

4 sprigs parsley, for garnish

1/2 cup Whole Wheat Cracker crumbs (pg.204)

(1 teaspoon Muhammad's Thai Sweet & Sour Sauce (pg.307) or 1/2 teaspoon Worcestershire Sauce)

1/2 stick butter

1/2 cup shallots, chopped

2 tablespoons unbleached flour

1/2 cup cold milk

2 tablespoons corn oil

Step 1: Wipe fillets with a damp cloth. Cut into 1-inch cubes.

Step 2: In a large skillet over a medium flame, heat butter until it sizzles, add shallots, green bell pepper, filleted fish cubes, salt and pepper; increase flame to low and sauté for 8 minutes;

Step 3: Meanwhile, whisk cold milk and flour in a bowl; when very smooth, pour into stainless steel bowl set over boiling water or the top section of a double boiler and cook 10 minutes or until sauce begins to thicken; stir in Thai Sauce; then add sautéed fish; lightly stir.

Step 4: Coat a casserole with corn oil; pour fish mixture in; sprinkle cheese evenly over top. Bake in a preheated 350°F oven for about 10 minutes, or until golden browned. Garnish with sprigs of parsley. Serve hot.

WHITING BROILED EN CASSEROLE
(A minimum of one hour before beginning this recipe marinate the fillets with the sweet & sour sauce, in a plastic bag, in the refrigerator.)

6 tablespoons olive oil

Juice of 1 lime

1 teaspoon salt

1/2 teaspoon black pepper

1 pound whiting fillets, skin removed, cut into 4-inch pieces

1 tablespoon chopped chervil

1 lime, sliced, for garnish

291

Step 1: Wipe fillets with a damp cloth. Blend the olive oil, lime juice, salt, pepper and chervil; In a plastic bag, marinate the fillets in the oil blend, in the refrigerator for a minimum of 1 hour.

Step 2: Remove fish from bag and drain off most of the excess marinade and reserve for basting, place fish in a casserole.

Step 3: Place in preheated broiling compartment , 350°F, 4 inches below flame; Broil for 10 minutes or until fish is golden brown and flakes easily. Basting with a little of the remaining marinade half way through the baking time. Serve hot on warm individual plates and with a rice dish (pg.121). Garnish with slices of lime.

BROILED FLAKY WHITING

6 tablespoons butter, melted	1 tablespoon chopped parsley
Juice of 1 lemon	1 lemon, sliced, for garnish
1 teaspoon salt	1 teaspoon Hungarian paprika
1/2 teaspoon black pepper	1/2 teaspoon garlic powder
4 eight-ounce whiting fillets	8 sprigs parsley, for garnish

Step 1: Wipe fillets with a damp cloth. Blend the butter, lime juice, paprika, garlic, salt, pepper and parsley; In a plastic bag, marinate the fillets in the butter blend, in the refrigerator for a minimum of 1 hour.

Step 2: Remove fish from bag and drain off most of the excess marinade and reserve for basting, place fish, skin side down, in a glass baking dish.

Step 3: Place in preheated broiling compartment, 4 inches below flame; Broil for 5 minutes on each side or until fish is golden brown and flakes easily. Basting with a little of the remaining marinade half way through the baking time. Serve hot on warm individual plates and with a rice dish (pg.121). Garnish with slices of lime and sprigs of parsley.

BOILED WHITING

2 pounds whiting fillets	1 cup Green Tomatillo Salsa (pg.115)
12 sprigs cilantro, for garnish	
1 quart Vegetable Stock or Bouillon (pg.81)	

Step 1: Wipe fillets with a damp cloth; tie fillets in a cheesecloth;

Step 2: Place in a large pot; pour stock or bouillon over, enough to cover all fish. Bring to boiling point over high flame; lower flame; cover; simmer gently for 10 to 12 minutes or until fillets flake easily.

Step 3: Carefully remove fillets from pot; arrange on preheated platter. Serve hot with Salsa. Garnish with sprigs of cilantro. Serve with Rice Dish (pg.121)

POACHED WHITING

4 eight-ounce whiting fillets

1/2 cup Lemon Butter Sauce (pg.107)

2 teaspoons salt

12 sprigs rosemary, for garnish

Step 1: In a large deep skillet or dutch oven, add enough cold water to cover the fillets.

Step 2: Put fillets & salt in cold water (about 2 cups). Bring just to a boil over high flame; lower flame and simmer, covered for 5 minutes; for thin fillets 3 minutes for thinner fillets; for thick steaks 7 to 8 minutes; use a slotted spoon to lift the fillets out of the water.

Step 3: Transfer the fillets to 4 dinner plates. Garnish each plate with 3 sprigs of rosemary. Serve with Lemon Sauce, Sautéed rice (pg.121) and Cauliflower (pg.72 & 145).

WHITING PLANKED

3 whole whiting, dressed

1/4 teaspoon chervil

1 lime, sliced

1/4 teaspoon white pepper

Juice of 1/2 lemon

3 cups turnips, steamed & seasoned (pg.74)

6 four-inch sprigs rosemary, for garnish

1/2 head semi-steamed cauliflower (pg.72)

4 whole tomatoes, baked (pg.162)

1 pound semi-steamed peas (pg.155)

1 teaspoon salt

Step 1: Utilize a well oiled hardwood plank or a buttered glass baking dish; place in cold oven and heat as oven preheats to 400°F.

Step 2: Clean fish and wipe with damp cloth; sprinkle fish inside and out with salt and white pepper; place on hot plank; bake in oven 35 minutes or until fish flakes easily; baste halfway through baking time with lemon juice.

Step 3: Remove fish from oven. Arrange tomatoes, turnips, cauliflower and peas around fish in an alternating pattern.

Step 4: Place plank with fish and vegetables back in oven to continue to bake for 10 more minutes or until turnips and cauliflower are done.

Step 5: Remove from oven; garnish with slices of lime and garnish with sprigs of rosemary. Serve immediately on plank.

WHITING WITH MARINARA SAUCE

FISH

1 1/2 pounds whiting fillets

MARINARA SAUCE

4 cups tomato pureé, strained

2 stalks celery, sliced

1 teaspoon fresh marjoram, minced

1 teaspoon salt

1/2 teaspoon black pepper

1 serano chili pepper, roasted , skin & seeds discarded, and finely chopped

2 cloves garlic, chopped

1/2 teaspoon fresh basil, minced

1/4 cup olive oil

GARNISH & ACCOMPANIMENT

8 sprigs cilantro, for garnish

2 tablespoons cream cheese

8 slices Whole Wheat Rosemary-Herb Bread, toasted (pg.189)

Step 1:For The Marinara Sauce: Heat olive oil in heavy skillet over a medium flame; add garlic and sauté a minute; add tomato pureé, celery, basil, marjoram, chili pepper, salt & black pepper; cover; simmer 20 minutes or until a thick sauce.

Step 2:For The Steamed Fish: Meantime, prepare fillets as instructed in (pg.269). Arrange fillets on plates.

Step 3: Pour hot marinara sauce over fillets. Garnish with sprigs of cilantro.

Step 4:For The Toast: Arrange Toasted bread slices on warm soup plates; spread cream cheese on top and pour a little marinara sauce over them.

17. BEVERAGES

There is an analogy that compares, a wrong done to someone which they've transformed into an opportunity, and the bitterness of a lemon made into a refreshing drink by sweetening it. "When life hands you lemons, make lemonade." This is further capitilized "When someone gives you 100 lemons; take 50 back to the store they purchased it from, exchange them for 150 limes; mix them with the lemons and make Citrusade, and get paid in the shade on a hot summer day."

LEMONADE
(Makes 2 1/2 quarts)

1 lemon, sliced, for garnish
1 1/4 cup sugar, dissolved in 2 cups boiling water
1 1/4 cup freshly squeezed & strained lemon juice, about10 lemons

Step 1: Hand squeeze lemons through a strainer.
Step 2: Combine lemon juice, dissolved sugar & 1 3/4 quarts of cold water in a 2 1/2 quart glass container; mix well; add 1 sliced lemon for garnish. Refrigerate. Serve cold or on ice.

√ Citrusade
Use a combination of *8 limes & 4 lemons,* instead of 10 lemons.
√ Pineapple Citrusade
Use a combination of *5 limes, 2 lemons, & 3 cups unsweetened pineapple juice* instead of 10 lemons.
Use 1 quart of water instead 1 3/4 quarts water.
√ Pink Lemonade
Add *10 large strawberries, halved & strained - through a fine mesh* along with lemon juice.

MUHAMMAD'S RED GRAPE JUICE™

1 quart jar, sterilized
2 quarts ripe black Concord grapes, washed & stemmed

Step 1: Place grapes into a juicer; process; fill jar within 1/2 inch of the top with juice; seal jar.
Step 2: Store in a cool place.

√ Muhammad's White Grape Juice™
Substitute The black Concord grapes with *pale green Muscats of Alexandria.*

TROPICAL PUNCH
FOR PARTIES
(prepare a day in advance)

3 cups mango pureé, finely strained

3/4 cup lemon juice, freshly squeezed

1 1/2 cup orange juice, freshly squeezed

1 quart ginger ale

1 pint sparkling water, Pierre™, club soda or seltzer

1 8-ounce can unsweetened crushed pineapple

1 cup strong hot tea

1 cup honey

Sprigs mint, for garnish

Step 1: Freeze the mango pureé in ice cube trays.

Step 2: Dissolve honey in the hot ice tea. Add lemon and orange juice. Refrigerate.

Step 3: Just before serving, add ginger ale, sparkling water and crushed pineapple.

Step 4: Place frozen mango cubes in a 3-quart punch bowl. Garnish with sprigs of mint. Serves 24 - in 4-ounce cups.

CITRUS FLOAT
FOR PARTIES
(prepare a day in advance)

1 cup lime juice

3 cups cold water

Sprigs of mint, for garnish

1 cup orange juice, freshly squeezed

1 cup honey or sugar, dissolved in 1 cup boiling water

1 cup Muhammad's Red Grape Juice™ (pg.295)

1 cup Muhammad's White Grape Juice™ (pg.295)

1 cup berry juice

2 oranges, sliced, for garnish

Step 1: Freeze the grape juices in ice cube trays.

Step 2: In a glass container add, dissolved honey or sugar, lime juice, berry juice, orange juice and 3 cups water; mix well.

Step 3: Place frozen grape cubes, orange slices in a 3-quart punch bowl; pour juice over all. Garnish with sprigs of mint. Serves 10 - in 8-ounce cups.

ORANGE COCKTAIL

2 cups orange juice, freshly squeezed

6 fresh apricots

5 carrots, peeled & sliced

6 pieces orange zest, 4-inch lengths, for garnish

Step 1: Mix orange juice, carrots and apricots in a blender on high speed until liquefied, about 1 minute. Refrigerate.

Step 2: Serve chilled; garnish with orange zest.

HEALTHY FRUIT DRINK

1 cantaloupe, peeled, seeded and diced

1/2 pint raspberries

3 ice cubes made of orange juice

6 pieces orange zest, 4-inch lengths, for garnish

1 cup apricot juice

1/2 pint red currants

Step 1: Mix cantaloupe, raspberries, red currants, apricot juice and frozen orange cubes in a blender on high speed until liquefied, about 1 minute. Refrigerate.

Step 2: Serve chilled; garnish with orange zest.

HEALTHY FRUIT SHAKE

(more creamy than the preceding drink)

1 cup cantaloupe chunks, frozen

1 cup mango chunks, frozen

4 tablespoon wheat germ

6 pieces orange zest, 4-inch lengths, for garnish

1 cup strawberries, frozen

1 1/2 cup orange juice

Step 1: Mix cantaloupe, strawberries, mango, orange juice and wheat germ in a blender on high speed until liquefied, about 1 minute. Refrigerate.

Step 2: Serve chilled; garnish with orange zest.

EMERALD COCKTAIL

1 cup unsweetened pineapple juice

1 tablespoon celery leaves or fennel

1 tablespoon parsley or chervil

1 tablespoon water cress leaves or sunflower sprouts

3 green lettuce leaves

Sprigs of mint, for garnish

Step 1: Mix all in a blender on high speed until liquefied, about 1 minute. Refrigerate.

Step 2: Serve chilled; garnish with sprigs of mint.

RED RUBY COCKTAIL

2 cups cranberry juice   2 cups pineapple juice

2 cups orange juice   2 cups apricot juice

1 lemon, juiced   Sprigs of mint

Step 1: Mix all together in a 2 1/2 quart glass container; refrigerate.

Step 2: Serve with ice; garnish with sprigs of mint.

ROSY YOGURT COCKTAIL

1 cup yogurt   2 cups tomato juice

1 teaspoon shallots, finely chopped   1/4 teaspoon fennel seed

1/2 teaspoon salt   2 ice cubes

Sprigs of mint

Step 1: Mix shallots, tomato juice, yogurt, and salt in a blender on high speed until liquefied, about 1 minute; add 2 ice cubes blend on high speed again until liquefied. Refrigerate.

Step 2: Serve chilled; garnish with sprigs of mint.

PINA COLADA

1 cup cream of coconut

3 cups crushed ice

3 cups unsweetened pineapple juice

6 pieces pineapple, 2-inch wedges, for garnishing glasses

Step 1: Mix cream of coconut & pineapple juice in a blender on high speed until liquefied, about 1 minute. Refrigerate.

Step 2: Serve chilled in tall glasses with crushed ice; garnish with pineapple wedges.

MINT SYRUP

2 cups Raw™ sugar

1 cup water

22 stalks fresh mint, crushed in a mortar

Step 1: Boil water in a saucepan over medium heat; add sugar and crushed mint; heat until the sugar dissolves; lower flame and simmer for 15 minutes.

Step 2: Strain; pour into a jar and seal; store in a cool dry place. Use this syrup with lemonade, iced tea, pineapple juice or citrusade.

18. COFFEE & TEA

INFO ON GREAT TASTING COFFEE

• Begin with freshly ground beans each time we make a pot.

• Do not store coffee in the refrigerator. Keep it in an airtight container, and in a cool, dry, dark area.

• Do not grind the beans too fine, if using an automatic drip maker, it will taste bitter. Use Drip for drip method; Regular for percolator; Fine or vacuum for espresso; steeped, and boiled coffee. The particular maker's instructional manual will describe the proper grind for their machine.

• Clean any residue in coffee pot and clean a drip coffee maker once a month with baking soda or one of the many coffee maker cleaners on the market.

• Porcelain and glass coffee makers are best. Metal, copper, etc. make the coffee taste bitter; Stainless steel has the least bad effect.

• Don't leave brewed coffee sitting on the grounds too long.

• Don't repour brewed coffee through the grounds.

• Never reheat coffee.

• Never allow brewed coffee to sit on a heater any longer than 18 minutes. The flavorful molecules will burn away. Store freshly brewed coffee in a thermal carafé.

• Use cold, clear water.

• The standard measurement is two level tablespoons of ground coffee per 6-ounces of water. Adjust to personal taste.

VARIOUS COFFEES

The type of coffee we like is a matter of personal taste.

When making Vienna Coffee The coffee and cream should be heated. For a very rich cup, put a couple of tablespoons of whipped cream in the cup and pour the very hot coffee over it; sprinkle a dash of ground vanilla bean on top.

An after-dinner coffee is generally stronger than a breakfast blend, especially if it is served in a demi-tasse. Simply double the strength of the usual brew of French or Italian coffee. Serve black in demitasse cups. And have an accompaniment of raw sugar or honey.

COFFEE RECIPES

THE MESSENGER'S COFFEE

6 cups boiling water
1 whole egg*, washed
1/8 teaspoon salt

1 cup gourmet coffee, ground
1 cup cold water

Step 1: In a saucepan, add coffee grinds to boiling water and cook 5 to 6 minutes.

Step 2: Meanwhile break the egg into a cup; add salt; beat with a whisk until fluffy; break egg shell into beaten egg; mix together. After coffee has boiled 5 to 6 minutes, drop beaten egg* plus shell into saucepan; allow to cook for 1 minute until egg is done; lower heat; add 1 cup of cold water to further help settle the grounds.

Step 3: After the coffee has somewhat cleared (its apt to be slightly muddy), about 3 minutes; strain and serve.

√ Old-School Camping Method

Mix egg (including shell) and coffee grinds in a saucepan; add 6 cups cold water & salt; bring just to a boil; remove from fire; pour 1 cup cold water on top; let settle a few minutes, then strain and serve.

*It helps the grounds to settle and absorbs some caffeine.

ICED COFFEE

Quart of double-strength or After Dinner Coffee (pg.300)
24 ice cubes made from regular coffee with a coffee bean* placed in each cube before freezing.

*For added flavor and appearance.

LEBANESE COFFEE

1 pint very strong coffee
1/4 teaspoon cinnamon
Dash of mace Raw sugar, maple syrup or honey
4 cinnamon sticks, for garnish

1 cup whipped cream
1 teaspoon grated orange peel

Step 1: Sweeten coffee with sugar or other sweetener; add orange peel; let cool.

Step 2: Stir in 3/4 cup whipped cream and cinnamon; chill in refrigerator.

Step 3: Pour into individual glasses; serve topped with a spoonful of whipped cream and a cinnamon stick inserted into each drink.

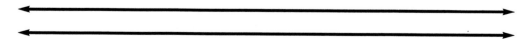

TEA

INFO ON GREAT TASTING TEA

Prep or warm the teapot (cup, or mug) by pouring boiling water in and swirling it around, then discard.

Perfected tea has freshly drawn and just boiled water poured on the leaves. Never use water which has been allowed to sit in a kettle. If the water over boils or does not boil at all, the tea leaves will be only half-opened and the flavor will be spoiled. The leaves must steep 10 to 12 minutes, 5 minutes for others.

FOR CONCENTRATE: Utilize 1 teaspoon of tea leaves per 1 cup of water. Put tea leaves into the tea pot; pour in 1 cup of boiling water; set it on a flame until just about to boil; turn off flame and allow to steep 10 to 12 minutes, some teas require 5 minutes of steeping—check instructions on package; FOR REGULAR STRENGTH: now fill up with as much boiling water as is required. Give a final stir, allow the leaves to settle; present hot to the table; pour through a strainer into serving cups.

Its best to use earthenware, china or porcelain. Tin is the only metal which should be used, but it must be new, clean and bright. Metal alters the flavor.

DO NOT add milk or sugar to tea. Connoisseurs drink tea plain. Milk causes sediment or particles to appear in tea. Slices lemon and a little honey are acceptable.

ICE TEA

Use black or green tea leaves; double the amount of tea leaves per cup, prepare the usual way; pour into a pitcher. Add ice when cool; if in a rush, triple the amount of tea leaves and add ice while the tea is hot, or if we have time pour some tea into ice trays with lemon zest and freeze to make ice cubes; add to regular strength cool tea. If the tea is left in the refrigerator it will become cloudy. Add lemon or orange slices, sprigs of mint to tea and serve with superfine sugar on the side for each person to sweeten according to preference.

HOT GINGER DRINK
(good to relieve an upset stomach or sea sickness)

1 quart water
2/3 cup raw sugar
Sprigs of mint, for garnish
1/2 cup ginger root, peeled & finely grated

Step 1:For Concentrate: Bring 3 cups of the water to a boil in a tea pot; add ginger root; boil for a few minutes.

Step 2:For Regular Strength: Pour into a pitcher with sugar, mix well until sugar is dissolved; fill up with remaining boiling water. Give a final stir, allow the roots to settle; present hot to the table; pour through a strainer into serving cups. Garnish with sprigs of mint.

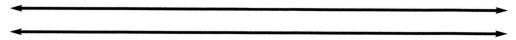

19. MILK DRINKS

HOT MILK COCOA

4 tablespoons unsweetened cocoa

3 tablespoons Raw™ sugar

Pinch of salt

Dash of Cinnamon

4 cups milk

1/8 teaspoon vanilla extract

Whipped cream

1/2 cup water

Step 1: Mix the cocoa, sugar, salt with 1/2 cup water in a saucepan and boil gently for 2 minutes.

Step 2: Add the milk and heat slowly just to the boiling point.

Step 3: Remove from heat; beat well with a whisk; add vanilla. Pour into mugs and top with a dollop of whipped cream; sprinkle with cinnamon.

HOT DOUBLE COCOA

2 tablespoons Raw™ sugar

1/2 cup water

1/4 teaspoon vanilla extract

Pinch of salt

Dash of cinnamon

1 1/2 tablespoons unsweetened cocoa powder

1 cup milk

1/2 cup half-and-half

1 ounce bittersweet chocolate

Whipped cream

Step 1: Mix the sugar, cocoa powder, salt and water in a bowl. Beat until smooth.

Step 2: Pour into a saucepan. Add milk, half-and-half and vanilla, and heat slowly just to the boiling point. Add bittersweet chocolate and stir well to melt.

Step 3: Pour into cups and top with a dollop of whipped cream; sprinkle with cinnamon.

MILK SHAKE

2 scoops ice cream

2 tablespoons strawberry syrup

3/4 cup milk

Step 1: Blend together ingredients in a blender. Serve immediately.

√ Chocolate Milk Shake

Use *2 tablespoons chocolate syrup* instead of strawberry syrup.

BANANA MILK SHAKE

2 cups milk

1 banana, mashed

2 tablespoons superfine sugar (optional)

1/2 cup powdered milk

Dash of mace

1/8 teaspoon salt

Step 1: Blend together ingredients in a blender. Serve immediately.

ORANGE EGG NOG

1 cup milk

1/4 cup powdered milk

2 tablespoons honey

2 eggs

1/2 cup orange juice

1/8 teaspoon salt

Step 1: Blend eggs in a blender for a few seconds; add remaining ingredients, continue blending.

Step 2: Serve immediately in tall glasses with crushed ice made from orange juice.

MOLASSES EGG NOG

2 cups milk, hot or cold

2 eggs, separated

Pinch ginger

3 tablespoons unsulphured molasses

1/8 teaspoon mace

Whipped cream

Step 1:whisk together egg yolks and molasses; gradually stir in ginger & milk.

Step 2:whisk egg whites until they form stiff peaks, stir in molasses & milk mixture.

Step 3: Pour into cups and top with a dollop of whipped cream; sprinkle with mace.

SMOOTHY

1 peach, peeled, cut in chunks & frozen

4 cherries, pitted, cut in halves & frozen

2 bananas, peeled, cut in chunks & frozen

2 mangoes, peeled, cut in chunks & frozen

Slices of lemon, for Garnish

Dash of cinnamon

Dash of nutmeg

2 tablespoons honey (optional)

8 ounces of milk or orange juice

Step 1: Blend ingredients in a blender until smooth and frothy.

Step 2: Pour into glasses and garnish with lemon slices.

POWER SHAKE

1 banana, peeled, cut in chunks & frozen

2/3 cup cantaloupe, peeled, cut in chunks & frozen

1/2 cup strawberries, cut in halves and frozen

8 ounces milk

1 tablespoon Tahini (pg.94)

1/8 teaspoon vanilla extract

Slices of orange, for Garnish

Step 1: Blend ingredients in a blender until smooth and frothy.

Step 2: Pour into glasses and garnish with orange slices.

SEASONINGS

All spices and seasonings should be stored in an airtight container in a cool dry place for up to 3 months; the pungent aroma begins to diminish after 3 weeks.

Item#01 MUHAMMAD'S SEASONING™

Ideal for accompanying fish, vegetable, rice and soup dishes.

Item#02 MUHAMMAD'S SEASONING II™

Ideal for accompanying fish, vegetable, rice and soup dishes.

Item#03 MUHAMMAD'S CAJUN SEASONING™

Ideal for accompanying fish, vegetable, veggy patties, rice and soup dishes.

Item#04 HOT CAJUN SPICE & HERB MIX™

Ideal for accompanying fish, vegetable, veggy patties, rice and soup dishes.

Item#05 MUHAMMAD'S CHILI POWDER™

Ideal for accompanying fish, vegetable, veggy patties, rice and soup dishes.

Item#06 MUHAMMAD'S MILD CHILI POWDER™

Ideal for accompanying Mexican fish, vegetable, veggy patties, rice and soup dishes.

Item#07 MUHAMMAD'S EXTRA HOT CHILI BLEND™

Ideal for accompanying Mexican fish, vegetable, veggy patties, rice and soup dishes.

Item#08 GARAM MASALA™

Ideal for accompanying Eastern Indian fish, vegetable, rice and soup dishes.

Item#09 MUHAMMAD'S CURRY POWDER™

Ideal for accompanying Eastern Indian and West Indian fish, vegetable, rice and soup dishes.

Item#10 MUHAMMAD'S LIGHT CURRY BLEND™

Ideal for accompanying Eastern Indian and West Indian breaded fish bake or fry.

Item#11 MUHAMMAD'S MILD CURRY POWDER™

Ideal for accompanying West Indian curries and breaded fish bake or fry.

Item#12 APPLE PIE SPICE™

Ideal for accompanying American desserts, especially pies and fruit bowls.

Item#13 MUHAMMAD'S DESSERT SPICE™
Ideal for accompanying desserts, especially pie crust, pies and fruit bowls.

Item#14 MUHAMMAD'S BEAN PIE SPICE™

Ideal seasoning for bean pies.

Item#15 SESAME SEASONING™
Ideal for accompanying Curried Sesame Sauce and East Indian dishes.

Item#16 JERK SPICE MIX™
Ideal for accompanying Jamaican style jerky.

√ Jerk Spice Rub™

Blend Jerk Spice Mix™ with *1 tablespoon mashed garlic* and *1 tablespoon lemon juice*. Rub on fish, corn on the cob or baked potatoes.

Item#17 BARBECUE SPICE & BASTING SAUCE™

Rub on fish to be grilled, or as seasoning in batter-fried seafood.

√ Barbecue Marinade I

Blend in Barbecue Spice Blend with *non-alcohol white wine & onions*.

√ Barbecue Marinade II

Blend in Barbecue Spice Blend with *vinegar & soy sauce*.

√ Barbecue Marinade III

Blend in Barbecue Spice Blend with a *Citrus Sauce*.

√ Barbecue Basting Sauce

Blend in Barbecue Spice Blend with *1 1/4 cup Ketchup (pg.___), 1/4 cup olive oil, & 1 tablespoon minced garlic*. Baste with the sauce during the last 10 minutes of cooking.

Item#18 SOUTHWESTERN AMERICAN HOT SPICE™
Ideal for accompanying Southwestern American vegetables and soups dishes.

Item#19 MUHAMMAD'S PEPPER FISH SEASONING™

Ideal for accompanying fish dishes.

Item#20 ETHIOPIAN HOT PEPPER SPICE MIX™ (Pg. __)
Ideal for accompanying Ethiopian soups and baked fish seasoning.

FINE HERBES

Item#21 LEMON HERB SEASONING™
Ideal for accompanying fish, vegetable, veggy patties, rice and soup dishes.

Item#22 HERB FISH SEASONING™

Ideal for accompanying fish dishes.

Item#23 MUHAMMAD'S SALAD TOPPING MIX™
Ideal for accompanying fish, vegetable, veggy patties, rice and soup dishes.

√ **®Muhammad's Vegetable Seasoning™**

Use *1 teaspoon* ®*Muhammad's Salad Topping Mix™* with *1 tablespoon non-alcohol dry white wine* as a flavoring ingredient in sautééd vegetables and fish.

√ **®Muhammad's Fish & Vegetable Marinade™**

Use *1 tablespoon* ®*Muhammad's Salad Topping Mix™* with *1/2 cup non-alcohol dry white wine* as a marinade for fish and vegetables.

SAUCES

Item#24 MUHAMMAD'S ROASTED RED CHILI SAUCE™ (Mexican)

Ideal for accompanying grilled foods, chilies, veggy patties, tacos, wraps, and soup dishes.

Item#25 ROASTED CHILI SAUCE™ (Central American)
Ideal for accompanying Central American vegetable and soup dishes.

Item#26 CARIBBEAN PEPPER SAUCE™
Ideal for accompanying fish or vegetable dishes.

Item#27 MUHAMMAD'S RED HOT SAUCE™

Ideal for accompanying fish, soups, eggs, cheese, sauces or vegetables.

CONDIMENTS

Item#28 NON-DAIRY TOMATO Ketchup™

A robust and rich Ketchup.

Item#29 COCKTAIL SAUCE™

A rich sauce with some zip, excellent with fish.

Item#30 MUHAMMAD'S THAI SWEET & SOUR SAUCE™

(VEGETABLE SAUCE & FISH MARINADE)

Use as a sauce or to marinate fish or raw vegetables in.

Item#31 MUHAMMAD'S THAI SOUR SAUCE & FISH MARINADE™

Use as a soup sauce or to marinate fish in.

Item#32 MUHAMMAD'S THAI STEAK SAUCE™

Use as a steak sauce for Burgers.

Item#33 MEDITERRANEAN VEGETABLE & FISH MARINADE™

Marinate fish or raw vegetables in.

Item#34 chilies IN ADOBO SAUCE™

Use as a soup or vegetable sauce or to marinate fish in.

Item#35 CHIPOTLE CHILI SAUCE™ (Complex)

Serve cold or hot with Mexican dishes.

Item#36 JALAPEÑO Ketchup™

A Mexican Ketchup that will give a Southwestern accent to any dish; perfect on Burgers.

Item#37 EASTERN CHILI SAUCE™

Add a brand new zest to our condiment tray with this unique sauce.

ENJOY AALIYAH'S JUICES

CALL 718-490-2267

ORDER FORM

(PLEASE CALL BEFORE ORDERING: 516-483-7673 Ask for Aubrey)

Item#	Quantity	Description of Sauce, Spice or Book	Unit Price	Total Price

TOTAL $

Add $4 Shipping & Handling for 1st item
and .50¢ for each additional item ordered

GRAND TOTAL

PAYMENT METHOD

☐ **Check or Money Order**

> **Please make check or money order payable to:**
> **AUBREY M. MILLER**
> **and mail to:**
> **Muslim Cookbook, Sauces & Spices**
> **600 Fulton Avenue 26F**
> **Hempstead, New York 11550**

Credit Card

☐ DISCOVER   ☐ AMERICAN EXPRESS

☐ VISA   ☐ MasterCard

Card# _____

3 or 4 digit Security Code* _____

Issue Date: _____ Expiry Date: _____

Zip Code where card was issued: _____

Name on Card: _____

Your Signature: _____

Bill to:

Name: _____

Street: _____

City: _____

State: _____ Zip: _____

Daytime Phone #: _____

Email: _____

Address To Be Sent:
If different from person placing order.

Name: _____

Street: _____
City: _____

State: _____ Zip _____
Daytime Phone #: _____

*Where to locate Security Codes on:

VISA   American Express

Visa and/or MasterCard cardholders should enter the last 3 digits that appear after the account number on the reverse side of the card

The 4-digit code on the front of the American Express Card is just above the account number

Thank you and may Allah(God) continue to bless us.

ABOUT THE AUTHOR

Aubrey M. Muhammad
Muslim Cookbook, Muhammad's Sauces & Seasonings™
600 Fulton Ave. 26F
Hempstead, New York 11550
Phone: 516-483-7673 or 516-481-4872
Email: Muslimcooking@Yahoo.com

Improve Your Quality of Life with Muslim Cooking With Muhammad™

Hempstead, New York—December 10, 2003—Tired of being "tired"? Need more energy? Want to live longer and start looking younger, have an aura of light emanating from your clearer skin? Want to lose weight? Move more briskly? Utilize more brain power? Heal our bodies by replenishing our cells with young ones filled with life, then Muslim Cooking With Muhammad: **Muslim Cookbook, Nutrition & Health Guide** By Rawiyah Sphere© is the answer.

Muslim Cooking With Muhammad™ has been compiled by the Rawiyah Sphere Of Writers© to assist those who desire to eat to live with the right foods and to demonstrate how to properly prepare them. A complement to the teachings of The Honorable Elijah Muhammad through his series of books titled How To Eat To Live©, this is book one of a five-part series of cookbooks which include unique sauces & seasonings available online, by mail order or supermarkets. We have a temporary website under construction, the address is greatcookbook.8m.com . This cookbook offers the person seeking healthy living a wide range of foods and meat alternatives that cleanse our digestive system instead of clogging it up and poisoning it with nutrient-depleted processed foods. Some of the recipes featured are the traditional bean soup, a variety of whole wheat breads, fish, the proper vegetables, fruit salads, beverages and, of course, desserts including the world famous bean pie.

About the publisher. Aubrey M. Muhammad was born and raised in the Village of Hempstead, New York. An unguided youth he hung out in the streets and got into trouble and on a bad path. But through the redeeming Program™ of Muhammad has been transformed into a beacon of light as a family counselor & community activist, actively participating in developing family cohesiveness to prepare our people to develop a community that will be equal in the human family. He was formally educated through New York public schools, York College, New York Institute Of Technology and Molloy College. Currently he is a cook, baker, producer, publisher, writer, motivational speaker, positive character developer, mentor and entrepreneur contributing to the development of local non-profit & profitable businesses and organizations. He says "These are a few characteristics and roles on the path to becoming one with Allah (God). But one must have peace with self first before helping others." The founder of Rawiyah Sphere Of Writers™, a group of aware brothers and sisters dedicated to presenting positive and encouraging information, education and entertainment to our people and then the entire human family and bring out of us the best of what Allah (God) has put in us as a blessing to a world seeking light and life. We currently have completed Part one of a positive motivational and people management course workbook. Rawiyah Sphere Of Writers™ are working on two screenplays, poetry, a sci-fi short story and a children's book which are proposed to be published this summer and fall of 2005.